THE NEW ENCYCLOPEDIA OF
AQUATIC LIFE

THE NEW ENCYCLOPEDIA OF
AQUATIC LIFE

VOLUME I

AQUATIC INVERTEBRATES AND FISHES

EDITED BY

ANDREW CAMPBELL
AND JOHN DAWES

Facts On File, Inc.

Published in North America by:
Facts On File, Inc.
132 West 31st Street,
New York NY 10001

THE BROWN REFERENCE GROUP PLC
(incorporating Andromeda Oxford Limited)
8 Chapel Place,
Rivington Street,
London EC2A 3DQ
www.brownreference.com

Editorial Director Lindsey Lowe
Project Manager Peter Lewis
Art Directors Martin Anderson, Chris Munday
Editor Rita Demetriou
Cartographic Editor Tim Williams
Picture Managers Claire Turner, Helen Sim
Picture Researchers Alison Floyd, Becky Cox
Production Director Alastair Gourlay
Production Controller Maggie Copeland
Editorial Consultant Graham Bateman
Indexer Ann Barrett

Library of Congress Cataloging in Publication Data available from Facts On File

Vol ISBN: 0-8160-6199-8
Set ISBN: 0-8160-5119-4

Facts On File books are available at special discounts when purchased in bulk quantities for businesses, associations, institutions or sales promotions. Please call our Special Sales Department in New York at (212) 967-8800 or (800) 322-8755.

You can find Facts On File on the World Wide Web at http://www.factsonfile.com

Cover design by Cathy Rincon

Printed in China

10 9 8 7 6 5 4 3 2 1

Photo page ii: *Sally Lightfoot crab and barnacles*
Daniel Cox/Oxford Scientific Films.

Advisory Editors

Dr. W. Nigel Bonner,
British Antarctic Survey,
Cambridge, England

Professor Fu-Shiang Chia,
University of Alberta,
Edmonton, Canada

Dr. Richard Connor,
University of Massachusetts at Dartmouth, North Dartmouth, Massachusetts

Dr. Peter Evans,
University of Oxford, England

Dr. John Harwood,
Gatty Marine Laboratory,
University of St. Andrews
Scotland

Dr. David Macdonald,
University of Oxford, England

Dr. John E. McCosker
Steinhart Aquarium
California Academy of Sciences
San Francisco, California

Dr R. M. McDowall
Ministry of Agriculture and Fisheries
Christchurch
New Zealand

Dr. Bernd Würsig
Texas A&M University
College Station
Texas

Contributors

PKA	Paul K. Anderson, University of Calgary, Canada
SSA	Sheila S. Anderson, British Antarctic Survey, England
RGB	Roland G. Bailey, University of London, England
GJB	Gerald J. Bakus, University of Southern California, Los Angeles
CCB	Carole C. Baldwin, National Museum of Natural History, Washington, D.C.
KEB	Keith E. Banister, (formerly) British Museum, London, England
RB	Robin Best, Instituto Nacional de Pequisas de Amazonia, Brazil
RCB	Robin C. Brace, University of Nottingham, England
BB	Bernice Brewster, British Museum, London, England
PB	Paul Brodie, Bedford Institute of Oceanography, Dartmouth, Nova Scotia, Canada
AC	Andrew Campbell, Queen Mary College, University of London, England
JEC	June E. Chatfield, Gilbert White Museum, Selborne, Hampshire, England
JD	Jim Darling, West Coast Whale Research, Fairbanks, Alaska
JD	John Dawes, Manilva, Málaga, Spain
GD	Gordon Dickerson, (formerly) Wellcome Research Laboratory, Beckenham, England

Artwork Panels
Mick Loates
Denys Ovenden
Colin Newman
Priscilla Barrett
S. S. Driver
Roger Gorringe
Richard Lewington
Kevin Maddison
Malcolm McGregor
Norman Weaver

GDi Guido Dingerkus, American Museum of Natural History, New York

DPD Daryl Domning, Howard University, Washington, D.C.

AWE Albert W. Erickson, University of Seattle, Seattle, Washington

PGHE Peter G.H. Evans, University of Oxford, England

SAF Svein A. Fosså, Akvariekonsulenten, Grimstad, Norway

RG Ray Gambell, International Whaling Commission, England

PRG Peter R. Garwood, University of Newcastle upon Tyne, England

DEG David E. Gaskin, University of Guelph, Canada

CG John Craighead George, North Slope Borough Dept. of Wildlife Management, Barrow, Alaska

JG Jonathan Gordon, WildCRU, University of Oxford, England

JH John Harwood, NERC Sea Mammal Research Unit, St. Andrews, Scotland

GJH Gordon J. Howes, British Museum, London, England

JJ Jack Jackson, Woking, Surrey, England

SDK Scott D. Kraus, New England Aquarium, Boston, Massachusetts

J-LP Johanna Laybourn-Parry, University of Lancaster, England

CL Christina Lockyer, British Antarctic Survey, England

HM Helene Marsh, James Cook University, Australia

AM Tony Martin, NERC Sea Mammal Research Unit, St. Andrews, Scotland

JMcC John E. McCosker, California Academy of Sciences, San Francisco, California

RMcD Bob McDowall, Ministry of Agriculture and Fisheries, Christchurch, New Zealand

JMP Jane M. Packard, University of Florida, Gainesville, Florida

VP Vassili Papastavrou, University of Bristol, England

LP Lynne R. Parenti, Smithsonian Institution, Washington, D.C.

TP Theodore W. Pietsch, University of Washington, Seattle, Washington State

PSR Philip S. Rainbow, Queen Mary College, University of London, England

GBR Galen B. Rathbun, California Academy of Sciences, Cambria, California

RR Randall Reeves, University of Quebec, Canada

AT Andrew Taber, Wildlife Conservation Society, New York, New York

PLT Peter L. Tyack, Northeast Fisheries Science Center, Woods Hole, Massachusetts

LW Lindy Weilgart, Dalhousie University, Canada

RSW Randall S. Wells, Moss Landing Marine Laboratories, Moss Landing, California

HW Hal Whitehead, Dalhousie University, Canada

IW Ian J. Winfield, Centre for Ecology and Hydrology, Cumbria, England

BW Bernd Würsig, Texas A&M University, College Station, Texas

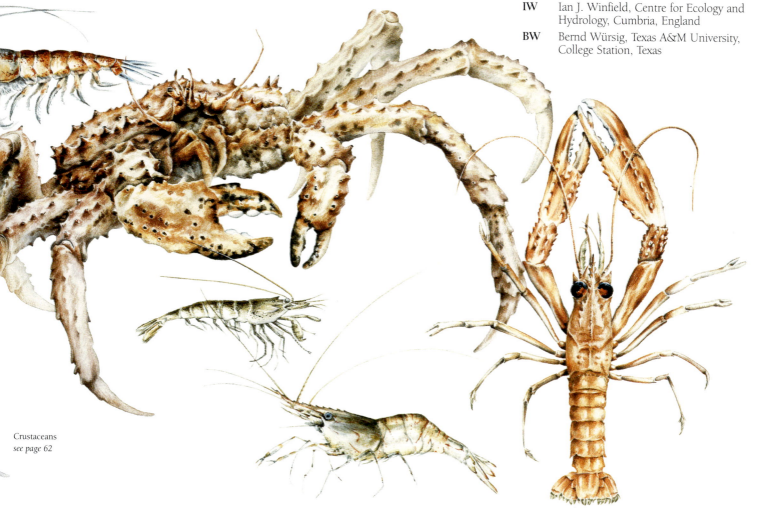

Crustaceans
see page 62

CONTENTS

IUCN CATEGORIES

Ex Extinct, when there is no reasonable doubt that the last individual of a taxon has died.

EW Extinct in the Wild, when a taxon is known only to survive in captivity, or as a naturalized population well outside the past range.

Cr Critically Endangered, when a taxon is facing an extremely high risk of extinction in the wild in the immediate future.

En Endangered, when a taxon faces a very high risk of extinction in the wild in the near future.

Vu Vulnerable, when a taxon faces a high risk of extinction in the wild in the medium-term future.

LR Lower Risk, when a taxon has been evaluated and does not satisfy the criteria for CR, EN or VU.

Note: The Lower Risk (LR) category is further divided into three subcategories: Conservation Dependent (cd) – taxa which are the focus of a continuing taxon-specific or habitat-specific conservation program targeted toward the taxon, the cessation of which would result in the taxon qualifying for one of the threatened categories within a period of five years; Near Threatened (nt) – taxa which do not qualify for Conservation Dependent but which are close to qualifying for VU; and Least Concern (lc) – taxa which do not qualify for the two previous categories.

Sturgeons and paddlefishes
see page 162

PREFACE

ALL LIFE ON EARTH ORIGINATED IN THE PRIMEVAL seas some 4,000 million years ago. After eons of evolution, the waters that cover over two-thirds of our planet are home to a bewildering array of creatures, from tiny single-celled animals to giant squid and monstrous sharks, and from beautiful and delicate sea anemones, corals, and sponges to grotesque angler fishes and other denizens of the deep.

The aim of the *New Encyclopedia of Aquatic Life* is – to hazard an obvious pun – to give the reader an "in-depth" insight into this largely hidden underwater world and reveal the secrets of its diverse inhabitants. Organized into two volumes, the *New Encyclopedia* proceeds from the microscopic to the gargantuan: Volume 1 treats the aquatic invertebrates and begins a comprehensive review of fishes, while Volume 2 completes the fishes section and covers the aquatic mammals. The common denominator of all the taxonomic groupings described is that they lead an entirely aquatic lifestyle.

Aquatic invertebrates are invertebrate animals that live in the sea, fresh water, or moist terrestrial habitats; they also include many parasites whose "aquatic" environment is that of the bodies of their hosts. The term "invertebrates" refers to the fact that none of these animals has a bony or cartilaginous backbone.

Some invertebrate phyla, while overwhelmingly aquatic in habits, contain groups that have terrestrial forms. For example, although segmented worms are mainly marine, the earthworms live in damp soil; also, slugs and snails are terrestrial variations of the mainly aquatic mollusks. For completeness, such terrestrial forms are also considered here. The diversities of form and biology are immense – a salmon and an elephant have more in common with one another than do many apparently related members of invertebrate phyla.

Thanks to the prominent part they play in our lives, birds and mammals are hugely popular subjects of study and amateur interest. By contrast, aquatic invertebrates are seen by some people as the poor relations of the animal kingdom. This is far from the case. For sheer beauty, the microscopic architecture of the diatoms and the sea anemones is not easily surpassed. For their capacity to cause devastating disease in humans, the malaria and bilharzia parasites are without equal. And, for complexity of structure and intelligence, the squids and octopuses rival fishes in their mastery of the water and in their fascinating behavior.

Molecular analysis has resulted in a major revision of invertebrate systematics, and our text endeavors to reflect the latest findings. However, some chapter groupings remain mere "flags of convenience" and should not be taken as indicating taxonomic affinities between the different groups described.

With over 24,000 species known to science, Fishes are found almost everywhere: from the cold lightless waters of the deepest oceans to lakes high in the Andes mountains, on land, in mud, underground, in the air, even in trees. There are luminous fishes, transparent fishes, and electric fishes. The size range is colossal, from species that are fully grown at 9mm (0.4in) to species reaching 12.5m (41ft)

in length. Some species are represented by countless millions of individuals, while others just manage to survive precariously with a handful of individuals.

Fish classification continues to be a matter of great debate among ichthyologists; as with the invertebrates, DNA studies have radically altered our understanding of relationships. While the present survey broadly adopts the scheme proposed by Joseph S. Nelson's authoritative volume *Fishes of the World* (3rd edn., 1994), we have given compilers of the individual accounts free rein to follow their preferred classifications. The meticulously compiled web resource FishBase (www.fishbase.org) has also been of invaluable help to the authors and editors of the current work, not least by supplying a standard set of common English species names.

Finally, the section on **Aquatic mammals** surveys two totally unrelated orders whose members are adapted to life at sea: the whales and dolphins (order Cetacea) and the dugong and manatees (order Sirenia). From a distance, the torpedo-shaped uniformity of marine mammals masks the character of each species; the illusion may be of animals with less individuality than some of the more familiar terrestrial mammals. But with closer study, that illusion is banished, and the ways of whale and dolphin spring intimately to life, and in so doing emphasize the subtlety and frailty of the natural web, and the dependence of the monumental upon the minute.

The bulk of the *New Encyclopedia* comprises general entries describing the biology, distribution, diet, breeding, and conservation status of particular groups; these groups are treated variously at the level of phyla (invertebrates), orders (fishes) or families (sea mammals). Each such entry incorporates a fact panel providing a digest of key data, and often including outline drawings to help the reader visualize the creatures in question. For large groups this information is consolidated in a separate table. In addition, special features focus in detail on subjects as diverse as the origin of malaria, Sockeye salmon breeding runs, and Dugong seagrass grazing.

As well as the outline drawings there are many color illustrations by highly gifted wildlife artists that vividly bring their subjects to life (because fishes vary widely in size, it is not possible to show them to scale in the plates). Throughout, color photographs from diverse sources complement and enhance the text and artwork.

We are much indebted to the contributors who updated the text of the original 1985 edition by Banister and Campbell; sadly, Keith Banister, who died in 1999, could not be among them. Thanks are also due to the design, editorial, and production team who have seen the *Encyclopedia* through to publication. For all involved in this undertaking, a major reward is in knowing that the work will help raise awareness about the fragility of life in our oceans, lakes, and rivers, and the pressing need to conserve it at all costs.

ANDREW CAMPBELL
QUEEN MARY COLLEGE, UNIVERSITY OF LONDON

JOHN DAWES
MANILVA, SPAIN

What is an Aquatic Invertebrate?

WHAT DO CRABS, SEA URCHINS, EARTH-worms, malaria parasites, and corals have in common? Until recently, it was believed that these very diverse groups had very few shared characteristics, apart from the fact that they all lack a backbone. Of the 1,300,000 or so known species of animals, about 1,288,550 – over 98 percent – are without a backbone. Invertebrates, then, make up the vast bulk of animals, measured both in terms of numbers of species recognized and numbers of individuals. Some invertebrates, such as garden snails and earthworms, are conspicuous and familiar animals, while others, although very abundant, pass unnoticed by most people.

However, recent research in the field of genetics has shown that in fact invertebrates, like the fruit fly *Drosophila*, share much genetic material with the higher vertebrates like man. Therefore, in terms of genes rather than conspicuous bodily structures, all members of the animal kingdom have a lot in common.

Invertebrate body forms range in size from the lowly microscopic *Amoeba*, which may be just one micrometer in diameter, to the Giant squid 18m (59ft) in length, a ratio of 1:18,000,000. They include life forms as diverse as the Desert locust and the sea anemones. They inhabit all regions of the globe, and all habitats, from the ocean abyss to the air. Life almost certainly originated in the

seas, and virtually all the major invertebrate groups, or phyla, listed (right) have marine representatives. Somewhat fewer (almost 14 phyla) have conquered freshwater. Fewer still (about 5 phyla) live on land and of these only the jointed-limbed groups (arthropods) have mastered the air and really dry places. Most numerous among arthropods are the uniramians (e.g. insects, millipedes, centipedes) and the chelicerates (e.g. scorpions, spiders, ticks, and mites).

Many invertebrates, like slugs (whether of the garden or sea), are free-living; others, such as barnacles, are attached to the substrate throughout their adult life: yet others live as parasites in or on the bodies of plants or other animals. Some

invertebrates are of great commercial significance, either as direct food for man (e.g. prawns and oysters), or as food for man's exploitable reserves (e.g. the planktonic copepods on which herring feed). Others (e.g. earthworms) are much appreciated because they improve the soil for agriculture. Many invertebrates live as parasites, either inside the human body or in the bodies of domestic animals and plants. Because they can cause considerable damage, parasitic invertebrates are of great medical and economic importance.

This great diversity of form and lifestyle in animals has led zoologists to classify animals according to type and evolutionary connections. To be certain that they are speaking of the same animals, they give each species a unique scientific name. These two-part names are known as Linnean binomials, from the 18th-century Swedish botanist Carolus Linnaeus, who devised this system of classification. Thus, the Common earthworm is *Lumbricus terrestris*. Every species is classified into one of the major groups, or phyla. A phylum comprises all those animals that are thought to have a common evolutionary origin. With one exception, the phyla are made up exclusively of invertebrate animals. The phylum Chordata includes all animals with a hollow dorsal nerve cord. Nearly all the chordates – including fishes, amphibians, reptiles, and birds – have a backbone, but some are invertebrate, such as the sea squirts. As new discoveries are made, and classification reassessed through new techniques of molecular analysis, the exact number of phyla is in a constant state of flux.

The technical classification that zoologists traditionally employ leads from the most primitive-

◖ *Left and below* Among the most well-known aquatic invertebrates are cephalopods like the Day octopus (Octopus cyanea), while at the other end of the scale, both in size and familiarity, are inconspicuous jelly animals such as hydras (Chlorohydra viridissima).

KINGDOM: PROTISTA – SINGLE-CELLED ANIMALS
Subkingdom Protozoa

<table>
<tr><td>FLAGELLATES Phylum Euglenida</td><td>p12</td></tr>
<tr><td>1,000 species</td><td></td></tr>
<tr><td>TRYPANOSOMES AND ALLIES
Phylum Kinetoplastida</td><td>p12</td></tr>
<tr><td>600 species</td><td></td></tr>
<tr><td>CILIATES Phylum Ciliophora</td><td>p12</td></tr>
<tr><td>8,000 species</td><td></td></tr>
<tr><td>MALARIAL PARASITES Phylum Apicomplexa</td><td>p12</td></tr>
<tr><td>5,000 species</td><td></td></tr>
<tr><td>DINOFLAGELLATES Phylum Dinoflagellata</td><td>p12</td></tr>
<tr><td>4,000 species</td><td></td></tr>
<tr><td>DIATOMS, SLIME NETS AND ALLIES
Phylum Stramenopila</td><td>p12</td></tr>
<tr><td>9,000 species</td><td></td></tr>
<tr><td>AMOEBAS AND ALLIES Phylum Rhizopoda</td><td>p12</td></tr>
<tr><td>200 species</td><td></td></tr>
<tr><td>RADIOLARIANS AND ALLIES Phylum Actinopoda</td><td>p12</td></tr>
<tr><td>4,240 species</td><td></td></tr>
<tr><td>FORMAMINIFERA Phylum Granuloreticulosa</td><td>p12</td></tr>
<tr><td>40.000 species</td><td></td></tr>
<tr><td>DIPLOMONADS Phylum Diplomonadida</td><td>p12</td></tr>
<tr><td>100 species</td><td></td></tr>
<tr><td>PARABASILIDS Phylum Parabasilida</td><td>p12</td></tr>
<tr><td>300 species</td><td></td></tr>
<tr><td>CRYPTOMONADS Phylum Cryptomonada</td><td>p12</td></tr>
<tr><td>200 species</td><td></td></tr>
<tr><td>MICROSPORANS Phylum Microspora</td><td>p12</td></tr>
<tr><td>200 species</td><td></td></tr>
<tr><td>ASCETOSPORANS Phylum Ascetospora</td><td>p12</td></tr>
<tr><td>c.30 species</td><td></td></tr>
<tr><td>CHOANOFLAGELLATES Phylum Choanoflagellata</td><td>p12</td></tr>
<tr><td>c.400 species</td><td></td></tr>
<tr><td>GREEN ALGAE Phylum Chlorophyta</td><td>p12</td></tr>
<tr><td>7,000–9,000 species</td><td></td></tr>
<tr><td>OPALINIDS Phylum Opalinida</td><td>p12</td></tr>
<tr><td>c.400 species</td><td></td></tr>
</table>

KINGDOM: ANIMALIA
Subkingdom Parazoa

<table>
<tr><td>SPONGES Phylum Porifera</td><td>p20</td></tr>
<tr><td>5,000 species in 8 families</td><td></td></tr>
<tr><td>SEA ANEMONES & JELLYFISHES
Phylum Cnidaria</td><td>p24</td></tr>
<tr><td>c.9,900 species in 3 classes</td><td></td></tr>
<tr><td>COMB JELLIES
Phylum Ctenophora</td><td>p36</td></tr>
<tr><td>100 species in 7 orders</td><td></td></tr>
<tr><td>GNATHOSTOMULIDS
Phylum Gnathostomulida</td><td>p38</td></tr>
<tr><td>80 species in 2 orders and 25 genera</td><td></td></tr>
<tr><td>ACOELOMORPHS
Phylum Acoelomorpha</td><td>p38</td></tr>
<tr><td>c.280 species in 2 orders</td><td></td></tr>
<tr><td>GASTROTRICHS
Phylum Gastrotricha</td><td>p38</td></tr>
<tr><td>c.450 species</td><td></td></tr>
</table>

<table>
<tr><td>ARROW WORMS
Phylum Chaetognatha</td><td>p38</td></tr>
<tr><td>c.100 species in 7 genera</td><td></td></tr>
<tr><td>WATER BEARS
Phylum Tardigrada</td><td>p40</td></tr>
<tr><td>Over 800 species in 2 classes and 15 families</td><td></td></tr>
<tr><td>VELVET WORMS Order Onychophora</td><td>p41</td></tr>
<tr><td>c110 species in 2 families</td><td></td></tr>
<tr><td>CRUSTACEANS
Subphylum Crustacea</td><td>p42</td></tr>
<tr><td>c.39,000 species in 6 classes</td><td></td></tr>
<tr><td>HORSESHOE CRABS
Subphylum Chelicerata</td><td>p64</td></tr>
<tr><td>4 species in 3 genera</td><td></td></tr>
<tr><td>SEA SPIDERS
Subphylum Pycnogonida</td><td>p65</td></tr>
<tr><td>c.1,000 species in 70 genera and 8 families</td><td></td></tr>
<tr><td>PRIAPULANS Phylum Priapula</td><td>p66</td></tr>
<tr><td>16 species in 6 genera and 3 families</td><td></td></tr>
<tr><td>KINORHYNCHS Phylum Kinorhyncha</td><td>p66</td></tr>
<tr><td>c.150 species in a single class</td><td></td></tr>
<tr><td>LORICIFERANS Phylum Loricifera</td><td>p66</td></tr>
<tr><td>10 species in 1 order and 2 families</td><td></td></tr>
<tr><td>HORSEHAIR WORMS Phylum Nematomorpha</td><td>p66</td></tr>
<tr><td>c.320 species</td><td></td></tr>
<tr><td>ROUNDWORMS Phylum Nematoda</td><td>p68</td></tr>
<tr><td>c.25,000 species in 2 classes</td><td></td></tr>
<tr><td>FLATWORMS Phylum Platyhelminthes</td><td>p72</td></tr>
<tr><td>c.18,500 species in 3 classes</td><td></td></tr>
<tr><td>RIBBON WORMS Phylum Nemertea</td><td>p72</td></tr>
<tr><td>c.900 species in 2 classes</td><td></td></tr>
<tr><td>MOLLUSKS Phylum Mollusca</td><td>p78</td></tr>
<tr><td>c.100,000 species in 7 classes</td><td></td></tr>
<tr><td>SIPUNCULANS Phylum Sipuncula</td><td>p102</td></tr>
<tr><td>c.250 species in 17 genera</td><td></td></tr>
<tr><td>ECHIURANS Phylum Echiura</td><td>p103</td></tr>
<tr><td>c.140 species in 34 genera</td><td></td></tr>
<tr><td>SEGMENTED WORMS Phylum Annelida</td><td>p104</td></tr>
<tr><td>c.16,500 species in 3 classes</td><td></td></tr>
<tr><td>ROTIFERS Phylum Rotifera</td><td>p112</td></tr>
<tr><td>c.1,800 species in 100 genera and 3 classes</td><td></td></tr>
<tr><td>SPINY-HEADED WORMS
Phylum Acanthocephala</td><td>p113</td></tr>
<tr><td>c.1,100 species in 3 classes</td><td></td></tr>
<tr><td>ENDOPROCTS Phylum Endoprocta</td><td>p114</td></tr>
<tr><td>c.150 species in 3 families</td><td></td></tr>
<tr><td>HORSESHOE WORMS Phylum Phoronida</td><td>p116</td></tr>
<tr><td>11 species in 2 genera</td><td></td></tr>
<tr><td>MOSS ANIMALS Phylum Bryozoa</td><td>p118</td></tr>
<tr><td>4,000 species in 1,200 genera and 3 classes</td><td></td></tr>
<tr><td>LAMPSHELLS Phylum Brachiopoda</td><td>p120</td></tr>
<tr><td>c.335 species in 69 genera and 2 classes</td><td></td></tr>
<tr><td>SPINY-SKINNED INVERTEBRATES
Phylum Echinodermata</td><td>p122</td></tr>
<tr><td>c.6,000 species in 5 classes</td><td></td></tr>
<tr><td>ACORN WORMS AND ALLIES
Phylum Hemichordata</td><td>p136</td></tr>
<tr><td>c.90 species in 3 classes</td><td></td></tr>
<tr><td>SEA SQUIRTS & LANCELETS Phylum Chordata</td><td>p138</td></tr>
<tr><td>c. 3,020 species</td><td></td></tr>
</table>

and simple animal types to the most complex and advanced. In order to achieve some form of system, various levels of organization are recognized, which give clear distinctions between phyla. The most fundamental of these organizational levels concerns the number of cells in the body. A cell is the smallest functional unit of an animal, governed by its own nucleus, which contains genetic material known as DNA (deoxyribonucleic acid). Other features are employed, such as the way the embryos develop, the number of layers of cells, the shape and symmetry of the larvae and adults, and the way the various internal cavities are formed. However, recent research into the structure of DNA, and particularly the way in which individual genes are arranged in the genetic code of animals, has revealed that most animals have much more in common with each other from a genetic standpoint than had previously been imagined. Also this study has provided some rather surprising information on the affinities of various animal groups.

◑ **Right** *The single protozoan cell may be quite a complex structure, with specialized parts called organelles responsible for different functions such as feeding and locomotion.*

◐ **Below** *Paramecia belong to a group of aquatic protozoans known as ciliates. These single-celled microorganisms reproduce by binary fission – dividing in half to form duplicates of themselves.*

The Simplest Animals
UNICELLULAR ORGANISMS

Animals with bodies made up of a single cell represent a separate level of organization from all the rest, for their body processes are performed by the one cell, which therefore itself cannot be specialized. In multicellular animals the responsibility for different life processes is shared out, different cells being specialized for different tasks, e.g. receiving stimuli (sensory cells), communication (nerve cells), movement (muscle cells) etc. Currently some 80,000 species of protozoa are known, but it is likely that many more remain to be discovered.

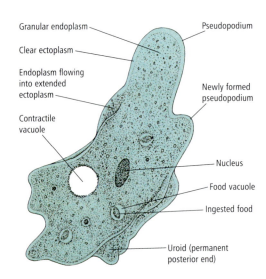

Granular endoplasm — Pseudopodium
Clear ectoplasm —
Endoplasm flowing into extended ectoplasm —
Contractile vacuole —
Newly formed pseudopodium
Nucleus
Food vacuole
Ingested food
Uroid (permanent posterior end)

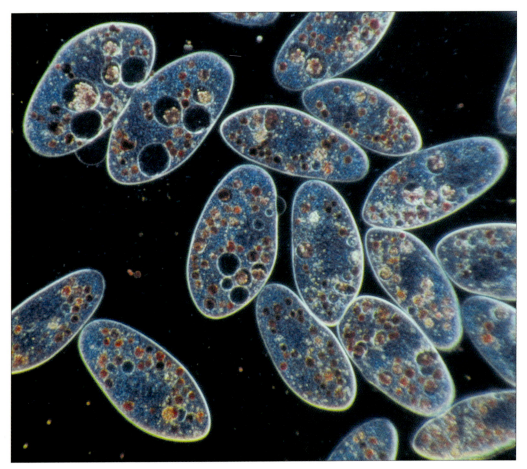

The single-celled animals or protozoans (sometimes referred to as acellular – without distinct cells) are assumed to be low on the scale of evolutionary sophistication. In reality their single cell is often large and complex. The essential life processes are carried out by special regions (organelles) within the cell – nucleus for government, bubblelike food vacuoles for energy acquisition, vacuoles that contract and expand to regulate water levels within the cell and so on.

Another fundamental question may be asked about single-celled animals. Are they in fact all animals? True animals derive their energy from relatively complex organic material that is plant or animal in origin – they are heterotrophic; they obtain their nourishment by a process of breaking down organic materials (are catabolic). However, some protozoans (e.g. the green flagellate *Euglena*

and the micro alga *Volvox*) have developed structures characteristic of plants, called chloroplasts, which are incorporated into their cells. The chloroplast enables the cell to synthesize organic materials, such as sugars, from mineral salts, carbon dioxide and water in the presence of sunlight (photosynthesis). Like green plants, these protozoans can subsist on inorganic food (are autotrophic) from which they synthesize organic material (are anabolic). Botanists consider such protozoans to be single-celled plants. The difficulty is that while some protozoans are clearly plants and others clearly animals, some, like Euglena, can feed by both autotrophy and heterotrophy. For reasons such as this some authorities believe that most protozoans warrant classification as an animal subkingdom, with obviously plantlike protozoans treated as members of the plant kingdom, outside it.

Recently scientists have proposed a new classification of the living world which overcomes the problem of whether protozoans are plants or animals. This reorganization proposes five kingdoms: Monera (bacteria and blue-green algae); Protista; Plantae (plants); Fungi and Animalia. The protozoans are included in the Protista as the subkingdom Protozoa, along with some other groups previously classified as algae by botanists.

Origins of Life
EVOLUTIONARY BEGINNINGS

Protozoans are most important because, as the "simplest animals" they are likely to provide important keys to two fundamental questions. These concern the origin of life, and the origin of multicellular metazoan animals. The origin of life is shrouded in scientific speculation. The biblical account of the origin of life as presented in Genesis is an historic attempt to answer one of man's most fundamental questions. Belief in the idea of a Divine creation is a matter of faith that cannot be tested by science. Nor can science yet tell us how life first began, although it has also been shown that primitive ideas such as spontaneous generation of life are completely wrong.

It is thought that the earth is not quite 5,000 million years old, and realistic estimates suggest that life began in its simplest form 4,000 million years ago. The first sedimentary rocks, not quite 4,000 million years old, contain fossils of simple cells which resemble those of present-day bacteria, that is, they lacked a distinct nucleus (i.e. were prokaryotes). These lived in a primeval atmosphere devoid of oxygen. The appearance of oxygen on the earth, 1,800 million years ago, brought with it many new evolutionary possibilities. The protozoans, green algae, higher plants and animals appeared a lot later, the earliest known fossils having been taken from rocks 1,000 million years old. All these organisms are made up of cells with nuclei (i.e. are eukaryotes). Thus the startling fact emerges that for three-quarters of the period for

○ *Above* The beautiful Christmas-tree worm (Spirobranchus giganteus) *is a member of the phylum Annelida –segmented worms – an ancient group that has existed at least since the Cambrian 500 million years ago.*

○ *Right* *The number and arrangement of cell layers distinguish various degrees of complexity in many-celled animals, from the single layer of the monoblastic sponges and mesozoans* **1** *through the diploblastic jellyfishes and comb jellies* **2** *to the three layers of most animals. The bulky middle layer (mesoderm) of triploblastic animals may be solid, as for example in flatworms and ribbon worms* **3**, *or divided into inner and outer parts separated by a cavity or coelom,* **4**. *Some groups, such as nematode worms, have a body cavity that is not formed within the mesoderm and is known as a pseudocoel* **5**.

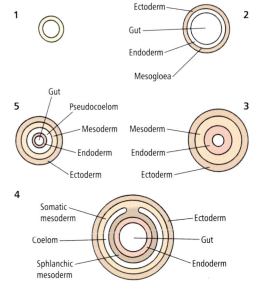

which life has existed on earth the only cells were prokaryotes, resembling bacteria. It was not until the Cambrian period 545–490 million years ago that invertebrates such as mollusks, trilobites, lampshells and echinoderms became established. Invertebrates with soft delicate bodies, such as segmented worms, flatworms, and sea squirts, have left a scant fossil record.

For life to have appeared, many conditions had to be fulfilled. It seems quite possible that the physical conditions prevailing on the surface of the early earth could have generated simple organic molecules such as amino acids, and then proteins, from inorganic molecules. The big unanswered question is how such substances could form themselves into organized living systems capable of reproducing their own kind.

Multicellular Animals
GROWING COMPLEXITY

The origins of multicellular animals are also speculative, but rather more can usefully be said about their possible early history. Because so many of the early animals had soft bodies they left very little fossil record. All theories about the early evolution of animals therefore rely mainly on the study of similarities between developing embryos and adults of animals in different groups. This allows inferences to be drawn about common ancestry. Two chief theories have been put forward.

According to one theory, protozoan animals gave rise to multicellular ones by colony formation. A number of types of colonial protozoan are known to exist, such as *Volvox*.

The famous 19th-century German biologist Ernst Haeckel proposed that a hollow *Volvox*-like ancestor could have developed into a two-layered organism. Views differ as to whether or not this was a planktonic or a bottom-dwelling organism, but it may have somewhat resembled the planula larvae of the sea anemones and jelly fishes and could have given rise to bottom-dwelling animals such as adult hydroids and sea anemones.

Although most animals are composed of three layers of cells, often in a highly modified form, there is evidence that the evolution from two-layered animals did occur in evolutionary history.

A different theory proposes that multicellular animals arose from single-celled animals containing many nuclei by the growth of cell walls between each nucleus. A number of protozoans, for example *Opalina*, are like this. According to this theory, the primitive multicellular animal would lack a gut, as in present-day gutless flatworms. However, the latter have three layers of cells, which raises the question – what is the origin of the two-layered animals? Because of this and other criticisms, this theory is now generally discarded in favor of the colonial one.

While it is not certain how the multicellular animals evolved from protozoan ancestors, it is possible to distinguish groups of metazoans on

⬗ Above Red slugs (Arion rufus) *mating. As triplo-blastic animals, mollusks such as slugs and snails have a coelom – a fluid filled body cavity that allows the body wall and gut muscles to move independently.*

⬗ Below Sea anemones may well have been some of *the earliest multicellular animals. Here, the tentacles of a group of sea anemones ensnare a* Mastagias sp. *jellyfish, another member of the phylum Cnidaria.*

the basis of relative simplicity or complexity of structure. (Some biologists divide invertebrates into protostomes and deuterostomes, see below.)

In metazoans there are three categories that can be used to determine level of complexity: how the cells are organized; how many layers of cells are to be found within the body; and whether or not a body cavity is present.

There are few types of cell in the most lowly metazoans and in sponges and these cells are never arranged into groups of similar cells (tissues). Such animals are said to have a cellular grade of organization. In the next step, as found in jellyfishes and allies and comb jellies, cells with similar functions are arranged together into tissues, each tissue having its own function or series of functions – these animals have a tissue grade of organization. In all animals apart from those just mentioned, requirements for functional specialization increase such that specific organs (often comprising a series of tissues) have evolved. Thus all animals from flatworms to man are said to have an organ grade of organization.

The second way to divide up multicellular animals is to look at the number of layers of cells that make up the animal's body. Those groups that are of the mesozoan type as well as the sponges consist of just one layer of cells, but in the jellyfishes and comb jellies two layers appear (ectoderm outside and endoderm inside). This "diploblastic" condition contrasts markedly with the single layer of cells seen in the protozoan colony Volvox, which is described as monoblastic. The two layers develop from the egg and remain throughout adult life, separated from each other by a sheet of jellylike mesogloea.

All animals "above" the jellyfishes and comb jellies are equipped with three layers of cells and are known as triploblastic. Here the ectoderm and endoderm are separated by a third cell layer, the mesoderm. The mesoderm forms the most bulky part of many animals, contributing the musculature of the body wall as well as that of the gut. In some of these triloblastic animals, e.g. flatworms (Platyhelminthes), the mesoderm is solid and not itself divided into two layers by a body cavity

⬤ **Above** *In common with many aquatic invertebrates, nudibranchs (shell-less sea slugs) are hermaphroditic. One of these colorful* Tambja verconis *has laid a rose-like egg mass (center).*

(coelom), so they are described as acoelomate. Without a body cavity these animals are at a disadvantage because the body movements affect the movements of the gut and vice versa. To be able to move the gut independently of the body wall is a great advantage, as it enables sophisticated digestive activities. Such a condition is reached only in coelomate animals, in which the mesoderm is divided into an outer section forming the body wall and an inner section forming the muscles of the gut, and the two are largely separated by a body cavity (coelom) within the mesoderm. The possession of a fluid-filled body cavity is the hallmark of all the more advanced invertebrates and the major phyla, including mollusks, annelids, the different arthropods, echinoderms and chordates, all have a coelom (are coelomates). Even so, improved techniques of research have changed our understanding of the form origin of body cavities

In some groups there is a body cavity between the body wall and the gut. This used to be called a pseudocoelom, not a true coelom, for it is not formed inside the mesoderm. Generally it arises from the blastocoel, an embryonic cavity which appears in the early stages of development, and contains fluid. In animals such as the nematode worms, it performs an important function as an incompressible, fluid skeleton. This cavity is not

"false" (i.e. pseudo) and many authorities now describe animals such as these as blastocoelomate.

Some evolutionary biologists suggest a different way of grouping invertebrates, believing that two main evolutionary lines have emerged in the animal world, the protostomes (first mouth) and deuterostomes (second mouth). In the early embryos of protostomes such as annelid worms and insects, the mouth is formed at or near the site of the blastopore. In deuterostomes such as the echinoderms (starfishes and sea urchins) and the chordates, the anus forms at the blastopore. Other distinctions can be seen by comparing the development of the two types. In the annelids the nerve cord is on the underside, a double, solid structure reminiscent of the nerve cord of insects. In the chordates it is a single hollow structure along the upper side of the animal. The annelid coelom is formed by the splitting of the mesoderm, but in the echinoderms and the chordates it develops from two pouches of the primitive gut. The sea-dwelling representatives of these two "lines" have characteristically different larvae.

Recent DNA sequence analysis of the different members of the animal kingdom has shown that the relationships believed to exist between different phyla, based on their structural organization, is now not likely to be correct, and different phyla have been repositioned within the scheme of an evolutionary tree accordingly. The sequence of the multicellular phyla, set out at the start of this section, reflects this new thinking. Here the genetic affinities between invertebrates that periodically molt their outer cuticle, and those that do not are particularly reflected.

These distinctions are not definite evidence of links between phyla, but do indicate possible evolutionary affinities. Certainly the chordates are likely to have arisen from a deuterostome type of ancestor, and the form of development shown by annelids and mollusks, as well as their DNA sequences, places them far from the echinoderms and chordates in any phylogeny or "family tree."

Symmetry
BODY PLANS

One of the most obvious differences separating the phyla of the animal kingdom is the overall appearance of the animals. The majority of animals, including the vertebrates, worms, and jointed-limbed forms, are bilaterally symmetrical: complementary right and left halves are mirror images. Their front and hind ends are however dissimilar. This is because in these animals there has been some specialization at the head end. In the lowly flatworms the head is only feebly developed, but it is identifiable. In the jointed-limbed animals, such as the insects, it is clearly defined. The evolution of a head end (cephalization) has come about in direct response to the development of forward movement. Clearly it is an advantage to have specialized sensory equipment (e.g. eyes, smelling and tasting receptors at the front of the body) to deal efficiently with environmental stimuli as they occur in the direction of travel. In this way, prey and predators can be quickly identified.

The position of sense receptors is often associated with the mouth opening. These factors have led to the development of aggregations of nervous tissue to integrate the messages coming from the receptors and to initiate a coordinated response (e.g. attack or flight) in the muscle systems of the body. This brain, be it ever so simple, came to lie at the front end of the body, often near the mouth, and the typical head arrangement was formed. In addition to a distinct head, other features of bilaterally symmetrical animals are thoracic regions (modified for respiration) and abdominal regions (modified for digestion, absorption and reproduction). The function of locomotion may be undertaken by either or both of the regions. In the mollusks the principles of bilateral symmetry are somewhat disguised by the unique style of body architecture, but if these animals are reduced to their simplest form, as in the aplacophorans and chitons, a basic bilateral symmetry is visible.

Some animals have, however, managed without a head. Despite their relatively high position in the table of phyla, the echinoderms (e.g. starfishes, sea urchins) are headless. This is all the more surprising when one realizes that the earliest echinoderms and their likely ancestors were bilateral animals. Still, they managed without a head, and in the present-day echinoderms the nervous tissue is spread fairly evenly throughout the body and all sensory structures are very simple and widely distributed. Modern adult echinoderms are fundamentally radially symmetrical; the body parts are equally arranged around a median vertical axis which passes through the mouth. There is no clear front end, nor left and right sides, in most of the species. Radial symmetry is best for a stationary lifestyle, in which food is collected by nets or fans of tentacles. This was almost certainly the lifestyle of the earliest echinoderms, as it is of most of present-day Cnidaria (jellyfishes and allies), the other phylum to display a clear radial symmetry. The radial symmetry in the Cnidaria is evident, whereas in the echinoderms a unique five-sided body form has been imposed on it, as seen in present-day starfishes and brittle stars.

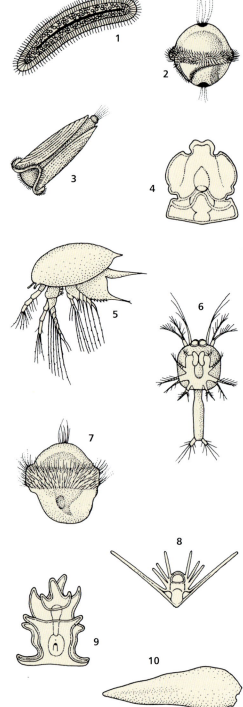

⬦ **Above** In most aquatic invertebrates a larva hatches from the egg, floats free, and metamorphoses into adult form. In some, an adult-like juvenile emerges. Adults with simple body architecture usually have larvae that are simple in form (e.g. the planula of sponges and jellyfishes). The tadpole-like sea squirt larva may have provided the evolutionary springboard from which vertebrates developed: **1** planula (sponge, jellyfishes, and other cnidarians); **2** trochophore (many worms); **3** cyphonautes (sea mat); **4** tornaria (hemichordates, including acorn worm); **5** nauplius (first stage of many crustaceans); **6** zoea (crabs and other decapods); **7** veliger (mollusk); **8** pluteus (brittle star, sea urchin); **9** auricularia (starfish, sea cucumber); **10** "tadpole' larva of a sea squirt.

⬤ Above and left *Most aquatic invertebrates have bilateral symmetry in common, however diverse their general appearance. For example, crabs and other crustaceans show a straightforward symmetry around a midline. Minor asymmetries may occur within this basic pattern, such as in the male Fiddler crab (Uca pugnax; left), which has evolved one claw far larger than the other. This outsized limb is used to attract the attention of females for mating, and to wrestle with other males during courtship struggles.*

Yet two major invertebrate groups show a different, radial symmetry without a head – the jellyfishes and their relatives, and the echinoderms, such as this Fromia sp. starfish (above). Five-pointed symmetry around the axis of the mouth is called pentamerism.

Finally, there are those animals which are essentially without regular form or are asymmetrical. These are the sponges, which grow in a variety of fashions, including encrusting, upright or plantlike, or even boring into rocks. While each species has a characteristic development of the canal system inside the body, its precise external appearance depends very much on prevailmg local conditions, such as exposure, currents and form of substrate. The simple body form of the sponges of course rules out the development of nerves and muscles, so a coordinating nerve system has not evolved.

The bilaterally symmetrical bodies of coelomate metazoans may be unsegmented (americ), divided into a few segments (oligomeric), or many units (metameric). The bodies of many types (e.g. ectoprocts or echinoderms) show division into a few segments during their development, but these may be masked in the adult. In the annelids and arthropods the repetition of structural units along the body (metamerism) allows for the modification of the segmental appendages to fulfil various functions. In the arthropods these appendages or limbs, often jointed, carry out a wide range of activities, from locomotion to copulation.   AC

DRIFTERS AND WANDERERS

The ecology of zooplankton

THE WORD PLANKTON MEANS "DRIFTER" OR "wanderer". It refers to those plants and animals that are swept along by water currents rather than by their own swimming ability. (Animals that swim and determine their own direction are called nekton.) The greatest diversity of plankton exists in the world's oceans, but lakes and some rivers also have their own plankton communities. Here, examples from the sea will be used. Plants of the plankton are known as phytoplankton and animals of the plankton as zooplankton. While many zooplankton are minute – less than 5mm (0.2in) long – a few are large, for example some jellyfishes, whose tentacles may be 15m (49ft) in length. Some zooplankton can actually swim, but not sufficiently well to prevent them from being swept along by currents in the water. However, their swimming ability may be sufficient to allow them to regulate their vertical position in the water, which can be very important as the position or depth of their food can vary around the daytime/nighttime cycle (for example, phytoplankton rises by day and sinks by night, whereas zooplankton does the reverse).

Seawater contains many nutrients important for plant growth, notably nitrogen, phosphorus and potassium. Their presence means that phytoplankton can photosynthesize and grow while they drift in the illuminated layers of the sea. Two forms of phytoplankton, dinoflagellates and diatoms, are particularly important as founders in the planktonic food webs, for upon them most of the animal life

of the oceans and shallow seas ultimately depends. By their photosynthetic activity the dinoflagellates and diatoms harness the sun's energy and lock it into organic compounds such as sugars and starch which provide an energy source for the grazers that feed on the phytoplankton.

Zooplankton comprises a wide range of animals. Virtually every known phylum is represented in the sea, and many examples of marine animals have planktonic larvae. Such organisms may be referred to as meroplankton or temporary plankton. Good examples are the developing larvae of bottom-dwellers such as mussels, clams, whelks, polychaete worms, crabs, lobsters, and starfish. These larvae ascend into the surface waters and live and feed in a way totally different from that of their adults. Thus the offspring do not compete with the adults for food or living space and the important task of dispersal is achieved by ocean currents. At the end of their planktonic lives, the temporary plankton must settle on the seabed and change into adult forms. If the correct substrate is missing then they fail to mature. Often complex physiological and behavioral processes occur

○ **Right** *Radiolarians have geometrically shaped skeletons made of silica. These minute protozoans form part of the vast oceanic plankton community.*

○ **Below** *Oncea are tiny holoplanktonic crustaceans; copepods such as these are the main source of protein in the oceans. This group is mating in midwater*

before satisfactory settlement is achieved, and many settling larvae have elaborate mechanisms for detecting textures and chemicals in substrates.

In addition to the temporary plankton there is a holoplankton: organisms whose entire lives are spent drifting in the sea. Of these the most conspicuous element (around 70 percent) are crustaceans. The most abundant class of planktonic crustaceans are the copepods, efficient grazers of phytoplankton especially in temperate seas. The euphausids make up another very important group of crustaceans, and in some regions, for example, the southern oceans, they can occur in enormous numbers as "krill," providing the staple diet of the great whales. All these crustaceans have mechanisms for straining the seawater to extract the fine plant cells from it. Other noncrustacean holoplanktonic forms that sieve water for food are the planktonic relatives of the sea squirts. Some rotifers live as herbivores in the surface waters of the sea, but they are a much more important component of the plankton of lakes and rivers. Along with many invertebrate larvae, these herbivorous holoplanktonic forms are important in harvesting the energy contained in the planktonic and pass it on to the carnivorous zooplankton by way of the food webs of the sea's surface.

There are many types of carnivorous zooplankton in the oceans and members of many phyla are involved. Protozoans feeding on bacteria or other protozoans occur. Some, like the foraminiferans and radiolarians, form conspicuous deposits on the seabed after they die, thanks to their durable mineralized shells or tests. Cnidarians provide a range of temporary and permanent planktonic carnivores. Many hydroid medusae spend only part of the lifecycle of the hydroids in the plankton, while others like the Portuguese man-of-war are permanent plankton dwellers, often taking food as large as fishes. The ctenophores, such as *Pleurobrachia* and *Beroë*, are efficient predators of copepods, often outcompeting fishes (for example, herrings) for them. Thus they are of economic significance as competitors of commercial fish stocks. Other carnivores include pelagic gastropods, polychaetes, and arrow worms.

Oceanographers regard the occurrence of certain species in surface waters as an indication of the origins of water currents. Thus, in Northwest Europe, plankton containing the arrow worm *Sagitta elegans* has been demonstrated to come from the clean open Atlantic, whereas water containing *S. setosa* is known to have a coastal origin. Different chaetognaths also appear at different depths in the ocean and are indicative of different animal communities.   AC

Protozoans

PROTOZOANS LIVE IN AN UNSEEN WORLD. *They are invisible to the naked eye, but occur all around us, beneath us and even within us – they are ubiquitous. Their overriding requirement is for free water, so they are mainly found in floating (planktonic) and bottom-dwelling communities of the sea, estuaries, and freshwater environments. Some live in the water films around soil particles and in bogs, while others are parasites of other animals, notably causing malaria and sleeping sickness in humans.*

Most protozoans are microscopic single-celled organisms living a solitary existence. Some, however, are colonial. Colony structure varies; in the green chlorophyte *Volvox* numerous individuals are embedded in a mucilaginous spherical matrix, while in other flagellates, for example *Diplosiga*, a group of individuals occurs at the end of a stalk. Branched stalked colonies are characteristic of some ciliates, such as *Carchesium*.

Basic Life Forms
FORM, FUNCTION AND DIET

Many protozoans have evolved a parasitic mode of life involving one or two hosts. Some species live in the guts and urogenital tracts of their hosts. Others have invaded the body fluids and cells of the host, for example the malarial parasite *Plasmodium*, which lives for part of its life cycle in the blood and liver cells of mammals, birds and reptiles and the other part in mosquitoes (see Malaria and Sleeping Sickness). Five of the seven protozoan phyla are exclusively parasitic, but among the mainly freeliving flagellates, amoebae and ciliates there are some species that have opted for parasitism. Notable among the parasitic flagellates are the haemoflagellates causing various forms of trypanosomiasis, including sleeping sickness. The opalinid gut parasites of frogs and toads are

another example. In most multicellular animals the essential life processes are carried out by specialized tissues and organs. In protozoans all life processes occur in the single cell and the building blocks for these specialized functions are small tubular structures termed microtubules. These have reached their most complex organization in the ciliates, the most advanced of all protozoans. Apart from a few flagellate groups, the ciliates are the only protozoans to possess a true cell mouth or cytostome. In addition, they typically have two types of nuclei (dimorphism), each performing a different role. The macronucleus – which is often large and may be round, horseshoe-shaped, elongated, or resemble a string of beads – controls normal physiological functioning in the cell, while the micronucleus is concerned with the replication of genetic material during reproduction. It is quite common for a ciliate to possess several micronuclei. Other protozoans have nuclei of one type only, although some species may have several. The exceptions are the foraminiferans, which show nuclear dimorphism at some stages in their life cycle. The most widely known and researched ciliates are species of the genera *Paramecium* and *Tetrahymena*, but these represent only a minute fraction of the 8,000 or so species so far described by science.

The majority of protozoans feed on bacteria, algae, other protozoans, microscopic animals and

○ **Right** *Slender filaments of a microscopic foraminiferan (Globigerinoides sp.) catch the light. The filaments, or pseudopodia, radiate out from the rest of the cell inside a hard shell or test. They are used to trap food and for movement.*

○ **Below** *Protozoan forms:* **1** *Actinophrys (heliozoan);* **2** *Opalina (opalinid);* **3** *Acineta (suctorian);* **4** *Euglena (phytoflagellate);* **5** *Elphidium (foraminiferan);* **6** *Trypanosoma (hemoflagellate);* **7** *Hexacontium (radiolarian).*

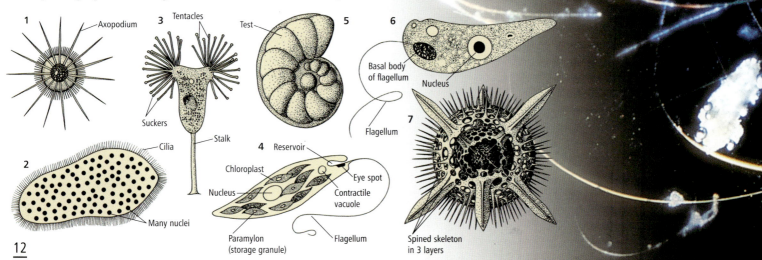

1 — Axopodium

3 — Tentacles — Suckers — Stalk

Test — 5

6 — Basal body of flagellum — Nucleus — Flagellum

Cilia

2 — Many nuclei

4 — Reservoir — Chloroplast — Nucleus — Eye spot — Contractile vacuole — Flagellum — Paramylon (storage granule)

7 — Spined skeleton in 3 layers

PROTOZOANS

Kingdom: Protoctista*

Subkingdom: Protozoa

About 80,000 species in 17 phyla.

Distribution Worldwide in aquatic and soil environments, parasitic in invertebrates and vertebrates.

Fossil record Earliest record of amoebalike organisms Precambrian, possibly up to 1,000 million years ago.

Size Microscopic, 1μ–5mm (most 5–250μm).

Features Unicellular, freeliving or parasitic; mostly solitary, some ciliates and flagellates colonial; move by means of pseudopodia, flagella or cilia; some amoebae with tests or shells; ciliates possess a mouth pore for ingestion (cystostome) and nuclei of two sizes; reproduction mainly asexual; sexual reproduction in some groups.

*Note: in earlier classifications the Protozoa were regarded as a phylum within the kingdom Animalia. This did not take into account that some protozoans have plantlike nutrition, and led to the situation where a single species could be classified as a plant by botanists and as an animal by zoologists. The recently proposed kingdom Protoctista, with one subkingdom, the Protozoa, resolves the problem by keeping all the singlecelled animals (whether plant- or animal-like) separate from the kingdom Animalia and the "plant" kingdoms.

FLAGELLATES Phylum Euglenida
1,000 species, including *Euglena*.

TRYPANOSOMES AND ALLIES
Phylum Kinetoplastida
600 species, including *Trypanosoma, Leishmania*.

CILIATES Phylum Ciliophora
8,000 species, including *Paramecium, Tetrahymena, Vorticella, Balantidium, Acineta, Didinium, Coldpidium*.

MALARIAL PARASITES Phylum Apicomplexa
5,000 species, including *Plasmodium, Coccidia*, the Gregarines and their allies.

DINOFLAGELLATES Phylum Dinoflagellata
4,000 species, including *Ceratium, Noctiluca*.

DIATOMS, SLIME NETS AND ALLIES
Phylum Stramenopila
9,000 species, including *Diatoma, Pinnularia*.

AMOEBAS AND ALLIES Phylum Rhizopoda
200 species, including *Amoeba, Arcella, Difflugia, Naegleria*.

RADIOLARIANS, HELIOZOANS AND ALLIES
Phylum Actinopoda
4,240 species, including *Actinophys, Actinosphaerium, Actipylina*.

FORAMINIFERA Phylum Granuloreticulosa
40,000 species, including *Elphidium, Globigerina, Pilulina*.

DIPLOMONADS Phylum Diplomonadida
100 species, including *Enteromonas, Giardia*.

PARABASILIDS Phylum Parabasilida
300 species, including *Trichonympha*.

CRYPTOMONADS Phylum Cryptomonada
200 species, including *Chilomonas*.

MICROSPORANS Phylum Microspora
800 species, including *Encephalitozoon*.

ASCETOSPORANS Phylum Ascetospora
c.30 species, including *Paramyxa, Marteilia*.

CHOANOFLAGELLATES Phylum Choanoflagellata
c.400 species, including *Monosiga*.

GREEN ALGAE Phylum Chlorophyta
7,000–9,000 species, including *Chlamydomonas, Eudorina, Volvox*.

OPALINIDS Phylum Opalinida
c.400 species, including *Opalina, Cepedea*.

in the case of parasites on host tissue, fluids and gut contents. Their diet incorporates complex organic compounds of nitrogen and hydrogen, and they are said to be heterotrophic. Some flagellates and green algae, such as *Euglena* (Phylum Euglenida) and *Volvox* (Phylum Chlorophyta) however, possess photosynthetic pigments in chloroplasts. These protozoans are capable of harnessing the sun's radiant energy in the chemical process of photosynthesis to construct complex organic compounds from simple molecules – they are said to be autotrophic. A number of such protozoans must, however, combine autotrophy with heterotrophy, in varying degrees. Such organisms lie on the boundary between an animal and plantlike nutrition .

Many protozoans are simply bound by the cell wall, but skeletal structures in the form of secreted shells or tests are common among the members of the phyla Rhizopoda, Actinopoda, and Granuloreticulosa and usually have a single chamber. The exclusively marine foraminiferans (phylum Granuloreticulosa) however, are exceptional in having shells with numerous chambers. Shells and tests may be formed of calcium carbonate or silica, or from organic substances such as cellulose or chitin.

Most freeliving and some parasitic species need to move around their environment to feed, to move toward and away from favorable and unfavorable conditions, and in some cases special movement is required in reproductive processes. The various protozoan groups achieve movement using different structures.

Members of the Phylum Rhizopoda (including the genus *Amoeba*) produce so-called pseudopodia – flowing extensions of the cell. These may be extended only one at a time, as in *Naegleria* or several at a time, as in *Amoeba proteus*, *Arcella*, and *Difflugia*. Heliozoan sarcodines (Phylum Actinopoda) which resemble a stylized sun, possess long slender pseudopodia, called axopodia, which radiate from central cell mass. Each axopodium is supported by a large number of microtubules arranged in a parallel fashion along the longitudinal axis. Heliozoans move slowly, rolling along by repeatedly shortening and lengthening the axopodia. A well-known example of these so-called sun organisms is *Actinosphaerium*. The foraminiferans, for example *Elphidium*, which bear complex chambered shells, have a complicated network of pseudopodial strands which branch and fuse with each other to produce a linking complex of what are called reticulopodia.

▶ ***Main picture*** *A colony of Volvox, a genus of microscopic unicellular organisms widely distributed in freshwater environments. Each colony is a hollow sphere composed of thousands of cells, and each cell has two flagella pointing outwards, which enable the colony to swim.*

▶ ***Right*** *Some representative species of protozoans:* **1** *A species of Difflugia. The shell is made up of foreign particles (microscopic);* **2** *A species of Acrinosphaerium, a microscopic sun animalcule (heliozoan);* **3** *A species of Amoeba, probably the best-known protozoan;* **4** *A genus of Stentor, a ciliate that lives attached to the substrate (microscopic);* **5** *A species of Arcella (microscopic);* **6** *Vorticella, a genus of microscopic sessile ciliates;* **7** *A species of Spirostomum, a genus of ciliates able to swim (microscopic).*

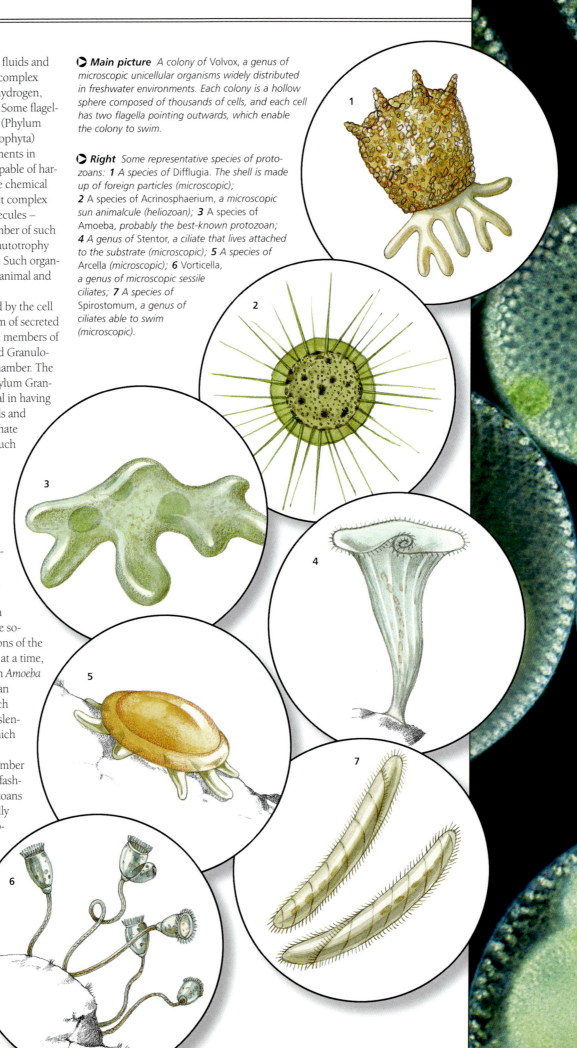

Like the axopodia of heliozoans the reticulopodia of foraminiferans are supported by microtubules.

The other means of movement is by the beating action of the filamentous cilia and flagella, which are permanent outgrowths of the cell rather than, like pseudopodia, its temporary pseudopodial extensions.

Cilia and flagella are structurally similar, but cilia are shorter. Normally flagellates carry only one or two flagella, while in the ciliates the cilia are numerous and usually arranged in ordered rows, each called kinety. The number of kinety is constant in each species and is used as an aid in identification. In some cases cilia may fuse to form cirri, which resemble short thick hairs, or structures which are sail-like. Each cilium and flagellum is about 0.15–0.3μm in diameter and is supported by a core (axoneme) made up of two centrally positioned microtubules surrounded and joined by cross-bridges to nine double microtubules. This 9+2 arrangement of microtubules is common in cilia and flagella throughout the living world – from amoebas to invaders of lung linings of humans. Movement in cilia and flagella involves the passage of waves along them from one axis to the other. Most flagella move in two-dimensional waves, while cilia move in three-dimensional patterns coordinated into waves that result from fluid forces (hydrodynamic forces) acting on the automatic beating of each cilium.

A Diversity of Strategies
REPRODUCTION

Reproduction in the protozoans does not usually involve sex or sexual organelles – it is asexual. In most freeliving species asexual reproduction occurs by a process called binary fission, whereby each reproductive effort results in two identical

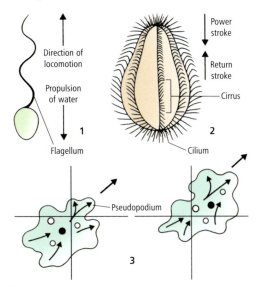

⬤ **Above** *Protozoans move in three ways:* **1** *By a sigle flagellum that pulls the cell through the water;* **2** *By rows of cilia coordinated to act like the oars of a rowboat, having a power stroke and a recovery stroke;* **3** *By amoeboid movement, whereby pseudopodia are extended and the rest of the body flows into them.*

daughter cells by the division of a parent cell. In the flagellates, including the parasitic species, the plane of division is longitudinal, while in the ciliates it is normally transverse and prior to division of the cytoplasm the mouth is replicated. Members of the phyla Rhizopoda, Actinopoda, and Granuloreticulosa do not normally have a fixed plane for division. In shelled and testate species the process is complicated by the need to replicate skeletal structures. In testate species of amoeba – for example *Difflugia* – cytoplasm destined to become the daughter is extruded from the aperture of the parent test. Preformed scales in the cytoplasm then form a test around the extruded cytoplasm. When the process is complete the two amoebae separate.

Most freeliving species normally reproduce asexually providing conditions are favorable. Sexual reproduction is usually only resorted to in adversity, such as drying up of the aquatic medium when the normal cells would not survive. The ability to undergo a sexual phase is not widespread in the amoebae and flagellates and is restricted to a limited number of groups. Some species may never have reproduced sexually in their evolutionary history, while others may have lost sexual competence. Both isogamous (reproductive cells or gametes alike) and the more advanced anisogamous (reproductive cells or gametes dissimilar) forms of sexual reproduction occur in protozoans.

The foraminiferans are unusual among freeliving species in having alternation of asexual and sexual generations. Here each organism reproduces asexually to produce many amoebalike organisms which secrete shells around themselves. When mature, these produce many identical gametes which are usually liberated into the sea, where they fuse in pairs to produce individuals which in turn secrete a shell, grow to maturity and repeat the cycle.

Almost all of the ciliates are capable of sexual reproduction by a process called conjugation, which does not result in an immediate increase in numbers. The function of conjugation is to facilitate an exchange of genetic materials between

Below *Asexual reproduction in protozoans is by simple division (binary fission). In flagellates* **1** *(e.g.* Euglena*) it is longitudinal. In ciliates* **2** *(e.g.* Tetrahymena*) division is complicated by the replication of the oral apparatus. In shelled amoebae* **3** *(e.g.* Euglypha*) the daughter is extruded from the parent. Amoebae* **4** *have no fixed plane of division.*

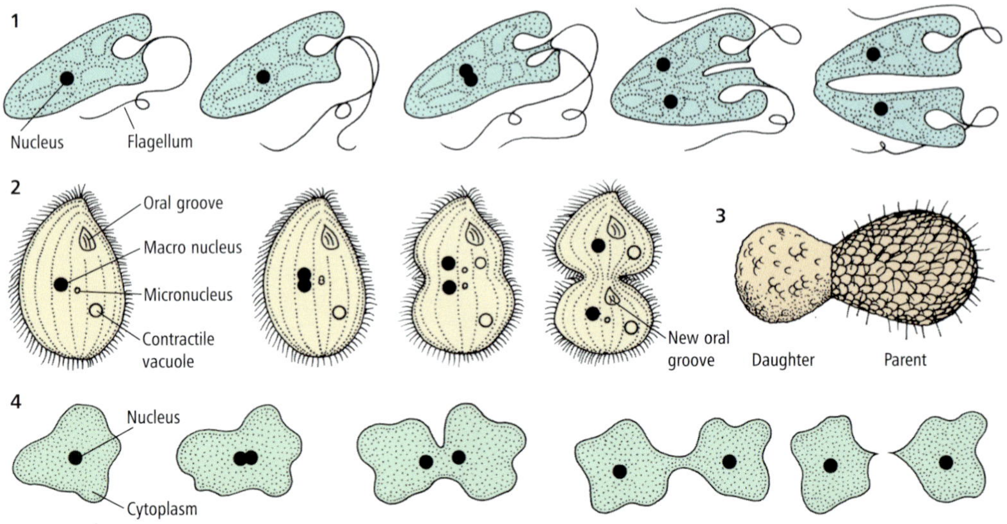

Prey Capture in Carnivorous Protozoans

Carnivorous protozoans prey on other protozoans, rotifers, members of the Gastrotricha and small crustaceans. The mode of capture and ingestion is often spectacular and frequently the prey are larger than the predators.

Among the ciliates the sedentary species of the subphylum Suctoria have lost their cilia, which have been replaced by tentacles, each of which functions as a mouth. When other ciliates, such as *Colpidium*, collide with a tentacle, they stick to it. Other tentacles move toward the prey and also attach. The cell wall of the prey is perforated at the sites of attachment and the prey cell contents are moved up the tentacle by microtubular elements within the tentacle. A single speciessuch as *Podophrya* can feed simultaneously on four or five prey. *Didinium nasutum* is a ciliate that feeds exclusively on *Paramecium*, which it apprehends using extrudable structures called pexicysts and toxicysts. The former hold the prey while the latter penetrate deeply into it ,releasing poisons. *Didinium* consumes the immobilized prey whole, its body becoming distended by the ingested *Paramecium*.

The heliozoan *Actinophrys* also feeds on ciliates captured, on contact, by the radiating axopodia. Once attached, the prey is progressively engulfed by a large funnel-shaped pseudopodium produced by the cell body. Occasionally when an individual *Actinophrys* has captured a large prey, other *Actinophrys* may fuse with the feeding individual to share the meal. In such instances, after digesting their ciliate victim, the heliozoan predators separate again.

The foraminiferan *Pilulina* has evolved into a living pitfall trap. This bottom-dwelling species builds a bowl-shaped shell or test with mud, camouflaging the pseudopodia across the entrance. When copepod crustaceans blunder onto the pseudopodia they get stuck and are drawn down into the animal. The radiolarians, which possess a silica-rich internal skeleton, deal with copepod prey by extending the waveflow along the axopodia the broad surfaces of the prey's exoskeleton, to and rupturing the prey by force. The axopodia then penetrate and prise off pieces of flesh which are directed down the axopodia to the main cell body for ingestion. JL-P/AC

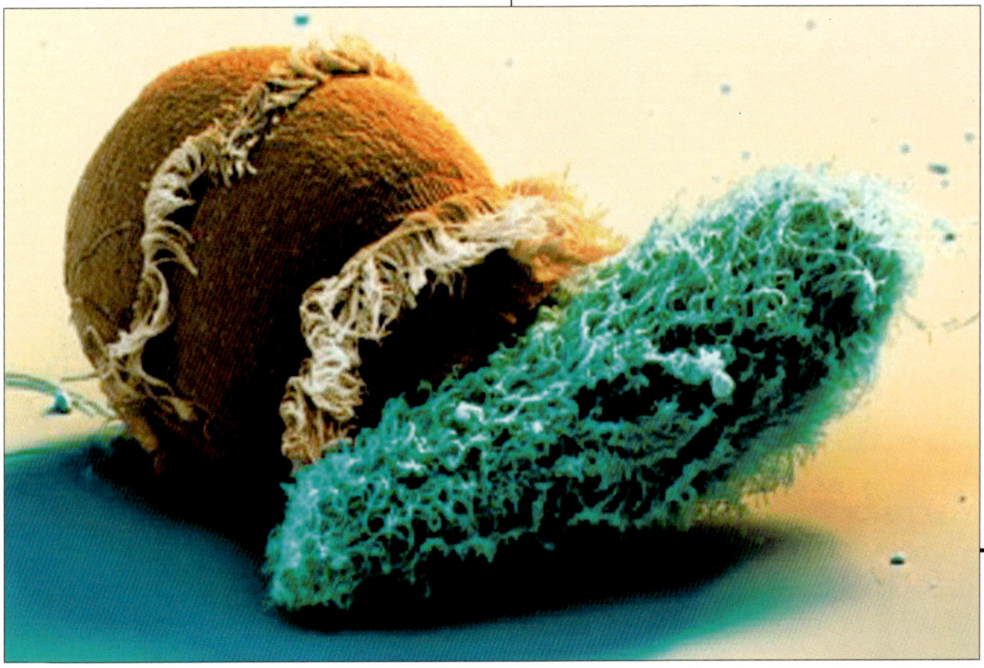

Left *As it maneuvers a* Paramecium *into a position where it is easier to devour, a* Didinium nasutum *expands its snout and gullet.*

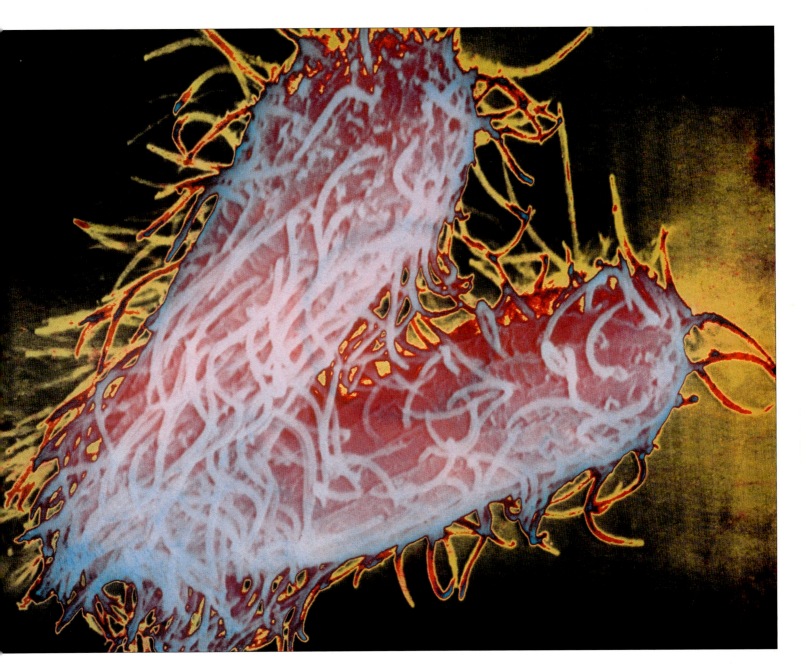

individuals. During this process two ciliates come together side by side and are joined by a bridge of cell contents (cytoplasm). A complex series of divisions of the micronucleus occurs, including a halving of the pairs of chromosomes (or meiosis).

In the final stages of conjugation, a micronuc-leus passes from each individual into the other. Essentially the micronuclei are gametes. Each received micronucleus fuses with an existing micronucleus in the recipient. The ciliates sepa-rate and, after further nuclear divisions, eventually undergo binary fission.

All members of the parasitic phyla, except for some groups in the Apicomplexa, produce spores at some stages in their lifecycles. The Apicomplexa contains a number of parasites of medical and vet-erinary importance, including the malarial para-sites *Plasmodium* and the *Coccidia* responsible for coccidiosis in poultry. Some species, like *Plasmod-ium*, have complex lifecycles involving two hosts with an alternation of sexual and asexual phases. In *Plasmodium* the sexual phase is initiated in humans and is completed in the mosquito;

following this many thousands of motile spores (sporozoites) are reproduced that are infective to humans, and which are transmitted when the mosquito feeds. In the human body, repeated phases of multiple asexual division take place with-in the red blood cells and liver cells (see Malaria and Sleeping Sickness). The phyla Microspora and Ascetospora are parasites of a wide range of verte-brates and invertebrates, while other forms para-sitize algae.

Recycling Agents
ECOLOGY

The ecology of protozoans is very complex, as one would expect in a group of ubiquitous organisms. They are found in the waters and soils of the world's polar regions. Some have adapted to warm springs and there are records of protozoans living in waters as warm as 68°C (154°F). Protozoans occur commonly in planktonic communities in marine, brackish, and freshwater habitats, and also in the complex bottom-dwelling (benthic) communities of these environments. Little is

known about protozoans in the marine deeps, but there is a record of foraminiferans living at 4,000m (13,000ft) in the Atlantic. Ciliates, flagellates and various types of amoebae are also common in soils and boggy habitats.

Since many protozoans exploit bacteria as a food source they form part of the decomposer food web in nature. Recent research indicates that protozoans may stimulate the rate of decomposi-tion by bacteria and thus enhance the recycling of minerals such as phosphorus and nitrogen. The exact mechanism is not entirely clear, but proto-zoans grazing on bacteria may maintain the bacte-rial community in a state of physiological youth and hence at the optimum level of efficiency. There is also evidence to suggest that some proto-zoans secrete a substance that promotes the growth of bacteria.   JL-P/AC

MALARIA AND SLEEPING SICKNESS

Protozoan diseases of humans

BETWEEN ONE AND THREE MILLION PEOPLE DIE annually from malaria, and another 500 million contract the disease – this statistic exemplifies the virulence of protozoan diseases. The most serious pathogens are *Plasmodium*, which produces malaria, and various trypanosome species responsible for diseases broadly called trypanosomiasis or sleeping sickness.

Malaria is caused by four species of the genus *Plasmodium*. The life cycle is similar in each species but there are differences in disease pathology. *Plasmodium falciparum* causes malignant tertian malaria and accounts for about 50 percent of all malarial cases. It attacks all red blood cells (erythrocytes) indiscriminately so that as many as 25 percent of the erythrocytes may be infected. In this species stages not involving the erythrocytes do not persist in the liver, so that relapses do not occur. *Plasmodium vivax* produces benign tertian malaria, which invades only immature erythrocytes so that the level of cells infected is low. Here, phowever, other stages remain in the liver, causing relapses. Benign tertian malaria is responsible for approximately 45 percent of malarial infections. The other two species are relatively rare. *Plasmodium malariae*, causing quartan malaria, attacks mature red blood cells and has persistent stages outside the blood cells. Little is known about *P. ovale* because of its rarity.

The diseases are named after the fevers which the parasites cause, tertian fevers occurring every three days or 48 hours and quartan fevers every four days or 72 hours. The naming practice is based on the Roman system of calling the first day one, whereas we would call the first day nought.

Once inside an erythrocyte, the parasite feeds on the red blood cell contents and grows. When mature it undergoes multiple asexual fission to produce many individuals called merozoites which, by an unknown mechanism, rupture the erythrocyte and escape into the blood plasma. Each released merozoite then infects another erythrocyte. The asexual division cycle in the red blood cells is well synchronized so that many erythrocytes rupture together – a phenomenon responsible for the characteristic fever which accompanies malaria. The exact mechanism producing the fever is not fully understood, but it is believed to be caused by substances (or a substance), possibly derived from the parasite, which

induce the release of a fever-producing agent from the white blood cells, which fight the disease. When the parasite has undergone a series of asexual erythrocytic cycles, some individuals produce the male and female gametocytes which are the stages infective to the mosquito host. The stimulus for gametocyte production is unknown.

Malaria is still one of the greatest causes of

○ *Below Life cycle of sleeping sickness: **1** Trypanosomes in human blood are taken up by the tsetse fly when feeding; **2** They enter the midgut, where division occurs before migrating forward after 48 hours to the foregut (proventriculus); **3** Trypanosomes remain in the proventriculus for 10–15 days before migrating to the salivary glands; **4** Over a 30–50-day period in the salivary gland, the trypanosomes change into crithidial forms and multiply before becoming infective metacyclic forms; **5** When the tsetse bites another human, metacyclic trypanosomes enter the victim's body and multiply at the site of infection; **6** Trypanosomes then invade the blood stream and reproduce by binary fission. They then may follow two courses (7 or 8); **7** They enter the tissue space of various organisms and lymph nodes and then invade the central nervous system to cause typical sleeping sickness symptoms. The trypanosomes do not enter cells, but remain between them; **8** They are taken up by further tsetse flies to continue the cycle.*

2

3

1

8

Tsetse fly

Human

4

5

7

6

death in humans. Tens of millions of cases are reported each year and many are fatal. Successful control measures are available, and in countries such as the USA, Israel and Cyprus the disease has been eradicated. In Third World countries, however, control measures have little impact on malaria. Broadly, eradication programs involve the use of drugs to treat the disease in humans, and a series of measures aimed at breaking the parasite's life cycle by destroying the intermediate mosquito host.

Like many insects, the mosquito has an aquatic larval stage. The draining of swamps and lakes deprives the mosquito of an environment for breeding and its larval development, but residual populations continue to breed in irrigation canals, ditches and paddy fields. Spraying of oil on the water surface asphixiates the larvae, which have to come to the water surface periodically to breathe. The poison Paris Green can effectively kill larvae when added to the water. Biological control using fish predators of mosquito larvae, such as the guppy, aid in reducing larval populations.

Adult mosquitoes can be killed by spraying houses with various insecticides such as hexachlorocyclohexane and dieldrin. In the past DDT was very successful but its toxicity to higher animals now precludes its use. Biological control measures involve releasing sterile male mosquitos into the population, thereby decreasing reproduction rates, and the introduction of bacterial, fungal and protozoan pathogens of the mosquito.Chemotherapy in humans involves four broad categories of treatment. Firstly, there are prophylactic drugs, such as Proguanil, which taken on a regular basis prevent recurring erythrocytic infections. Secondly, there are drugs such as Chloroquine which destroy the blood stages of the parasite. Thirdly there are drugs which destroy gametocytes. Lastly there are drugs which, when taken up by the mosquito during feeding on humans, prevent further development of the parasite in the insect. Drug resistance by *Plasmodium* does occur and is

⚑ **Above** *Thousands of the motile spores (sporozoites) of* Plasmodium vivax *in a blood sample. This species is responsible for producing benign tertian malaria, by far the commonest form.*

increasing; *P. falciparum* has become resistant to Chloroquine in some parts of Africa and South America, and has to be treated by a combination of quinine and sulfonamides.

The flagellates *Trypanosoma rhodesiense* and *T. gambiense* cause African trypanosomiasis or sleeping sickness. The two-host lifecycle involves a tsetse fly (genus *Glossina*) and humans. In man, the trypanosomes live in the blood plasma and lymph glands, progressing later to the cerebrospinal fluid and brain. The disease is typified by mental and physical apathy and a desire to sleep. The disease is fatal if untreated, *T. rhodesiense* running a more acute course than *T. gambiense*. Control measures include insecticide use, introduction of sterile males, clearing vegetation in which *Glossina* spends the whole of its life cycle, and the use of drugs in humans. Control is complicated by the fact that *T. rhodesiense* also infects game animals, so that a reservoir population of the parasite persists. JL-P/AC

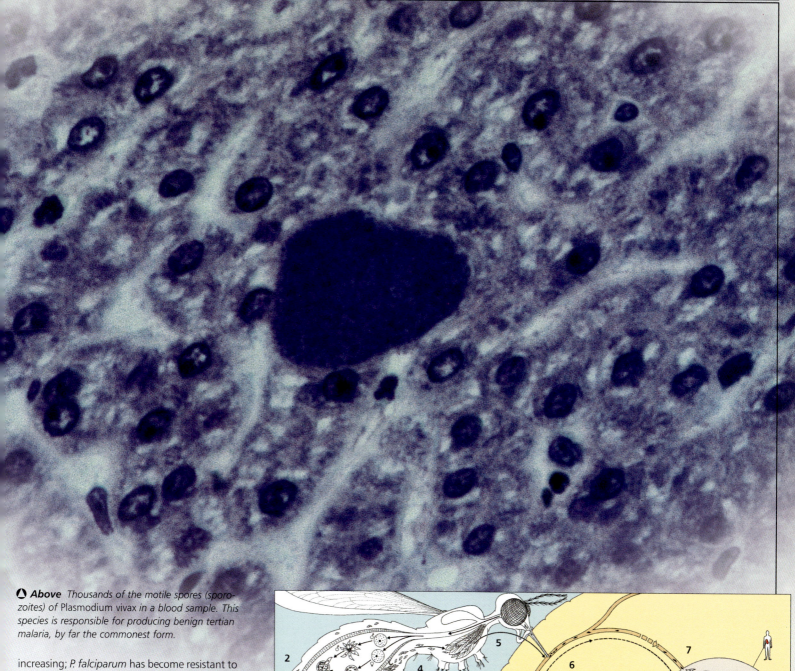

⚑ **Above** *Life cycle of malaria:* **1** *In a blood meal a mosquito takes up gametocytes, which enter its stomach;* **2** *The gametocytes mature to produce either thin motile male gametes or larger female gametes. The male gametes fertilize the female gametes to produce a zygote;* **3** *The zygote penetrates the stomach wall, where it develops into an oocyst;* **4** *The oocyst ruptures, releasing many sporozoites into the mosquito's body cavity;* **5** *The sporozoites migrate to the mosquito's salivary glands;* **6** *When the insect next feeds, it releases sporozoites into the human blood stream;* **7** *The sporozoites migrate through the blood stream* and enter the liver to start the "pre-erythrocitic" cycle; **8** *In the liver cell, the parasite reproduces, producing masses of merozoites;* **9** *In some species, released merozoites may reinfect other liver cells, which act as a reservoir of the parasite;* **10** *Merozoites in the blood stream enter red blood cells;* **11** *Within the red blood cell division occurs to produce masses of merozoites which reinfect other red blood cells. Cell rupture is synchronized – a characteristic fever develops, repeated on each release every 48 or 72 hours, depending on species;* **12** *Some merozoites form gametocytes, taken up by mosquitos to renew the infection cycle.*

Sponges

S INCE ANCIENT TIMES, THE HUMBLE BATH
sponge has been harvested and used by people,
particularly in the Mediterranean region. Bath
sponge species are the best known of a group of animals whose relationship to other organisms is still
a matter of debate.

Until the early 19th century sponges were regarded as plants, but they are now generally considered to be a group (phylum Porifera) of animals
placed within their own subkingdom, the Parazoa.
They probably originated either from flagellate
protozoans or from related primitive metazoans.

A Simple Structure

FORM, FUNCTION, AND DIET

Sponges range in size from the microscopic up to
2m (6.6ft). They often form a thin incrustation on
hard substrates to which they are attached, but
others are massive, tubular, branching, amor-
phous or urn-, cup- or fan-shaped. They may be
drab or brightly colored, the colors derived from
mostly yellow to red carotenoid pigments.

All sponges are similar in structure. They have
a simple body wall containing surface (epithelial)
and linking (connective) tissues, and an array of
cell types, including cells (amoebocytes) that
move by means of the flow of protoplasm (amoeboid locomotion). Amoebocytes wander through
the inner tissues, for example, secreting and
enlarging the skeletal spicules and laying down
spongin threads. Sponges are not totally immov-
able but the main body may show very limited
movement through the action of cells called
myocytes, but they often remain anchored to the
same spot.

Although sponges are soft-bodied, many are
firm to touch. This solidity is due to the internal
skeleton comprised of hard rod- or star-shaped
calcareous or siliceous spicules and/or of a meshwork of protein fibers called spongin, as in the
bath sponge. Spicules may penetrate the sponge
surface of some species and cause skin irritation
when handled.

⬖ **Above** A freshwater sponge (Ephydatia fluviatilis);
its green color is the result of action of micro-algae
such as Chlorella.

⬗ **Right** Clearly visible on this group of Yellow tube
sponges (Aplysina fistularis) is the large exhalent
opening, or osculum.

Sponges are filter-feeders straining off bacteria
and fine detritus from the water. Oxygen and dissolved organic matter are also absorbed and waste
materials carried away. Water enters canals in the
sponge through minute pores in their surface and
moves to chambers lined by flagellate cells called
choanocytes or collar cells. The choanocytes
ingest food particles, which are passed to the
amoebocytes for passage to other cells. Eventually
the water is expelled from the sponge surface, often
through volcanolike oscules at the surface. Water
is driven through the sponge mainly by the waving action of flagella borne by the choanocytes.

Different Strategies

SEXUAL REPRODUCTION

Sponges reproduce asexually by budding off new
individuals, by fragmentation of parts which grow
into new sponges and, particularly in the case of
freshwater sponges, by the production of special

gemmules. These gemmules remain within the
body of the sponge until it disintegrates, when
they are released. In freshwater sponges, which
die back in winter in colder latitudes, the gemmules are very resistant to adverse conditions,
such as extreme cold. Indeed, they will not hatch
unless they have undergone a period of cold.

In sexual reproduction, eggs originate from
amoebocytes and sperms from amoebocytes or
transformed choanocytes, usually at different
times within the same individual. The sperms are
shed into the water, the eggs often being retained
within the parent, where they are fertilized. Either
solid (parenchymula) or hollow (amphiblastula)
larvae may be produced; many swim for up to several days, settle, and metamorphose into individuals or colonies that feed and grow. Others creep
on the substrate before metamorphosis. Some
mature Antarctic sponges have not grown over a
period of 10 years.

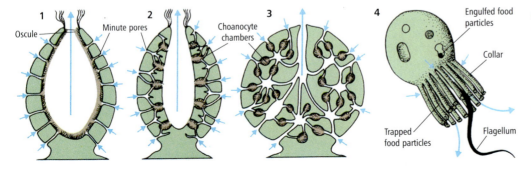

⬗ **Left** 1, 2 and 3: Water enters canals in the sponge
through minute pores in their surface and moves to
chambers lined by flagellate cells called choanocytes or
collar cells 4. The choanocytes ingest food particles,
which are passed to the amoebocytes for passage to
other cells. Eventually the water is expelled from the
sponge surface. Water is driven through the sponge
mainly by the beating action of the flagellae borne on
the choanocytes. Choanocytes may line the body cavity
1, or the wall is folded so these cells line pouches
1, 2 connected to more complicated canal systems.

SPONGES

Subkingdom: Parazoa

Phylum: Porifera

About 5,000 species in 790 genera and 80 families.

Distribution Worldwide, freshwater and marine, intertidal to deep sea.

Fossil record Originated in Cambrian 570–500 million years ago; 390 genera identified from Cretaceous (135–65 m.y.a.).

Size From microscopic to 2m (6.6ft); the largest sponges occur in the Antarctic and the Caribbean.

Features Form variable; solitary or colonial; mostly porous, filter-feeding organisms mostly attached direct to substrate, without "stem"; lack organs and have little in way of definite tissues, but with complex array of cell types; skeleton lacking or of siliceous or calcareous spicules, or of organic spongin fibers; generally hermaphrodite; sexual and asexual reproduction.

GLASS OR SILICEOUS SPONGES
Class Hexactinellida (Hyalospongiae)
About 600 species. Marine, below tidal levels but more common in deeper waters. Skeleton of complex silica spicules, with basic pattern of 6 rays. Genera and species include: *Aphrocallistes*, **Venus' flower basket** (*Euplectella aspergillum*), *Holascus*, *Pheronema*.

CALCAREOUS SPONGES Class Calcarea
About 400 species. Marine. Skeleton of calcareous spicules which are needlelike or 3- or 4-rayed. Genera include: *Acyssa*, *Clathrina*, *Leucilla*, *Leucosolenia*, *Scypha*.

TYPICAL SPONGES Class Demospongiae
About 4,000 species. Marine and freshwater. Skeleton lacking or of silica spicules, spongin fibers or both. Spicules when present not 6 rayed. Genera and species include: *Aplysina*, *Cliona*, **Caribbean sponge** (*Cribochalina vasculum*), *Ephydatia*, *Haliclona*, **Bath sponge** (*Hippospongia communis*), **Caribbean fire sponge** (*Neofibularia nolitangere*), *Siphonodictyon*, **Bath sponge** (*Spongia officinalis*), *Spongilla*.

CORALLINE SPONGES Class Sclerospongiae
About 15 species. Marine, in tropical, shallow, subtidal caves or underneath corals. Skeleton with calcareous base and entrapped silica spicules and organic fibers. Sponge forms thin layer over calcareous base. Genera include: *Ceratoporella*, *Stromatospongia*.

Abundant on the Continental Shelf

ENVIRONMENT AND CONSERVATION

Sponges are found in large numbers in all the seas of the world. They occur in greatest abundance on firm substrates, relatively few being adapted to life on unstable sand or mud. Their vertical range includes the lowest part of the shore subject to tidal effects and extends downwards as far as the abyssal depths of 8,600m (27,000ft). One family of siliceous sponges, the Spongillidae, has invaded freshwater lakes and rivers throughout the world.

Sponges living between tide marks are typically confined to parts of the shore that are seldom exposed to the air for more than a very short period. Some occur a little higher up the shore, but these are only found in shaded situations or on rocks facing away from the sun.

Some sponges are killed by even a relatively

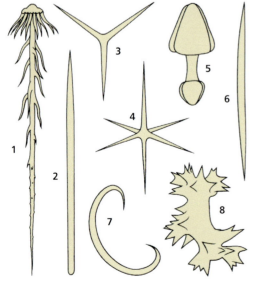

○ *Above* A species of Axinellida *sponge (Demospongiae) growing on the trunk of a fan coral. Large examples of sponges of this genus are commonly known as 'Elephant's ear sponges'.*

○ *Right* *Finger sponges (Suberites sp.) off the Australian coast. Even within a single genus, sponges may take a huge variety of forms.*

○ *Left* *Sponge spicules, which are made of calcium carbonate or silica, help support the body of the sponge. Their various shapes may characterize particular types of sponge and can be important in identifying them.* **1** *Monaxon spicule with barbs (Farrea beringiana);* **2** *Monaxon spicule (Mycale topsenti);* **3** *Triaxon spicule (Leucoria heathi);* **4** *Hexaxon spicule (Auloraccus fissuratus);* **5** *Monaxon spicule with terminal processes (Mycale topsenti);* **6** *Monaxon spicule (Raspaigella dendyi);* **7** *Monaxon spicule with recurved ends (Sigmaxinella massalis);* **8** *Polyaxon spicule (genus Streptaster);*

▷ **Right** *Boring sponges (here, Siphono-dictyon sp.) are widespread within tropical stony corals, to which they can cause considerable damage.*

short exposure to air, and it is in the shallow waters of the continental shelf that sponges achieve their greatest abundance in terms both of species and individuals.

Cavernous sponges are often inhabited by smaller animals, some of which cause no harm to the sponge, although others are parasites. Many sponges contain single-celled photosynthetic algae (zoochlorellae), blue-green algae. and symbiotic bacteria, which may provide nutrients for the sponge. Sponges are eaten by sea slugs (nudibranchs), chitons, sea stars (especially in the Antarctic), turtles, and some tropical fishes.

Usually more than half of the species of tropical sponges living exposed rather than under rocks are toxic to fish. This is believed to be an evolutionary response to high-intensity fish predation, nature having selected for noxious and toxic compounds that prevent fish from consuming sponges. Some toxic sponges are very large, such as the gigantic Caribbean sponge (*Cribochalina vasculum*), while others, such as the Caribbean fire sponge (*Neofibularia nolitangere*), are dangerous to the touch – in humans they cause a severe burning sensation lasting for several hours. Toxins probably play an important role in keeping the surface of the sponge clean, by preventing animal larvae and plant spores from settling on them. Some sponge toxins may prevent neighboring invertebrates from overgrowing and smothering them.

Sponge toxins have been used in studies on the transmission of nerve impulses. They show con-

siderable potential as biodegradeable antifouling agents and possibly as shark repellants.

Bath sponges owe their usefulness to the water-absorbing and retaining qualities of a complex lattice of spongin fibers; the fibers are also elastic enough to allow water to be squeezed out of the sponge. A number of species are harvested (mainly off Florida and Greece), principally *Spongia officinalis*, with a fine-meshed skeleton, and *Hippospongia equina*, with a coarser skeleton. These grow on rocky bottoms from low-tide level down to great depths and may be collected either by using a grappling hook from a boat, or by divers. Curing sponges simply involves leaving them to dry in the sun, allowing the soft tissues to rot, pounding and washing them, leaving only the spongin skeleton.

Cultivation of sponges from cuttings has been successfully used although such projects are probably less viable than making synthetic products.

Sponges contain various antibiotic substances, pigments, unique chemicals such as sterols, toxins, and even anti-inflammatory and antiarthritis compounds. Boring sponges of the family Clionidae may cause economic loss by weakening oyster shells. These sponges excavate chambers both chemically and mechanically.　　　　GJB/AC

ANIMALS OF THE MESOZOAN PLAN

Mesozoan animals are a taxonomic enigma, here they are regarded as an assemblage of animals showing similar evolutionary attainments. Ever since they were first discovered in 1883, scientists have been changing their opinions about their evolutionary position and relations with other animals. Now they are thought to comprise four phyla (Phylum Placozoa, Phylum Monoblastozoa, Phylum Rhombozoa, and Phylum Orthonectida) containing about 90 species, free-living or parasitic on marine invertebrates. None is larger than about 8mm (0.3in) in length. They are multicellular animals constructed from two layers of cells, and are therefore distinct from the protozoa, but their cell layers do not resemble the endoderm and ectoderm of the metazoans (see Aquatic Invertebrates). The features of these animals mean that they cannot be assigned to any other animal phylum. Some scientists believe that certain species may be degenerate flatworms, in other words they may have been previously more complex; the other more widely held opinion, however, is that they are simple multicellular organisms holding a position intermediate between Protozoa and Metazoa.

The Dicyemida, members of the phylum Rhombozoa are all parasites in the kidneys of cephalopods (for example *Octopus*), while the Orthonectida infect echinoderms (starfish, sea urchins etc), mollusks (snails, slugs etc.), Annelida (earthworms etc.) and ribbon worms (see Flatworms and Ribbon Worms). Despite their simple morphology, the Dicyemids have evolved complex lifecycles involving several generations. The first generation, called a nematogen, occurs in immature cephalopods. Repeated similar generations of nematogens are produced asexually by repeated divisions of special central (axial) cells which give rise to wormlike (vermiform) larvae **1**. When the host attains maturity the parasite assumes the next generation or rhombogen, which looks superficially similar to the nematogen, but differs in its cellular makeup. The individuals are hermaphrodite and produce infusariiform larvae which look superficially like ciliate protozoans. The fate of the larvae is uncertain, but it is believed that another intermediate host is involved in the lifecycle. Genera included in the Phylum Rhombozoa are *Dicyema*, *Dicyemmerea* and *Conocyema*.

The Orthonectids **2**, live in the tissues and tissue spaces of their marine invertebrate hosts, for example nemerteans, polychaetes, ophiuroids and bivalves. The asexual phase looks like an amoeboid mass and is called a plasmodium because it resembles the protozoan *Plasmodium*.　　　GJB/AC

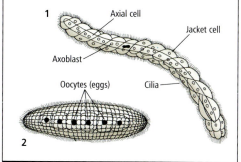

Sea Anemones and Jellyfishes

SEA ANEMONES, CORALS AND JELLYFISHES ARE *perhaps the most familiar members of the phylum Cnidaria. This diverse assemblage, whose name derives from the Greek* cnidos, *meaning "stinging nettle," contains an enormous number of animals, many of which are characterized by their possession of stinging cells (nematocysts). Cnidarians are mainly marine animals; there are only a few freshwater species, of which the best known are the hydras.*

The cnidarians are multicellular animals and have a two-layered (diploblastic) construction, in which both the differences between cells and organ development are limited. These restrictions have, however, been partially offset in colonial types by the specialization of individuals (polymorphism).

Cnidarians
FORM AND FUNCTION

There are two life-history phases: polyp and medusa. The polyp is the sedentary phase and consists of three regions: a basal disk or pedal disk which anchors it; a middle region or column within which is the tubular digestive chamber (gastrovascular cavity); and an oral region which is ringed by tentacles. In colonial types a tubular stolon links adjacent polyps. The medusa is the mobile phase and is effectively an inverted polyp. By virtue of the fluid (water) it contains the digestive cavity plays an important role in oxygen uptake and excretion. This fluid additionally acts as a hydrostatic skeleton through which body wall muscles can antagonize one another.

Since the medusa is the sexual phase, and it can be argued that it is the original life form, with the predominantly bottom-living (benthic) polyp acting as an intermediate, multiplicative asexual stage. However, in the class Hydrozoa the medusa is frequently reduced or even lost, and in the class Anthozoa totally absent. Emphasis in the class Scyphozoa lies, to the contrary, with the medusa stage, as the evolution of the highly mobile and graceful jellyfish testifies; the polyp phase in jellyfish is a relatively inconspicuous component in the lifecycle.

The outer (ectodermal) and inner (endodermal) cell layers of the body are cemented together by the jellylike mesogloea which in the jellyfish forms the bulk of the animal. The mesogloea contains a matrix of elastic collagen fibers which aid both the change and maintenance of body shape. This is particularly obvious in the pulsating swimming movements characteristic of jellyfish, during which contractions of the swimming bell brought about by radial and circular muscles are counteracted by vertically running, elastic fibers. Muscle contraction results in an increase in bell depth and hence fiber stress; fiber shortening subsequently restores the bell to its original shape. In the medusae of hydrozoans the resulting water jets are concentrated and directed by the shelflike velum projecting inwards from the rim of the bell, where there are tentacles, towards the mouth. Structural support in the relatively large anthozoan polyps is also provided by septa (mesentaries) which contain retractor muscles. When mobile, polyp locomotion may be brought about in a number of ways: by creeping upon the pedal disk, by looping or, rarely, by swimming (for example the anemones, *Stomphia, Boloceroides*).

◔ **Left** *A delicate, featherlike colony of Ostrich-plumed stinging hydroids (Aglaophenia cupressina). All species of this genus have modified side branches (corbulae) that act as reproductive structures.*

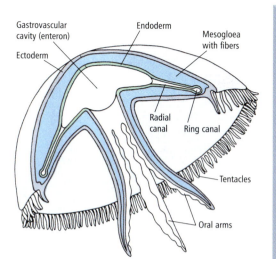

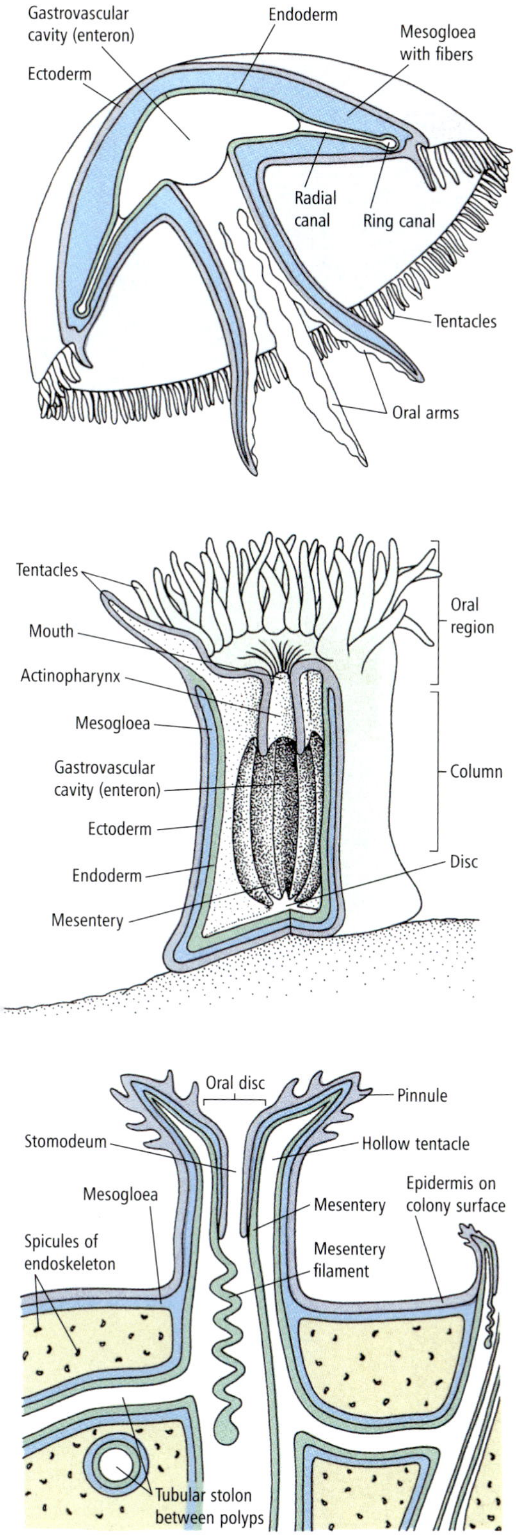

Gastrovascular cavity (enteron)
Endoderm
Mesogloea with fibers
Ectoderm
Radial canal
Ring canal
Tentacles
Oral arms

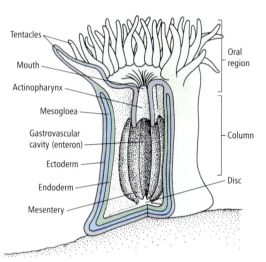

Tentacles
Mouth
Actinopharynx
Mesogloea
Gastrovascular cavity (enteron)
Ectoderm
Endoderm
Mesentery
Oral region
Column
Disc

FACTFILE

SEA ANEMONES AND JELLYFISHES

Phylum: Cnidaria

Classes: Hydrozoa, Scyphozoa, Anthozoa

About 9,900 species in 3 classes.

Distribution Worldwide, mainly marine free-swimming and bottom-dwelling.

Fossil record Precambrian (about 600 million years ago) to present.

Size Width microscopic to several meters.

Features Radially symmetrical animals with cells arranged in tissues (tissue grade); possess tentacles and stinging cells (nematocysts); body wall of two cell layers (outer ectoderm and inner endoderm) cemented together by a primitively noncellular jellylike mesogloea and enclosing a digestive (gastrovascular) cavity not having an anus; there are two distinct life history phases: free-swimming medusa and sedentary polyp.

HYDRAS AND ALLIES Class Hydrozoa
About 3,200 species in about 6 orders .Fossil record: some hydroids: many hydrocorals. Features: of 4- (tetramerous) or many- (polymerous) fold symmetry; solitary or colonial; life-cycle can include polyp and medusa or exclusively one or other; mesogloea without cells; digestive (gastrovascular) system lacks a stomodeum (gullet); stinging cells (nematocysts) and internal septa absent; sexes separate or individuals bisexual; gametes mature in the ectodermis which frequently secretes a chitinous or calcareous external skeleton; medusa has shelf-to-bell rim (velum); tentacles generally solid. Orders: Actinulida; Hydroida (hydroids, sea firs): Milleporina; Siphonophora; Stylasterina; Trachylina.

JELLYFISHES Class Scyphozoa
About 200 species in 5 orders (4 if Cubomedusae are elevated to class level, see main text). Fossil record: minimal. Features: dominant medusa form with 4-fold (tetramerous) symmetry; polyp phase produces medusae by transverse fission; solitary (either swimming or attached to substrate by stalk); mesogloea partly cellular; digestive (gastrovascular) system has gastric tentacles (no stomodeum) and is usually subdivided by partitions (septa); sexes usually separate; gonads in endodermis; complex marginal sense organs; skeleton absent; tentacles generally solid; exclusively marine.
Orders: Coronatae; Cubomedusae; Rhizostomae; Semaeostomae; Stauromedusae.

SEA ANEMONES, CORALS Class Anthozoa
About 6,500 species in probably 14 orders in 2–3 subclasses. Fossil record: several thousand species known. Features: exclusively polyps; predominantly with 6-fold (hexamerous) or 8-fold (octomerous) symmetry; pronounced additional tendency to bilateral symmetry; solitary or colonial; have flattened mouth (oral) disk with an inturned stomodeum; cellular mesogloea; sexes separate or hermaphrodite; gonads in endodermis; digestive (gastrovascular) cavity divided by partitions (septa) bearing gastric filaments; skeleton (when present) is either a calcareous external skeleton or a mesogloeal internal skeleton of either calcareous or horny construction; some forms specialized for brackish water; tentacles generally hollow.

SUBCLASS ALCYONARIA (OR OCTOCORALLIA)
Orders include: **soft corals** (Alcyonacea); **blue coral** (Coenothecalia); **horny corals** (Gorgonacea); **sea pens** (Pennatulacea); Stolonifera; Telestacea. One species, the **Broad sea fan** (*Eunicella verrucosa*; order Gorgonacea), is listed as Vulnerable.

SUBCLASS ZOANTHARIA (OR HEXACORALLIA)
Orders include: **anemones** (Actinaria); **thorny corals** (Antipatharia); Ceriantharia; Corallimorpharia; **hard or stony corals** (Madreporaria); Zoanthidea. The **Starlet sea anemone** (*Nematostella vectensis*; order Actinaria) is classed as Vulnerable by the IUCN Red List.

Hydras and Allies

CLASS HYDROZOA

The hydras and their allies (class Hydrozoa) are considered to be the group that exhibits the most primitive medley of features. The class contains a plethora of medusa and polyp forms which are, for the most part, relatively small. We can plausibly imagine the early hydrozoan lifecycle as being similar to that of the hydrozoan order Trachylina. Here the medusae have a relatively simple form and the typical cnidarian larva, the planula, gives rise in turn to a hydralike stage which buds-off the next generation of medusae. Significantly this stage is predominantly free-swimming (pelagic), but in other hydrozoan orders subsequent polyp elaboration has resulted in the interpolation of bottom-living, hydralike colonies. Further evolution in specialized niches where dispersal is not at a premium has led in turn to the secondary reduction of medusae; indeed most hydroids lack or almost totally lack a medusoid phase.

Early hydroids were probably solitary inhabitants of soft substrates. Subsequent evolution produced types living in sand (Actinulida) and fresh water (Hydridae – hydras). Most colonial types, however, occur on hard surfaces, anchored by

Oral disc
Pinnule
Stomodeum
Hollow tentacle
Mesogloea
Epidermis on colony surface
Mesentery
Mesentery filament
Spicules of endoskeleton
Tubular stolon between polyps

� Above *The three main forms of cnidarians: **1** A medusa (jellyfish); **2** A solitary polyp (sea anemone); **3** A colonial polyp (soft coral). While medusae are free-swimming, polyps are usually sessile. The single exterior opening to the enteron acts as both mouth and anus.*

☞ Right *Green hydra (Hydra viridissima), a freshwater polyp, showing asexual budding. Unlike those of the colonial hydroids, these buds detach themselves from the parent to form new organisms.*

rooting structures. The interconnecting stems (stolons) are protected and supported by a chitinous casing (perisarc), which may or may not enclose the polyp heads. The functional interconnection of members of these colonies permits a division of labor between polyps and an associated variety in form (polymorphism). While one form (gastrozooid) retains both tentacles and a digestive cavity, the form that defends the colony (dactylozooid) has lost the cavity. Another form, the gonozooid, is dedicated solely to the budding-off of medusae or, in species lacking medusae, to producing gametes for reproduction. The delicate branching of hydroid colonies is extremely variable, but universally serves to space out member polyps and to raise them well above the substrate, thereby reducing the chance of clogging by silt and sediments.

The evolution of various forms in the class Hydrozoa has culminated in the formation of the complex floating siphonophore colonies (oceanic hydrozoans), each colony composed of a diverse array of both medusae and polyps; they are characteristic of warmer waters. Essentially each individual within the colony is interlinked by a central stolon. In addition to the three polyp forms found in hydroids, there can be up to four forms of medusae: **1** muscular swimming bells that propel the entire colony (for example, *Muggiaea*, *Nectalia*); **2** gas-filled flotation bells (for example, the Portuguese man-of-war – *Physalia physalis*); **3** bracts which play either a supportive or protective role, or both; **4** medusa buds. Freed from the substrate, these colonies are able to reach large sizes with, for example, the trailing colonial stemwork of the Portuguese man-of-war often extending for several meters below the apical float. Such colonies are capable of paralyzing and ingesting relatively large prey items such as fish, and can even deliver a potentially dangerous sting to humans. Recent research indicates that some species (for example, those of the genus *Agalma*) may attract large prey by moving tentaclelike structures, which are replete with stinging cells (nematocysts) and

⬤ **Right** Physalia physalis, *the Portuguese man-of-war, Atlantic (diameter of float 30cm/12in).*

which bear a remarkable resemblance to small zooplankton (copepods).

At one time it was thought that the pinnacle of this evolutionary line was illustrated by animals such as the by-the-wind-sailor (*Vellela vellela*), which has a disklike, apical float bearing a rigid "sail" that catches the wind, thus facilitating drifting. It is now thought, however, that these organisms simply consist of one massive polyp floating upside-down, and that they are related to gigantic bottom-living hydroids. The large size of these bottom-living giants – up to 10cm (4in) in *Corymorpha* and 3m (10ft) in *Branchiocerianthus* – has been permitted by their adoption of a deposit-feeding life style, often at great depth in still water.

Finally, two groups of hydrozoans produce a calcareous external skeleton resembling that of corals: these are the tropical milleporine and stylasterine hydrocorals.

Left *Sea anemones and jellyfishes:* **1** Cyanea lamarckii, *a jellyfish, N Atlantic (diameter 20cm/8in);* **2** Aurelia aurita, *the common jellyfish, medusa phase, Mediterranean and N Atlantic (diameter 25cm/10in);* **3** Actinia equina, *the beadlet anemone, Mediterranean and N Atlantic in intertidal zone (height 7cm/2.8in);* **4** Metridium senile, *the Plumose anemone (height 8cm/3in);* **5** Obelia geniculata, shallow rocky habitats of NW Europe (colony height 4cm/1.6in); **6** Sertularia operculata, *a hydroid, a colony of polyps (height of colony 45cm/17.7in);* **7** Eunicella verrucosa, *a sea fan, Mediterranean and N Atlantic (height 30cm/12in);* **8** Peachia hastata, *a "sit-and-wait" burrowing anemone, Mediterranean and N Atlantic (height 10cm/4in);* **9** Corynactis viridis, *an anemone-like animal, N Atlantic (diameter 5cm/2in);* **10** Alcyonium digitatum, *or "dead man's fingers" a colony of polyps, Mediterranean and N Atlantic (colony height 20cm/7.9in).*

⬤ **Above** *The Sea nettle* (Chrysaora fuscescens) *is named for the powerful sting that its tentacles can deliver. Dense swarms of this species may gather off the coasts of California and Oregon in fall and winter.*

⬤ **Below** *Jellyfish polyps attached to the bed of a landlocked marine lake on Kakaban Island off Borneo. This lake is renowned for its abundance of jellyfishes, of four different stingless species.*

Jellyfishes

CLASS SCYPHOZOA

Among cnidarians, it is the jellyfishes that have most fully exploited the free-swimming mode of life though the members of one scyphozoan order (the Stauromedusae) are bottom-living, with an attached, polyplike existence. Jellyfish medusae have a similar though more complex structure than the medusae of hydroids with the disk around the mouth prolonged into four arms, a digestive system comprising a complex set of radiating canals linking the central portion (stomach) to a peripheral ring element, and a relatively more voluminous mesogloea. The mesogloea in some genera (for example *Aequoria*, *Pelagia*) helps buoyancy by selectively expelling heavy chemical particles (anions) (such as sulfate ions), which are replaced by lighter ones (such as chloride ions). A wide size range of prey organisms are taken, though many species, including the common Atlantic semaeostomes of the genus *Aurelia*, are feeders on floating particles and thus concentrate on small items. The arms of *Aurelia* periodically sweep around the rim of the bell, gathering up particles that accumulate there after deposition on the animal's upper surface. In contrast the arms around the main mouth of the Rhizostomae have become branched, and have numerous sucking mouths, each capable of ingesting small planktonic organisms such as copepods. Within this group are the essentially bottom-living, suspension-feeding forms of the genus *Cassiopeia*, which lie upside down on sandy bottoms, their frilly arms acting as strainers. The bell shapes of members of two orders are distinctive: coronate medusae have bells with a deep groove and cubomedusae have bells that are cuboid in shape.

The gametes of jellyfish are produced in gonads that lie on the floor of the digestive cavity and are initially discharged into it. Fertilization normally occurs after discharge. Many species, however, have brood pouches located on the undersurface where the larvae are retained. After release larvae settle and give rise to polyps, which produce additional polyps by budding. These polyps also produce medusae by transverse division (fission), a process that results in the formation of stacks (strobilae) of ephyra larvae. When released the ephyra larvae feed mainly on protozoans and grow and change into the typical jellyfish.

To trap prey cnidarians normally employ stinging cells (nematocysts). The discharge of these is now thought to be under nervous control. Discharge involves a collagenous thread being rapidly shot out, uncoiling and turning inside-out, sometimes to expose lateral barbs. Hollow stinging cells often contain a toxin that can enter the body of the prey. The released toxins can be very potent; especially dangerous are those of the cubomedusan sea wasps (e.g., genus *Chironex*), which have been responsible for killing several humans, particularly off Australian coasts. Victims usually succumb rapidly to respiratory paralysis. Nematocysts may be pirated by sea slugs and used for their own protection. Some authorities treat these jellyfish, with their box-shaped medusae and powerful stinging cells, as a separate class, the Cubomedusae.

Corals and Sea Anemones
CLASS ANTHOZOA

Corals and sea anemones (class Anthozoa) only exist as polyps. Sea anemones (order Actiniaria) always bear more than eight tentacles and usually have both tentacles and internal partitions (mesenteries) arrayed in multiples of six.

Many anemone species, especially the more primitive ones, are burrowers in mud and sand but most dwell on hard substrates, cemented there (permanently or temporarily) by secretions from a well-differentiated disk. The disk around the mouth (oral disk) is equipped with two grooves (siphonoglyphs) richly endowed with cilia, which serve to maintain a water flow through the relatively extensive, digestive cavity. The oral disk extends inward to produce a tubular gullet or stomodeum which acts as a valve, closing in response to increases in internal pressure. In common with jellyfish some anemones feed on particles suspended in the seawater for which leaflike tentacles, prodigious mucus production and abundant food tracts lined with cilia are required; a good example is the common plumose anemone, genus *Metridium*. Asexual reproduction occurs by budding, breaking up or fission, while sexual reproduction may involve either internal or external fertilization of gametes. Some species brood young, either internally or externally at the base of the column.

Members of two other orders are also anemone-like: the cerianthids have greatly elongated bodies adapted for burrowing into sand, but have only one oral groove (siphonoglyph). Zoanthids lack a pedal disk, are frequently colonial and often live attached to other organisms (epizoic).

Also included in the subclass Zoantharia are the hard (stony) corals (order Madreporaria) whose polyps are encased in a rigid, calcium carbonate skeleton. The great majority of hard corals live in colonies which are composed of vast numbers of small polyps (about 5mm, 0.2in), but the less abundant solitary forms may be large (*Fungia* up to 50cm, 20in, across); most are tropical or subtropical in distribution. In colonial forms the polyps are interconnected laterally; they form a superficial living sheet overlying the skeleton, which is itself secreted from the lower outer (ectodermal) layer.

◗ *Overleaf Sandalled anemones* (Actinothoe sphyrodeta) *customarily attach themselves to rocks or other hard substrates.*

ASSOCIATIONS AND INTERDEPENDENCE IN ANEMONES, CRABS, AND FISHES

Cnidarians are involved in a variety of associations with other animals, ranging from obtaining food or other benefits from another animal (commensalism) to being interdependent (symbiosis).

An example of commensalism occurs between the hydroid genus *Hydractinia* and hermit crabs, particularly in regions deficient in suitable polyp attachment sites. This is understandable since the shells inhabited by such crabs provide substitute sites and, moreover, the relationship provides *Hydractinia* with the opportunity for scavenging food morsels. Whether the crab benefits is unclear, though the development of defensive dactylozooids in *H. echinata* specifically in response to a chemical stimulus emanating from crabs suggests that it does and that there is therefore a mutually beneficial coexistence (mutualism). The association between the cloak anemone *Adamsia palliata* and the crab *Pagurus prideauxi* is, to the contrary, far more intimate. These species normally form a partnership when small. Over time the crab outgrows its shelly refuge, but by secreting a horny foot (pedal) membrane the anemone progressively enlarges the shell lip, thus obviating any need for the crab to change shells. A crab lacking an anemone will, upon contact with *Adamsia*, recognize it and attempt to transfer it to its shell.

A range of intermediate degrees of association is provided by the anemone *Calliactis parasitica*, which associates with hermit crabs but also frequently lives independently. An interesting, one-sided association is that of the Hawaiian crab genus *Melia*, which has the remarkable habit of carrying an anemone in each of its two chaelae, thereby enhancing its aggressive armament; the crab even raids their food.

Clown fishes (*Amphiprion* spp.) live in the tentacles of sea anemones. Their hosts protect these fishes and the fishes protect the anemones from would-be predators (chiefly other fishes, deterred by the territorial behavior of the clown fish). Clown fishes also apparently act as anemone cleaners. Although it has been suggested that inhibitory substances are secreted by these fishes to reduce the discharge of stinging cells, recent work has failed to confirm this. It is more likely that stinging is avoided by the secretion of a particularly thick mucous coat, which during acclimatization of the fish to its host anemone may become modified, with the levels of certain excitatory (acidic) components being reduced.   RB/AC

🌑 **Above** *Sea pens (order Pennatulacea) live on soft seabeds. The large, stemlike, primary polyp houses a skeletal rod that becomes embedded in the substrate as a result of waves of contractions. Secondary polyps are arranged laterally on this stem.*

◗ **Right** *Coral bleaching and death, perhaps caused by rising sea temperatures and lower salinity, is a growing problem. This coral is* Acropora sp.

🌑 **Below** *The octocorallian Mushroom soft coral* (Anthomastus ritteri) *is a deep-sea species found off the US west coast and Baja California. When threatened, with all its tentacles retracted, it resembles a fungus.*

Corals exhibit a great diversity of growth forms, ranging from delicately branching species to those whose massive skeletal deposits form the building blocks of coral reefs. An interesting growth variant is shown by *Meandrina* and its relatives in which polyps are arranged continuously in rows, resulting in a skeleton with longitudinal fissures – hence its popular name, the brain coral.

Closely related to the hard corals are the members of the order Corallimorpharia which lack a skeleton. These include the jewel anemone (genus *Corynactis*), so named because of its vivid and highly variable coloration. Since it reproduces asexually, rock faces can become covered by a multicolored quiltwork of anemones. The black or thorny corals (order Antipatharia) form slender, plantlike colonies bearing polyps arranged around a horny axial skeleton; they have numerous thorns.

Octocorallian corals comprise a varied assemblage of forms, but all possess eight featherlike (pinnate) tentacles. The polyps project above and are linked together by a mass of skeletal tissue called coenenchyme, which consists of mesogloea permeated by digestive tubules. Thus in contrast to hard corals, the octocorallians have an internal skeleton. This assemblage includes the familiar gorgonian (horny) corals, sea whips and fans, and the precious red coral, genus *Corallium*. Most of these have a central rod composed of organic material (gorgonin) around which is draped the coenenchyme and polyps, the former frequently containing spicules which may impart a vivid coloration. Such is the case with *Corallium*, whose central axis consists of a fused mass of deep red calcareous spicules; this material is used in jewelry. The tropical organ pipe coral, genus *Tubipora* (order Stolonifera) produces tubes or tubules of fused spicules which are crossconnected by a regular series of transverse bars. In contrast, the soft corals (order Alcyonacea) only contain discrete spicules within the coenenchyme (for example dead man's fingers, genus *Alcyonium*). The order Coenothecalia is solely represented by the Indo-Pacific blue coral, genus *Heliopora*, which has a massive skeleton composed of crystalline aragonite fibers fused into plates (lamellae): its blue color is imparted by bile salts. Many species in most of these groups have several forms (especially gastrozooids, dactylozooids and gonozooids). Many polyps (siphonozooids) act as pumps, promoting water circulation through the colonial digestive system. Familiar examples are the sea pansy (genus *Renilla*) and the sea pen (genus *Veretillum*), both of which when disturbed emit waves of phosphorescence. These are controlled by the nervous system and are inhibited by light. Their role is unclear, though it is likely that they are a response to intrusion by would-be predators.

The cnidarian nervous system shows a certain amount of organization and local specialization. This is especially evident in anemones where nerve tracts accompany the retractor muscles responsible for protective withdrawals. The marginal ganglia of scyphomedusae and the circumferential tracts of hydromedusae have been found to contain pacemaker cells which are responsible for initiating and maintaining swimming rhythms. In *Polyorchis* it has been found that the giant nerves controlling movement are all coupled together electrically, ensuring that they function collectively as a giant ring nerve fiber capable of initiating synchronously muscle contraction from all parts of the bell.

Similarly the behaviors of individual polyps in hydroid and coral colonies are integrated by the activities of colonial nerve nets. Additional powers for integrating control are provided by conduction pathways created by sheets of electrically coupled, epithelial cells. For example, the shell-climbing behavior of anemones of the genus *Calliactis* seems to depend upon the interplay of activities between two epithelial systems – one on the outside (ectodermal), the other inside (endodermal) – and the nerve net, though conclusive evidence as to the exact cellular locations of these additional systems has been difficult to obtain.   RB/AC

AGGRESSION IN ANEMONES

A number of anemones display a well-defined aggressive sequence which, for the most part, is used in confrontation with other anemones. These anemones all possess discrete structures located at the top of the column which contain densely packed batteries of stinging cells (nematocysts): they are called acrorhagi. They can be inflated and directed at opponents.

The common intertidal beadlet anemone (*Actinia equina*), whose distribution encompasses the Atlantic seaboards of Europe and Africa and which also occurs in the Mediterranean, is an example upon which attention has been focused. Although this species can vary considerably in color (red to green), the acrorhagi are always conspicuous thanks to their intense bluish hue. Aggression is triggered by the contact of tentacles. One individual usually displays column extension and bends so that some of its simultaneously enlarging acrorhagi make contact with the opponent (after 5–10 minutes). There follows a discharge of the stinging cells (nemato-

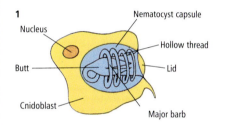

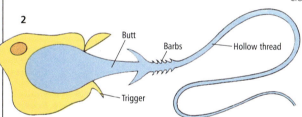

cysts) which normally results in a rapid withdrawal by the victim.

Experiments suggest that in common with more advanced animals contest behavior is ritualized, but that in these lowly forms it depends on simple physiological rules rather than on complex behavioral ones. The "rules" apparently decree that larger anemones should act aggressively more rapidly than smaller ones, and so win contests.

The North American anemone *Anthopleura elegantissima* reproduces asexually by fission. In consequence intertidal rocks can become entirely covered by a patchwork of asexually produced anemones. Close inspection reveals that each densely packed clone – the mass of asexually produced offspring – is separated from its neighbors by anemone-free strips, and that these are maintained by aggressive interactions involving acrorhagi. It is clear, therefore, that the aggressive behavior of individuals constituting the boundary of a clone serves to provide territorial defense for the entire clone, the central members of which, significantly, are more concerned with reproduction than aggression. Thus there is, as in hydroid colonies, a functional division of labor, despite the lack of physical interconnection between the clonal units. Individuals at the interclonal border have more and larger acrorhagi than centrally placed members, a difference apparently dependent solely on the former experiencing aggressive contact with non-clonemates. Such a dichotomy is thought to indicate the presence of a sophisticated self/nonself recognition system.   RB/AC

◑ **Left** The stinging cell (cnidoblast) of a cnidarian: **1** before discharge of the nematocyst and **2** after discharge.

◓ **Below** A corallimorph (Pseudocorynactis *sp.*) attacking a Sea star (Linckia laevigata).

THE LIVING AND THE DEAD

The origins and biological organization of coral reefs

CORAL REEFS ARE EXTRAORDINARY OASES IN the midst of oceanic deserts, for they support immensely rich and diverse faunas and floras but occur primarily in the tropics where the marked clarity of the water indicates a relative dearth of planktonic organisms and other nutrients. "Coral" consists of the skeletons of hard or stony coral.

The success of reef-building (hermatypic) corals in tropical waters, where high light intensities prevail throughout the year, is strictly dependent upon the nutrient-manufacturing (autotrophic) activities of interdependent (symbiotic) algae (zooxanthallae) which live within each polyp. Such dependence also necessarily restricts the algae to these

waters. Moreover, since these algae flourish best at temperatures higher than 20°C (68°F), reef development is further limited to depths of less than 70m (230ft), where light intensities are greatest. Corals do, however, survive both at higher latitudes and in deeper waters, but where they do their capacity to secrete limestone for reef building is found to be severely curtailed as a result of the reduced metabolic support provided by the algae. Finally, restrictions on the distribution of corals are

also imposed by the deposition of silt, freshwater runoff from land and cold, deepwater upwelling. The two former factors, for example, restrict reef development in the Indo-Pacific Ocean towards offshore island sites, while the last hinders coral growth off the west equatorial coast of Africa, where the Guinea current surfaces. It should not be forgotten, though, that in the development of most reefs, encrusting (calcareous) algae (for example, *Lithophyllum*, *Lithothamnion*) normally

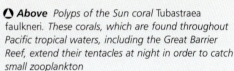

Above *Polyps of the Sun coral* Tubastraea faulkneri. *These corals, which are found throughout Pacific tropical waters, including the Great Barrier Reef, extend their tentacles at night in order to catch small zooplankton*

Left *Colonies of sea fans may be several meters high, as with these* Melithea *sp. fans off Fiji in the Southern Pacific. Sea fans can fall prey to several diseases, including aspergillosis and red-band disease.*

the last 100,000 years. Core drillings taken at Eniwetok atoll in the Pacific have extended downwards for up to 1.6km (1mile) before hitting bed rock: from analyses of both the fauna and flora in cores obtained, it has proved possible to reconstruct past fluctuations in sea level. The majority of the world's coral reefs started development during the Cenozoic era (not later than 65 million years ago) and consist predominantly of corals of the order Madreporaria.

All coral reefs have a similar biological organization, with the reef plants and animals, as on rocky shores, lying in zones in accordance with their tolerances to physical factors. This is most evident on the exposed, windward faces of those reefs subject to continuous wave crash where especially prolific growths of both corals and algae develop. However, a reef can only grow outwards if debris accumulates on the reef slope; with increasing water depths, such material tends to slide down the slope and thus becomes unavailable. Below 30–50m (100–165ft), hermatypic corals are replaced by nonhermatypic ones, and by fragile, branching alcyonarians (gorgonians, etc.). Above the slope is the reef crest which, in the most exposed situations, is dominated by encrusting calcareous algae (for example, the genus *Porolithon*). These algae form ridges which are full of cavities thereby providing numerous recesses which are colonized by a multitude of invertebrates, including zoanthids, sea urchins and vermetid gastropods. Where wave action is not too severe, windward reef crests are usually dominated by a relatively small number of coral species, notably stout *Acropora* and hydrocoralline *Millepora* species.

Zonation is far less marked on the leeward side of the reef crest, where a different set of problems has to be faced of which sediment accumulation from land runoff is perhaps the most acute. Nevertheless, the relatively sheltered nature of this habitat permits the rapid proliferation of branched corals. In common with the coral faunas of windward slopes, those of leeward faces display dramatic changes of coral form with increasing depth, changes which can either be attributable to the replacement of species by others or to changes in species forms. For example, on Caribbean reefs, dominant species such as *Monastrea annularis* display both stout (shallow-water) and branching (deepwater) growth forms. Recent work on *M. cavernosa* has indicated that forms found at equivalent depths are distinctive: the polyps of the shallow-water form are open continuously, while those of the deepwater form (which house far fewer zooxanthellae) are open only at night. **RB**

play an extremely important part. In many cases the limestone they produce acts as a cement.

In 1842 Charles Darwin distinguished three main geomorphological categories of reef which are still in use today: fringing reefs, barrier reefs and atolls. As the name suggests, the first are formed close to shore, on rocky coastlines. Barrier reefs are, on the contrary, separated from land by lagoons or channels which have usually been produced as a result of subsidence. (The best known and largest barrier reef is the Great Barrier Reef off the northeast coast of Australia, though the name is somewhat misleading as along its length (1,900km/1,200 miles) occur a host of different reef configurations – more than 2,500. Finally, atolls are found around subsiding volcanoes.

The continuation of coral growth is heavily dependent upon changes in water level. At present the world is in a period between glaciations and the rising sea level permits vertical growth to continue at about 0.3–1.5cm (0.1–0.6in) per year, a rate that has apparently been maintained over

Comb Jellies

SMALL, TRANSLUCENT, GLOBULAR ANIMALS, comb jellies float through the open seas, like ghosts, capturing prey with their whiplike tentacles. The order name Ctenophora was derived from the Latin for "comb bearers" to reflect their most distinct feature – the rows of comb plates.

The comb jelly's body consists of three zones – a voluminous mesogloea sandwiched, as in sea anemones and jellyfishes, between thin ectodermal (outer) and endodermal (inner) cell layers. Most noticeable, however, are the eight rows of plates of cilia (comb rows) whose activities serve to propel the animal while it is searching for zooplanktonic prey.

Combing the Sea
MOVEMENT

The waves of movement of the comb plates responsible for swimming are initiated and synchronized by impulses arising within the apical sense organ which functions primarily as a statocyst, detecting tilting, although it is also sensitive to light. It contains a sensory epithelium bearing four groups of elongate sensory "balancer" cilia, upon which a calcareous ball (statolith) perches.

The orientation of the animal is controlled very simply: irrespective of whether the comb jelly is swimming upward or downward, deflection of the balancer cilia away from an upright position brought about by the statolith results in a change in the frequency of beating of the cilia which is spontaneously generated. The overall effect exerted through the differential activation of the four groups of "balancer cilia," and subsequently the four pairs of comb rows to which they are electrically connected, is to ensure that the animal swims vertically rather than obliquely. Since the power stroke of the individual comb plates is

opposite to direction of waves of activity passing along the comb rows, the animal normally travels mouth forward. However, this activity is also under control exerted by the nerve net, which upon receipt of a mechanical stimulus can cause either a cessation or reversal of beating. There is also some evidence to suggest that the synchronization of beating of the comb plates within any one row might be partially dependent upon direct mechanical coupling.

Angling with Tentacles
FORM, FUNCTION AND DIET

Most comb jellies resemble species in the common genus *Pleurobrachia* (order Cydippida) which occurs in the colder waters of both the Atlantic and Pacific oceans, and is often found stranded in tidal pools. Its globular body is up to 4cm (1.5in) in diameter, and has two pits into which the tentacles can be retracted. These tentacles function as drift nets, catching passing food items while the animal hovers motionless. When extended these appendages may be up to 50cm (20in) in length. They have lateral filaments and bear numerous adhesive cells (colloblasts) each of which has a hemispherical head fastened to the core of the tentacle by a straight connective fiber and by a contractile spiral one, the latter acting as a lasso. Once caught prey is held by the colloblasts, which produce a sticky secretion, until transferred to the central portion (stomach) of the digestive system following the wiping of the tentacles over the mouth. When feeding upon pipefishes of a similar size to itself, *Pleurobrachia* will play them in much the same way as an angler tires out a hooked fish.

The stomach, in which digestion commences, leads to a complex array of canals where there is further digestion and intake of small food particles which are subsequently broken down by intracellular digestion. These canals are especially routed

◗ *Right* *While most comb jellies feed on zooplankton the large-mouthed* Beroë cucumis *feeds exclusively on other jellies* (Bolinopsis infundilbulum). *It has been referred to as the "Jaws of the midwater jelly world."*

alongside those body regions having high energy consumption levels, notably the eight comb rows. The gonads lie in association with the lining of the gastric system; gametes pass out through the mouth. Following external fertilization a larva – a miniature version of the adult – is produced.

The common comb jellies of temperate waters are all like *Pleurobrachia*, which has the most primitive body form; shape in the other orders departs from this. The elongate lobate comb jellies are laterally compressed and have six lobes projecting from their narrow mid region, four of which are delicate and two stout. These serve to capture food: the tentacles are small and lack sheaths. *Mnemiopsis* (order Lobata), which is about 3cm (1.2in) in size and occurs in immense swarms, has, in association with the production of these lobes, four long and four short comb rows. Elongation and compression have been carried much further in the Cestida, resulting in organisms resembling thin gelatinous bands. Species in the two genera concerned (*Cestum, Velamen*) are collectively referred to as Venus's girdle, and are found in tropical waters and the Mediterranean, only occasionally straying into northern waters. The graceful swimming of these forms is mostly dependent upon undulations of the whole body, brought about by muscle fibers embedded in the mesogloea. They feed entirely by means of tentacles set in grooves running along the oral edge.

In the order Beroidea, the thimble-shape body is similarly laterally compressed, but mainly occupied by the greatly enlarged stomodeum rather than mesogloea. Species in this group are up to 20cm (8in) in length and often have a pinkish color. There are no tentacles; instead food is caught by lips which curl outwards to reveal a glandular and ciliated (macrocilia) area. Relatively large food items are rapidly taken in by a combination of suction pressure from the contraction of radial muscles in the mesogloea and ciliary action. The common North Sea species *Beroë gracilis* feeds exclusively upon *Pleurobrachia pileus*.

The very small order Ganeshida includes one genus *Ganesha* with two pelagic species somewhat intermediate in form between members of the Cydippida and Lobata. The order Platyctenida is a curious group which, contrary to other flattened ctenophores, are compressed from top to bottom and have, for the most part, assumed a benthic

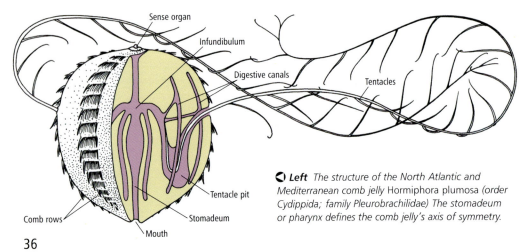

Sense organ

Infundibulum

Digestive canals

Tentacles

Comb rows

Tentacle pit

Stomadeum

Mouth

◖ *Left* *The structure of the North Atlantic and Mediterranean comb jelly* Hormiphora plumosa (*order Cydippida; family Pleurobrachilidae*) *The stomadeum or pharynx defines the comb jelly's axis of symmetry.*

FACTFILE

COMB JELLIES

Phylum: Ctenophora

Orders: Beroida, Cestida, Cydippida, Ganeshida, Lobata, Platytecnida, Thalassocalycida

About 100 species in 7 orders.

Distribution Worldwide, marine

Fossil record None

Size Length from very small about 0.4cm (0.15in) to over 1m (3.3ft).

Features Basically radially symmetrical but masked by superimposed bilateral symmetry; body wall 2-layered (diploblastic) with a thick jellylike mesogloea and nerve net (these features making them similar to sea anemones and jellyfishes); 8 rows of plates of fused cilia (comb plates) upon whose activity locomotion predominantly depends; tentacles when present help in the capturing of zooplankton; digestive/gastrova scular system with a stomodeum (gullet), stomach and a complex array of canals; one phase in lifecycle (not equivalent to polyp or medusa); hermaphroditic.

ORDER BEROIDA (class Nuda)
Includes the species *Beroë gracilis*.

ORDER CESTIDA
Includes: Venus's girdle (genera *Cestum, Velamen*).

ORDER CYDIPPIDA
Includes: *Pleurobrachia, Dryodora, Ctenella*.

ORDER GANESHIDA
One genus *Ganesha*.

ORDER LOBATA
Includes: *Mnemiopsis, Deiopea, Ocyropsis*.

ORDER PLATYCTENIDA
Includes: *Coeloplana, Ctenoplana, Tjalfiella, Gastrodes*.

ORDER THALASSOCALYCIDA
One species *Thalassocalyce inconstans*.

creeping lifestyle. Their ciliated undersurface is derived from part of the stomodeal wall. Of the four genera involved *Coeloplana* and *Tjalfiella* are flattened creeping forms, the latter being practically sessile – attached to the substrate. In contrast *Ctenoplana* is partially planktonic, having become adapted to creeping on the water's surface also. The most specialized, though, is *Gastrodes* which is a parasite of the free-swimming sea squirt genus *Salpa*. The flattened adult stage is a freeliving, benthic form, but the planula-type larva bores into the tunicate test and develops into a bowl-shaped, intermediate parasitic stage. The final, small order Thalassocalycida contains comb jellies with extremely fragile bodies and an umbrella shaped expansion at one end. *Thalassocalyce inconstans* is the sole species of the order.   RB/AC

◗ **Right** *Usually found on soft corals in warm waters, this* Ctenoplana *species (order Platyctenida) is in its larval stage. A highly modified ctenophore species it is sometimes mistaken for a nudibranch or a flatworm.*

Gnathostomulids, Acoelomorphs, Gastrotrichs, and Arrow Worms

tHIS DISPARATE GROUPING OF ORGANISMS *embraces a huge variety of marine worms, ranging in size from the small arrow worms down to the infinitesimally tiny gnathostomulids, which can live in the gaps between sand grains.*

Gnathostomulids
PHYLUM GNATHOSTOMULIDA

These microscopic acoelomate marine worms are commonly found in shallow saltwater to a depth of several hundred meters. Members of the order Filospermoidea have a lengthy tapering rostrum (front end lies in front of the mouth), and the adult males lack a penis and the adult females lack a vagina. In the Bursovaginoidea members have less elongated bodies lacking the slender rostrum, and the adults have a penis, bursa, and vagina. These animals were first described from meiofaunal samples in 1956 and accorded phylum status in 1969. While they are undoubtedly acoelomate, their relationships with other animal groups are far from clear. Their outer surface bears cilia (one cilium per epithelial cell) and they glide through the sediment by a combination of ciliary action and flexure of the body brought about by muscular activity. They feed on bacteria and the microscopic jaws aid in the ingestion of food. On account of their minuscule size, diffusion plays an important part in the absorption of oxygen, the removal of carbon dioxide and the distribution of nutrients around the body. Sensory structures, often pitlike, on the outer surface, associated with cilia detect environmental stimuli and connect with the superficial nervous system. Many aspects of the biology of these animals are not well understood and the identification and classification of species is a specialist task.

Acoelomorphs
PHYLUM ACOELOMORPHA

Scientists are constantly reviewing the taxonomic positions and evolutionary relationships of various animal groups. Formerly thought to be basal among the Protostomes (flatworms), acoelomorphs, on the basis of molecular evidence, are now believed to belong to the Lophotrochozoa, except for the orders Acoela and Nemertodermatida, which occupy a unique position as the most basal extant group of bilaterians (bilaterally symmetrical animals).

For many years the lowly gutless flatworms have been classified as an order, the Acoela, within the class Turbellaria of the problematic flatworms. In light of the molecular evidence there is now a suggestion that these apparently simple yet remarkable animals, which have a mouth but no gut, and which frequently associate with symbiotic algae, may constitute a new phylum. This phylum also includes the Acoela's sister order Nemertodermatida, where the similarities between the two involve their ciliation, body-wall structure, reproductive organs and the relation of the statocyst to the nervous tissue. The phylum has been called the Acoelomorpha. Evidence for this view is consolidated by the fact that the acoelomorphs display some structural details and specialized characteristics that set them apart from the other flatworms. Were the acoelomorphs to be removed from the group, those animals remaining would show a clear affinity with each other and would appear to have been evolved from a single evolutionary line. Thus, creating a separate phylum for the acoelomorphs is as much a recognition of the integral similarities of the other flatworms as it is of the differences shown by the acoelomorphs. (See also Flatworms and Ribbon Worms.)

⬤ **Above** *Acoelomorphs of the order Acoela. Formerly grouped with the platyhelminthes (flatworms), new molecular and morphological evidence has caused them to be reclassified.*

▷ **Right** *Body plans showing the principal features of **1** a gnathostomulid (an adult Problognathia minima), **2** a gastrotrich (genus Chaetonotus), and **3** an arrow worm.*

Gastrotrichs
PHYLUM GASTROTRICHA

Gastrotrichs are minute animals often found in habitats shared with rotifers. They are "wormlike" and live among detrital particles in both fresh and seawater. Gastrotrichs show bilateral symmetry but have a pseudocoel and not a true coelom.

The genus *Chaetonotus* has a rounded head attached to the trunk by an elongated neck; the tail is usually forked and the outer surfaces of the body are covered with sticky knobs (papillae). The underside bears hairs (cilia) arranged in bands whose coordinated beating causes the animal to glide over the substrate. The upper surface of the animal is usually armed with spines and scales.

The gastrotrich pharynx generates a sucking action which is employed to draw food into the gut. It takes single-celled algae, bacteria and protozoans. The reproductive strategies vary according to the groups of gastrotrichs. Males are unknown in the class Chaetonotoidea where reproduction is by parthenogenesis among females. Here two types of egg are laid. In one, hatching takes place very quickly and the young mature in about three days. In the other case eggs can lie dormant, surviving desiccation, and will hatch when more favorable circumstances prevail. The members of the class Macrodasyida are hermaphrodites. Gastrotrichs are of little ecological or economic importance.

Arrow Worms
PHYLUM CHAETOGNATHA

Arrow worms are small, inconspicuous marine animals that were unknown before 1829. Their torpedo-shaped bodies, combined with their

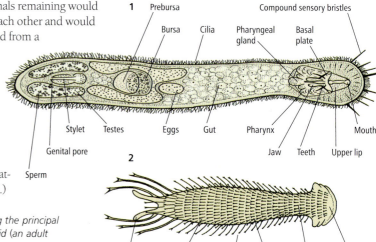

1 Prebursa — Compound sensory bristles
Bursa — Cilia — Pharyngeal gland — Basal plate
Stylet — Testes — Eggs — Gut — Pharynx — Mouth
Genital pore — Jaw — Teeth — Upper lip
Sperm — **2**
Forked tail — Papillae — Cilia — Trunk — Neck — Head

◁ **Left** *Arrow worms in marine plankton (of which they form a significant part). This group of animals was not known until the early 19th century, when fine-meshed towed nets capable of sieving out plankton from sea water were developed.*

FACTFILE

GNATHOSTOMULIDS, ETC.

Phyla: Gnathostomulida, Acoelomorpha, Gastrotricha, Chaetognatha.

GNATHOSTOMULIDS Phylum Gnathostomulida
About 80 species in 2 orders and 25 genera. **Distribution:** worldwide, exclusively marine, inhabiting sediments like anoxic sands and muds from coastal regions down to several hundred meters. **Fossil record:** apparently none. **Size:** up to 2mm (0.1in) long. **Features:** adults: freeliving, acoelomate, bilaterally symmetrical, unsegmented wormlike microscopic animals, with bodies divisible into head, trunk and tail regions. There is a unique pharyngeal region armed with jaws (hence the phylum name meaning jaw mouthed). The gnathostomulids are either protandric hermaphrodites (starting adult life as males and becoming females later) or they are simultaneous hermaphrodites being male and female at the same time. The fertilized eggs develop in the protostome fashion and the young develop directly into adults without a larval phase. Order Filospermoidea; Order Bursovaginoidea.

ACOELOMORPHS Phylum Acoelomorpha
Controversial phylum with over 280 species in 2 orders – Acoela and Nemertodermatida. Genera and species include: *Convoluta convoluta* (order Acoela), *Meara* (order Nemertodermatida).

GASTROTRICHS Phylum Gastrotricha
About 450 species. **Distribution:** widespread, marine and fresh water. **Fossil record:** none. **Size:** microscopic, less than 3 mm (0.12in). **Features:** freeliving usually with some external areas covered with cilia; body unsegmented, blastocoelomate but body cavity filled with cells; body of three layers (triploblastic) often with one or more pairs of adhesive organs; excretory protonephridia when present consist of a single flame cell; cuticle covered with spines, scales or bristles.

CLASS CHAETONOTOIDA
Mainly fresh water. Front end of body usually distinct from trunk; adhesive tubes at rear; protonephridia present; mainly parthenogenetic (asexually reproducing) females. Genera include: *Chaetonotus.*

CLASS MACRODASYIDA
Marine, chiefly reported from Europe. Bodies straight with adhesive tubes on front, rear and sides of the body; no protonephridia; hermaphrodite. Genera include: *Macrodasys.*

ARROW WORMS Phylum Chaetognatha
About 100 living species in 7 genera. **Distribution:** all oceans, planktonic apart from 1 benthic genus. **Fossil record:** one dubious record. **Size:** length between 0.4cm (0.16in) and 10cm (4in), most less than 2cm (0.8in). **Features:** small bilaterally symmetrical freeliving animals, formerly believed to have deuterostome development, but new research suggests they are basal protostomes; lack circulatory and excretory systems; body torpedo-shaped with paired lateral fins and tail fin; mouth at front and armed with strong grasping spines. Genera: *Bathyspadella, Eukrohnia, Heterokrohnia, Krohnitta, Pterosagitta, Sagitta, Spadella.*

ability to dart rapidly forward through the water for short distances, explain their common name.

Arrow worms are transparent and almost all are colorless. All known species are similar in appearance and all live in the plankton, except *Spadella*, which lives in the sea floor. Their evolutionary position remains unclear despite various attempts to show relationships with other phyla. Today they are generally supposed to be without close affinities, lying at the base of the protostome line.

The long, narrow body carries a head at the front which bears curved hooks of chitin. These grasp prey and maneuver it into the mouth. Small planktonic animals form the diet, especially crustaceans such as copepods, but occasionally larger food such as other arrow worms and fish larvae may be taken. The mouth carries small teeth which assist in the act of swallowing. A pair of small, simple eyes is also borne on the head. These may or may not be pigmented and serve mainly as light detectors rather than as organs that actually form an image.

The trunk carries two pairs of lateral fins and the body terminates in a fishlike tail segment. The gut runs straight through from mouth to anus and has two small pouches or diverticula at the front.

Arrow worms are hermaphroditic and their sex organs are relatively large for the overall body size. The ovaries lie in the trunk region and the testes and seminal vesicles lie toward the tail, separated by a partition. The form of the seminal vesicles, where sperm is stored, is used to identify the various species. The breeding cycle varies in length according to distribution. It is completed rapidly in tropical waters, in about six weeks in temperate latitudes, and it may take up to two years in polar regions. Fertilization takes place internally and fertilized eggs are released into the sea where they develop as larvae before maturing into adults. The larvae resemble small adults. In the genus *Eukrohnia* the larvae are brooded in special pouches.

The outside of the body is equipped with small mechanoreceptors that respond to vibrations in the water such as are generated by certain prey species. This facility allows the arrow worms to detect prey and engulf them. If they themselves are damaged, for example in an attack by a predator, lost parts, including the head, can regrow.   AC

3

Hood

Rear teeth

Front teeth

Eyes

Grasping spines

Pharynx

Intestine

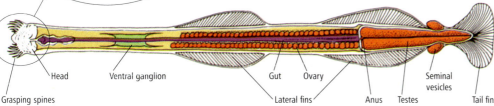

Head | Ventral ganglion | Gut | Ovary | Seminal vesicles

Grasping spines | Lateral fins | Anus | Testes | Tail fin

Water Bears

tARDIGRADES (LITERALLY "SLOW WALKERS") *are minute fat-bodied animals, measuring some 0.1 to 1.0 mm in length. Because of the perceived similarity of their body shape to that of bears, they are commonly referred to as "water bears" (a term first coined by the 18th-century German naturalist Johann August Goeze). Their customary habitat is in ditches, lakes and shallow coastal waters. They can often be found in the water film that clings to damp clumps of moss or lichen – hence their alternative common name of "moss bears" – and also occur in soil, freshwater and marine sediments.*

Resilient Survivors
LOCOMOTION AND BIOLOGY

Water bears move by slow crawling, attaching themselves with claws at the end of each leg. In addition to their four pairs of short, unjointed legs (which are known as lobopodial limbs, and are also found in velvet worms), there are further signs of segmentation in their muscles and nervous system. In *Echiniscus* species the cuticle is arranged in segmental plates. Most water bears feed by piercing plant cells with two sharp stylets and sucking out the contents via a muscular pharynx. Some feed on

○ **Above** *An electron micrograph image of a water bear of the genus* Macrobiotus *shows clearly the characteristic segmented, cylindrical body form of the marine tardigrades.*

detritus, while others are predatory. There are two, probably salivary, glands leading into the mouth. Defecation may be associated with molting, as in *Echiniscus,* which leaves its feces in its cast cuticle.

The three "Malpighian" glands leading into the gut are believed to serve an excretory function. Water bears have no respiratory organs, blood vessels, or heart, because diffusion is sufficient for transport of essential foods in such small animals. The nerve cord along the underside is well organized with ganglia, and the sense organs include two eyespots and sensory bristles.

Water bears have separate sexes, the females usually being the more numerous. However, certain species are hermaphrodite, while males have yet to be discovered in other species. In some species the females breed asexually (namely, by parthenogenesis). In general, reproduction involves copulation with subsequent internal fertilization; some females store transferred sperm in seminal receptacles. Between one and 30 eggs are laid at a time. These may be thin-shelled and hatch soon after laying, or thick-shelled to resist hazardous environmental conditions.

The newly hatched young resemble adults and grow by increasing the size, but not the apparently fixed number of their constituent cells – a feature that may be associated with their very small size. Legs increase from two pairs to four before adulthood. Maturity is reached in about 14 days and they live between three and 30 months, passing through up to 12 molts.

Because the environments they inhabit are subject to extreme temperature changes, water bears have developed great resilience to severe conditions. They can survive desiccation and, experimentally at the other extreme, immersion into chemicals or liquid helium at −227°C. Their body covering, or cuticle, is not made of chitin like the exoskeleton of arthropods, but rather is composed of a water-permeable protein compound that is capable of shrinkage and swelling.

Thus, when drought occurs, tardigrades contract their bodies into a "barrel" (or "tun") state of dehydrated suspended animation, known as cryptobiosis, that can last for several years. When conditions improve, they swell up and return to life once more. PSR

FACTFILE

WATER BEARS

Phylum: Tardigrada

Over 800 species in 2 classes and 15 families.

DISTRIBUTION Worldwide, particularly on damp moss, also in soil, freshwater and marine sediments. Fossil record: species from the Cretaceous period, 136–65 million years ago.

SIZE Microscopic to minute – 50μm to 1.2mm (under 0.05in).

FEATURES Fat-bodied, with a soft, chitinous cuticle, periodically molted; 4 pairs of stout, unjointed, clawed legs; sucking mouthparts with paired stylets; simple gut; segmented muscles; nerve cord on underside, with swellings (ganglia); no circulatory or respiratory organs; 3 "Malpighian" glands are possibly excretory; probably a fixed number of cells; only sense organs are 2 eyespots; remarkable suspended animation (anabiosis) during desiccation; sexes distinct, internal fertilization (some asexual reproduction).

CLASS EUTARDIGRADA
Species include: *Macrobiotus* species (family Macrobiotidae).

CLASS HETEROTARDIGRADA
Genera and species include: *Batillipes* species (family Batillipedidae); genus *Echiniscus* (family Echiniscidae).

Velvet Worms

tHE SEGMENTED BODIES OF THE VELVET *worms, or onycophorans, recalls the body structure of the annelid worms and the arthropods (insects and crustacea) and a study of their features reveals that they lie somewhere between these two major invertebrate groups. For this reason, some biologists have tended to regard the onycophorans as "missing links" or "living fossils."*

Voracious Predators
FORM AND FUNCTION

Unlike these annelids and the arthropods the onycophorans today are a small group with restricted distribution. They are almost all carnivores, feeding on smaller invertebrates such as insects like termites, annelid worms and snails. They frequently capture prey by spraying it with the secretion of their slime glands which discharge via the oral papillae. Jets of adhesive secretion can be discharged over remarkable distances which harden on exposure to air and entangle the victims. These can then be dealt with at leisure, the jaws being effective in cutting up the

prey prior to swallowing. The circulation system is like that of the arthropods, with blood bathing the organs as it passes through the various compartments of the haemocoel. The blood is pumped around the body by a dorsal heart. The transfer of gases to and from the tissues is the responsibility of many tubular tracheae, which open at the surface via small openings known as spiracles (as in the insects). The trachaea run inwards from the spiracles and pass down into the tissues. The transfer of oxygen into the body and of carbon dioxide out, is effected by diffusion and the blood is not involved directly in delivering respiratory gases. Although this system is very similar to that seen in the insects it is thought to have evolved independently. Water balance and excretion are controlled by pairs of nephridia carried in most of the leg bearing body segments. Onycophorans are dioecious (separate sexes). Mating between adults occurs but has rarely been observed. Some strange mechanisms exist for the acceptance of sperms by the female. For example in one African species, a bundle of sperm is deposited on the external surface of the female and the cuticle breaks down so the sperms can enter her body and pass into the blood stream and eventually pass into the ovaries where the eggs are fertilized. In some species eggs with protective shells are laid and develop externally (ovipary). In others the embryo develops and is nurtured inside the mother's body, using food supplied by the mother, so that young ony-

◑ Above *Onycophorans occur in Africa, Southeast Asia, South America, and (most numerously) in Australia, where many new species are being identified. This is* Peripatus acacioi, *from Brazil.*

◐ Below *A tropical velvet worm (Macroperipatus torquatus) from the island of Trinidad, West Indies, captures its prey by entangling it in a mass of sticky threads produced by its slime glands.*

cophorans are born resembling miniature adults (vivapary). In others the eggs develop inside the mother's body depending on the yolk supply they contain (ovovivipary). The young then emerge as miniature adults. There are no larval phases in onycophorans.   AC

FACTFILE

VELVET WORMS

Phylum: Onycophora

About 110 species in 2 families.

DISTRIBUTION Circumtropical (family Peripatidae) and temperate southern hemisphere (circumaustral) (family Peripatopsidae), freeliving, generally in leaf litter.

FOSSIL RECORD A number of fossil species date from the Lower Cambrian (530 mya), but unlike the modern species many of these were marine.

SIZE About 5mm to 15 cm (0.4 – 6 inches).

FEATURES Caterpillarlike "worms" with poorly developed heads, and serially arranged lobe-like walking legs. The head carries three pairs of ornaments or appendages, the well developed antennae, one pair of jaws and a pair of oral or mouth papillae. The mouth opens by way of circular lips and there are small eyes at the base of the antennae. The outer surface of the body is covered with a thin cuticle formed from chitin, and appears segmented or annulated in many cases, as do the antennae and the legs. There is a true coelom, but it is restricted to the cavities of the gonads, as in the insects and crustacea, and the body organs, gut etc. are bathed in blood which circulates through the spaces of the haemocoel.

FAMILY PERIPATIDAE
Genus *Peripatus*.

FAMILY PERIPATOPSIDAE
Genus *Peripatopsis*.

Crabs, Lobsters, Shrimps, and Allies

WITH THEIR TOUGH EXOSKELETONS RICH *in chitin – which require molting for growth to take place – and their paired jointed appendages, or limbs, arranged on segments down the body, crustaceans are clearly arthropods. They are primarily aquatic, mostly marine, but also include freshwater representatives.*

This chapter deals with the more familiar – and by far the most speciose – order of crustaceans, the decapods, which comprise the crabs, lobsters and shrimps. In many cases, these are the larger crustaceans exploited worldwide by humans for food. However, also treated here are the krill (order Euphausiacea) – the tiny organisms that, in their millions, constitute the diet of Earth's largest mammals, the baleen whales.

Segmented and Armored

ANATOMY AND PHYSIOLOGY

The numerous segments of crustaceans are usually grouped into three functional units (tagmata) – the head, thorax, and abdomen. The head is made up of five segments while the thorax and abdomen (which often ends in a nonsegmental telson) vary in number of segments. Some of the smaller crustaceans contain up to 40 segments, whereas the decapods (shrimps, crabs, lobsters), the biggest crustaceans, have 19 – five in the head, eight in the thorax and six in the abdomen. Some thoracic appendages may fuse to the back of the head, forming a cephalothorax, and a shield-like carapace may cover the head and part or all of the thorax: crustacean evolution is the story of reduction in the number of segments and their grouping into tagmata, with consequent specialization of the appendages for specialized roles. Although the fossil record goes back well over 500 million years, it tells us little about the origin of crustaceans.

The cuticle of crustaceans provides a tough, protective layer that also serves as an external skeleton (exoskeleton). The cuticle is rich in chitin, a polysaccharide similar in structure to the cellulose found in plants, and is secreted by the underlying single layer of living cells, the epidermis. The endocuticle of a decapod is comprised of an outer pigmented and inner calcified and uncalcified layers. The thin outermost epicuticle is secreted by tegumental glands.

The cuticle, which is initially soft and flexible, is progressively hardened inward from the epicuticle by the deposition of calcium salts and by sclerotization (tanning), involving the chemical

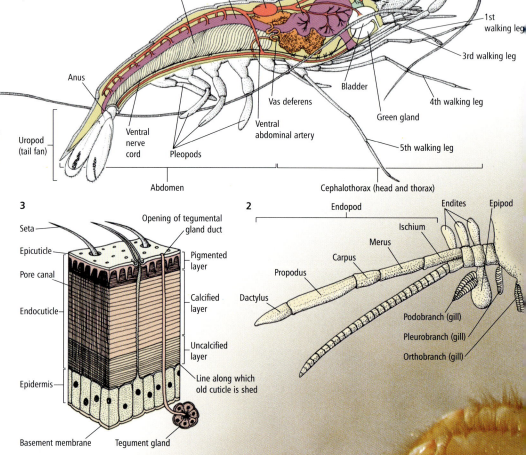

1

Anus / Uropod (tail fan) / Ventral nerve cord / Pleopods / Abdomen / Abdominal wall muscles / Intestine / Heart / Pyloric stomach / Testis / Cardiac stomach / Brain / Compound eye / Antenna / Antennule / 2nd walking leg / 1st walking leg / 3rd walking leg / 4th walking leg / 5th walking leg / Vas deferens / Ventral abdominal artery / Bladder / Green gland / Cephalothorax (head and thorax)

3
Seta / Epicuticle / Pore canal / Endocuticle / Epidermis / Basement membrane / Tegument gland / Opening of tegumental gland duct / Pigmented layer / Calcified layer / Uncalcified layer / Line along which old cuticle is shed

2
Endopod / Endites / Epipod / Ischium / Merus / Carpus / Propodus / Dactylus / Podobranch (gill) / Pleurobranch (gill) / Orthobranch (gill)

◔ *Above* **1** *Body plan of a decapod (free-swimming prawn of the genus* Palaemon*); in the inset,* **2**, *a typical thoracic appendage of this order of crustaceans is illustrated. The cross-sectional diagram* **3** *shows the different layers of the crustacean cuticle.*

◑ *Right* *The Ghost crab (*Ocypode quadrata*) inhabits sandy burrows on beaches along the east coast of the USA. Its large eyes are sensitive to changes in the intensity of light, and it is mainly nocturnal.*

cross-linking of cuticular proteins to form an impenetrable meshwork.

A rigid exoskeleton prevents a gradual increase in size, and so a crustacean grows, stepwise, in a series of molts involving the secretion of a new cuticle by the epidermis and the shedding of the old. before a molt, food reserves are accumulated and calcium is removed from the old cuticle and much of its organic material resorbed. It is then split along lines of weakness as the crustacean swells (usually by an intake of water) before hardening of the new cuticle. The rest of the old exoskeleton may then be eaten to reduce energy loss.

During and immediately after molting, the

temporarily defenseless crustacean hides to avoid predators. Some adult crabs cease molting, but many adult crustaceans molt throughout life.

Crustaceans' body organs lie in a bloodfilled space – the hemocoel, and the blood often contains hemocyanin, a copper-based respiratory pigment which bears oxygen and is equivalent to hemoglobin in vertebrates. The coelom, the major body cavity of many animals, is restricted to the inner cavity of the coxal glands – paired excretory and osmoregulatory organs each consisting of an end sac and a tubule that opens out at the base of the second antenna (antennal gland) or the second maxilla (maxillary gland).

The "typical" crustacean head bears five pairs of appendages. Each of the first two segments bears a pair of antennae – the first antennae (antennules) and the second antennae (antennae). All crustaceans have two pairs of antennae. The antennae have probably shifted in the course of evolution, since they now lie in front of the mouth, which may have been terminal in a pre-crustacean ancestor. They are typically sensory,

although in some crustaceans they are employed in locomotion or even used by a male to clasp the female when mating.

Situated behind the mouth is the third segment bearing the mandibles, the main jaws developed from jawlike extensions (gnathobases) at the base of the appendages, while the remainder of the limb has been lost, or reduced to a sensory palp. The fourth and fifth head segments bear the first maxillae (maxillules) and second, or true, maxillae respectively; these accessory jaws assist mastication and are similarly derived by partial or complete reduction of the limb to a gnathobase.

The alimentary canal of crustaceans consists of a cuticle-lined foregut and hindgut, with an intermediate midgut giving rise to blind pockets (ceca), perhaps modified as a hepatopancreas combining the functions of digestion, absorption, and storage. The nervous system consists of a double ventral nerve cord, primitively with concentrations of the cord (ganglia) in each segment, but often further concentrated into a number of large ganglia.

FACTFILE

CRABS, LOBSTERS, SHRIMPS, ETC.

Superorder: Eucarida

About 8,600 species in 154 families.

Distribution Worldwide; marine, some in fresh water.

Fossil record Crustaceans appear in the Lower Cambrian, over 530 million years ago.

Size From tiny (0.5–5cm/0.2–2in) krill to lobsters 60cm (24in) long.

KRILL Order Euphausiacea
About 90 species in 2 families of marine pelagic filter feeders. Species include whale krill (*Euphausia superba*).

DECAPODS Order Decapoda
About 8,500 species in 151 families. Species include Common shrimp (*Crangon crangon*), cleaner shrimps (families Stenopodidae and Hippolytidae), American lobster (*Homarus americanus*), American spiny-cheeked crayfish (*Orconectes limosus*), Caribbean spiny lobster (*Panulirus argus*), Robber crab (*Birgus latro*), Christmas Island crab (*Geocarcoidea natalis*).

See Decapod Suborders and Infraorders ▷

From Swimming to Walking

EVOLUTION AND BREEDING BIOLOGY

The ancestors of crustaceans were probably small marine organisms living on the sea bottom but able to swim, with a series of similar appendages down the length of a body not divided into thorax and abdomen; all appendages would have been used in locomotion, feeding, and respiration. The limbs of early crustaceans were two-branched (biramous), with an endopod (inner limb) and exopod (outer limb) branching from the base (protopodite). The ancestral limb would have had two flat leaflike lobes, as in several living crustaceans of the order Branchiopoda (for example, fairy shrimps and brine shrimps). Such limbs are usually moved in rhythm to create swimming and feeding currents, food being passed along the underside of the body to the mouth – so promoting the evolution of jaws from limb gnathobases. Extensions from the outer side of the limb bases often act as respiratory surfaces.

One major line of crustacean evolution has produced large walking animals. The two-branched swimming and filtering leg has evolved into an apparently one-branched (uniramous) walking leg (stenopodium) strictly the endopod alone, the exopod being reduced and lost during larval development or previously in evolution. Such cylindrical legs have a reduced surface area and are not suitable as respiratory surfaces, which are particularly necessary in large crustaceans. Exites or extensions of the body wall at the base of the legs are therefore used as gills. The decapods (shrimps, crabs, lobsters) also show increased development of the head (cephalization). The first three pairs of thoracic limbs are adapted as accessory mouthparts (maxillipeds) and a carapace shields the cephalothorax.

Crustaceans typically have separate sexes and the fertilized egg as it divides shows a characteristic modified spiral cleavage pattern. Crustaceans usually develop through a series of larval stages of increasing size and numbers of segments with their associated limbs. The simplest larval stage is the nauplius larva, with three pairs of appendages – the first and second antennae and the mandibles. It occurs in many living crustaceans, often as a pelagic dispersal stage that swims and suspension-feeds with the three pairs of appendages. These limbs therefore have different functions in larva and adult, usually relinquishing their larval roles to other appendages that develop further down the body. Nauplius larvae are followed by a variety of larger larvae, according to the type of crustacean, although many crustaceans bypass the nauplius equivalent by developing within the egg.

The following account covers the more important crustacean groups. For a complete list of classes within the phylum Crustacea, see The 6 Classes of Crustaceans table on p.61.

Krill and Decapods – the Eucarids

SUPERORDER EUCARIDA; ORDER EUPHAUSIACEA

The planktonic krill and the decapods (shrimps, lobsters, crabs) are classified in the superorder Eucarida. They have a well-developed carapace, fused dorsally with all thoracic segments, and stalked eyes. Fertilized eggs are usually carried beneath the abdomen of the female and hatch as planktonic zoeae, with a large carapace, prominent eyes and well-developed thoracic appendages. Krill and primitive decapods, however, hatch as nauplius larvae.

Krill (order Euphausiacea) have primitive features of generalist members of the class Malacostraca. All are marine; the eggs hatch as nauplii. None of the thoracic appendages are adapted as

◀ **Left** *Representative crustacean species from the sea shores and shallow seas of NW Europe:* **1** *A sea slater* Ligia oceanica *(order Isopoda; 2.5cm/1in), which dwells high on sea shores;* **2** Gammarus locusta, *an amphipod from the lower shore (order Amphipoda; 1.4cm/0.5in);* **3** Pseudocuma longicornis, *a tannaid living on the lower shore an in shallow waters;* **4** Lepas anatifera, *goose barnacles (5cm/2in);* **5** Carcinus maenas, *the Shore crab, common in shallow water (4cm/1.6in);* **6** Semibalanus balanoides, *the Acorn barnacle, which grow on rocks on the middle and lower shore (1.5cm/0.6in);* **7** Palinurus vulgaris, *a sea crayfish, found in rocky crevices down to 70m/230ft (50cm/20in);* **8** Scyllarides latus, *a flattened deca-pod living on rocks, stones, and sand (35cm/14in);* **9** Homarus gammarus, *a lobster living in crevices from the extreme lower shore to shallow water (45cm/18in);* **10** Crangon vulgaris, *a shrimp living on sandy substrates on the lower shore and in shallow water (5cm/2in);* **11** Eupagurus bernhardus, *a hermit crab living in the disused shell of* Buccinum undatum *(6cm/2.4in).*

maxillipeds, and all have fully developed exopods. The thoracic appendages also bear epipodites which take the form of external gills not covered by the carapace.

Most krill have luminescent organs, usually on the eyes, at the bases of the seventh thoracic limbs, and on the underside of the abdomen. They are probably used for communication in swarming and reproduction. Krill are pelagic and filter feed when phytoplankton conditions are suitable, otherwise preying on larger planktonic organisms. The first six pairs of thoracic appendages are adapted as a filter basket. Phytoplankton-rich sea water enters at the tips of the legs and is strained as it passes between the leg bases. Whale krill reach about 5cm (2in) long, dominate the zooplankton of the Antarctic Ocean and are the chief food of many baleen whales (see Drifters and Wanderers).

In decapods, the first three pairs of thoracic appendages are adapted as auxiliary mouthparts (maxillipeds), theoretically leaving five pairs as legs (pereiopods) – hence deca poda "ten legs." (In fact, the first pair of pereiopods is often adapted as claws.) Historically decapods have been divided into swimmers (natantians) and crawlers (reptantians) – essentially the shrimps and prawns on the one hand and the lobsters, crayfish and crabs on the other. More modern divisions rely on morphological characteristics, and decapods are now divided between the suborders Dendrobranchiata and Pleocyemata.

Members of the Dendrobranchiata are all shrimplike, characterized by their laterally compressed body and many-branched (dendrobranchiate) gills. Their eggs are planktonic and hatch as nauplius larvae. The Pleocyemata have gills which lack secondary branches, being platelike (lamellate) or threadlike (filamentous) and their eggs are carried on the pleopods of the female before hatching as zoeae.

Prawns and Shrimps
SUPERORDER EUCARIDA; ORDER DECAPODA

The terms shrimp and prawn have no exact zoological definition, and are often interchangeable.

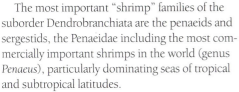

⬖ **Above** *The larger crustaceans are of great economic importance. Here, langoustines (Nephrops norvegicus) from the North Sea, a great seafood delicacy, await transport to market.*

⬗ **Below** *Tiny krill such as this (note the luminescent organs) make up a large proportion of the marine zooplankton that sustain filter-feeding whales. Krill themselves feed on diatoms, which they filter from the water.*

species) complete their entire lifecycles in freshwater, but many shrimps living in rivers return to estuaries to breed and release their zoea larvae.

In addition to the totally pelagic species, many shrimps are essentially bottom-dwellers, only swimming intermittently. In adult shrimps the thoracic pereiopods are responsible for walking (and/or feeding) and the five pairs of abdominal pleopods for swimming. Flexion of the abdomen is occasionally used for rapid escape. Shrimp zoea larvae have two-branched thoracic appendages, the exopods being used for swimming; the pleopods take over the swimming function in postlarval and adult stages as the exopods are

reduced. By the adult stage the "walking" pereiopods are single-branched.

Most pelagic shrimps are active predators feeding on crustaceans of the zooplankton, such as krill and copepods. Bottom-dwelling species are usually scavengers, but range from catholic carnivores to specialist herbivores.

Shrimps usually have distinct sexes, although in some species, including *Pandalus borealis*, some of the females pass through an earlier male stage (protandrous hermaphroditism). Successful copulation usually requires molting by the female immediately before mating, when spermatophores are transferred from the male. Eggs are spawned

The most important "shrimp" families of the suborder Dendrobranchiata are the penaeids and sergestids, the Penaeidae including the most commercially important shrimps in the world (genus *Penaeus*), particularly dominating seas of tropical and subtropical latitudes.

Among the "shrimp" families in the much larger suborder Pleocyemata, the Stenopodidae comprise cleaner shrimps, which remove ectoparasites from the bodies of fish. Carideans (infraorder Caridea) are typified by possessing a second abdominal segment of which the lateral edges overlap the segments to either side. They are the dominant "shrimps" of northern latitudes although present throughout the world's oceans, from the intertidal zone down to the deep sea. Some shrimps (for example, *Macrobrachium*

between two and 48 hours later and are fertilized by sperm from the spermatophore. The eggs of penaeids are shed directly into the water, but in most shrimps the eggs are attached to bristles on the inner branches (endopods) of pleopods 1–4 of the female. The incubation period usually lasts between one and four months, during which time the female does not molt. Most shrimp eggs hatch as zoeae and pass through several molts over a few weeks, to postlarval and adult stages. Most shrimps are mature by the end of their first year and typically live two to three years. (See also The Economic Importance of Crustaceans)

Lobsters and Freshwater Crayfish

ORDER DECAPODA; INFRAORDER ASTACIDEA

Lobsters and freshwater crayfish belong to a group known historically as the macrurans ("large-tails") but now divided into three infraorders – the Astacidea (lobsters, freshwater crayfish, scampi), the Palinura (spiny and Spanish lobsters) and the Thalassinidea (mud lobsters and mud shrimps). All have well-developed abdomens, compared with, for example, anomurans or brachyurans. For the group's importance as a source of food for humans, see Economic Importance of Crustaceans, page 60–61.

Lobsters and freshwater crayfish walk along the substratum on their four back pairs of single-branched thoracic legs (pereiopods). The first pair of pereiopods is adapted as a pair of formidable claws for both offense and defense. The abdomen bears pleopods, but these cannot move the heavy body and have become variously adapted for functions which include copulation or eggbearing.

Lobsters are marine carnivorous scavengers, usually living in holes on rocky bottoms. The commercially important American lobster reaches 60cm (2ft) in length and weighs up to 22kg (48lb). Lobsters are very long lived and they may survive 100 years.

MIGRATIONS ALONG THE SEABED

The spiny lobsters of the family Palinuridae (also sometimes called rock lobsters or sea crayfish) lack claws but have defensive spines on the carapace and antennae. Among the best known are two American species, *Panulirus argas*, found in the shallow seas off Florida and the Caribbean, and *P. interruptus*, which lives off California. (The European spiny lobster is *Palinurus elephas*, the generic name a curious anagram of that of the American species.) Spiny lobsters spend their days in rock or coral crevices, emerging by night to forage for invertebrate prey. They return from their wanderings to one of several dens within a feeding range of hundreds of meters, and after several weeks may move several kilometers to a new location. The homing capacity of *P. argas* is now known to involve the use of a magnetic map, for the lobsters can somehow derive enough positional information from the earth's magnetic field to determine the direction home. *Panulirus. argas* is in fact the first invertebrate confirmed to use a magnetic map sense for navigation. Many spiny lobsters also take part in spectacular mass migrations. *Panulirus argas*, for example, will abandon its normal behavior in the fall and as many as 100,000 individuals move south, by both day and night, in single files of up to 60 individuals (BELOW). They may cover 15km (9.3 miles) a day and travel for 50km (31 miles) at depths between 3 and 30m (10–100ft). The lobsters may be primed to migrate by annual changes in temperature and daylight length, but the immediate trigger is a sharp temperature drop associated with a fall storm – usually the first strong winter squall. The spiny lobsters maintain alignment in the queue by touch but may respond initially by sight, recognizing the rows of white spots along the abdomens of their companions.   PSR

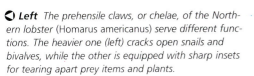

◖ Left *The prehensile claws, or chelae, of the Northern lobster* (Homarus americanus) *serve different functions. The heavier one (left) cracks open snails and bivalves, while the other is equipped with sharp insets for tearing apart prey items and plants.*

◗ Right *The White-clawed crayfish* (Austropotamobius pallipes) *was once common in European freshwater streams, but is now threatened by the larger American Signal crayfish* (Pacifastacus leniusculus)*, which carries a fungal disease fatal to the native species.*

Freshwater crayfish, however, are more omnivorous. There are more than 500 species of freshwater crayfish, mostly about 10cm (4in) long, and since they typically require calcium they are often restricted to calcareous waters. Because of their marine ancestry, their internal fluids have an osmotic pressure higher than that of the surrounding medium and water will enter by osmosis across gill and gut membranes. The cuticle covering the rest of the body is made impermeable by tanning and calcification. The convoluted tubule of each antennal (green) gland is very long and resorbs ions from the primary urine (filtered from the blood at the end sac of the gland). A dilute urine, one tenth the osmotic pressure of the blood, may be produced, eliminating water that has entered osmotically. Any salts still lost with the urine are replaced by ions actively taken up by the gills.

Reproduction involves pairing, in which either sperm from the male flows down along the grooves on the first pleopods into a seminal receptacle in the female, or a spermatophore is transferred. Fertilized eggs are incubated on the pleopods of the female and hatch as mysis larvae bypassing in the egg the stages equivalent to nauplius and zoea.

Squat Lobsters and Hermit Crabs

ORDER DECAPODA; INFRAORDER ANOMURA;
SUPERFAMILY GALATHEOIDEA

Squat lobsters, hermit crabs, and mole crabs are part of a collection of probably unrelated groups intermediate in structure and habit between lobsters and crabs. The abdomen is variable in structure – often being asymmetrical or reduced and held in a flexed position (anom ura: odd-tailed – hence the scientific name Anomura given to these crustaceans). The fifth pair of pereiopods is turned up or reduced in size.

Hermit crabs are thought to have evolved from ancestors which regularly used crevices for protection, eventually specializing in the use of the discarded spiral shells of gastropod mollusks. The abdomen is adapted to occupy the typically righthanded spiral of such shells although rarer lefthanded shells may also be used. The pleopods are lost at least from the short side of the asymmetric abdomen, but those on the long side of females are adapted to carry fertilized eggs. At the tip of the abdomen, the uropods are modified to grip the interior of the shell posteriorly, and toward the front of the animal thoracic legs may be used for purchase. One or both claws can block up the shell opening. The shell offers excellent protection and still affords mobility (see Househunting Hermits).

Not all species of hermit crabs live in gastropod shells. Some occupy tusk shells, coral, or holes in wood or stone. The hermit crab *Pagurus prideauxi* lives in association with a sea anemone, *Adamsia carciniopados*, whose horny base surrounds the crab's abdomen and greatly overflows the

HOUSEHUNTING HERMITS

Hermit crabs typically occupy the empty shells of dead sea snails (BELOW *Aniculus maximus* in a tun shell), so gaining protection while at the same time keeping their mobility. They can discriminate if offered a selection of shells, and will differentiate between shells of different sizes and species, to choose the one that fits their body most closely. Hermit crabs (family Paguridae) change shells as they grow, although in some marine environments there may be a shortage of available shells, and a hermit crab may be restricted to a shell smaller than is ideal. Some hermit crabs are aggressive and will fight fellows of their own species to effect a shell exchange: aggression is often increased if the shell is particularly inadequate.

Hermit crabs may encounter empty shells in the course of their day-to-day activity but the vacant shell is usually "spotted" by sight; the hermit crab's visual response increases with the size of an object and its contrast against the background. The hermit crab then takes hold of the shell with its walking legs and will climb onto it, monitoring its texture. Exploration may cease at any time, but if the shell is suitable the hermit crab will explore the shell's shape and texture by rolling it over

between the walking legs and running its opened claws over the surface. Once the shell aperture has been located, the hermit crab will explore it by inserting its claws one at a time, occasionally also using its first walking legs. Any foreign material will be removed before the crab rises above the aperture, flexes its abdomen and enters the shell backward. The shell interior is monitored by the abdomen as the crab repeatedly enters and withdraws. The crab will then emerge, turn the shell over and re-enter finally.   PSR

originally occupied shell. This hermit crab avoids the risk of being eaten when transferring from one shell to another, for the protecting anemone moves simultaneously with its associate. The crab is protected by the stinging tentacles of the anemone, which in turn profits from food particles which its crustacean partner releases into the water during feeding.

Hermit crabs live as carnivorous scavengers on sea bottoms ranging from the deep sea to the seashore. They have also taken up an essentially terrestrial existence in the tropics. Land hermit crabs range inland from the upper shore, often occupying the shells of land snails. The Coconut crab has abandoned the typical hermit crab form, and appears somewhat crablike, but with a flexed abdomen. It lives in burrows and holes in trees, which it can climb, feeding on carrion and vegetation, and can drink. Land hermit crabs have reduced the number of gills that would tend to dry out in the air and collapse under surface tension. The walls of the branchial chamber are richly supplied with blood, which enables them to act as lungs, and some species have accessory respiratory areas on the abdomen enclosed in the humid microclimate provided by the shell. Land hermit

Left *The Coconut crab (Birgus latro), a hermit crab relative, is a terrestrial species from Pacific islands that is especially partial to coconuts. Scavenging widely, these large crabs are perfectly capable of scaling palms in search of their favorite food.*

Right *Some 120 million Christmas Island crabs (Gecarcoidea natalis) live on this small island in the Indian Ocean. At the beginning of each wet season, the adults migrate en masse from the forests to the coast, where they breed and release eggs into the sea.*

crabs are not fully terrestrial, for they have planktonic zoea larvae. The adults must return therefore to the sea for reproduction.

Squat lobsters are well named, for they have relatively large symmetrical abdomens flexed beneath the body. They typically retreat into crevices. Porcelain crabs are anomuran relatives of squat lobsters which look remarkably like true crabs. Mole crabs are anomurans that by flexing the abdomen burrow into the sand when waves break low on warm sandy shores. The first antennae form a siphon channeling a ventilation current to the gills and the setose (bristly) second antennae filter plankton.

True Crabs
ORDER DECAPODA; INFRAORDER BRACHYURA

There are 4,500 species of true crabs which all possess a very reduced symmetrical abdomen held permanently flexed beneath the combined cephalothorax (brachyuran: short-tailed). The terminal uropods are lost in both sexes: four pairs of pleopods are retained on the female's abdomen to brood eggs and in the male only the front two pairs remain to act as copulatory organs. The crabs have a massive carapace extended at the sides, and the first of the five pairs of thoracic walking legs is adapted as large claws. Typically crabs are carnivorous walkers on the sea bottom.

The reduction of the abdomen has brought the center of gravity of the body directly over the walking legs, making locomotion very efficient and potentially rapid. The sideways gait assists to this end. The shape of a crab is therefore the ultimate shape in efficient crustacean walking. Mainly as a result, the brachyurans have enjoyed an explosive adaptive radiation since their origin in the Jurassic era (206–144 million years ago) and various anomurans (for example, mole crabs and porcelain crabs) approach or duplicate the crablike form.

Crabs live in the deep sea and extend up to and beyond the top of the shore. The blind crab *Bythograea thermydron* is a predator in the unique faunal communities surrounding deepsea hydrothermal vents, regions of activity in the earth's crust which emit hot sulfurous material 2.5km (1.6 miles) below the surface of the sea. On the other hand, crabs of the family Ocypodidae, such as the burrowing ghost and fiddler crabs, live at the top of tropical sandy and muddy

⬥ **Above** *One of the largest crabs on the Pacific coast of North America, the Puget Sound King crab* (Lopholithodes mandtii), *can grow up to 30cm (12in) across. It feeds on seastars and other echinoderms.*

⬥ **Below** *The true crab species* Caphyra laevis, *found around the Philippines, lives in a commensal relationship with the soft coral* Xenia elongata, *which it uses for camouflage.*

shores and the distribution of the genus *Sesarma* extends well inland. Crabs have also invaded the rivers – the common British shore crab extends up estuaries – and in the tropics crabs of the family Potamidae and some Grapsidae are truly freshwater in habit.

Most crabs burrow to escape predators – descending backfirst into the sediment, and several typically remain burrowed for long periods. Of these the Helmet crab has long second antennae which interconnect with bristles to form a tube for the passage of a ventilation current down into the gill chamber of the buried crab. Some crabs have become specialist swimmers, with the last pair of thoracic legs adapted as paddles. The more terrestrial crabs like the ghost crabs are very rapid runners – their speed and night-time activity contributing to their common name. Other crabs, particularly spider crabs (see Japanese Spider Crabs), cover themselves with small plants and stationary animals (e.g. sponges, anemones, sea mats) for protective camouflage. Pea crabs may live in the mantle cavities of bivalve mollusks, feeding on food collected by the gills of the host, and female coral gall crabs become imprisoned by surrounding coral growth. The female crab is left with just a hole to allow entry of plankton for food and the tiny male for reproduction.

Decapod Suborders and Infraorders

SUBORDER DENDROBRANCHIATA

7 families of free-swimmers with many-branched gills and free-floating eggs hatching as nauplius larvae; carnivorous, 0.5–20cm (0.2–8in) long. The family Penaeidae includes: Banana prawn (*Penaeus merguiensis*), Brown shrimp (*P. aztecus*), Giant tiger prawn (*P. monodon*), Green tiger prawn (*P. semisulcatus*), Indian prawn (*P. indicus*), Kuruma shrimp (*P. japonicus*), Pink shrimp (*P. duorarum*), White shrimp (*P. setiferus*), and Yellow prawn (*Metapenaeus brevicornis*).

SUBORDER PLEOCYEMATA

144 families; gills platelike (lamellate) or threadlike (filamentous), not many-branched; eggs carried by female before hatching as zoeae.

BANDED OR CLEANER SHRIMPS
INFRAORDER STENOPODIDEA

2 families of bottom-dwelling cleaners of fish, about 5cm (2in) long. Species include: *Stenopus* species.

SHRIMPS, PRAWNS, PISTOL SHRIMPS
INFRAORDER CARIDEA

36 families of marine, brackish and freshwater swimmers and walkers; predatory scavengers, dominant shrimps in N oceans; 0.5–20cm (0.2–8in) long. Species include: Brown shrimp (*Crangon crangon*), Pink shrimp (*Pandalus montagui*), Brown pistol shrimp (*Alpheus armatus*), Sand shrimp (*Crangon septemspinosa*), Pederson cleaner shrimp (*Periclimenes pedersoni*), Common shore shrimp (*Palaemonetes vulgaris*).

Suborder Dendrobranchiata

Suborder Pleocyemata

Infraorder Stenopodidea
Banded or Cleaner shrimps

Infraorder Caridea
Shrimps, prawns, pistol shrimps

Infraorder Astacidea
Lobsters, freshwater crayfish, scampi

Infraorder Palinura
Spiny and Spanish lobsters

LOBSTERS, FRESHWATER CRAYFISH, SCAMPI
INFRAORDER ASTACIDEA

7 families of mostly marine, some freshwater, bottom walkers, hole dwellers; predatory scavengers; up to 60cm (2ft) long. Species include: American lobster (*Homarus americanus*), European lobster (*H. gammarus*) and Dublin Bay prawn or Norway lobster (*Nephrops norvegicus*).

SPINY AND SPANISH LOBSTERS
INFRAORDER PALINURA

4 families, of marine bottom walkers or hole dwellers; often spiny but lack permanent rostrum (frontal spine) of Astacidea; predatory scavengers up to 60cm (2ft) long. Species include: American spiny lobsters (*Panulirus argus* and *P. interruptus*) and European spiny lobster (*P. elephas*).

Infraorder Thalassinidea
Mud shrimps, mud lobsters

Infraorder Anomura
Anomurans

Superfamily Paguroidea
Hermit crabs

Superfamily Galatheoidea
Squat lobsters, porcelain crabs

Superfamily Hippoidea
Mole crabs

Infraorder Brachyura
Crabs, spider crabs

MUD SHRIMPS, MUD LOBSTERS
INFRAORDER THALASSINIDEA

11 families; bear a carapace up to 9cm (3.5in) long. Live in shallow water in deep burrows in sand or mud. Species include: *Callianassa subterranea*.

ANOMURANS
INFRAORDER ANOMURA

13 families, including:

Hermit crabs
Superfamily Paguroidea

6 families; carapace to 19cm (7.5in); inhabiting marine and terrestrial gastropod shells; scavengers feeding on detritus. Species include: *Pagurus bernhardus*, stone crabs (*Lithodes* species), land hermit crabs and coconut crab (*Birgus latro*).

Squat lobsters, Porcelain crabs
Superfamily Galatheoidea

4 families with carapace to 4cm (1.6in); marine, in holes, under stones; scavenging detritivores. Species include: squat lobster (*Galathea* species), porcelain crab (*Porcellana platycheles*).

Mole crabs
Superfamily Hippoidea

1 family with carapace to 5cm (2in), marine sand burrowers, filter feeders. Species include: mole crab (*Emerita talpoida*).

CRABS, SPIDER CRABS
INFRAORDER BRACHYURA

71 families with carapace up to 45cm (18in); mostly bottom dwellers, walking on seabed, but some parasitic/commensal with fish, some burrowers, some swimmers; predaceous scavengers. Groups, families and species include: 7 families of spider crabs, including *Macrocheira kaempferi* (family Majidae), Edible crab (*Cancer pagurus*) and Dungeness crab (*C. magister*) (family Cancridae); helmet crabs (family Corystidae), including *Corystes cassivelaunus*; swimming crabs (family Portunidae), including Blue crab (*Callinectes sapidus*), Henslow's swimming crab (*Polybius henslowi*), and Shore or Green crab (*Carcinus maenas*); Chinese mitten crab (*Eriocheir sinensis*), *Sesarma* species (family Grapsidae); pea crabs (family Pinnotheridae), including *Pinnotheres* species; and ghost crabs (*Ocypode* species) and fiddler crabs (*Uca* species) (family Ocypodidae).

Most crabs are carnivorous scavengers although the more terrestrial ones may eat plant matter. The fiddler crabs process sand or mud in their mouthparts, scraping off the nutritious microorganisms with specialized spoon- or bristle-shaped setae.

Reproduction involves copulation. The second pair of pleopods on the male's abdomen acts like pistons within the first pair to transfer sperm to the female for storage. The eggs are fertilized as they are laid and are held under the broad abdomen of the female. They hatch as prezoea larvae, molting immediately to the first of several planktonic zoea stages. Zoea larvae have a full complement of head appendages, but only the first two pairs of thoracic appendages (destined to become the first two or three pairs of adult maxillipeds), used by the zoea for swimming. After several molts the megalopa stage is reached, with abdominal as well as thoracic appendages. This settles on the sea bottom and metamorphoses into a crab.   PSR

JAPANESE SPIDER CRABS

Spider crabs belong to a superfamily (7 families) of true (brachyuran) crabs with long legs and a superficial resemblance to spiders. Included in their number is the world's largest crustacean, the giant spider crab (*Macrocheira kaempferi*), whose Japanese name is *Takaashigani* – the "tall-leg crab".

This remarkable animal may measure up to 8m (26.5ft) between the tips of its legs when these are splayed out on either side of the body. Its claws may be 3m (10ft) apart when held in an offensive posture. The main body (cephalothorax) of the crab is, however, relatively small and would not usually exceed 45cm (18in) in length or 30cm (12in) in breadth.

Giant spider crabs have a restricted distribution off the southeast coast of Japan. They live on sandy or muddy bottoms between 30–50m (100–165ft) deep. They have poor balance and so live in still waters, hunting slow-moving prey that includes other crustaceans as well as echinoderms, worms and mollusks. Little detail is known of their life history, but they probably pass through zoea and megalopa larval stages before they metamorphose into juvenile crabs. Large specimens are probably more than 20 years old.

The crabs are caught relatively infrequently, but they are used for food. Because of their size they command respect, and their nippers can inflict a nasty wound.

The existence of the giant crabs was first reported in Europe by Engelbert Kaempfer, a physician for the Dutch East India Company who visited Japan in 1690, in his *History of Japan* published in English in 1727 (although he himself died in 1716). The crabs were given their Latin name in honor of Kaempfer in the 19th century by C. I. Temminck, the director of the Leiden Museum, which received much of the natural history collections of the Dutch East India Company.   PSR

Other Crustaceans

aSIDE FROM THE MORE FAMILIAR DECAPODS, *the crustaceans also include a host of smaller, less commonplace arthropods, some of which are major components of plankton. Certain branchiopod genera, such as* Daphnia *and* Artemia, *are well-known to aquarium hobbyists as commercial fish food.*

The small crustaceans are predominantly aquatic, and mostly marine, but include freshwater representatives. One group, the woodlice, has even successfully colonized land.

Branchiopods
CLASS BRANCHIOPODA

Fairy shrimps and water fleas are among the branchiopods, small, mostly freshwater, crustaceans. They have leaflike trunk appendages used for swimming and filter-feeding. Flattened extensions (epipodites) from the first segment (coxa) of these limbs act as gills, giving the class its scientific name of "gill legs" (Branchiopoda).

Fairy shrimps (order Anostraca) live in temporary freshwater pools and springs, (some, the brine shrimps, in salt lakes), typically in the absence of fish. Unlike other branchiopods they lack a carapace (hence an ostraca). They have elongated bodies with 20 or more trunk segments, many bearing appendages of the one type. They are usually about 1cm (0.4in) long, but some reach 10cm (4in). Fairy shrimps swim upside-down, beating the trunk appendages in rhythm, simultaneously filtering small particles with fine slender bristles (setae) on the legs. Collected food particles are then passed along a groove on the underside to the mouth.

When mating, a male fairy shrimp clasps the female with its large second antennae. The female lays her eggs into a brood sac. The eggs on release are extremely resistant to drying out (desiccation). Some eggs will hatch when wetted, but others require more than one inundation – a successful evolutionary strategy, ensuring that populations are not wiped out when insufficient rain falls to maintain the pool long enough to complete the fairy shrimp life cycle. Fairy shrimps hatch as nauplii and grow to maturity in as little as one week.

Brine shrimps are found in salt lakes, the brackish nature of which eliminates possible predators. The eggs similarly resist drying out and are sold as aquarium food. *Artemia salina* has a remarkable resistance to salt, surviving immersion in saturated salt solutions. The gills absorb or excrete ions as appropriate and this brine shrimp can produce a concentrated urine from the maxillary glands.

Water fleas (suborder Cladocera) are laterally compressed with a carapace enclosing the trunk but not the head, which projects on the underside as a beak. Overall length is just 1–5mm (0.04–0.2in). The powerful second antennae are used for swimming. The trunk is usually reduced to about five segments, of which two may bear filtering appendages. Most water fleas, including *Daphnia* species, live in freshwater and filter small particles, but some marine cladocerans are carnivorous.

Water fleas brood their eggs in a dorsal chamber and asexual reproduction (parthenogenesis) is common. Populations may consist only of females reproducing parthenogenetically for several generations until a temperature change or limitation of food supply induces the production of males. The brood chamber, which now encloses fertilized eggs, may be cast off at the next molt and can withstand drying, freezing and even passage through the guts of vertebrates. Some Daphnia species show cyclomorphosis, cyclic seasonal changes in morphology, often involving a change in head shape.

In the clam shrimps (suborder Spinicaudata), most of which are some 1cm (0.4in) in length, the remarkably clamlike bivalve carapace encloses the whole body, but in tadpole shrimps (order Notostraca) part of the trunk extends behind the large shieldlike carapace and the overall body length may reach 5cm (2in). Either may be found with fairy shrimps in temporary rain pools.

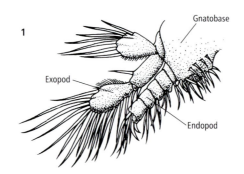

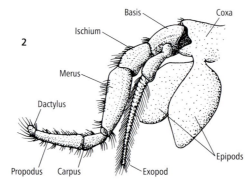

Remipedes
CLASS REMIPEDIA

The first extant remipede crustacean (*Speleonectes lucayensis*) was described only in 1981, after its discovery in an anchialine cave on Grand Bahama Island. Since then, another eleven species have also been found in such caves which lack a surface connection to the sea and appear to act as a reservoir for relict crustacean taxa. Living remipedes are indeed very similar to a fossil arthropod (*Tesnusocaris*) from the Carboniferous period, and can therefore be considered as 'living fossils'.

Remipedes may therefore have a body form closest to that of the earliest crustaceans. They are small and elongate with 20 to 30 similar body segments each with biramous appendages beating in metachronal rhythm. They are believed to be carnivorous, injecting digestive fluids into their prey, before sucking up the semifluid remains.

Cephalocarids
CLASS CEPHALOCARIDA

Cephalocarids were first described in 1955, and all those so far discovered are minute inhabitants of marine sediments, feeding on bottom detritus. The body, under 4mm (0.2in) in length, is not divided into thorax and abdomen, and the leaf-shaped body appendages are very similar to each other and indeed to the second maxillae.

Branchiuran fish lice and Tongue worms
CLASS MAXILLOPODA; SUBCLASS BRANCHIURA

Branchiurans are ectoparasites living on the skin or in the gill cavities of fish, feeding on the blood and mucus of the host, and are therefore commonly called fish lice. They have a large shieldlike carapace for protection, and have large claws on the antennules and large suckers (modified first maxillae) with which they hang on tight.

Tongue worms (pentastomids) are the most unlikely looking crustaceans and in the past have

Above The Common water flea (Daphnia pulex) *is widespread, and can be found in many eutrophic (oxy-gen-poor, nutrient-rich) environments such as stagnant ponds and ditches, feeding on bacteria and fine algae.*

◁ Left *Crustacean limbs exhibit great diversity: these diagrams show the thoracic appendages of* **1** Hutchinsoniella (class Cephalocarida) *and* **2** *a mala-costracan of the superorder Syncarida.*

been put into their own phylum. It is now believed, however, particularly from DNA evidence, that they are indeed crustaceans, probably related to branchiurans. Tongue worms are worm-like parasites in the respiratory tracts of carnivorous vertebrates, typically reptiles, although six species are found in mammals, including man, and two in birds. The life cycle usually involves a herbivorous vertebrate intermediate host for the developing larvae, such as a fish or a rabbit.

The front end of a tongue worm has five short protuberances bearing, respectively, the mouth and four hooks used by the animal to anchor itself and in feeding. (Once it was thought that there was a mouth on each of the five – hence the name pentastomid.) The mouth is modified for sucking

CRUSTACEANS

Subphylum: Crustacea

About 39,000 species in 6 classes.

Distribution Worldwide, primarily aquatic, in seas, some in fresh water, woodlice on land.

Fossil record Crustaceans appear in the Lower Cambrian, over 530 million years ago.

Size From microscopic (0.15 mm/0.006in) parasites to goose barnacles 75cm (30in) and lobsters 60cm (24in) long.

Features 2 pairs of antennae; typically segmented body covered by plates of chitinous cuticle subject to molting for growth; body divided into head, thorax and abdomen; head and front of thorax may fuse to form cephalothorax often covered by shieldlike carapace; segments from 19 in decapods to 40 in some smaller species; compound eyes; paired appendages on each segment typically include the antennae, main and 2 accessory pairs of jaws (mandibles, maxillules, maxillae), and typically 2-branched limbs on tho-rax (called pereiopods) and abdomen (generally called pleopods) usually jointed, variously adapted for feeding, swimming. walking, burrowing, respiration, reproduction, defense (pincers); breathing typically by gills or through body surface; body organs in blood-filled hemocoel; double nerve cord on underside; foregut, midgut, hindgut; sexes typically separate; development of young via series of larval stages.

BRANCHIOPODS Class Branchiopoda
Comprises around 1,001 species in 23 families, 3 orders and 2 subclasses. Mostly small freshwater filter feeders.

REMIPEDES Class Remipedia
2 species in 2 families and 1 order Nectiopoda. Blind swim-mers in marine (anchialine) caves without surface connection to the sea. **Length** 5mm (0.4in).

CEPHALOCARIDS Class Cephalocarida
9 species in 4 genera and 1 family and 1 order. Bottom-dwellers feeding on deposited detritus

MAXILLOPODS Class Maxillopoda
Over 9,705 species in 6 subclasses.

MUSSEL SHRIMPS AND SEED SHRIMPS
Class Ostracoda
5,650 species in 43 families and 4 orders. **Length** Small, 1–3mm 0.04–0.12in), mostly bottom dwelling, with two-valved carapace.

MALACOSTRACANS Class Malacostraca
23,000 species in 497 families and 16 orders.

See The 6 Classes of Crustaceans ▷

55

the host's blood. The worm shape is an adaptation to life in confined passages that must not be blocked, or the host will suffocate. The adults move little, and the nervous system is reduced, as befits a parasite. There are no excretory or respiratory organs, or heart. Fertilized eggs are released in the host's feces or by the host sneezing, and lie in vegetation before being ingested by a herbivore.

In the case of *Linguatula serrata*, the eggs are eaten by a rabbit or hare and the larvae hatch out under the action of digestive juices. The larva bores through the gut wall and is carried in the blood to the liver. Here it forms a cyst and grows through a series of molts to approach adult form. If the rabbit is eaten by a dog or wolf, the larva is released and passes up the dog's esophagus to the pharynx, and so to its adult location in the host's nasal cavity. *Porocephalus crotali* lives in snakes, with mice as intermediate hosts, and other tongue worms live in crocodiles with fish intermediate hosts. Ancestral pentastomids may have been parasitic on fish much as branchiurans today. It is a plausible evolutionary step for the parasite to have been stimulated to leave this host when eaten by a crocodile, to take up residence in the mouth of the predator.

Barnacles

CLASS MAXILLOPODA; SUBCLASS THECOSTRACA; INFRACLASS CIRRIPEDIA

Barnacles are sedentary marine crustaceans, permanently attached to the substrate. For protection barnacles have carried calcification of the cuticle to an extreme and have a shell resembling that of a mollusk. The shell is a derivative of the cuticle of the barnacle head and encloses the rest of the body. Stalked goose barnacles, which commonly hang down from floating logs, are more primitive than the acorn barnacles that abut directly against the rock and dominate temperate shores. (For barnacles' economic impact, see Cemented Crustaceans).

Barnacles (infraclass Cirripedia) feed with six pairs of thoracic legs (cirri) which can protrude through the shell plates to filter food suspended

△ **Above** *Exposed in the intertidal "barnacle zone" of the shore, these* Chthalamus entatus *barnacles keep their shell plates firmly closed to avoid dehydration.*

in the seawater. Goose barnacles trap animal prey, but most acorn barnacles have also evolved the ability to filter fine material, including phytoplankton and even bacteria, with the anterior cirri.

Barnacles are hermaphrodites. They usually carry out crossfertilization between neighbors. Fertilized egg masses are held in the shell until release as first-stage nauplii. Indeed it was J. Vaughan Thompson's observations (1829) of barnacle nauplius larvae of undoubted crustacean pedigree that removed lingering suspicions regarding the possible molluskan nature of barnacles. There are six nauplius stages of increasing size which swim and filter phytoplankton over a period of a month or so, before giving rise to a nonfeeding larva – the cypris larva, named for its similarity to the mussel shrimp genus *Cypris*. This is the settlement stage of the life cycle, able to drift and swim in the plankton before alighting, and choosing a settlement site in response to environmental factors which the larva detects by an array of sense organs.

Barnacles colonize a variety of substrates, including living animals such as crabs, turtles, sea snakes and whales – with a moving host the barnacle does not need to use

◁ **Left** *An exoparasitic fish louse attached to its host, a Variegated lizardfish (*Synodus variegatus*). Parasitic copepods grow far larger than their free-living relatives.*

energy in beating its cirri. Some barnacles have evolved to become parasites, which bear little similarity to their freeliving relatives, except as larvae. Members of the superorder Rhizocephala (literally "root-headed") parasitize decapod crustaceans.

Copepods

CLASS MAXILLOPODA; SUBCLASS COPEPODA

The class Copepoda includes 220 families of mostly minute sea- and freshwater inhabitants which provide a major source of food for fish, mollusks, crustaceans and other aquatic animals. As dominant members of the marine plankton, copepods of the order Calanoida may be among the most abundant animals in the world. On the other hand, members of the order Harpacticoida are common inhabitants of usually marine sediments, and species of the order Cyclopoida may be either planktonic or bottom-dwelling (benthic) in the sea or fresh water. Some copepods are parasitic, infesting other invertebrates, fish (often as fish lice on the gills) and even whales. Some of these attain 30cm (12in) in length.

Free-living copepods are small and capable of rapid population turnover. The large first antennae may be used for a quick escape, but more usually they act as parachutes against sinking, while the thoracic limbs are the major swimming organs.

Many calanoid copepods can filter feed on phytoplankton, using the feathery second maxillae to sieve a current driven by the second antennae which beat at about 1,000 strokes per minute. The setae on the second maxillae are adapted to trap a particular size of microscopic plant organisms (phytoplankton) and the first pair of thoracic limbs (maxillipeds) scrape off the filtered material.

In fact calanoid copepods cannot survive in the marine planktonic ecosystem by filtering alone. Filter feeding is an energy-sapping process that requires the driving of large volumes of water through a fine sieve. There must therefore be a minimum level of phytoplankton in the sea simply to repay the cost of filtering. Phytoplankton populations in temperate oceans only reach such concentrations for brief periods in the year – in the North Atlantic, during the spring bloom and perhaps again in the fall. For much of the year, therefore, the calanoid copepod feeds raptorially – seizing large prey items including other members of the zooplankton. During the rich spring "bloom," filtering becomes worthwhile and the copepods can pass through several generations, multiplying very quickly, before returning to low metabolic tickover, often using fat reserves for the rest of the year. The number of copepod generations per year is related to the time period of the phytoplankton bloom.

Copepods pair, rather than copulate directly, the male transferring a packet of sperm (spermatophore) to the female, perhaps in response to a "chemical message" (pheromone) from her. The

CEMENTED CRUSTACEANS

Barnacles are the most successful marine fouling organisms and more than 20 percent of all known species have been recorded living on artificial objects, including ships, oil rig legs (RIGHT) and power station outlets. Goose barnacles (*Lepas* species) once attached themselves in enormous clumps to slow-moving sailing ships. They have been supplanted today by acorn (or rock) barnacles (*Balanus* species) on motor-powered vessels, although stalked whale barnacles (*Conchoderma* species, which grow, as their common name indicates, on whales' skins) are also found on the hulls of supertankers.

The minute planktonic (nauplius) larvae of barnacles, which feed on phytoplankton, are dispersed in the sea and build up fat reserves to support the non-feeding settlement (cypris) stage through further dispersal, site selection and metamorphosis. The cypris larva, a motive pupa according to Charles Darwin in the 1850s, has a low metabolic rate and lasts as long as a month before alighting on a chosen substrate. The cypris then walks, using sticky secretions on the adhesive disks of the antennules, responding to current strength and direction, light direction, contour, surface roughness and the presence of other barnacles, as it monitors the suitability of a site for future growth. Finally, cypris cement is secreted from paired cement glands down ducts to the adhesive disks so that they become embedded permanently, whereupon the cypris metamorphoses to the juvenile barnacle which feeds and grows, developing its own cement system.

Barnacles on a ship's hull create turbulence and drag, slowing the vessel down and increasing its fuel consumption. To counter this, antifouling paint is used, which releases toxin in sufficient concentration to kill settling larvae or spores. Copper, the most common antifouling agent, is very toxic and must be released at a rate of 10 micrograms per sq cm per day to prevent barnacle settlement and growth.

Barnacles accumulate heavy metals, specifically zinc as detoxified granules of zinc phosphate. Barnacles are therefore suitable monitors of zinc availability in the marine environment, their high concentrations being easily measurable. Thames estuary barnacles, for example, have been found to contain an almost incredible zinc concentration of 15 percent of their dry weight. PSR

eggs are fertilized as they are laid into egg sacs carried by the female. Eggs hatch as nauplii and pass through further nauplius and characteristic copepodite stages before adulthood.

It is the larval stages that ensure the dispersal of parasitic copepods. Copepods that are parasitic on the exterior of their host (exoparasites) may show little anatomical modification, but endoparasites often consist of little more than an attachment organ and a grossly enlarged genital segment with large attendant egg sacs.

Mussel shrimps
CLASS OSTRACODA
Mussel shrimps or ostracods (class Ostracoda) are small bivalved crustaceans widespread in sea and fresh water. Some are planktonic, but most live near the bottom, plowing through the detritus on which they feed. Algae are another favored food.

The rounded valves of the carapace completely enclose the body, which consists of a large head

and a reduced trunk, usually with only two pairs of thoracic limbs. The antennae are the main locomotory organs. Both pairs may be endowed with long bristles (setae) to aid propulsion when swimming, or the first antennae may be stout for digging, or even hooked for climbing aquatic vegetation.

Malacostracans
CLASS MALACOSTRACA
Including more than half of all living crustacean species, the class Malacostraca is very important in marine ecology and has also successfully invaded freshwater and land habitats.

Malacostracans are modifications of a shrimp-like body plan. The thorax consists of eight segments bearing limbs, of which up to three of the front pairs are accessory mouthparts or maxillipeds. A carapace typically covers head and thorax, though this may have been lost in some peracarids (see below). Members of the primitive superorder Syncarida also lack a carapace but this absence may be of more ancient ancestry: the anaspidaceans are bottom-dwelling feeders on detritus in Southern Hemisphere fresh waters, and the bathynellaceans are minute, blind detritivores living in freshwater sediments.

◁ **Left** Peering out from its burrow under a coral head, a mantis shrimp (Odontodactylus scyallarus) waits to strike at its next prey.

Most adult malacostracans are bottom-dwellers (benthic), and the single-branched (uniramous) thoracic legs are adapted for walking. Some malacostracans can swim using pleopods, the limbs of the first five abdominal segments. The appendages of the sixth abdominal segment are directed back as uropods to flank the terminal telson and form a tail fan.

The gills of malacostracans are usually situated at the base of the thoracic legs in a chamber formed by the carapace, and are aerated by a current driven forward by a paddle on the second maxillae. Malacostracans typically ingest food in relatively large pieces. The anterior part of the stomach is where the large food particles are masticated before they pass to the pyloric stomach, where small particles are filtered and diverted to the hepatopancreas for digestion and absorption. Remaining large particles pass down the midgut and hindgut to be voided.

The most primitive malacostracans are to be found in the order Leptostraca. They are marine feeders on detritus, with a bivalved carapace, leaflike thoracic limbs and eight abdominal segments. Mantis shrimps (order Stomatopoda) are marine carnivores that wait at their burrow entrances for unsuspecting prey, including fish, before striking rapidly with the enormous claws on the second thoracic appendages.

The vast majority of the remaining malacostracans are grouped within the two superorders Peracarida and Eucarida. The peracarids are a superorder of malacostracans containing nine orders of which the isopods (woodlice or pill bugs and others) and amphipods (sand hoppers and beach fleas) contain about 10,000 species between them. Peracarids hold their fertilized eggs in a brood pouch formed on the underside of the body by extensions from the first segments (coxae) of the thoracic legs, the eggs hatching directly as miniature versions of their parents. The carapace, when present, is not fused to all the thoracic segments. The first thoracic segment is joined to the head.

The small sediment-dwelling peracarid crustaceans of the order Thermosbaenacea inhabit thermal springs, fresh and brackish lakes, and coastal ground water. Opossum shrimps (order Mysida), although typically marine, are common also in estuaries, where they may be found swimming in large swarms and may constitute the major food of many fish. They filter small food particles with their two-branched thoracic limbs, and on many species a balancing organ (statocyst) is clearly visible on each inner branch of the pair of uropods. Their common name comes from the large brood pouch on the underside of the female's thorax.

⬧ **Above** *Representative types of planktonic crusta-ceans:* **1** *A freeliving copepod. It swims by using its well-developed antennae (5cm/2in);* **2** *A phyllosoma larva of a crawfish. This delicate planktonic larva dev-elops into the massive bottom-dwelling spiny lobster Palinurus vulgaris (pictured on the artwork plate in the foregoing Crustaceans chapter);* **3** *A caprellid, a minute bottom-dwelling crustacean. These are often less than 1mm (0.4 in) long and often live in associa-tion with other invertebrates or plants;* **4** *A zoea larva, i.e. the early larval stage of a crab. It has a full comple-ment of head appendages but only the first two pairs of thoracic appendages. After several molts it develops into* **5** *a megalopa, the late larval stage, which has a head, and thoracic and abdominal appendages.*

act as the respiratory surface. *Porcellio* and *Armadillidium* species tolerate dryer conditions than can *Oniscus* species and use the outlying exopods of the first pair of pleopods for respiration. The danger of desiccation is reduced, for these exopods have intuckings of the cuticle (pseudotracheae) as sites of respiratory exchange.

Most isopods are scavenging omnivores, some tending to a diet of plant matter, especially the woodlice which contain bacteria in the gut to digest cellulose. Of the more carnivorous, *Cirolana* species can be an extensive nuisance to lobster fishermen, devouring bait in lobster pots.

Isopods have also evolved into parasites. Ectoparasitic isopods attach to fish with hooks, and pierce the skin with their mandibles to draw the blood on which they feed. Those isopods (e.g., *Bopyrus* species) that live in the gill chambers of decapod crustaceans (crabs, shrimps, lobsters) are more highly modified and may cause galls. Some isopods even hyperparasitize rhizocephalan barnacles, themselves parasitic on decapods.

Beach fleas and Other Amphipods

SUPERORDER PERACARIDA; ORDER AMPHIPODA

Amphipods are laterally compressed peracarids that often lie on their flattened sides. The most familiar are the beach fleas or sand hoppers found on sandy shores, and the misnamed "Freshwater shrimp" common in European streams. Amphipods are mainly marine and bottom-dwelling (benthic), but some are free-swimming (pelagic).

Like the isopods, amphipods have no carapace, their eyes are stalkless, they have one pair of maxillipeds, seven pairs of single-branched walking legs (pereiopods) and a brooding pouch on the underside. Unlike the isopods, they have gills on the thoracic legs, and on the six abdominal segments there are usually three pairs of pleopods and three pairs of backward-directed uropods.

Most amphipods are scavengers of detritus, able to both creep using the thoracic pereiopods and swim with the abdominal pleopods. Many burrow or build tubes and feed by scraping sand grains or filtering plankton with bristle-covered limbs. Beach fleas, which have a remarkable ability to jump, burrow at the top of sandy shores or live in the strand line. This proximity to dry land has helped terrestrial amphipods volve in moist forest litter, though to a more limited extent than in isopods.

Amphipods of the family Hyperiidae are pelagic carnivores that live in association with gelatinous organisms, such as jellyfish, on which they prey. *Phronima* species are often reported to construct a house from remains of salp tunicates in which the animal rears its young. Skeleton shrimps (family Caprellidae) are predators of hydroid polyps, and the atypical, dorsoventrally flattened whale lice are ectoparasites of whales.   PSR

🔵 *Above* The freshwater shrimp Spinacanthus parasiticus *is endemic to Lake Baikal in Siberia, where it lives in symbiosis with the* Lubomiskiya *sponge.*

🔵 *Below* A marine relative of the woodlouse is the Sea slater (Ligia oceanica), *which lives in seashore rock crevices, emerging at night to feed on detritus.*

Woodlice and Other Isopods

SUPERORDER PERACARIDA; ORDER ISOPODA

Woodlice (or pill bugs) are the crustacean success story on land. They are the most familiar members of the order Isopoda. Like other isopods, they are flattened top-to-bottom (dorsoventrally) and lack a carapace covering the segments. The first pair of thoracic limbs is adapted as a pair of maxillipeds, leaving seven pairs of single-branched thoracic walking legs (pereiopods). The five pairs of abdominal pleopods are adapted as respiratory surfaces. Isopods typically molt in two halves, the exoskeleton being shed in separate front and rear portions.

Most isopods walk on the sea bed, but some swim, using the pleopods, and others may burrow. The woodboring gribble used to destroy wooden piers along the coasts of the North Atlantic by rasping with its file-like mandibles, a major pest until concrete replaced wood. Isopods are also to be found in freshwater, and sea slaters live at the top of the intertidal zone, indicating the evolutionary route of the better known woodlice to life on land.

The direct development characteristic of reproduction in the superorder Peracarida (see above) avoids the release of planktonic larvae, and is a major adaptive preparation for terrestrial life. Woodlice have behavioral responses, for example to changes in

humidity, to avoid desiccatory conditions and often therefore select damp microhabitats. Members of the pill bug genus *Armadillidium* are able to roll up, as the generic name suggests.

Woodlice have adapted their respiratory organs to take up oxygen from air. Members of the genus *Oniscus* show only little change from the ancestral aquatic isopod arrangement of pleopods as gills. Each of the five pairs of pleopods is two-branched and overlaps the one behind. The exopods of the first pair are extensive enough to cover all the remaining pleopods. The innermost fifth pleopods therefore lie in a humid microchamber and the endopods are well supplied with blood to

The 6 Classes of Crustaceans

A TOTAL OF 420 CRUSTACEAN SPECIES ARE threatened in some measure, with 1 species – the Socorro isopod (*Thermosphaeroma thermophilum*; order Isopoda) – Extinct in the Wild. 56 species are Critically Endangered, including the Florida fairy shrimp (*Dexteria floridana*; order Anostraca), *Atlantasellus cavernicolus* (order Isopoda), Noel's amphipod (*Gammarus desperatus*; order Amphipoda), Tree hole crab (*Globonautes macropus*) and the Big-cheeked cave crayfish (*Procambarus delicatus*; order Decapoda); 73 are Endangered, including the Peninsula fairy shrimp (*Branchinella alachua*; order Anostraca), *Lepidurus packardi* (order Notostraca), Clifton cave isopod (*Caecidotea barri*; order Isopoda), Hay's spring amphipod (*Stygobromus hayi*; order Amphipoda), and the Red-black crayfish (*Cambarus pyronolus*; order Decapoda); 280 species are Vulnerable, including 5 species of fairy shrimp (genus *Branchinella*; order Anostraca), Wilken's stenasellid (*Mexistenasellus wilkensi*; order Isopoda), and 37 species of the cave amphipod *Stygobromus* (order Amphipoda); and 10 species are classified as Lower Risk.

CLASS BRANCHIOPODA

Branchiopods

About 1,001 species in 23 families, 3 orders and 2 subclasses.

SUBCLASS SARSOSTRACA

FAIRY SHRIMPS ORDER ANOSTRACA
180 species in 7 families. Genera and species include: brine shrimps (*Artemia* species)

SUBCLASS PHYLLOPODA

TADPOLE SHRIMPS ORDER NOTOSTRACA
11 species in 1 family. Genera and species include: *Triops* species.

ORDER DIPLOSTRACA
810 species in 15 families. Suborders: clam shrimps (suborder Spinicaudata), including *Cyzicus* species; water fleas (suborder Cladocera), including *Daphnia* species.

CLASS REMIPEDIA

Remipedes

12 species in 2 families and 1 order (Nectiopoda). Species include: *Speleonectes lucayensis*.

CLASS CEPHALOCARIDA

Cephalocarids

9 species in 4 genera and 1 family (Hutchinsoniellidae) and 1 order (Brachypoda). Species include: *Hutchinsoniella macracantha, Lightiella serendipita*.

Class Branchiopoda
Branchiopods

Class Cephalocarida
Cephalocarids

Class Maxillipoda
Subclass Cirripedia
Barnacles

Subclass Branchiura
Branchiurans

CLASS MAXILLOPODA

Maxillopods

Over 9,705 species in 6 subclasses.

SUBCLASS THECOSTRACA

INFRACLASS FACETOTECTA
Arguably the biggest remaining mystery of crustacean classification. Single genus *Hansenocaris* accommodating curious "y-larvae" not yet assigned to a particular maxillopodan taxon.

INFRACLASS ASCOTHORACIDA
45 species in 6 families and 2 orders (Laurida, Dendrogastrida), very small parasites on echinoderms and soft corals. Species include: *Ascothorax* species.

BARNACLES INFRACLASS CIRRIPEDIA
980 species in 3 superorders. Adults parasitic or permanently attached to substratum, most with long, curved filter-feeding "legs." Superorder Acrothoracica: 50 species in 3 families and 2 orders. Small (0.4mm/0.16in) filter-feeders boring into calcareous substrates (e.g. shells). Species include: *Trypetesa* species. Superorder Rhizocephala: 230 species in 9 families and 2 orders. Internal parasites of decapods (lobsters, shrimps, crabs). Species include: *Sacculina carcini*. Superorder Thoracica: 700 species in 29 families and 2 orders. Filter-feeding barnacles on rocks and other substrates. Up to 75cm (30in) long. Species include: goose barnacles (*Lepas* species), acorn or rock barnacles (*Balanus* species) and whale barnacles (*Conchoderma* species).

SUBCLASS TANTULOCARIDA

29 species in 5 families. Microscopic (0.15mm/0.006in) ectoparasites on deep sea bottom-dwelling crustaceans. Species include: *Basipodella harpacticola*.

Subclass Mystacocarida

Subclass Copepoda
Copepods

Class Ostracoda
Mussel shrimps and seed shrimps

Class Malacostraca
Malacostracans

SUBCLASS BRANCHIURA

150 species in 1 order. Bloodsucking fish lice some 7mm (0.3in) long, ecoparasitic on marine or freshwater fish. Species include: *Argulus foliaceus*.

TONGUE WORMS
SUBCLASS PENTASTOMIDA

90 species in 9 families and 2 orders. Worm-like parasites in respiratory tracts of carnivorous vertebrates (especially reptiles). Genera and species include: *Linguatula* species.

SUBCLASS MYSTACOCARIDA

11 species in 1 family. Minute (0.5mm/0.02in) in sediments of seabed feeding on detritus. Species include: *Derocheilocaris typicus*.

COPEPODS
SUBCLASS COPEPODA

Over 8,400 species in 220 families and 10 orders. Mostly minute components of plankton and sediment fauna. Orders and species include: order Calanoida with 2,300 species in 43 families, including *Calanus finmarchicus*; order Harpacticoida with 2,800 species in 54 families, including *Harpacticus* species; order Cyclopoida with 450 species in 15 families, including *Cyclops* species; order Poecilostomatoida with 1,320 species in 61 families of fish lice, including *Ergasilus sieboldi*; order Siphonostomatoida with 1,430 species in 40 families of fish lice, including *Caligus* species.

CLASS OSTRACODA

Mussel shrimps and Seed shrimps

5,650 species in 43 families and 4 orders. Species include: *Cypris* species.

CLASS MALACOSTRACA

Malacostracans

23,000 species in 497 families, 16 orders and 3 subclasses.

SUBCLASS PHYLLOCARIDA

ORDER LEPTOSTRACA
3 families containing 25 species of pelagic or bottom-dwelling feeders on detritus. Species include: *Nebalia bipes*.

SUBCLASS HOPLOCARIDA

ORDER STOMATOPODA
17 families containing 350 species of bottom-dwelling carnivorous mantis shrimps. Species include: *Squilla empusa*.

SUBCLASS EUMALACOSTRACA

SUPERORDER SYNCARIDA
Order Anaspidacea: 15 species in 4 families. S Hemisphere freshwater bottom-dwelling detritus feeders up to 5cm (2in) long. Species include: *Anaspides tasmaniae*. Order Bathynellacea: 100 species in 2 families, inhabiting freshwater sediments feeding on detritus, blind, 0.5–1.2mm (0.02–0.04in) long. Species include: *Parabathynella neotropica*.

SUPERORDER PERACARIDA
9 orders, including:
Order Thermosbaenacea: 9 species in 4 families of sediment-dwellers in marine and fresh water, and in hot-spring groundwater. About 3mm (0.12 in) long. Species include: *Thermosbaena mirabilis*.
Order Mysida: (Opossum shrimps): 4 families. Free-swimming and bottom-dwelling filter feeders 1–3cm (0.4–1.2in) long. Species include: *Neomysis integer*.
Order Isopoda (Sea slaters, woodlice, pill bugs and sow bugs): 4,000 species in 120 families. Marine, freshwater and terrestrial, typically omnivorous crawlers but some parasites (e.g. *Bopyrus* species) and wood-boring gribbles (*Limnoria* species). 0.5–1.5cm (0.2–0.6in) long. Genera include: *Armadillidium, Oniscus, Porcellio*.
Order Amphipoda (Sand hoppers and beach fleas): 6,000 species in 155 families. Mostly marine bottom-dwelling scavengers, 0.1–1.5cm (0.04–0.6in) long. Species include: skeleton shrimps (*Caprella* species), whale lice (*Cyamus* species) and the "freshwater shrimp" (*Gammarus pulex*).

SUPERORDER EUCARIDA
Order Euphausiacea (Krill): 85 species in 2 families of marine pelagic filter feeders, 0.5–5cm (0.2–2in) long. Species include: whale krill (*Euphausia superba*).
Order Amphionidacea: 1 marine free-swimming species, *Amphionides reynaudii*, up to 3cm (1.2in) long.
Order Decapoda (Shrimps, lobsters, crabs): 10,000 species in 151 families.*

*See p. 53 for Table of Decapods.

THE ECONOMIC IMPORTANCE OF CRUSTACEANS

Human food and foulers of vessels

THE ECONOMIC IMPORTANCE OF CRUSTACEANS is twofold – their commercial value as food items and the costs caused by their effects as foulers of ships or coastal structures.

Crustaceans, especially the decapods (shrimps, lobsters, crabs), are important as food products, whether cropped from the wild or reared by aquacultural processes. Whale krill of the Antarctic Ocean are now being harvested and processed as food, not only for humans, but more particularly for agricultural livestock. In the Gulf of Mexico and off the southeastern United States, fishing boats trawl for the Brown shrimp which, with the White shrimp and the Pink shrimp, make up the world's largest shrimp fishery. In Southeast Asia, in Indonesia and the Philippines and in Taiwan, shrimps of the same genus *Penaeus* have been reared for food in brackish ponds for 500 years. Popular species are the Banana prawn, the Indian prawn, the Giant tiger prawn, the Green tiger prawn and the Yellow prawn. The shrimps are trapped in pools at high tide and cultured for several months, often with mullet or milkfish. In Singapore ponds are usually constructed in mangrove swamps and in India rice paddies are used. Typical yields vary from 300 to 1,600kg of edible shrimp per hectare (1,650–8,700lb/acre). In Japan there is an intensive culture of the Kuruma shrimp. Eggbearing females are supplied by fishermen and

shrimps are reared over two weeks, from eggs through successive larval stages with differing food requirements, to postlarvae before transfer to production ponds. Harvesting takes place 6–9 months later at yields which may attain 6,000kg per ha (32,600lb/acre).

In British waters the Caridean shrimp (also called the Pink shrimp) is fished by beam trawl in spring and summer in the Thames estuary, the Wash, Solway Firth, and Morecambe Bay – the Thames fishery dating back to the 13th century. The Brown shrimp is fished off Britain, Germany, Holland and Belgium; boats work a pair of beam trawls and total landings reach 30,000 tons a year. *Palaemon adspersus* is taken off Denmark and off south and southwest Britain.

Another caridean, the tropical Indo-Pacific freshwater prawn *Macrobrachium rosenbergi*, is

⬤ **Right** *Barnacle fishing on the coast of Galicia, Spain. Risking life and limb, fishermen clamber over tidal rocks in high surf and use poles to lever off their their tightly clinging catch. Their reward is the high price that barnacles command in local restaurants.*

⬤ **Below** *Important species of fished crustaceans:*
1 Krill (Euphausia superba); 2 King crab (Paralithodes sp.); 3 Common shrimp (Crangon crangon); 4 Northern prawn (Pondulus borealis); 5 Norway lobster (Nephrops norvegicus).

a giant reaching 25cm (10in) long; it is therefore attractive to aquaculturists, but its larvae are hard to rear and dense populations do not occur naturally.

Lobsters and crabs are usually caught in traps, enticed by bait to enter via a tunnel of decreasing diameter opening into a wider chamber. Most are predators or scavengers: lobsters prefer rotting bait but crabs are attracted to fresh fish pieces. Crab or lobster meat usually consists of muscle (white meat) from the claws and legs, and lobster abdominal muscle is also used. The hepatopancreas (brown meat) may be taken in some species. The meat is processed as a paste or canned, or the crustacean may be sold fresh or frozen.

The Dublin Bay prawn or Norway lobster supplies scampi – strictly the abdominal muscle. It burrows in bottom mud and is collected by trawling. Most lobsters, however, are caught in lobster pots. American lobsters and European lobsters are of commercial value in temperate seas but are replaced by spiny lobsters in warmer waters: *Panulirus argus* and *P. interruptus* are trapped off Florida and California respectively, *P. versicolor* in the Indo-Pacific and *Jasus* species off Australia.

Freshwater crayfish are consumed with enthusiasm in France. The habit has transferred to Louisiana, United States, where between 400,000 and 800,000kg (from 880,000 to 1,960,000lb) of wild Red and White crayfish are trapped each year, and a further 1.2 million kg (2.6 million lb) reared in artificial impoundments.

The Edible crab is taken in pots off European coasts. The British annual catch reaches 6,500 tonnes, boats laying out 200–500 pots daily in strings of 20–70 buoyed at each end. The crabs are usually sold to processing factories, to be killed by immersion in freshwater or by spiking, boiled in brackish water and then cooled to room temperature to set the meat, which is extracted by hand picking or with compressed air. The related Dunge-ness crab is fished off the west coast of North America, and the Blue crab is taken off the east coast by trap or line or by fishing with a trawl net.

On the negative side, one year's growth of fouling organisms can increase the fuel costs of ships by 40 percent, and barnacles are the most important foulers. Their presence impedes the smooth flow of water over a ship's hull and their shell plates disrupt paint films, so promoting corrosion. Barnacles are cemented to the substratum and necessitate expensive dry docking for removal. Barnacles have swimming larvae that disperse widely, ready to alight on passing ships. Barnacles and tube-building crustaceans may also clog water-cooling intake pipes of industrial installations by the coast, such as power stations.

The commercial importance of woodboring crustaceans such as the gribbles has decreased since concrete has replaced wood as a major pier construction material.   PSR

Horseshoe Crabs

t HE SUBPHYLUM CHELICERATA, OF WHICH
horseshoe crabs form a small part, is more commonly represented by its terrestrial members –
the arachnids (spiders, scorpions,an their relatives).
The horseshoe crabs' primordial appearance hints at
the fact that they form of the most ancient surviving
groups of organisms.

All chelicerates are typified by having a pair of pincerlike mouthparts (chelicerae), which are positioned in front of the mouth opening. They have
no biting jaws and two distinct parts of the body
are recognizable, the prosoma (front part) and
opisthosoma (rear part). Since they fit this
description and in spite of their common names
and sea-dwelling habit, horseshoe crabs are therefore more closely related to terrestrial arachnids
than to crustaceans. They have remained more or
less unchanged for some 300 million years, since
the Permian period. The fact that extant species
occur in two widely separated areas of the world
(the eastern seaboard of the USA, and South and
Southeast Asia) suggests that they are relicts of a
far more extensive distribution.

Horseshoe crabs have a protective hinged carapace, whose domed

◔ Above During spring tides in Delaware Bay, New
Jersey, thousands of male horseshoe crabs gather on
the shoreline to await the arrival of females for spawning. The annual migration of shorebirds to this location
has evolved to coincide with the resulting superabun-
dance of crab eggs, on which the birds feed.

shield of horseshoe form covers the prosoma and
the first part of the opisthosoma; a long caudal
spine protrudes behind. They have compound
eyes on the carapace and median simple eyes.
Beneath the dark brown carapace lie the chelicerae and five pairs of walking legs, comparable in
evolution to the chelicerae, pedipalps, and four
pairs of walking legs of spiders.

Horseshoe crabs live on sandy or muddy bottoms in the sea, plowing their way through the
upper surface of the sediment. During burrowing,
the caudal spine levers the body down while the

◑ Right Limulus polyphemus, the horseshoe crab species found in US waters, is
threatened by human activity. Since the
late 1990s, overharvesting of the crabs
for use as whelk and eel bait has caused
a major decline in their numbers.

fifth pair of walking legs acts as shovels, the form
of the carapace facilitating passage through the
sand. The animal also uses the caudal spine to
right itself if accidentally turned over.

Horseshoe crabs are essentially scavenging carnivores. There are jawlike extensions on the bases
of the walking legs, used to trap and macerate
prey, such as clams and worms, before it is passed
forward to the mouth. The stout bases of the sixth
pair of legs can also act like nutcrackers to open
the shells of bivalve mollusks which are seized
during burrowing.

The appendages on the rear part (opisthosoma)
are much modified. The first pair forms a protective cover over the remainder, each of which is
expanded into about 150 delicate gill lamellae
resembling the leaves of a book, in an adaptation
unique to horseshoe crabs. The movement of the
appendages maintains a current over the respiratory surfaces of the gill books which are well supplied with blood, which in turn drains back to the
heart for pumping around the body. Small horseshoe crabs can swim along upside down, using
the gill books as paddles.

At night at particular seasons of the year, male
and female horseshoe crabs congregate at the
intertidal zone for reproduction. The female lays
200–300 eggs in a depression in the sand, to be
fertilized by an attendant clasping male. The eggs
hatch after several months as trilobite larvae, so
called because of their similarity to the fossil trilobites of the Paleozoic era (545–248 million years
ago). Initially 1cm (0.4in) long, the larvae develop
to reach maturity in their third year. PSR

FACTFILE

HORSESHOE OR KING CRABS

Subphylum: Chelicerata (part)

Class: Merostomata

Order: Xiphosura

4 species in 3 genera: *Trachypleus gigas, T. triden-
tatus, Carcinoscorpius rotundicauda, Limulus
polyphemus.*

Distribution Marine, Atlantic coast of N America
(genus *Limulus*), coasts of SE Asia (*Tachypleus, Carcinoscorpius*).

Fossil record First appear in the Devonian period,
417–354 million years ago.

Size Larvae about 1cm (0.4in) long, adults up to 60cm
(2ft) long.

Features Pair of pincerlike mouthparts (chelicerae) in
front of mouth; carapace covers the back of the prosoma
(front portion of body) and part of the opisthosoma (rear
portion of body); prosoma has 6 pairs of appendages:
chelicerae and 5 pairs of walking legs; opisthosoma
bears 6 pairs of flattened limbs (a modified genital operculum or lid, and 5 pairs of leaflike or lamellate gillbooks
for respiration) and a rear spine; excretion is by coxal
glands at limb bases; circulatory system well developed;
sexes distinct, with external fertilization; larva has three
divisions, like a trilobite.

Sea Spiders

d ESPITE THEIR COMMON NAME, THIS CLASS of marine arthropods is only distantly related to terrestrial spiders. Sea spiders are for the most part extremely small, from 1mm to 1cm (0.04-0.39 in). A few larger species occur mainly in the abyssal zone – for example, some species of the genus Colossendeis have a leg span of 70cm (28in).

Exclusively marine animals, sea spiders are to be found from the intertidal zone to the deep sea, down to an extreme depth of 7,000m (23,000ft). They have an exaggerated hanging stance, like larger examples of their terrestrial namesakes, and are typically to be found straddling their sessile prey. Sea spiders grip the substratum with claws as they sway from one individual of their colonial prey to another without shifting leg positions. Although they mostly move slowly over the seabed, many sea spiders are capable swimmers.

Sea spiders typically have four pairs of long legs arising from lateral protuberances along the sides of the small, narrow trunk. There are some ten- and twelve-legged species. The paired chelifores and palps border the proboscis, the size and shape of which varies between species (this feeding structure is not found in terrestrial spiders).

The diet of sea spiders comprises soft-bodied invertebrates, for example cnidarians (jellyfish soft corals, and sea anemones), bryozoans, small ragworms and lugworms, hydroid polyps, sponges, and sea mats. The customary feeding technique is either to suck up their prey's body tissues through the proboscis or to cut off pieces of tissue from

○ **Above** A sea spider feeding on a soft coral. It displays the spindly legs, reduced body, and skeletal appearance that is characteristic of the group as a whole. Indeed, the name of the class, Pantopoda, means literally "all legs."

the prey with the chelifores, then transfer them to the mouth at the tip of the proboscis. A few sea spiders feed on algae.

In addition to the walking legs, there is a further pair of small legs, which is particularly well developed in males. As eggs are laid by the female they are fertilized and collected by the male, which cements them on to the fourth joint of each of its small eggbearing (ovigerous) legs, where they are brooded. The eggs hatch later as protonymphon larvae and develop through a series of molts, adding appendages to the original three larval pairs, the forerunners of the chelifores, palps and ovigerous legs.

Body colors are variable, being generally white to transparent, but bright red in deep-sea species. The high surface-area-to-volume ratio of the narrow body means that it is only a short distance to the outside from anywhere in the body and respiratory gases and other dissolved substances can be moved efficiently by diffusion. There is therefore no need for specialized excretory, osmoregulatory, or respiratory organs. The lack of storage space in the body does, however, mean that reproductive organs and gut diverticula have to be partly accommodated in the relatively large legs.   PSR

Priapulans, Kinorhynchs, Loriciferans and Horsehair Worms

tHIS DISPARATE GROUPING CONTAINS FOUR *different phyla of marine worms. Due to similarities in their cuticles, kinorhynchs and loriciferans are seen by biologists as closely related. Lacking the well-defined, non-inversible mouth cone that characterizes these two phyla, priapulans are seen as their sister phylum in the grouping cephalorhynchs. Horsehair worms are closely related to nematode worms, but, unlike nematodes, do not parasitize mammals.*

Priapulans
PHYLUM PRIAPULA

The priapulans are ancient marine animals about which very little is known. They are found mostly in colder waters. They are wormlike, but their bodies are not segmented as in annelid worms. In the past, they have sometimes been considered alongside echiurans and sipunculids; however, they are not related to these groups.

The priapulans comprise a small phylum of uncertain affinities, composed of exclusively marine species inhabiting soft sediments. The more familiar forms are the relatively large family Priapulidae, but recently the small sand-living genus *Tubiluchus* and the small tube-dwelling *Maccabeus* have been described.

The trunk of priapulans bears warts and spines, and although it may have rings, no true segmentation is present. A tail consisting of one or two projections may be present, though there is no tail in *Halicryptus* or *Maccabeus*. In *Priapulus* the tail is in the form of a series of vesicles which constantly change shape and volume and may be involved in respiration. In *Acanthopriapulus* the tail is muscular, bearing numerous hooks, and may serve as an anchor during burrowing. In *Tubiluchus* the tail is a long, tubular structure.

The pharynx is eversible and muscular, armed with numerous teeth, or, in *Maccabeus*, bristles (setae). In the Priapulidae, the pharynx is used to capture living prey, but in *Tubiluchus* a scraping function is more likely. The intestine is in the trunk, the anus opening at its rear, with no part of the gut in the tail.

The sexes are separate, with differences in size between the sexes in *Tubiluchus*, probably associated with copulation.

The free-living larval stage of priapulans may be extremely long, the larva feeding in surface sediment layers for two years or more before changing to the adult condition.

The Priapula are considered to be related to the Kinorhyncha because of the body armature, lack of cilia and the molting of the cuticle.   PRG/AC

Kinorhyncha
PHYLA KINORHYNCHA

Some authorities used to group the kinorhyncha along with the gastrotrichs, roundworms, horsehair worms, rotifers, and priapulids in one phylum, known as the Aschelminthes, thanks to certain common developmental and structural features. Others believe that they are best treated as a phylum in their own right, since the criteria for grouping them together are debatable. This is especially true in the light of DNA sequencing studies, which indicate that the Kinorhynchs now have less in common with the rotifers.

These animals show bilateral symmetry and a body cavity formed from the blastocoel (formerly referred to as a pseudocoel) lying between the body wall and the gut. It is not a true coelom. The animals are not segmented and the body is supported by a layer of skin (cuticle) which is shed periodically when the animals molt. The alimentary tract is usually 'straight through,' with a mouth,

esophagus, intestine, rectum and anus. Excretion is carried out through structures known as protonephridia. Reproductive strategies vary from group to group although the sexes are usually separate. Development is along protostome lines.

The kinorhynchs are poorly known marine "worms" reaching up to 1mm (0.04in) in length. They probably exist worldwide but most of the 150 or so known species have been recorded from European coastal sands and muds – a reflection probably of where people have searched for them rather than of their actual distribution. Their bodies appear segmented but the divisions are only "skin-deep", so their segmented condition is the subject of some debate, and they are quite unrelated to the annelid worms or arthropods. They creep about in sand and mud using the spines of the head to gain a hold while the rear of the body is contracted forward. Then the tail spines dig in and the head is advanced and so the process is repeated. The head is not well developed. Male and female kinorhynchs have a similar appearance and sexual reproduction occurs year round. A larva emerges at hatching which molts several times before becoming an adult.

Loriciferans
PHYLUM LORICIFERA

Despite their small size, the Loriciferan body contains many cells – up to 10,000 – and comprises some complex structures, including muscle bands, protonephridia for excretion (actually located within the reproductive organs), a long gut, a nervous system, and reproductive organs. The head bears a number of spine-like structures, arranged in rings, and other ornaments, as well as an invertible oral cone, which carries the mouth. In some species the mouth is equipped with stylets, which presumably assist in feeding.

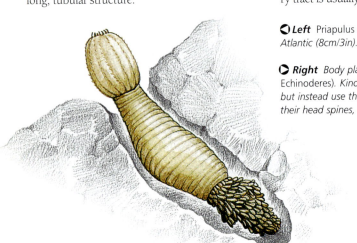

◖ **Left** *Priapulus caudatus, a priapulan, North Atlantic (8cm/3in).*

◗ **Right** *Body plan of a kinorhynch (genus Echinoderes). Kinorhynchs do not have external cilia, but instead use the spines along their bodies, plus their head spines, for locomotion.*

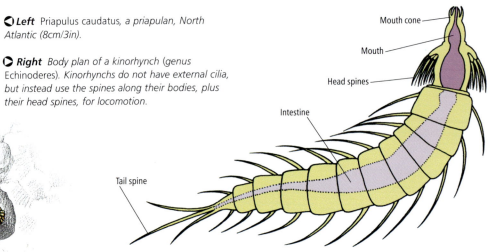

Mouth cone
Mouth
Head spines
Intestine
Tail spine

Loriciferans exist as separate males and females, each with a distinct appearance. The males carry a pair of testes and the females a pair of ovaries. Fertilization is believed to take place internally but little is known of the early development of the young. In most types a special larval type known as a Higgins larva forms. This is able to move around using specially developed 'toes' somewhat similar to the toes of the adult body. The larval cuticle is shed periodically and eventually molts into an adult. In some deep-sea species the larva become precociously sexually mature (neoteny) which can produce more larvae, thus speeding up the life cycle. In others the larva may pass through a dormant period before metamorphosing into adults.

Horsehair Worms

PHYLUM NEMATOMORPHA

Adult horsehair worms typically live in the soil around ponds and streams and lay their eggs in the water, attaching them to water plants. The larvae are parasitic and usually attack insects. One mystery about their lifecycle is that many of the insects acting as hosts for the horsehair worm larvae are terrestrial, not aquatic, for example, crickets, grasshoppers, and cockroaches. It may be that these animals become infected by drinking water containing the larvae. The development inside the host can take several months and the larvae usually leave the host insect when it is near water to lead a free existence in the moist soil. The adults probably do not feed.   AC

⬆ **Above** A 'Gordian knot' of horsehair worms (Gordius sp.). These worms are often found in drinking troughs used by horses, a fact that gave rise to the myth that they were horsehairs come to life.

⬇ **Below** Body plan of an adult female loriciferan (Nanaloricus mysticus). In this diagram, the abdomen, which is covered by a girdle of spiny plates known as a lorica, has been cut away to show the ovaries. For protection, the animal can retract its head, neck, and thorax into the lorica.

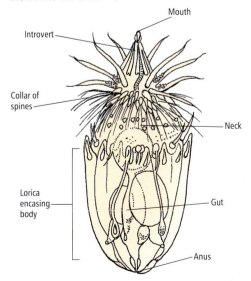

Mouth
Introvert
Collar of spines
Neck
Lorica encasing body
Gut
Anus

FACTFILE

PRIAPULANS, KINORHYNCHS ETC.

Phyla: Priapula, Kinorhyncha, Loricifera, Nematomorpha.

About 496 species across the 4 phyla.

PRIAPULANS Phylum Priapula
16 species in 6 genera and 3 families. **Distribution:** exclusively marine, intertidal and subtidal. **Size:** 0.55mm–20cm (0.03–16in). **Features:** unsegmented blastocoelomate worms; body divided into 2 or 3 regions; introvert at front with terminal mouth and eversible pharynx; trunk may have tail attached; possess chitinous cuticle which is periodically molted; cilia lacking; sexes separate; produce freeliving lorica larva.

FAMILY PRIAPULIDAE
Genera include: *Priapalus, Prialuposis, Acanthopriapulus, Halicryptus.*

FAMILY TUBILUCHIDAE
Genus *Tubiluchus.*

FAMILY MACCABEIDAE (CHAETOSTEPHANIDAE)
Genus *Maccabeus.*

KINORHYNCHS Phylum Kinorhyncha
About 150 species in the class Echinoderida. **Distribution:** worldwide in marine coastal areas, mostly living between sediment particles. **Fossil record:** none. **Size:** less than 1mm (0.04in). **Features:** free-living or epizoic; blastocoelomate, body segmented (13 segments) and covered in spines (no cilia); excretion via a pair of protonephridia, each fed by a single flame cell. Genera include: *Antigomonas, Echinoderes.*

LORICIFERANS Phylum Loricifera
About 10 species in 1 order and 2 families. **Distribution:** exclusively marine, inhabiting sediments like anoxic sands and muds usually in depths of 300–8,000m.
Fossil record: according to some authorities suitable habitats for these animals have existed since the Cambrian era, 500 m.y.a. **Size:** minute 115–383 microns, 0.115–0.383 mm (around 0.015 inches). **Features:** adults: free living, unsegmented and probably blastocoelomate, bilaterally symmetrical animals, with bodies divisible into head, neck, thorax and abdominal regions. The abdomen is encased in a strongly developed cuticle known as a lorica, hence the phylum name, meaning 'corset bearing'! The lorica is made from 6 plate-like structures and is also ornamented with minute projections, the number and disposition of which can vary between the sexes. The first three parts can be withdrawn, almost telescopically, into the abdomen.

HORSEHAIR WORMS Phylum Nematomorpha
About 320 species. Also called Gordian or threadworms. **Distribution:** worldwide; adults freeliving and primarily aquatic in freshwater; juveniles parasitic in arthropods; *Nectonema* is an aberrant pelagic form found in marine coastal environments. **Fossil record:** none. **Size:** 5–100cm (2–39in) long. **Features:** unsegmented worms with thick external cuticle which is molted; front end slender; body cavity blastocoelomate (a pseudocoel); through gut with mouth and anus present, but may be degenerated at one or both ends; lack circular muscles, cilia, excretory system; sexes separate with genital ducts opening into common duct with gut (cloaca). Genera include: *Gordius, Nectonema, Paragordius.*

Roundworms

rOUNDWORM INFESTATION IN HUMANS *affects some one thousand million people world-wide; elephantiasis (lymphatic fliariasis) is a disfiguring disease of the tropics inflicted upon over 250 million individuals. These diseases are just two of the many caused by roundworms (Nematoda).*

The nematodes are among the most successful groups of animals. They have exploited all forms of aquatic environment and many live in damp soil. Some are even hardy enough to survive in hostile environments like hot springs, deserts and cider vinegar. Furthermore, by parasitizing both animals and plants they have widely extended their habitat ranges. Thus they are significant food and crop pests and the agents of disease in plants, animals, and man.

Free-livers and Parasites
FORM AND FUNCTION

There are many types of nematode, but these animals are all quite similar. They are typically worm-shaped. Their bodies are not divided into segments or regions and generally taper gradually toward both the front and back. The mouth lies at the front and the anus almost at the tail. In cross

Dorsal cord
Muscle layer
Pseudocoel
Cuticle
Epidermis
Pharyngeal glands
Anus
Pharynx wall
Pharynx
Lateral cord
Ventral cord

Ovary
Uterus
Vaginal muscles
Vulva
Pharynx
Mouth
Ovary
Excretory pore
Nerve ring
Stylet

◁ **Left** *The body plan of a nematode, showing in cross-section the internal organs of the worm in the region of the pharynx.*

▷ **Right** *Magnified image of Trichinella spiralis roundworms. Mammals, including humans, are infested by these parasites, if raw meat containing the cysts of the larval worm is ingested.*

section, they are perfectly circular and their outer skin is protected by a highly impermeable and resistant cuticle the secret of the success of this group. The cuticle is complex in structure and is made up of several layers of different chemical composition, each with a different structural layout. The precise form of the cuticle varies from

◐ **Below** *A female roundworm (Mermis sp.) above ground in damp weather. Adults of the family Mermithidae are free-living, but the larvae are parasitic on various insects, including grasshoppers. This fact has been expolited for the purpose of pest control.*

species to species, but in the common gut parasite of man and domestic animals, *Ascaris*, it comprises an outermost keratinized layer, a thick middle layer and a basal layer of three strata of collagen fibers which cross each other obliquely. These flex with respect to each other and allow the animal to make its typical wavelike movements, brought about by longitudinal muscle fibers. The high pressure of fluid maintained in the blastocoelomate body cavity (pseudocoel) counteracts the muscles and keeps the worms' cross section round at all times.

Both freeliving and

ROUNDWORMS

Phyla: Nematoda

About 25,000 species in 2 classes.

ROUNDWORMS, EELWORMS, THREADWORMS OR NEMATODES Phylum Nematoda

About 25,000 named species in 2 classes, but many may remain to be discovered. **Distribution:** worldwide; mostly freeliving in damp soil, freshwater, marine: some parasites of plants and animals. **Fossil record:** sparse; around 10 species recognized in insect hosts from Eocene and Oligocene (54–26 million years ago). **Size:** from below 0.05mm to about 1m (0.02in–3.3ft) but mostly between 0.1 and 0.2mm (0.04–0.008in). **Features:** round unsegmented worms sheathed in resistant external cuticle which is molted from time to time; body tapers to head and tail; show blastocoelomate (pseudocoelomate) cavity between gut and body wall; mouth and anus present; lack circular muscles, cilia, excretory flame cells and a circulatory system; nervous system quite well developed; sexes separate.

CLASS APHASMIDA
About 14 orders; genera include: *Trichinella*.

CLASS PHASMIDA
About 6 orders; genera include: *Ascaris, Loa, Mermis, Onchocera, Wucheria*.

parasitic forms may have elaborate mouth structures associated with their food-procuring activities and ways of life. The gut has to function against the fluid pressure of the pseudocoel and in order to do so may depend on a system of pumping bulbs and valves.

In primitive forms excretion is probably carried out by gland cells on the lower surface located near the junction of the pharynx and the intestine. In the more advanced types, there is an H-shaped system of tubular canals with the connection to the excretory pore situated in the middle of the transverse canal.

The nervous system of nematodes provides a very simple brain encircling the foregut and supplying nerves forward to the lips around the mouth. Other nerves are supplied down the length of the body. The body bears external sensory bristles and papillae.

Freeliving nematodes are mostly carnivores feeding on small invertebrates including other nematodes. Some aquatic forms feed on algae and some are specialized for piercing the cells of plant tissue and sucking out the contents. Others are specialized to consume decomposing organic matter such as dung and detritus and/or the bacteria that are feeding on these substances. Nematodes parasitic in man and animals are responsible for many diseases and are therefore of considerable medical and veterinary significance. In humans among other diseases they cause river blindness (*Onchocera* species), roundworm (*Ascaris lumbricoides*) and elephantiasis (*Wucheria* species). Very spectacular is the eye worm *Loa* which can sit on the cornea. Nematode diseases are more common in the tropics.

Parasitic nematodes feed on a variety of body tissues and fluids which they obtain directly from their hosts. Roundworm of man is one of the largest and most widely distributed human parasites. Infections are common in many parts of the world and the incidence of parasitism in populations

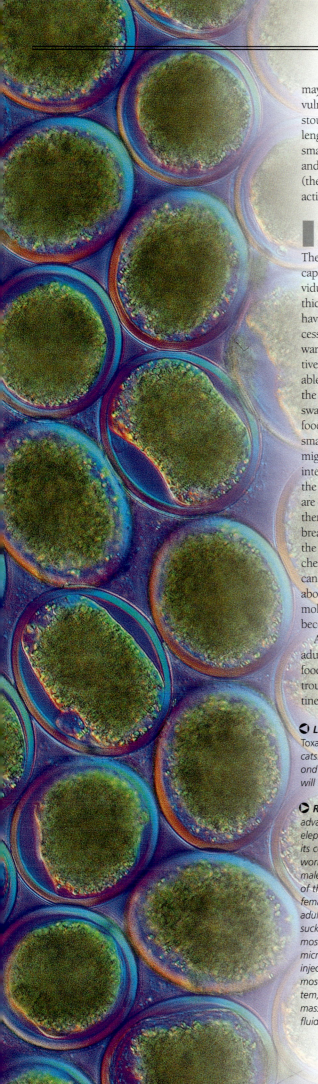

may exceed 70 percent; children are especially vulnerable to infection. The adult parasites are stout, creamcolored worms that may reach a length of 30cm (1ft) or more. They live in the small intestine, lying freely in the cavity of the gut and maintaining their position against peristalsis (the rhythmic contraction of the intestine) by active muscular movements.

Debilitating Diseases
HUMAN INFECTION

The adult female has a tremendous reproductive capacity and it has been estimated that one individual can lay 200,000 eggs per day. These have thick, protective shells, do not develop until they have been passed out of the intestine and for successful development of the infective larvae a warm, humid environment is necessary. The infective larva can survive in moist soil for a considerable period of time (perhaps years), protected by the shell. Man becomes infected by accidentally swallowing such eggs, often with contaminated food or from unclean hands. The eggs hatch in the small intestine and the larvae undergo an involved migration around the body before returning to the intestine to mature. After penetrating the wall of the intestine the larvae enter a blood vessel and are carried in the bloodstream to the liver and thence to the heart and lungs. In the latter they break out of the blood capillaries, move through the lungs to the bronchi, are carried up the trachea, swallowed and thus return to the alimentary canal. During this migration, which may take about a week, the larvae molt twice. The final molt is completed in the intestine and the worms become mature in about two months.

An infected person may harbor one or two adults only and, as the worms feed largely on the food present in the intestine, will not be greatly troubled, unless the worms move from the intestine into other parts of the body. Large numbers of

◁ **Left** *Eggs of the parasitic filarial nematode worm* Toxascaris leonina, *which commonly affects dogs and cats. This parasite has a very simple life cycle; the second stage larvae are ingested by the dog or cat, and will mature in the animal's intestinal tract.*

▷ **Right** *The elephant-like skin folds that characterize advanced cases of parasitic infection give the disease elephantiasis (properly known as lymphatic filariasis) its common name. Elephantiasis is caused by roundworms of the genera* Wuchereria *or* Brugia. *The adult male* **1** *and female* **2** *worm parasitize the lymph ducts of their victim, to which they attach themselves, the female by papillae* **3** *and the male by a spine* **4**. *The adults produce larvae called microfilariae* **5** *which are sucked up from the blood of an infected person by mosquitoes* **6** *when they feed. Inside the insect the microfilariae develop into infective larvae* **7** *which are injected into the blood of another person when the mosquito feeds. There they move to the lymphatic system, completing the cycle. Adults form the tangled mass of worms that cause the build-up of lymphatic fluids resulting in the characteristic swellings* **8**.

adults, however, give rise to a number of symptoms and may physically block the intestine. As in trichinosis, migration of the larvae round the body is a dangerous phase in the lifecycle and, where large numbers of eggs are swallowed, severe and possibly fatal damage to the liver and lungs may result. Chronic infection, particularly in children, may retard mental and physical development.

Elephantiasis is a disfiguring disease of man restricted to warm, humid regions of the world and occurs in coastal Africa and Asia, the Pacific and in South America.

The blood of humans infected with the parasite contains the microfilaria stage of the worm, that is, the fully developed embryos still within their thin, flexible eggshells, that have been released from the mature female worms. During the day the microfilariae accumulate in the blood vessels of the lungs, but at night, when mosquitoes are feeding, the microfilariae appear in the surface blood vessels of the skin and can be taken up by the insects as they feed. The daily appearance and disappearance of the microfilariae in the peripheral blood is controlled by the activity pattern of the infected person and is reversed when the person is active at night and asleep during the day.

It is an impressive example of the evolution of close interrelationships between parasites and their hosts and ensures maximum opportunity for the parasite to complete its lifecycle. Microfilariae

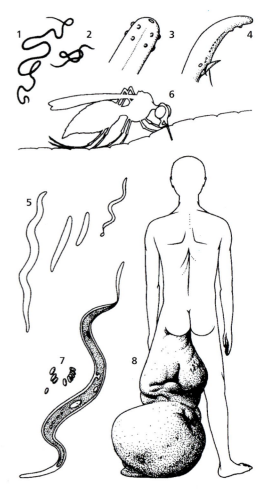

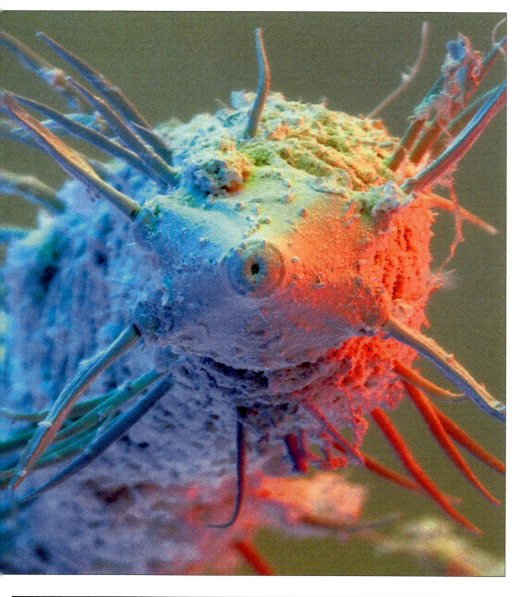

taken up by a mosquito undergo a period of development in the body muscles of the insect before becoming infective to man. As the mosquito feeds, larvae may once again enter the human host.

The adult worms may reach a length of 10cm (4in), but are very slender. They live in the lymphatic system of the body, often forming tangled masses and their presence may cause recurrent fevers and pains.

In long-standing infections, however, far more severe effects may be seen, caused by a combination of allergic reactions to the worms and the effects of mechanical blockage causing accumulation of lymph in the tissues. Certain regions of the body are more commonly affected than others, notably the limbs, breasts, genitals, and certain internal organs, which become swollen and enlarged. The skin in these areas becomes thickened and dry and eventually resembles that of an elephant. In severe cases the affected organ may reach an enormous size and thus engender debilitating or even fatal secondary complications.

Drug treatment for the elimination of the worms is useful in the early stages of infection, but little can be done where chronic disease has produced true elephantiasis. Indeed, the parasites may no longer be present at that time.   AC

◁ **Left** *A marine roundworm (order Desmoscolecida). These worms, which live among sand grains on coastal beaches, are covered with spines that protect them from abrasion and enable them to withstand the pull of incoming and outgoing tides.*

◑ **Below** *A microscopic nematode worm is lassoed by the predatory fungus Arthrobotrys abchonia. The fungus forms a three-celled ring some 20–30 microns in diameter; when the worm enters the ring, the cells inflate instantly and hold it fast.*

EELWORM TRAPS

In a reversal of the roles played by certain gnat larvae and the fungal fruiting bodies on which they feed above ground, soil-living nematodes face the hazard of predatory fungi. Eelworms, active forms that thread their way through the soil particles, fall prey to over 50 species of fungi whose hyphal threads penetrate the eelworms' bodies.

There are several ways by which the hyphae penetrate the eelworms. Some fungi form sticky cysts which adhere to the eelworm, then germinate and enter its body. Other fungi form sticky threads and networks, like a spider's web, which trap the eelworms.

Some fungi form lassolike traps. These consist of three cells forming a ring on a side branch of a hypha. An eelworm may merely push its way into the ring and become wedged or the trap may be "sprung," the three cells suddenly expanding inward in a fraction of a second, to secure the eelworm (see right).

It is interesting that these fungi do not need to feed on eelworms: they only develop traps if eelworms are present in the soil.   AC

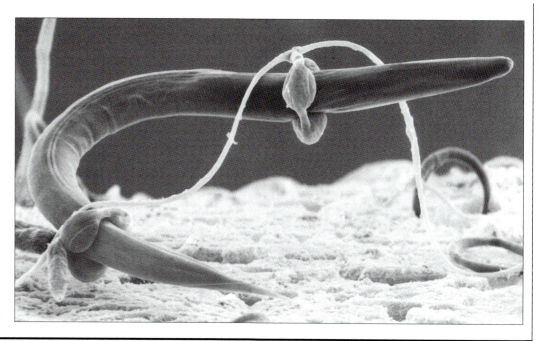

Flatworms and Ribbon Worms

LATWORMS ARE THOUGHT TO HAVE BEEN THE *first animals to evolve distinct front and rear ends. The most remarkable groups are the parasitic flukes and tapeworms, but many species are free-living. Ribbon worms are commonly considered as being most closely related to the turbellarian flatworms, but are more highly organized. As might be expected for these completely soft-bodied groups, the fossil record is virtually non-existent.*

Flatworms are the simplest animals with a three-layered (triploblastic) arrangement of body cells. Their flat shape derives from the fact that, having no body cavity other than the gut, they must respire by diffusion, and so no cell can be too far from their exterior surface. The ribbon worms (phylum Nemertea) are almost entirely free-living, marine worms, often highly colored, with only a few forms living on land or in freshwater, and one group as external parasites on other invertebrates.

Flatworms

PHYLUM PLATYHELMINTHES

With taxonomy constantly under review, the position of some groups of aquatic invertebrates is not always static. This is certainly the case with the order Acoela, which has until recently been considered as a flatworm within the class Turbellaria. Some scientists now believe that these gutless flatworms should be put in a new solitary phylum – Acoelomorpha (see also Gnathostomulids etc.).

The turbellarians are a widely distributed group of mostly free-living flatworms with a ciliated epidermis. They usually have a gut but no anus, and are classified by the shape of the digestive tract. Best known are the planarians, which may be black, gray, or brightly colored, live in fresh or sea water, and feed on protozoans, small crustaceans, snails, and other worms. *Convoluta* has no gut and depends on symbiotic algae for its food. Some members of the order Rhabdocoela (e.g. *Temnocephala* spp.) attach to crustaceans and other invertebrates and feed on free-living organisms, but most have become parasitic, such as *Fecampia* species, which live inside crustaceans.

Some planarians regenerate complete worms

◐ **Left** *An Indo-Pacific species of planarian,* Pseudoceros ferrugineus, *off Komodo Island, Indonesia. Brightly colored flatworms such as these are often mistaken for nudibranchs (sea slugs).*

from any piece. The more sophisticated parasitic flatworms, however, are unable to replace lost parts. In general the lower the degree of organization of an animal, the greater its ability to replace lost parts. Even a small piece, cut from such an animal usually retains its original polarity: a regenerated head grows out of the cut end of the piece which faced the front end in the whole animal. The capacity for regeneration decreases from front to rear: pieces from forward regions regenerate faster and form bigger and more normal heads than pieces from further back. In some planarians only pieces from near the front are able to form a head; those further back effect repair but do not regenerate a head.

The head of a planarian is dominant over the rest of the body. Grafts of head pieces reorganize the adjacent tissues into a whole worm in relation to themselves. Grafts from tail regions, on the other hand, are generally absorbed. However, the dominance of the head over the rest of the body is limited by distance, for example, if the animal grows to a sufficient length. This is what happens when planarians reproduce asexually: the rear part starts to act as if it were "physiologically isolated" and then finally constricts off as a separate animal.

True parasitism is universal in the two other classes, the Trematoda and Cestoda. The majority of monogenean trematodes are external parasites living on the outer surface of a larger animal, many on the gills of fishes. A few inhabit various internal organs and are true internal parasites, such as *Polystoma* in the urinary bladder of a frog and *Aspidogaster* in the pericardial cavity of a mussel species. The digenean trematodes, including the flukes, are all internal parasites. The adults inhabit in most cases the gut, liver or lungs of a vertebrate animal, swallowing and absorbing the digested food, blood or various secretions of their host. Among these are *Fasciola* species in the liver of sheep and cattle, *Schistosoma* in the blood of man and cattle, and *Paragonimus* in the lungs of man. The internal parasites are parasitic throughout the greater part of their life. After an initial short period as a freeliving ciliated larva known as a miracidium, the young enters a state of parasitism as a sporocyst or redia in a second host, and after a second free interval as a tadpole-shaped cercaria, may enter the body of a third host to become encysted. The second host is often a mollusk, and the cercaria may complete its lifecycle by becoming encysted in the same animal or a fish.

The cestodes are the most modified for a parasitic existence, as the adults remain internal parasites throughout life. They invariably inhabit the gut of a vertebrate. The intermediate host is often also a vertebrate – commonly the prey of the final host. As an adult, *Taenia crassicollis* is parasitic in the intestine of the cat; the cysticercus larval stage occurs in the livers of rats and mice. The adult tapeworm *Echinococeus granulosus* inhabits the gut

of dogs and foxes; its hydatid cyst larval stage may be found in the liver or lungs of almost any mammal, but especially sheep and sometimes man.

Flatworms are bilaterally symmetrical animals without true segmentation. The shape is leaflike or ribboned in the planarians, or cylindrical in some rhabdocoels. While a distinct head is rarely developed, there is often a difference marking the anterior end, – the presence of eyes, a pair of short tentacles, a slight constriction to form an anterior lobe. The mouth is on the underside, mostly toward the front. In some polyclads there is a small ventral sucker on the underside, and in some rhabdocoels there is an adhesive organ at the front and rear. In *Temnocephala* species, a row of tentacles is often present. The trematodes closely related to the Turbellaria in internal organization resemble them externally, with further

FACTFILE

FLATWORMS AND RIBBON WORMS

Phyla: Platyhelminthes, Nemertea

About 19,400 species in total. Platyhelminthes contains 3 classes and Nemertea contains 2 classes.

FLATWORMS

Phylum Platyhelminthes

About 18,500 species in 3 classes(some experts believe that the two subclasses of trematodes warrant elevation to class status). **Distribution:** worldwide; freeliving aquatic; parasitic in invertebrates and vertebrates. Fossil record: earliest in Mesozoic era 225–65 million years ago. **Size:** microscopic (1μm) to 4m (13ft), mostly 0.01–1cm (0.04–0.4in). **Features:** bilaterally symmetrical, usually flattened, possibly the first animals to have evolved front and rear ends and upper and lower surfaces; triploblastic, having a third layer of cells (mesoderm) which, by itself or in combination with ectoderm or endoderm, gives rise to organs or organ systems; without skeletal material, true segmentation, apparent body cavity (acoelomate) or blood-vascular system; defined head with a concentration of sense organs and a central nervous system; excretory vessels originate in ciliary flame cells; gut may be absent, rudimentary or highly developed but there is no anus; sexual and asexual reproduction. male and female organs often in the same animal, often hermaphrodite; development sometimes direct, sometimes accompanied by metamorphosis.

RIBBON WORMS (OR PROBOSCIS WORMS)

Phylum Nemertea

About 900 species in 2 classes. **Distribution:** worldwide; freeliving, mostly marine but some in freshwater and damp soil. **Fossil record:** as for platyhelminths. **Size:** 0.2cm–26m (0.08in–85ft). **Features:** bilaterally symmetrical, unsegmented worms with flattened elongated body; with a ciliated ectoderm; scientists disagree over status of the body cavity , may be truly coelomate; similar to flatworms but more highly organized; eversible proboscis in a sheath; gut with an anterior mouth, distinct lateral diverticula and anus at rear; there is a blood-vascular system and excretory vessels with ciliary flame cells; reproduce mostly by sexual means, occasionally asexual (by fragmentation), sexes separate; development in some direct, in others accompanied by metamorphosis.

See The Classes and Orders of Flatworms and Ribbon Worms ▷

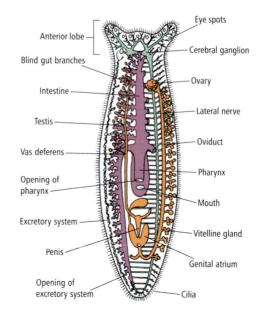

Anterior lobe
Blind gut branches
Intestine
Testis
Vas deferens
Opening of pharynx
Excretory system
Penis
Opening of excretory system

Eye spots
Cerebral ganglion
Ovary
Lateral nerve
Oviduct
Pharynx
Mouth
Vitelline gland
Genital atrium
Cilia

MEMORY AND LEARNING IN PLANARIANS

Planarians are capable of learning and have a memory. They acquire a conditioned reflex in response to a bright light followed by an electric shock. If animals trained in this way are cut into two, both halves regenerate into a whole organism, which retains its acquired learning, indeed both "heads" and "tails" show as much retention as uncut animals.

Similar results are found in planarians taught to find their way through a simple maze. Further experiments indicate that sexually mature worms fed on trained animals learn quicker than "control" animals kept on a normal diet. Two-headed planarians, which have been produced by surgery, learn more quickly than others, while animals whose brains have been removed are incapable of learning.

The memory of the animals cannot therefore be located in its brain and nervous system alone; it must be represented by chemical changes in cells throughout the body. It has been suggested that in the head of the planarian, memory is retained by neuron circuitry, whereas in the rest of the body it is retained in the form of a chemical imprint. This hypothesis has been confirmed by an experiment in which trained worms were cut in two and made to regenerate in a liquid containing a chemical "memory eraser" known as ribonucleic acid ASE. The "heads" were not affected by it, but the "tails" forgot eveything they had learned. Planarians show, beyond reasonable doubt, inheritance of acquired learning in animals that reproduce asexually.   GD

◁ **Left** Body plan of a planarian flatworm (genus Planaria), showing the digestive, excretory, reproductive, and nervous systems. The blind gut is highly branched in order to transport food to all parts of the body

modifications to accommodate the parasitic existence. They are generally leaflike with a thicker, more solid body. Suckers on the underside fix the parasite to its host. Usually there is a set at the front, or a single sucker surrounding the mouth and a rear set, or a single large rear sucker. Among trematodes, monogeneans often have more numerous suckers. Cestodes are ribbonlike, the anterior end is, in most cases, attached to the host by means of suckers and hooks placed on a rounded head (scolex). The hooks are borne on a retractile process, the rostellum. In the order Pseudophyllidea a pair of grooves takes the place of suckers and there are no hooks. In many cestodes parasitic in fishes, the head bears four prominent flaps, the bothridia. In *Tetrarhynchus* species there are four long narrow rostella covered with hooklets. The cestodes are mouthless, and nothing distinguishes upper and lower surfaces. The body or strobila, which is narrower at the front, is made up of a series of segmentlike proglottides which become larger toward the rear.

The outer surface of the body wall of parasitic flatworms is differently modified in the three classes and the underlying layers of muscle are also differently arranged. A characteristic of flatworms is the mesenchyme, a form of connective tissue filling the spaces between the organs. There is an alimentary canal in the turbellarians (except the Acoela) and in the trematodes, which also have a muscular pharynx and an intestine. There is no gut in the cestodes, which take in nutrients through the surface of the body wall. Flatworms have a bilateral nervous system involving nerve fibers and nerve cells. The degree of development of the brain varies in the different groups, being greatest in the polycladids and some monogenean trematodes: there is a grouping of nerve cells at the front end into paired cerebral ganglia, especially in the free-living forms. Sense organs in

⬤ **Below left** *The Rodrigues nemertine (Geonemertes rodericana) is a rare terrestrial ribbon worm. Living on the Indian Ocean islands of Rodrigues and Mauritius, it eats small invertebrates and (unlike its marine relatives) uses its proboscis to aid locomotion.*

⬤ **Below right** *Body plan of a ribbon worm, showing the proboscis in prey-capture position, outside of the rhynchocoel. The piercing barb, or stylet, on its tip is characteristic of the order Metanemertini.*

adult free-living turbellarians include light, chemosensory and chemotactic receptors, and these may also occur in the free-living stages of trematodes and cestodes. An excretory system exists in nearly all flatworms except the Acoela. There is usually a main canal running down either side of the body, with openings to the exterior. Opening into the twin canals are small ciliated branches that finally end in an organ known as a flame cell. There is no circulatory-vascular system.

Both male and female reproductive organs occur in the one animal, which is usually hermaphrodite, one of the exceptions being the trematode genus *Schistosoma*. The reproductive organs are most complex in the parasitic forms. The testes are often numerous, their united ducts leading into a muscular-walled penis resting in the genital opening. The female reproductive organs comprise the ovaries, which supply the ova, and the vitellarium, which supplies the ova with yolk and a shell. The ovaries discharge their ova into an oviduct which later forms a receptacle where fertilization occurs. The oviduct next receives the vitalline ducts which lead into the genital atrium. The location and arrangement of the genital opening in relation to the exterior are such to prevent self-fertilization and ensure crossfertilization. Development in rhabdocoels and monogenean trematodes is direct. In digenean trematodes, cestodes and some planarians a metamorphosis occurs. Asexual reproduction occurs commonly in

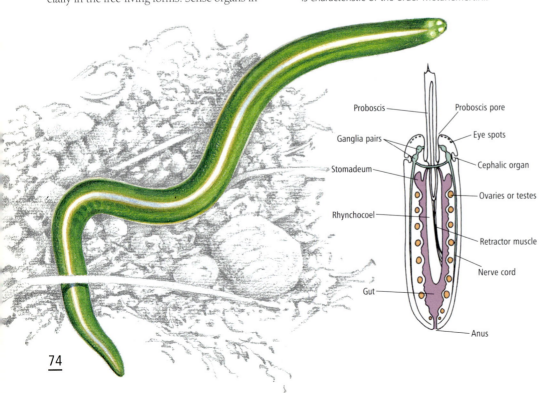

Proboscis
Ganglia pairs
Stomadeum
Rhynchocoel
Gut

Proboscis pore
Eye spots
Cephalic organ
Ovaries or testes
Retractor muscle
Nerve cord
Anus

the turbellarians by a process of budding. Other planarians may fragment into a number of cysts each of which develops into a new individual.

Ribbon Worms

PHYLUM NEMERTEA

Ribbon worms are often found burrowing in sand and mud on the shore or in cracks and crevices in the rocks. Some are able to swim by means of undulating movements of the body. Nearly all are carnivorous, either capturing living prey, mostly small invertebrates, or feed on dead fragments. The body is nearly always long, narrow, cylindrical or flattened, unsegmented and without appendages. The entire surface is covered with cilia and with gland cells secreting mucus which may form a sheath or tube for the creature. Beneath the ectoderm cell layer are two or three layers of muscle. There is no true coelom or body cavity, the space between organs being filled with mesenchyme. The proboscis, the most characteristic organ, lies in a cavity (rhynchocoel) formed by the muscular wall of the proboscis sheath. The proboscis may be everted for feeding. In members of the order Metanemertini – *Drepanophorus* species – there are stylets on the proboscis, providing formidable weapons. In other nemerteans, such as *Baseodiscus*, there are no stylets, but the prehensile proboscis can be coiled round its prey and conveyed to the mouth underneath the front end. The gut is a straight tube from mouth to anus, but various regions are recognizable in some species. There is a blood-vascular system, the blood being generally colorless, with corpuscles. The excretory system resembles that of ribbon worms, but the nervous system is more highly

developed. The brain is composed of two pairs of ganglia, above and below, just behind or in front of the mouth. Certain ganglia are probably related to special sense organs on the anterior end of the worm, and most ribbon worms have eyes. From the brain a pair of longitudinal nerve cords runs back down the body and there is a nerve net the complexity of which varies in the three orders. In most species the sexes are separate. The ovaries and testes are situated at intervals between the intestinal ceca and each opens by a short duct to the surface. Most ribbon worms develop directly, but some have a pelagic larva stage (pilidium), ending with a remarkable metamorphosis – the young adult develops inside the larva, from which it emerges.

Although very common, ribbon worms generally are of little economic or ecological importance. GD/AC

Above A ribbon worm foraging. Ribbon worms are almost entirely carnivorous, feeding on small crustaceans and annelid worms. Some species have a toxic secretion in the proboscis that helps immobilize prey.

The Classes and Orders of Flatworms and Ribbon Worms

FLATWORMS
PHYLUM PLATYHELMINTHES

Freeliving flatworms
Class Turbellaria

About 4,500 species. Orders include:
Order Acoela*; genera include: *Convoluta*
Order Nemertodermatida*; genera include: *Meara*.
Order Rhabdocoela; genera include: *Dalyellia, Fecampia, Mesostoma, Temnocephala*.
Order Tricladida (planarians); genera include: *Dendrocoelum, Planaria, Polycelis, Procerodes, Rhynchodemus*.
Order Polycladida (planarians); genera include: *Planocera, Thysanozoon*.
The Lake Pedder planarian (*Romankenkius pedderensis*; order Tricladida) was recently declared as extinct by the IUCN.

*Note: There is now consensus among some scientists that this order may constitute a new phylum – the Acoelomorpha (see also Gnathostomulids etc.).

Parasitic flatworms
Class Trematoda

About 9,000 species.

SUBCLASS MONOGENEA*
MONOGENEANS
Order Monopisthocotylea; genera include: *Gyrodactylus*.
Order Polyopisthocotylea; genera include: *Polystoma*.

SUBCLASS ASPIDOGASTREA
Genera include: *Aspidoyaster*

SUBCLASS DIGENEA*
FLUKES, DIGENEANS
Order Strigeatoidea; genera include: *Alaria, Schistosoma*.
Order Echinostomida; genera include: *Echinostoma, Fasciola*.
Order Opisthorchiida; genera include: *Heterophyes, Opisthorchis*.
Order Plagiorchiida; genera include: *Paragonimus, Plagiorchis*.

* Some authorities believe these groups warrant class status.

Right Head of a Hymenolepis nana tapeworm. The smallest of the cestodes, this is the only tapeworm species that parasitizes humans without an intermediate host.

Tapeworms
Class Cestoda

About 5,000 species.

SUBCLASS CESTODARIA
Order Amphilinidea; genera include: *Amphilina*.
Order Gyrocotylidea; genera include: *Gyrocotyle*.

SUBCLASS EUCESTODA
Order Tetraphyllidea; genera include: *Phyliobothrium*.
Order Protocephala; genera include: *Proteocephalos*.
Order Trypanorhyncha; genera include: *Tetrarhynchus*.

Order Pseudophyllidea; genera include: *Dibothriocephalus, Ligola*.
Order Cyclophyllidea; genera include: *Echinococcus, Taenia, Hymenolepis*.

RIBBON WORMS
PHYLUM NEMERTEA

Unarmed proboscides
Class Anopla

Order Hoplonemertea; genera include: *Amphiphorus, Hubrechtonemertes*.

Armed proboscides
Class Enopla

Order Bdellonemertea; genera include: *Malocobdella*.

PATHOGENIC PARASITES
Lifecycles and medical significance of digenean flukes

FEW ANIMALS AFFECT PEOPLE SO ADVERSELY AS flukes of the subclass Digenea. They include creatures that cause one of the most prevalent human diseases – schistosomiasis or bilharzia, and others that cause serious losses of livestock. These digenean flukes can be divided into blood flukes (e.g. *Schistosoma* spp.), lung flukes (e.g. *Paragonimus westermani*), liver flukes (e.g. *Fasciola* and *Opisthorchis* spp.), and intestinal flukes (e.g. *Fasciolopsis buskii, Heterophyes heterophyes*). Liver flukes can cause serious losses of sheep and cattle.

Other groups of parasitic flatworms contain representatives that, directly or indirectly, are harmful to people. Some monogenean parasites of fish often cause serious losses in fish-farming stocks kept in overcrowded conditions. Human cestode disease caused by adults of the tapeworm species *Taenia solium, T. saginata* and *Diphyllobothrum latum* is relatively nonpathogenic, but hydatid disease produced by the hydatid cysts of *Echinococcus granulosus*, cysticercosis caused by the cysticerus larval stage of *T. solium*, and sparganosis caused by the plerocercoid larvae of the genus *Spirometra* can be pathogenic.

The Common liver fluke (*Fasciola hepatica*) of

◐ **Below** *Life cycle of the Liver fluke (Fasciola hepatica) in sheep:* **1** *Eggs of flukes living in the sheep are passed from the body in droppings;* **2** *In wet or damp pastures, the eggs hatch into miracidia larvae;* **3** *Free-swimming miracidium penetrates the snail* Lymnaea truncata, *where it develops into a sporocyst;* **4** *The sporocyst develops into redia larvae in the digestive gland of the snail;* **5** *The redia develop into cercaria larva, which leave the snail via the pulmonary aperture;* **6** *The cercariae encyst on the grass;* **7** *Encysted cercariae are eaten by sheep where they migrate to the liver, where the fluke* **8** *matures within 10–14 weeks.*

sheep and cattle, almost worldwide in its distribution, is replaced by *F. gigantica* in parts of Africa and the Far East. Young flukes live in the liver tissue feeding mainly on blood and cells, while the adults live in the bile ducts. The flukes are hermaphrodite, with male and female organs in the same worm. Large numbers of eggs are produced and pass out in the feces onto the pasture. After a variable period, depending on the temperature, a miracidium hatches out. Moving on its cilia, this first-stage larva seeks out and penetrates the appropriate snail host, which in Europe and the United States is the Dwarf pond snail (*Lymnaea truncatula*), an inhabitant of temporary pools, ditches and wet meadows. The miracidium develops in its secondary host into a sporocyst which produces two or three generations of multiple rediae. Each redia produces freeliving cercariae, the number being determined by temperature. From one miracidium therefore many thousands of infective cercariae are produced. The tadpole-shaped cercariae leave the snail and may encyst on grass as metacercariae until eaten by a suitable primary host, which may be a sheep, cow, donkey, horse, camel and may even be a human eating, for example, infected watercress.

Spectacular losses due to acute fluke infestation can occur in sheep but are rarer in cattle. In some years the annual economic losses from fascioliasis in cattle and sheep in the United Kingdom for example have been estimated to be in the region of £10m and £50m respectively. Annual total losses in The Netherlands, the United States, and Hungary

can reach proportionally equivalent figures. It is possible in some countries to predict or forecast outbreaks of fascioliasis by using a meteorological system relying on monthly rainfall, evaporation and temperature data. In some countries chemical control of the snail host is possible, but in others reliance has been placed on periodic and strategic dosing of infected animals with such drugs as rafoxanide, oxyclozanide and nitroxynil. In the early 1980s a new breakthrough in treatment was made with the development of triclabendazole, which is very effective against early immature and mature *F. hepatica* in sheep and cattle.

Schistosomiasis or bilharzia affects the health of over 250 million people in over 70 developing countries, and it is estimated that another 600 million people are at risk. There are three principal schistosome species affecting humans. *Schistosoma haematobium* causes disease of the bladder and reproductive organs in various parts of Africa, especially Egypt, and the Middle East; *S. mansoni*, affecting mainly the liver and intestines, occurs in many parts of Africa, the Middle East, Brazil, Venezuela, Suriname, and some Caribbean islands; *S. japonicum*, also affecting the liver and intestines and sometimes the brain, occurs in China, Japan, the Philippines and parts of Southeast Asia.

Schistosomes live in the blood vessels feeding on the cells and plasma. They do little damage themselves but are prolific egglayers. The eggs pass through the veins into the surrounding tissues of the bladder, intestines or liver, causing severe damage. The long cylindrical adult females live permanently held in a ventral groove of the more muscular males, laying eggs which eventually pass out in the host's urine or feces. Adult schistosomes possess adaptations which enable them to evade the immunological defenses of the host

8

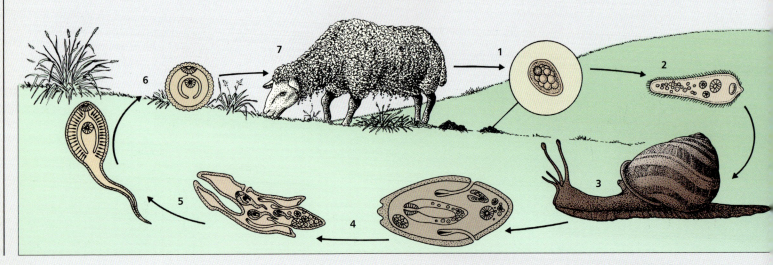

and they may live and reproduce in one person for up to 30 years. Should the eggs reach fresh water they hatch, releasing a freeswimming miracidium which actively seeks out and penetrates the appropriate intermediate freshwater snail host – a pulmonate (e.g. *Bulinus*, *Physopsis*) or, for *S. japonicum*, a prosobranch snail. The parasite multiplies asexually inside the snail and after a period of between 24 and 40 days has produced a large number of infective cercariae. These escape from the snail and need to burrow through human skin or into another suitable host for the parasite to develop into either a male or female worm.

The geographical range of each species of schistosome is confined to the distribution of suitable snail hosts. The most important factor affecting the spread of schistosomiasis is the implementation of water-resource development projects in developing countries – primarily the construction of hydroelectric dams and also irrigation systems. The Aswan High Dam in Egypt, and Lake Volta in Ghana have already aggravated and increased the spread of a disease already endemic in these countries. The debilitating disease schistosomiasis and

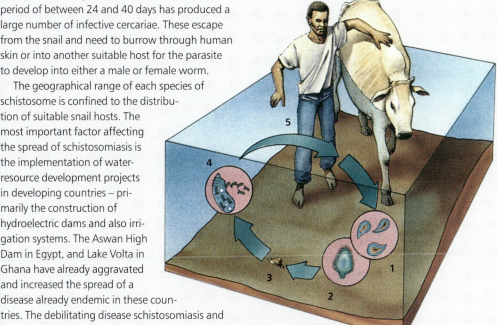

malaria are the two most prevalent diseases of the world and have received much attention from the World Health Organization (WHO), which stimulates research into the basic problems related to the spread and control of these important diseases. The WHO claims that schistosomiasis could be eliminated by a combination of clean-water

programs and the intensive use of drugs such as metrifonate and praziquantel against the appropriate schistosomes. Some experts believe that a vaccine is needed too, and some promising developments are being made in that direction as a result of applying new technology using monoclonal antibodies.   GD/AC

◗ **Above** *The parasitic blood fluke* Schistosoma japonicum. *Symptoms of bilharzia include anaemia, diarrhoea, dysentery, cirrhosis of the liver, and enlargement of the liver and spleen.*

◖ **Left** *Life cycle of the human blood fluke (*Schistosoma *spp.), which cause urinary or vesical schistosomiasis (bilharzia) through damage to the bladder wall as its eggs bore through to escape from the host. Freshwater snails, for example* Oncomelania *spp., form the host for the larval stage: **1** The eggs are passed from the human into the water in urine or faeces; **2** The eggs hatch into free-swimming miracidia larvae; **3** The miracidia larvae invade the snail host, each developing into a sporocyst, which finally gives rise to many cercariae larvae; **4** Cercariae larvae are released and penetrate unbroken human skin, particularly on the hands and the feet; **5** Paired adult flukes live within the blood vessels (veins) of the human intestine. The fatter male worm holds the female within the groove of its body wall.*

Mollusks

tHE DIVERSITY OF MOLLUSKS IS EXPRESSED IN *their exploitation for food, pearls, and dyes, and their role as hosts to pathogens and parasites, and as garden pests. This great variety is reflected in the range of body forms and ways of life. Mollusks include coat-of-mail shells or chitons, marine, land and freshwater snails, shell-less sea slugs and terrestrial slugs, tusk shells, clams or mussels, octopuses, squids, cuttlefishes and nautiluses.*

In addition to the 90,000–100,000 living species, the many extinct species include the ammonites and belemites. Today's mollusks occur throughout the world, living in the sea, fresh, and brackish water, and on land. Apart from those that float, swim weakly (e.g. sea butterflies), or powerfully (e.g. squids), or burrow (e.g. clams), mollusks live either attached to or creeping over the substrate, whether seabed or ground, or vegetation.

Mantled Mollusca
FORM AND FUNCTION

The molluskan body is soft and is typically divided into head (lost in the bivalves), muscular foot and visceral hump containing the body organs. There are no paired jointed appendages or legs, a feature distinguishing mollusks from the arthropods. Most species have their soft parts protected by a hard calcareous shell.

Two key features of the molluskan body are the mantle, an intucking of skin tissue that forms a protective pocket, and the toothed tongue or radula.

Right *Flaps from the mantle extending to envelop the glossy shell of a Mole cowrie* (Cypraea talpa)*. These protect the shell from abrasion, and continually deposit enamel onto it.*

Below *Alarmed by a diver, a Giant Pacific octopus* (Octopus dofleini) *emits a cloud of ink. Cephalopods such as this have highly developed brains and eyes.*

Mollusks have a gut with both mouth and anus, associated feeding apparatus, a blood system (usually with a heart), nervous system with ganglia, reproductive system (which in some is very complex), and excretory system with kidneys. The epidermal (skin) tissues of mollusks are generally moist and thin, and prone to drying out. Gills are present in most aquatic species, which are used to extract oxygen from water. In most bivalves and some gastropods, however, the gills are also used in feeding, when they strain out organisms and detritus from the water or silt with minute flickering cilia on the gills. These particles are then conveyed by tracts of cilia to the mouth.

In land and some freshwater snails, the walls of the mantle cavity act as lungs, exchanging respiratory gases between the air and body. Many mollusks have a free-floating (pelagic) larval stage, but this is absent in land and some freshwater species.

Lack of an internal skeleton has kept most mollusks to a relatively small size. Cephalopods have achieved the greatest size in the Giant squid, which can be 20m (60ft) long, including tentacles. Giant ammonites with shells up to 2m (6.6ft) across existed in the Jurassic period 195–135 million years ago. The largest living bivalves are the tropical giant clams, which can reach 1.5m (4.5ft) in shell length. A substantial number of species measure less than 1cm (0.4in). Some of the smallest, like the tiny gastropod *Ammonicera rota*, are only 1mm (0.04in) long when fully grown.

Inbuilt Protection
THE MANTLE

The back of a mollusk is covered by a fold of skin, the mantle, which forms a pocket housing the gills, osphradium (a chemical sensory organ), hypobranchial gland (secreting mucus), anus, excretory pore and sometimes the reproductive opening. This special feature of mollusks has been adapted in many different ways and is present in all molluskan classes.

The cells of the mantle, particularly at the thickened edge of the mantle skirt, secrete the shell and may also produce slime, acids and ink for defense. Mucus for protection and for cohesion of food particles is secreted by the gill and the hypobranchial glands. Products of the mantle can be defensive, acting to deter predators. The purple gland in the mantle of the sea hare expels a purple secretion when the animal is disturbed. Several species of dorid sea slugs or sea lemons can expel acid from glands in the mantle, while on land the Garlic snail gives off a strong aroma of garlic from cells near the breathing pore.

The mantle wall may be visible and in some sea slugs it is brightly colored and patterned – acting as either warning coloration or camouflage. The glossy and colored shells of cowries are usually hidden by a pair of flaps from the mantle.

Protection of the delicate internal organs was probably an early function of the mantle, which also provides a space into which the head and foot can be retracted when the animal withdraws into its shell. Within the mantle cavity, the gills are protected from mechanical damage (from rocks, coral etc.) as well as from silting. At the same time the gills must have ready access to sea water from which to extract oxygen. In some mollusks, special strips of mantle tissue are developed as tubular siphons which help to separate two currents of water that pass over the gills – the inhalant and exhalant water currents. Fleshy lobes to the mantle, as in freshwater bladder snails of the genus

FACTFILE

MOLLUSKS

Phylum: Mollusca

About 90,000–100,000 species in 7 classes.

DISTRIBUTION Worldwide, primarily aquatic, in seas mainly, some in fresh and brackish water, some on land.

FOSSIL RECORD Appear in Cambrian rocks about 530 million years ago, modern classes distinct by about 500 million years ago; abundant extinct nautiloids, ammonites, belemites.

SIZE Often smaller than crustaceans, but ranging from tiny 1mm (0.04in) gastropods to Giant squid up to 20m (60ft) long.

FEATURES Body soft, typically divided into head (lost in bivalves), muscular foot and visceral hump containing body organs; protected by hard calcareous shell in most species; no paired jointed appendages; fold of skin (mantle) protects soft parts; mouthparts include usually a toothed tongue (radula); breathing mostly by gills, which may serve also in filter feeding; heart usually present; cephalopods have veins; nervous system of paired ganglia; sexes typically separate (not land species), fertilization external or by copulation; young develop via larval stages (not land or freshwater species) including often a free-floating trochophore and/or veliger before settling to an often bottom-dwelling life.

MONOPLACOPHORANS Class Monoplacophora
25 species of deepsea segmented limpets.

SOLENOGASTERS, CHAETODERMS Class Aplacophora
c. 370 wormlike marine species in 2 subclasses.

CHITONS OR COAT-OF-MAIL SHELLS
Class Polyplacophora
c. 1,000 species.

SLUGS AND SNAILS (GASTROPODS) Class Gastropoda
c. 60,000–75,000 species in 3 subclasses.

TUSK OR TOOTH SHELLS Class Scaphopoda
c. 900 species of marine sand burrowers.

CLAMS AND MUSSELS (BIVALVES)
Class Bivalvia (or Pelecypoda)
c. 20,000 species in 7 orders in sea, brackish and freshwater.

CEPHALOPODS Class Cephalopoda
c. 900 marine, mostly pelagic, species in 3 subclasses.

See The 7 Classes of Mollusks ▷

Physa, may function as extra respiratory surfaces.

Fertilization of eggs may take place within the mantle cavity of bivalves, and eggs are brooded there in, for example, the small pea shells of fresh-water habitats.

The versatile molluskan mantle can become muscular and serve in locomotion. Some sea slugs employ their leaflike mantle lobes in swimming. Some scallops, such as the Queen scallop, swim by expelling water from the mantle cavity.

Shedding Teeth
THE RADULA

The radula, a toothed tongue, is typically present in all classes of mollusk except the bivalves. It is secreted continuously in a radula sac and is composed of chitin, the polysaccharide also found in arthropod exoskeletons. The oldest teeth are toward the tip: when a row of teeth becomes worn, they detach and are often passed out with the feces. A new row of teeth then moves into position. Inside the mouth is an organ, the buccal mass, which contains and operates the radula during feeding. The radula is carried on a rod of muscle and cartilage (odontophore) that projects into the mouth cavity, while further complexes of muscles and cartilage in the walls of the buccal mass operate the radula, usually in a circular motion.

The form of the radula depends on feeding habits and is used in identifying and classifying individual species. Herbivores, such as land snails and slugs, have a broad radula with many small teeth, while carnivores, including whelks, have a narrow radula with a few teeth bearing long pointed cusps. Limpets, which browse algae off rocks,

◗ *Right* *Representative mollusk species:* **1** *A species of* Dentalium, *or Elephant's tusk shell (5cm/2in);* **2** Solen marginatus, *a razor shell (12.5cm/4.9in);* **3** *A chiton (class Polyplacophora). Chitons are flattened sedentary mollusks with eight overlapping shell plates;* **4** Nucella lapillus, *a dog whelk; rocky shores of NW Europe (3cm/1.2in high);* **5** Buccinum undatum, *the large European whelk (8cm/3in);* **6** *A species of* Neopilina, *a genus of limpet-like mollusks (4cm/1.6in);* **7** *A species of* Aplysia, *or sea hare (15cm/5.9in);* **8** Tridacna gigas, *the largest living mollusk, or giant clam (1.35m/4.4ft);* **9** *A common octopus (genus* Octopus); **10** Falcidens gutterosus, *a chaetoderm, Mediterranean (1.5cm/0.6in).*

have an especially hard rasping radula and a few very strong teeth in each row; they leave scratch marks on the surface of rock.

In the carnivorous cone shells each tooth is separated from the membrane, and is a harpoon-like structure delivered into the body of the prey (often a fish or a worm) to facilitate penetration of an accompanying nerve poison. The tiny sacoglossan sea slugs feed on threadlike algae – their radula teeth are adapted to pierce individual algal cells.

A Wealth of Variety
THE SHELL

Mollusks usually hatch from the egg complete with a tiny shell (protoconch) that is often retained at the apex of the adult shell. This calcareous shell, into which the animal can withdraw, is often regarded as a hallmark of a mollusk. For the living mollusk, the shell provides protection from predators and mechanical damage, while on land and on the shore it helps prevent loss of body water. Empty shells have long been a source of fascination, and many people collect them.

New growth occurs at the shell lip in gastropods and along the lower or ventral margin in bivalves. Shell is secreted by glandular cells, particularly along the edge of the mantle. This is easy to demonstrate in young land snails, by painting

waterproof ink along the outside of the lip. After a few days new shell will be seen in front of the ink mark. Newly secreted shell is thin, but gradually attains the same thickness as the rest. Although, in the event of damage, a repair can be made further back from the mantle edge, it will be a rough patch and not contain all the layers of normal shell. When growth stops for a while during cold weather, in drought, or a time of starvation, a line forms on the shell which continues to be visible after resumption of growth. A number of mollusks (e.g. cockles) normally have regular marks recording interruptions of their growth.

The cross-lamellar component of the shell, revealed by high magnification, consists of different layers of oblique crystals, each layer with a different orientation, rather like the structure of radial car tyres. This is thought to give greater strength without extra weight or bulk.

Shell is mostly composed of calcium carbonate, in calcite form (in the prismatic layer) and in argonite form (in the cross-lamellar layers), together with some sodium phosphate and magnesium carbonate. The mineral component of the shell is laid down in organic crystalline bodies in a matrix of fibrous protein and polysaccharides (conchiolin) secreted by the mantle. Snails can store calcium salts in cells of the digestive gland (hepatopancreas).

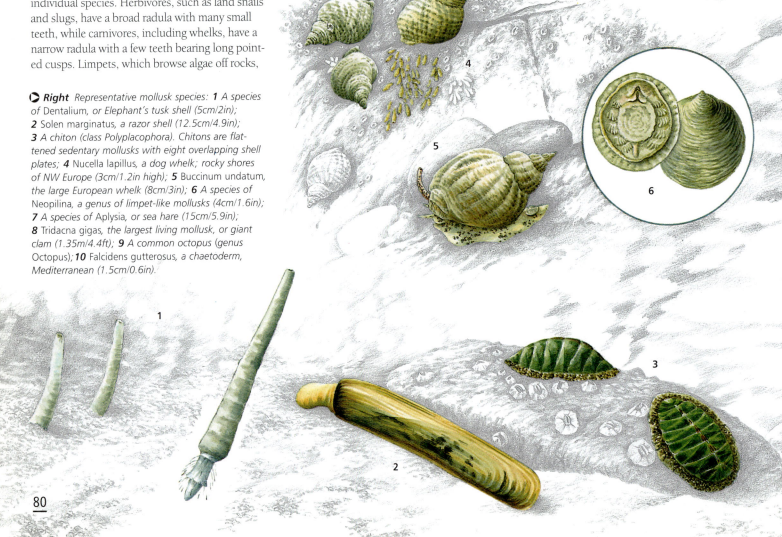

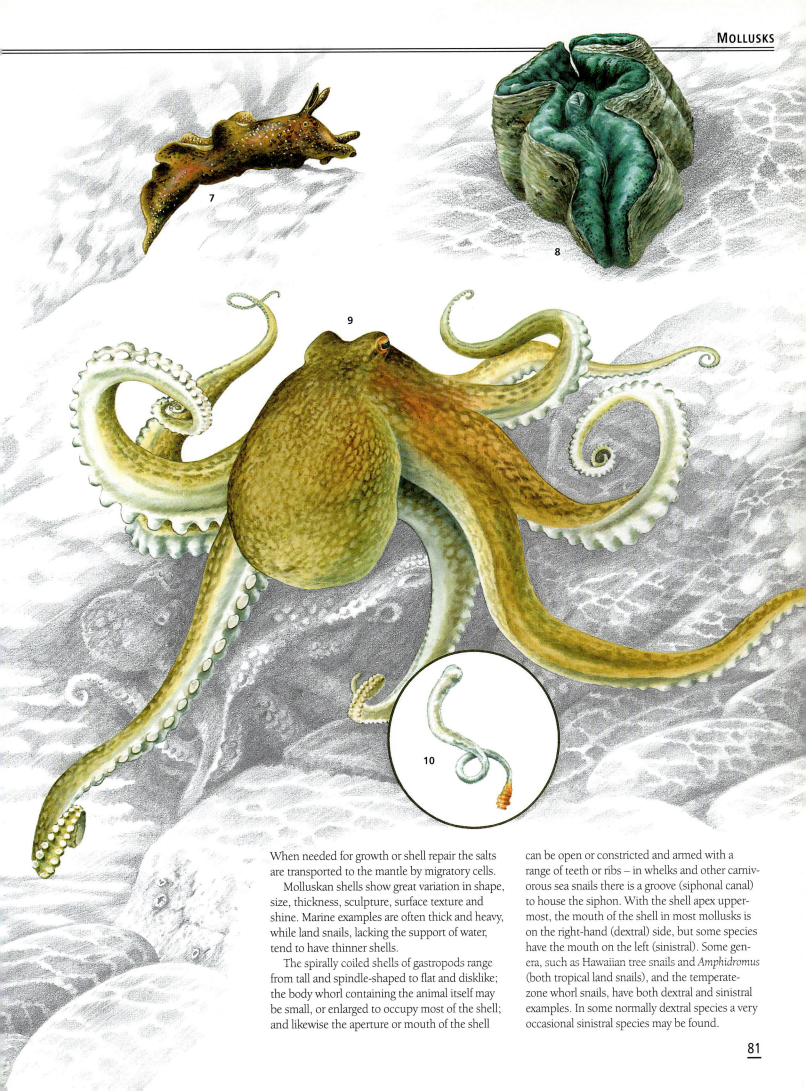

7

8

9

10

When needed for growth or shell repair the salts are transported to the mantle by migratory cells.

Molluskan shells show great variation in shape, size, thickness, sculpture, surface texture and shine. Marine examples are often thick and heavy, while land snails, lacking the support of water, tend to have thinner shells.

The spirally coiled shells of gastropods range from tall and spindle-shaped to flat and disklike; the body whorl containing the animal itself may be small, or enlarged to occupy most of the shell; and likewise the aperture or mouth of the shell can be open or constricted and armed with a range of teeth or ribs – in whelks and other carnivorous sea snails there is a groove (siphonal canal) to house the siphon. With the shell apex uppermost, the mouth of the shell in most mollusks is on the right-hand (dextral) side, but some species have the mouth on the left (sinistral). Some genera, such as Hawaiian tree snails and *Amphidromus* (both tropical land snails), and the temperate-zone whorl snails, have both dextral and sinistral examples. In some normally dextral species a very occasional sinistral species may be found.

The nautilus, an exception among living cephalopods, has a light, brittle, spiral shell. In section this is seen to be divided, behind the outermost body chamber, by thin walls into progressively smaller earlier body chambers. Each wall (septum) has a central perforation which in the living animal is traversed by a threadlike extension of the body – the siphuncle – which extends to the shell apex. The pressure of gas in the chambers affects buoyancy.

Many shells are strongly sculpted into ribs, lines, beading, knobs, or spectacular spines. Such detail, prized by shell collectors, is also used in the identification of species. The surface of the shells is sometimes rough, but in certain examples, such as cowries and olive shells, it may be smooth and glossy. Many tropical shells are very colorful and may also have attractive patterns and markings.

A number of mollusks in different groups have a reduced shell or none at all. Some sea slugs retain external shells, others have thin internal shells and some (the nudibranchs) like land slugs are without any shell. Shell-less sea slugs have evolved to swim as well as crawl, to squeeze into small crannies, and to develop secretions and body color as means of defense. An external shell is also lacking in some parasitic gastropods, in the wormlike aplacophorans and in most cephalopods.

Convergent Development
THE EVOLUTION OF MOLLUSKS

The success of the mollusks has been due to their adaptability of structure, function, and behavior. Mollusks are thought to be derived from either an ancestor of the Platyhelminthes (planarians, flukes, tapeworms) or from the arthropod annelid line, the latter having trochophore larvae, as do most mollusks.

There is fossil evidence of mollusks in some of the oldest fossil-bearing rocks , dating back over 530 million years to the Cambrian period. Mollusks soon evolved in different directions and the modern classes had largely separated out by the end of the Cambrian, 490 m.y.a. The earliest fossils are all of marine species. Land snails appeared in the coal-measure forests of 300 m.y.a., but land snail fossils are rare until deposits of the Tertiary (65–1.8 m.y.a.).

The original molluskan shell was probably cap-like. Many families, such as limpets, have reverted to that form from the spiral coiling that was widespread in gastropods (and still is) and in the few remaining shelled cephalopods. Nautiloids (now represented by only six living species) gave rise to some 3,000 known fossil species, many of which flourished in the Paleozoic seas, but they dwindled in the Mesozoic (248–65 m.y.a.) when

◑ Above *Mollusks exhibit a wide diversity of shell shapes. The Wavy-top shell* (Astraea undulosa; *main picture), derives its name from the pronounced undulations at the edge of its shell. The cross-section of a Pearly nautilus* (Nautilus pompilus; *inset) shows the chambers into which this animal's distinctively beautiful shell is divided.*

ammonites expanded. After a successful period, ammonites suddenly vanished in their turn at the end of the Cretaceous, along with the dinosaurs.

There is no central theme to molluskan evolution. Different groups of mollusks have adapted to similar habitats, often adopting similar characteristics (convergent evolution). Among bivalves, for example, both true piddocks and the False piddock bore into mudstone but, although the outsides of their shells are similar, the latter is more closely related to venus shells and its shell-hinge teeth are quite different. The bivalve shell of members of the class Bivalvia even has its counterpart in a different class, the bivalve gastropods.

Isolated islands, as in the Pacific, show a high level of speciation (evolution of new species) and forms that are endemic – for example the Partula snails (limited to that island) – because of the separation of the snail population from other larger populations. In Hawaii there are even local color forms of tree snails in isolated valleys.

Gills and Lungs
RESPIRATION AND CIRCULATION

Mollusks originated in the sea – and their basic method of breathing is by gills which extract dissolved oxygen from the surrounding water. The typical molluskan gill (ctenidium) consists of a central axis from which rows of gill filaments project on either side (bipectinate). Blood vessels enter the filaments and the surface of each filament is covered with cells bearing cilia; some of these cells create a current in the water with their long cilia, and others pick up food particles. An inhalant current of water enters the gill on one side, passes between the filaments and goes out as an exhalant current on the other side.

In some mollusks the gill serves only for respiration, while in others (e.g. most bivalves) the two enlarged gills have a dual role of feeding as well as respiration. Gills are delicate structures, which need to be kept clear of clogging particles: the ciliary devices evolved for cleaning the gills later became adapted for feeding. The mantle is often developed at the rear end into a tube (siphon) which projects and takes in water, testing it with sensory cells and tentacles on the way; in some bivalves (e.g. the tellinids) there is a separate siphon for the exhalant current.

Blood is pumped around the molluskan body by a heart, and is distributed to the tissues by arteries but, in all except cephalopods, it has to make a slow passage back through blood spaces (hemocoel).

Monoplacophorans and chitons have several pairs of gills in the mantle cavity. In prosobranch or operculate gastropods there is typically one pair of gills, but in the more highly evolved groups the gill is reduced and lost on one side, so winkles and whelks have only one gill in the mantle cavity. The more primitive prosobranchs (e.g. slit shells, ormers, slit and keyhole limpets) still have two gills. These limpets have lost the typical molluskan ctenidium, replacing it by numerous secondary gills of different structure which hang down around the mantle cavity. Most prosobranchs are aquatic, breathing by gills, although some have adapted to life on land and breathe by a vascularized mantle cavity or lung.

During periods of drought, land prosobranchs can spend long spells of time inactive inside the shell, sealed off by an operculum. Some tropical land species of the family Annulariidae have developed a small tube of shell material behind the operculum that enables the snail to obtain air when the operculum is enclosed. The tropical apple snails live in stagnant water, and these have long siphons that reach above the surface of water to breathe air.

Among the sea slugs and bubble shells, the primitive shelled species such as *Acteon* and the sea hares have a gill within the mantle cavity, but in the shell-less forms there are either secondary gills, as in the sea lemons, or respiration takes

● ❍ **Above and below** *Consisting of four folds of tissue, the gills of oysters (above, a Rock oyster,* Chama *sp.) serve both for respiration, pumping water through the mantle cavity, and for feeding, gathering food particles. The octopus' siphon has a triple function, not only drawing water across the gills, but also propelling it through the water and dispensing ink for defense.*

place directly through the skin, which may have its surface area increased by numerous papillae.

The pulmonates (land snails and slugs, pond snails), as their name implies, are essentially lung-breathers, having lost the gill, and breathe air from a highly vascularized mantle wall. The finely divided blood vessels of the respiratory surface can often be seen as silvery lines through the thin shell. The entrance to the mantle cavity is sealed off and opens by a breathing pore (pneumostome) whenever an exchange of air is needed. The pulmonate pond snails usually breathe air and come up to the surface to open the breathing pore above water.

Some deepwater pond snails of lakes have reverted to filling the mantle cavity with water and no longer use air. While freshwater prosobranchs breathe by gills and are more often found in the oxygenated waters of rivers and streams, the pulmonates, breathing air, are better adapted for living in the stagnant, deoxygenated water of ponds and ditches.

Bivalves are excusively aquatic and breathe by gills. In primitive families, including the nut shells, the gills are relatively small, and are only used for breathing, not feeding.

Cephalopods breathe by gills in the mantle cavity. The system is highly efficient, since there is a greater flow of water through the mantle cavity due to its use in jet propulsion, and faster blood circulation through a closed blood system with veins as well as arteries. The branchial hearts of most cephalopods are not present in nautiluses, which rely instead on duplication of gills to meet their respiratory needs.

rock shells, volutes, olives, cones, auger and turret shells (neogastropods) are specialized for a carnivorous diet – the shell has a siphonal canal housing a siphon which directs water over taste cells in the osphradium (a chemoreceptor in the mantle cavity), which helps in the detection of food. Certain carnivorous gastropods, like the Dog whelk and the necklace shells, drill holes in the shells of other mollusks which are then consumed. The murex or rock shells bore mechanically, but necklace shells use acid to soften the shell before excavating with the radula.

The sea slugs and bubble shells include herbivores, suspension feeders, carnivores and parasites, but the majority are carnivores feeding on encrusting marine animals. The sea slug *Melibe leonina*, from the west coast of the USA, is an active swimmer and adapted to feeding on crustaceans, which it catches with the aid of a large cephalic hood: the radula is absent. Shelled opisthobranchs, like species of canoe shell, lobe shell and cylindrical bubble shell, feed on animals in the sand, including mollusks. The inside of the gizzard is lined with special plates which they use to crush the prey. The curious pyramidellids with small coiled shells are parasitic in a range of marine animals.

Pulmonates are chiefly herbivorous, although many of them feed on dead rather than living plant material, and pond snails often consume detritus and mud on the bottom. In these animals the radula is broad, with large numbers of small teeth. There is no style nor chitinous gizzard plates as found in bubble shells. The smaller land snails retain a microphagous diet, while a few species from different families have become carnivorous. These include the shelled slugs that eat earthworms, and a number of tropical land snails, such as the family Streptaxidae and genus *Euglandina*, which eat other snails. Some glass snails (family Zonitidae) have carnivorous tendencies and the large glass snail *Aegopis verticillus* of eastern Europe readily eats land snails.

The more primitive bivalves feed on detritus, which is pushed into the mouth by labial palps, but most modern bivalves are ciliary feeders, making use of phytoplankton, while others take in detritus from the surface of the substrate with siphons. In the more adanced bivalves, the gills are used for filtering food and conveying it to the mouth by wrapping it in mucus and passing it along food grooves to the mouth. The crystalline style and stomach plates are well developed in bivalves. The woodboring shipworms have cellulase enzymes used to digest wood shavings.

▌ Herbivores, Carnivores, Parasites
▌ FEEDING

Primitive mollusks probably fed on small particles, the macrophagous habit (eating large particles) developing only later. Most mollusks, except bivalves, feed using the radula (see above). The bivalves and some gastropods (e.g.slipper limpets of the USA, ostrich foot of New Zealand, and river snails of Europe) are ciliary feeders, either straining food from seawater (filter feeding) or sucking in sludge off the bottom (deposit feeding).

Another typical molluskan feature, which is found in some prosobranchs and bivalves, is the stomach, its wall protected by chitinous plates

from a pointed, forward-projecting style which winds round and brings the string of food from the esophagus into the stomach. The style also secretes digestive enzymes.

The gastropods include browsing herbivores, ciliary feeders, detritus feeders, carnivores and parasites. The muscular mouthparts (buccal mass) and gut show adaptions reflecting this variety. Limpets, top shells and winkles browse on algae and other encrustations on rocks, while the Flat periwinkle eats brown seaweed and the Bluerayed limpet rasps at the fronds and stems of oarweed (*Laminaria* species). Some will eat carrion while others attack live animals. The whelks, murexes or

Above *Young of the Australian octopus (Octopus australis) hatching. After attaching her eggs to the roof of her lair, the female octopus aerates them with gentle water jets from her siphon.*

Below *An egg ribbon of the Spanish dancer nudibranch (Hexabranchus sanguineus). These striking agglomerations, which may contain thousands of eggs, are laid on reefs by this species of sea slug.*

The curious group of bivalve septibranchs – clams of the family Cuspidariidae – have lost the gill and have reduced labial palps and style. They are scavengers, sucking juices of dead animals. Species of the bivalve genus *Entovalva* are parasites inside sea cucumbers, and some of the freshwater mussels are parasitic in fish in the early stages of their life history.

The carnivorous cephalopods mostly catch fish, although the slower-moving octopus takes crustaceans. The radula is relatively small, but the prey is seized by jaws with a hard beak. In cephalopods, enzymes are secreted by gland cells into the tubules of the digestive gland where extracellular digestion takes place: this contrasts with the ingestion of food particles by cells of the digestive gland (intracellular digestion) in other mollusks. Extracellular digestion is a feature in which cephalopod body organization is in advance of the rest of the mollusks and parallels the situation in vertebrates.

Regulating Waste
EXCRETION

In mollusks there is a kidney next to the heart which extracts nitrogenous waste from the blood. The excretory duct runs alongside the rectum to the pore at the mantle edge in pulmonates, but in prosobranchs there is a simple opening on the side of the kidney directly into the mantle cavity. In some mollusks certain minerals are selectively resorbed. There is little water regulation in marine mollusks but considerable activity in those of freshwater. Land mollusks conserve their water and little goes out with the excreta, nitrogenous waste being in an insoluble crystalline form and often stored in the kidney. Bivalves give off their nitrogenous waste as ammonia or its derivatives. In some opisthobranchs excretory waste is discharged into the gut.

Egglayers
BREEDING

Eggs of mollusks vary considerably. Some are shed into water before fertilization as in bivalves. Many mollusk eggs are very small but those of cephalopods are large and yolky. When fertilization is internal, elaborate egg cases may be secreted and very often gastropods lay eggs in large clutches. Some winkles and water snails deposit eggs in a jellylike matrix often attached to vegetation. Necklace shells form stiff collars of egg cases which are large for the size of the mollusk, while whelks and murexes deposit eggs in leathery capsules attached to rocks and weed. Land snail eggs tend to be buried in soil: some are contained in a transparent envelope but others have a limy eggshell, and the eggs of one of the large African land snails, *Archachatina marginata*, are of the size and appearance of a small bird's egg. Egg masses of sea slugs can be quite spectacular when found in rock pools.

In aquatic mollusks there is usually a planktonic larva, the primitive trochophore, of short duration, and/or the characteristic veliger larva that develops from it (often within the egg capsule), with shell and ciliary lobes. Some retain the egg inside the body of the female, or in the capsule, from which the young emerge as miniature adults. The veliger lives in the plankton, feeding on algae

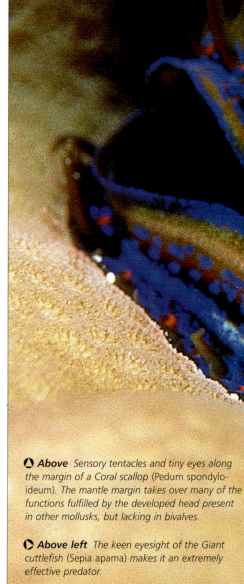

for a day to several months before settling. Vast numbers of molluskan larvae are present in the oceanic plankton and many of them are eaten by other members of the zooplankton or by filter-feeders, or perish when they fail to find a suitable habitat to settle.

In land and freshwater prosobranchs, the veliger stage is suppressed, and a snail hatches directly from the egg. Pulmonates also lack the veliger stage, and floating larvae occur in only some freshwater bivalves. The pelagic larva was important in establishing the freshwater Zebra mussel that first came to Britain in the first half of the 19th century. Freshwater or river mussels brood the eggs in the gills and release them as glochidia larvae parasitic on fish.

It is in the sea snails and limpets (prosobranchs) and sea slugs and bubble shells (opisthobranchs) that the veliger is most varied. Chitons and more primitive prosobranchs such as slit shells and ormers have a trochophore larva, with a horizontal band of ciliated cells, which only lasts for a few days. Mollusks with veligers in the plankton for several weeks have a better opportunity for dispersal. At metamorphosis the ciliated lobes (velum) by which the veliger swims and feeds are engulfed, the mollusk ends its planktonic life and sinks to the bottom. Bivalve veliger larvae also occur in the plankton but in some, such as the small midshore *Lasaea rubra*, the young hatch as bivalves and establish themselves near the parent colony. Following the bivalve veliger stage is an intermediate pediveliger when the larva searches for a suitable place to settle; if none is found, the velum can be reinflated and the larva is carried to other sites.

Advanced and Sensitive
NERVOUS SYSTEM AND SENSE ORGANS

The brain and eye of the cephalopod are the most highly developed of any invertebrate. The molluskan nervous system essentially consists of pairs of ganglia (masses of nerve tissue), each ganglion linked by nerve fibers. In the more primitive groups, the individual ganglia are well separated, but in more highly evolved mollusks, such as land snails and whelks, there is both a shortening of the connectives, bringing the ganglia into closer association, and a concentration of most of the ganglia in the head. The ring of ganglia round the front part of the gut (esophagus) in mollusks, compares with the nervous system of annelids and arthropods. The main pairs of ganglia in mollusks are the cerebral, pleural, pedal, parietal, visceral, and buccal (receiving impulses from the head, mantle, foot, body wall and internal organs), and there is a pedal "ladder" arrangement in monoplacophorans, chitons and the more primitive prosobranchs such as slit shells. In prosobranch gastropods there is the further complication of torsion.

The majority of mollusks are sensitive to light, which can be detected by sensors in the shell plates of chitons, the black eyespots associated with the tentacles of most gastropods, and the extremely elaborate cephalopod eye. The balance of the animal is maintained by special fluid-filled sacs, known as statocysts, containing mineral grains. Prosobranchs have a special chemosensory organ, the osphradium, but there are less specialized patches of chemosensory cells in other mollusks. The terrestrial slugs have a sense of smell, which they use to locate food.

Mollusks are also sensitive to touch: the suckers of octopuses can discriminate texture and pattern (see Learning in the Octopus), while the lower pair of tentacles of land pulmonates are largely tactile and function in feeling the way ahead.

The Foot
MOVEMENT

Some mollusks (e.g. mussels and oysters) anchor themselves to one place, but most move around in pursuit of food, for mating and to escape enemies. The octopus crawls, using suckers on its arms, modifications of the foot. Despite the mollusks' slow image, some, like cephalopods, can swim surprisingly fast.

Usually the foot is the organ involved in locomotion, which involves gliding over the surface of seabed, rock or plant. Land snails and slugs, particularly, lay down a lubricating and protective

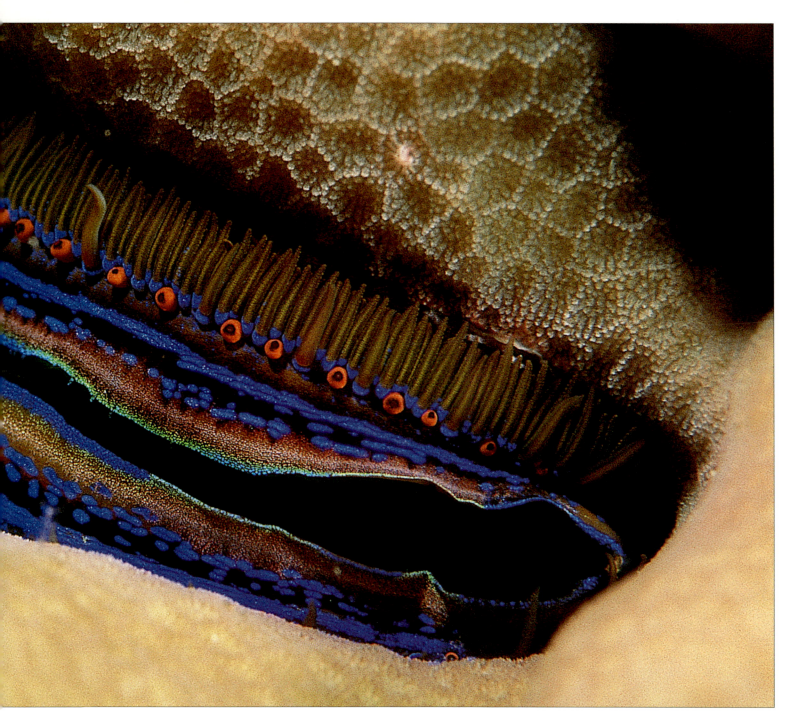

film of slime or mucus – the silvery trails seen on garden paths and walls. Some species "leap" with long stretches of the foot; the head lunges forward and attaches to ground ahead. Lobes of the foot (parapodia), are often developed for swimming in the sea slugs, and the pelagic thin-shelled *Limacina* and sluglike *Clione* species also have swimming "wings." The sea slugs, freed from the restrictions of a shell, can swim by lateral movements using muscles in the body wall.

Planktonic larvae and some small gastropods move primarily by the beating action of cilia. Veliger larvae of gastropods and bivalves have minute, hairlike cilia on the lobes of the enlarged

◗ **Right** *Gastropods, such as the Roman snail (Helix pomatia) move forward by creating undulating contractions of the foot. This species can cover around 7cm/min.; aquatic species are generally faster.*

velum which are used for feeding, respiration, and locomotion. They are also able to adjust their depth by retreating into the shell to sink, then re-expanding the velum to halt the descent. Many pond snails move by cilia on the sole of the foot, and can glide along the surface film of water by this method . On land, where the body weight is not supported by water, snails moving by ciliary means are more likely to be the smaller species. Bivalves may swim by shell-flapping (scallops), they may "leap" across the surface (cockles), or burrow. Cockles use the pointed foot for moving the shell across the surface of the sand. Most bivalves, however, use the foot (which can be of considerable size) for burrowing; it is pushed forward and expanded by blood entering the pedal hemocoel (blood space); the muscles of the foot also contract and it then changes shape, often forming an anchor. Further contraction brings the shell down into the sand; as the shell closes, water jetted out of the mantle cavity can help to loosen the sand ahead. The digging cycle then starts again.

The Ubiquitous Mollusk

ECOLOGY

Mollusks have colonized the sea, fresh water, and land. Tropical regions tend to have a more diverse fauna than temperate belts, although temperate New Zealand has one of the richest molluskan land faunas.

Marine habitats can include rocky, coral, sandy, muddy, boulder and shingle shores and also the transitions between freshwater, sea and land found in salt marshes, brackish lagoons, mangrove swamps and estuaries. Beyond the molluskan fauna of the shores is that of the ocean, with communities below the lowtide mark in comparatively shallow water of continental shelves. There is a mosaic of different types of communities on the sea floor, mostly relating to differences in bottom materials. Certain mollusks, like squids, can form part of the free-swimming animal population (nekton) in open water. The veliger larvae of most marine mollusks float passively in the upper waters of the sea, part of the plankton. A few prosobranchs (violet sea snails and heteropods) and opisthobranchs (pteropods or sea butterflies) spend their entire adult lives on or just below the surface as part of the pelagic community. Deep waters of the abyss were once thought to be devoid of life but investigations have revealed a limited but characteristic fauna. With some exceptions (e.g. squids) abyssal mollusks are small.

Freshwater habitats colonized by mollusks include running waters of streams and rivers, still waters of lakes, ponds, canals, and temporary waters of swamps, all with their own range of species. There are both bivalves and gastropods living in freshwater, the latter including both prosobranchs and aquatic pulmonates. Foreign species can spread dramatically like the freshwater

fingernail clam *Corbicula manilensis*, introduced from Asia to the USA, where it now clogs canals, pipes and pumps. Only the gastropods have successfully colonized land; they include both prosobranchs and pulmonates, although the latter, as both slugs and snails, are the most common in temperate climates.

In the food chains of the sea, mollusks are eaten by other mollusks, as well as by starfish and by bottom-living fish such as rays. Some starfish are notorious predators of commercial mollusks such as oysters and mussels. Some whales eat large quantities of squid. On the shore seabirds probe in mud for mollusks which can form a substantial part of their diet. Such predation by animals which are part of the natural ecosystem can usually be tolerated by mollusks, as they can be prolific breeders.

A few mollusk species have adopted the parasitic way of life. They are nearly all gastropods, with a few bivalves. Among the prosobranchs are parasites on the exterior of the host (ectoparasites), such as needle whelks (eulimids), which are parasites of echinoderms but look like normal gastropods. Internal parasites (endoparasites) are less active and have reduced body organs and less shell. The caplike genus *Thyca* lives attached to the underside of starfish, in the radial groove under the arms. *Stilifer*, which penetrates the skin of echinoderms, has a shell but it is enclosed in fleshy flaps of proboscis (pseudopallium) outside the skin of the host. The further inside the host a parasite is, the more the typical molluskan structure is lost.

Empty gastropod shells are often used by hermit crabs. Commensalism, in which one partner feeds on the food scraps of the other, is shown by the small bivalves *Devonia perrieri*, *Mysella bidentata*, and *Montacuta* species ,which live with sea cucumbers, brittle stars, and heart urchins respectively. Symbiosis is shown by the presence of algae (zooxanthellae) in the tissues of sea slugs such as *Elysia* and *Tridachia* species and also in the mantle edge of the Giant clam.

Mollusks are also hosts to their own parasites, many of which may have become established via commensalism. Most parasites of mollusks are larvae of two-suckered flukes. Two commercially and medically important parasites are the liver fluke of sheep and cattle (*Fasciola hepatica*) and blood flukes or bilharzia of humans (see Pathogenic Parasites). Mollusks can also be parasitized by arthropods. Familiar examples are the small white mites *Riccardoella limacum* found crawling on the skin of slugs and snails and the small pea crab, *Pinnotheres pisum*, living in the mantle cavity of the Edible mussel.

Mollusks have long been used in human culture for food, fishing bait and hooks, currency, dyes, pearl, lime, tools, jewelry and ornament. Mother-of-pearl buttons were once manufactured from the shells of freshwater mussels, particularly

in the USA, where these mussels were originally common in the rivers. Most pearls come from marine pearl oysters, but at one time fine pearls were obtained from the Freshwater pearl mussel which occurred notably in upland rivers of Wales, Scotland and Ireland. Today pearls are cultured commercially by inserting a "seed pearl" inside the mantle skirt of the oyster.

Mediterranean cooks are famous for their seafood dishes which utilize gastropods such as necklace shells, top shells, ormers, murexes and occasionally limpets; bivalves such as mussels, scallops, date mussels, venus shells, carpet shells, wedge shells, and razor shells; and also cephalopods including cuttlefishes, squids and octopuses. The traditional "escargot" of French cuisine is the pulmonate Roman snail. On the east coast of the USA the hardshell clams used by

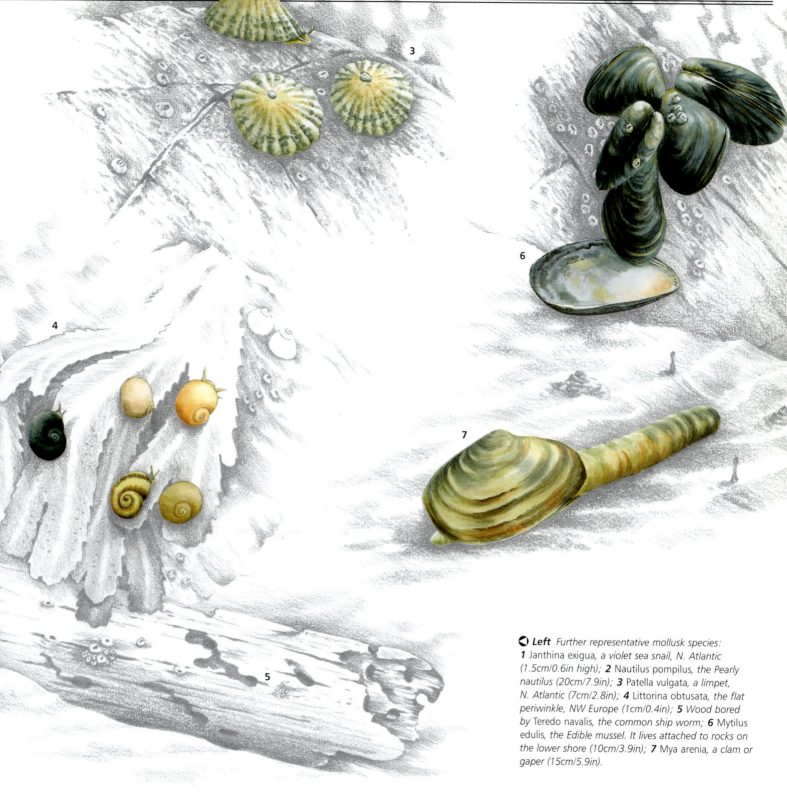

⟨⟩ **Left** *Further representative mollusk species:*
1 Janthina exigua, *a violet sea snail, N. Atlantic
(1.5cm/0.6in high);* **2** Nautilus pompilus, *the Pearly
nautilus (20cm/7.9in);* **3** Patella vulgata, *a limpet,
N. Atlantic (7cm/2.8in);* **4** Littorina obtusata, *the flat
periwinkle, NW Europe (1cm/0.4in);* **5** *Wood bored
by* Teredo navalis, *the common ship worm;* **6** Mytilus
edulis, *the Edible mussel. It lives attached to rocks on
the lower shore (10cm/3.9in);* **7** Mya arenia, *a clam or
gaper (15cm/5.9in).*

cooks are quahogs (introduced from waste fom the galleys of transatlantic liners to the Solent in southern England), while softshell clams are from a range of genera including gapers, carpet shells and trough shells.

Both slugs and snails can be pests of agriculture and horticulture. The mollusks are controlled by biological, cultural and chemical methods, the latter being the ones most usually employed.

A few marine mollusks also affect human activity. Bivalves like the shipworm bore into marine timbers, and gastropods – including the slipper limpet and oyster drill – are pests of oyster beds.

The major threats to mollusks are habitat destruction and pollution – the latter being more important for aquatic species, which are subject to crude oil spills, heavy metals, detergents, fertilizer in agricultural runoff, and acid rain from distant industry. Native land snails of deciduous woodland in the American Midwest, for example, often cannot cope with the more rigorous conditions of cleared land. In consequence, much North American farmland has been colonized by European mollusks, especially slugs, introduced with plants.

In addition to the harvesting of natural populations and measures limiting trade in shells, others aim to prevent introductions of non-native species. The Red List compiled by the World Conservation Union (IUCN) collates data on endangered species that can be used in their conservation.

Little is known of the molluskan fauna of some of the potentially richest and most threatened habitats, many of which are delicate and intolerant of disturbance. Hundreds of snail species are likely to be exterminated before they are even described and studied.

The 7 Classes of Mollusks

THIS TAXONOMIC ACCOUNT INCLUDES ALL species, genera, and families mentioned in the text. For reasons of space, divisions such as suborder sand superfamilies, important in some groups, have been omitted. The sequence of families reflects their relationships. The Gastropoda and Bivalvia are the 2 classes which between them contain around 1,048 threatened species.

CLASS MONOPLACOPHORA

Monoplacophorans
25 species, including *Neopilina galathea*.

CLASS APLACOPHORA

Solenogasters, Chaetoderms
About 370 species in 2 subclasses: Solenogastres, including *Epimenia verrucosa*; and Caudofoveata.

CLASS POLYPLACOPHORA

Chitons or Coat-of-mail shells
About 1,000 species, including the Giant Pacific chiton (*Amicula stelleri*) and *Mopalia* species.

CLASS GASTROPODA

Slugs and Snails (gastropods)
About 60,000–75,000 species in 3 subclasses. In this class alone there are over 1,000 threatened species, mostly within the Monotocardia, Basommatophora, and Stylommatophora.

PROSOBRANCHS OR OPERCULATES
SUBCLASS PROSOBRANCHIA

ORDER DIOTOCARDIA
Families, genera and species include: Slit shells (family Pleurotomariidae), including *Pleurotomaria* species; ormers and abalones (family Haliotidae), including *Haliotis* species; slit and keyhole limpets (family Fissurellidae), including *Diodora*, *Fissurella* species, Great keyhole limpet (*Megathura crenulata*); true limpets (family Patellidae), including Common limpet (*Patella vulgata*), Bluerayed limpet (*Patina pellucida*); top shells (family Trochidae), including Thick top shell (*Monodonta lineata*); turban shells (family Turbinidae), including Tapestry turban (*Turbo petholatus*); pheasant shells (family Phasianellidae), including Pheasant shell (*Tricolia pullus*), Australian pheasant shell (*Phasianella australis*).

ORDER MONOTOCARDIA
Mesogastropods: Apple snails (family Ampullariidae), including *Pila*, *Pomacea* species; river snails (family Viviparidae), including *Viviparus viviparus*; winkles or

periwinkles (family Littorinidae), including Dwarf winkle (*Littorina neritoides*), Flat winkle (*L. littoralis*), Edible winkle (*L. littorea*); roundmouthed snails (family Pomatiidae), including *Pomatias elegans*; spire snails (family Hydrobiidae), including Jenkins' spire shell (*Potamopyrgus jenkinsi*); family Omalogyridae, including *Ammonicera rota*; vermetids (family Vermetidae), including *Vermetus* species; sea snails (family Janthinidae), including Violet sea snail (*Janthina janthina*); family Styliferidae (parasites), including *Stylifer*, *Gasterosiphon* species; family Eulimidae (parasites), including *Eulima*, *Balcis* species; family Entoconchidae (parasites), including *Entoconcha*, *Entocolax*, *Enteroxenos* species; slipper limpets, cup-and-saucer and hat shells (family Calyptraeidae), including Atlantic slipper limpet (*Crepidula fornicata*); family Capulidae (parasites), including *Thyca* species; ostrich foot shells (family Struthiolariidae), including *Struthiolaria* species; conch shells (family Strombidae), including Pink conch shell (*Strombus gigas*); cowries (family Cypraeidae), including Money cowrie (*Cypraea moneta*), Gold ringer (*C. annulus*); necklace and moon shells (family Naticidae), including *Natica* species. About 369 species are threatened: 3 *Aylacostoma* species are Extinct in the Wild, including *A. stigmaticum*; 40 species are Critically Endangered, including 7 species of the pebblesnail *Somatogyrus*; and 100 species are Endangered, including *Beddomeia fallax*, *Graziana klazenfurtensis*, *Jardinella pallida*, *Lanistes solidus*.
Neogastropods: Whelks (Buccinidae), including Edible whelk (*Buccinum undatum*); dog whelks (family Nassariidae), including *Bullia tahitensis*; spindle shells (family Fasciolariidae), including *Fasciolaria* species; rock shells or murexes (family Muricidae), including *Murex* species, Common dog whelk (*Nuceila lapillus*), Oyster drill (*Urosalpinx cinerea*); volutes (Volutidae), including *Voluta* species; olives (family Olividae), including *Oliva* species; turret shells (family Turridae); cones (family

Conidae), including Courtly cone (*Conus aulicus*), Geographer cone (*C. geographicus*), Marbled cone (*C. marmoreus*), Textile cone (*C. textile*), Tulip cone (*C. tulipa*); auger shells (family Terebridae), including *Terebra* species.
7 species are listed as threatened by the IUCN: 4 *Conus* species are Vulnerable, including *C. africanus*, and 3 are Lower Risk/Near Threatened, including *Latiaxis babelis* and 2 *Ranella* species.

SEA SLUGS AND BUBBLE SHELLS
SUBCLASS OPISTHOBRANCHIA

BUBBLE SHELLS ORDER BULLOMORPHA
Acteon shells (family Acteonidae), *Acteon* species; bubble shells (family Hydatinidae), including *Hydatina* species; cylindrical bubble shells (family Retusidae), including *Retusa* species; bubble shells (family Bullidae), including *Bullaria* species; lobe shells (family Philinidae), including *Philine* species; canoe shells (family Scaphandridae), including *Scaphander* species.

ORDER PYRAMIDELLOMORPHA
Pyramid shells (family Pyramidellidae).

ORDER THECOSOMATA
Sea butterflies or pteroptods (family Spiratellidae), including *Limacina* species.

ORDER GYMNOSOMATA
Sea butterflies or pteropods (family Clionidae), including *Clione* species.

ORDER APLYSIOMORPHA
Sea hares (family Aplysiidae), including *Aplysia* species.

ORDER PLEUROBRANCHOMORPHA

ORDER ACOCHLIDIACEA
Family Hedylopsidae, including *Hedylopsis* species; family Microhedylidae, including *Microhedyle* species.

ORDER SACOGLOSSA
Bivalve gastropoids (family Julidae), including *Berthelinia limax*; family Elysiidae, including *Elysia*, *Tridachia* species; family

Stiligeridae, including *Hermaea* species; family Limapontiidae, including *Limapontia* species.

SHELL-LESS SEA SLUGS
ORDER NUDIBRANCHIA
Sea slugs (family Dendronotidae), including *Dendronotus* species; sea lemons (suborder Doridacea); family Tethyidae, including *Melibe leonina*; family Aeolidiidae, including Common gray sea slug (*Aeolidia papillosa*); floating sea slugs (family Glaucidae), including *Glaucus atlanticus*, *G. marginata*.

LUNGBREATHERS OR PULMONATES
SUBCLASS PULMONATA

TROPICAL SLUGS
ORDER SYSTELLOMMATOPHORA
Genera include: *Veronicella*.

POND AND MARSH SNAILS
ORDER BASOMMATOPHORA
Operculate pulmonates (family Amphibolidae), including *Salinator* species; dwarf pond snails (family Lymnaeidae), including *Lymnaea trunculata*; bladder snails (family Physidae), including *Physa* species, Moss bladder snail (*Aplexa hypnorum*); ramshorn snails (family Planorbiidae), including *Bulinus*; freshwater limpets (family Ancylidae).

Class Monoplacophora
Monoplacophorans

Class Aplacophora
Solenogasters, chaetoderms

Class Polyplacophora
Chitons or coat-of-mail shells

Class Gastropoda
Slugs and snails (gastropods)

▶ **Right** *The Panama Horse conch (Fasciolaria princeps), a gastropod, is an aggressive predator that feeds on other mollusks.*

Class Scaphopoda
Tusk or tooth shells

Class Bivalvia (Pelecypoda)
Clams and mussels (bivalves)

Class Cephalopoda
Cephalopods

Arctica islandica; Zebra mussel (family Dreissenidae), *Dreissena polymorpha*; Ruddy lasaea (family Erycinidae), *Lasaea rubra*; family Galleomatidae, including *Devonia perrieri*; montagu shells (family Montacutidae), including *Montacuta* species, *Mysella bidentata*; venus and carpet shells (family Veneriidae), including Venus shells (*Venus* species) – quahog or Hard-shell clam (*V. mercenaria*), smooth Venus (*Callista* species) – carpet shells (*Venerupis* species); False piddock (family Petricolidae), *Petricola pholadiformis*, oval piddocks (*Zirfaea* species); wedge shells or bean clams (family Donacidae), including *Donax* species; Tellins (family Tellinidae), including *Tellina folinacea*.

4 species of *Tridacna* are classed as Vulnerable by the IUCN, including *T. gigas* and *T. rosewateri*.

ORDER ADEPEDONTA

Trough shells (family Mactridae), including *Spisula* species; razor shells (family Solenidae), including *Ensis* species; gapers (family Myidae), including *Mya, Platyodon* species; Rock borer or Red nose (family Hiatellidae), *Hiatella arctica*; flask shells (family Gastrochaenidae), including *Gastrochaena* species; piddocks (family Pholadidae), including *Pholas* species, wood piddocks (*Xylophaga* species); shipworms (family Teredinidae), including *Teredo* species.

SEPTIBRANCHS
ORDER ANOMALODESMATA

Dipper clams (family Cuspidariidae), including *Cuspidaria* species.

CLASS CEPHALOPODA

Cephalopods
About 900 species in 3 subclasses.

NAUTILOIDS
SUBCLASS NAUTILOIDEA

Includes Pearly nautilus, *Nautlius* species.

AMMONITES†
SUBCLASS AMMONOIDEA

Including Giant ammonite (*Titanites titan*).

SUBCLASS COLEOIDEA

CUTTLEFISHES ORDER DECAPODA
Cuttlefishes, including *Sepia, Sepiola* species; squids, including *Loligo* species, flying squid (*Onycoteuthis* species), Giant squid (*Architeuthis harveyi*); also extinct belemites.

ORDER VAMPYROMORPHA
Including *Vampyroteuthis infernalis*.

OCTOPUSES ORDER OCTOPODA
Including *Octopus* species, Paper nautilus (*Argonauta* species).

About 39 species are endangered: 8 are Critically Endangered, including *Gyraulus cockburni, Lantzia carinata*; 5 are Endangered, including *Afrogyrus rodriguezensis, Glyptophysa petiti*; 15 are Vulnerable, including *Bulinus nyassanus*.

LAND SNAILS AND SLUGS
ORDER STYLOMMATOPHORA

Hawaiian tree snails (family Achatinellidae), including *Achatinella* species; whorl snails (family Vertiginidae), including *Vertigo* species; african land snails (family Achatinidae), including *Archachatina maryinata*; family Oleacinidae, including *Euglundina* species; shelled slugs (family Testacellidae), including *Testacella* species; glass snails (family Zonitidae), including Garlic snail (*Oxychilus alliarius*), *Aegopis verticillus*; family Limacidae, including Gray field slug (*Deroceras reticulatum*), Great gray slug (*Limax maximus*); family Chamaemidae, including *Amphidromus* species; family Helicidae, including Brownlipped snail (*Cepaea nemoralis*), Common garden snail (*Helix lucorum*), Roman snail (*H. pomatia*), Desert snail (*Eremina desertorum*), *Eobania vermiculata, Otaila lactea*; carnivorous snails (family Streptaxidae).

About 620 species are threatened: 9 species (all genus *Partula*) are Extinct in the Wild, including *P. hebe*; 116 species are Critically Endangered, including 24 species of

Achatinella, 9 species of *Opanara*, and 7 species of *Belgrandiella*; 101 species are Endangered including *Ampelita julii, Bellamia robertsoni, Hirasea insignis, Thapsia snelli*, and *Victaphanta compacta*.

CLASS SCAPHOPODA

Tusk or Tooth shells
About 900 species. Family Dentaiiidae, including Elephant tusk shell (*Dentalium elephantinum*); family Cadulidae, including *Cadulus* species.

CLASS BIVALVIA (PELECYPODA)

Clams and Mussels (bivalves)
About 20,000 species in 7 orders. 157 species are listed as threatened by the IUCN.

ORDER PROTOBRANCHIA

Includes nut shells (family Nuculidae), including *Nucula* species.

ARK SHELLS, DOG COCKLES
ORDER TAXODONTA

Includes dog cockles (family Glycimeridae), including *Glycimeris* species.

ORDER ANISOMYARIA

Mussels (family Mytilidae), including Date mussels (*Lithophaga* species), Edible m

ussel (*Mytilus edulis*), *Botulus, Fungiacava* species; pearl oysters (family Ptetiidae), including *Pinctada martensii*; scallops (family Pectinidae), including *Pecten* species, Queen scallop (*Aequipecten opercularis*); file shells (family Limidae), including *Lima* species; saddle oysters (family Anomiidae), including Window oyster (*Placuna placenta*), oysters (family Ostreidae), including *Ostrea, Crassostrea* species.

ORDER SCHIZODONTA

Freshwater pearl mussel (family Margaritiferidae), *Margaritifera margaritifera*; freshwater or river mussels (family Unionidae), including *Unio, Anodonta, Lampsilis* species; tropical freshwater mussels (family Aetheriidae), including *Aetheria* species. Around 52 species are Critically Endangered, including the Oyster mussel (*Epioblasma capsaeformis*), Marshall's mussel (*Pleurobema marshalli*); 28 are Endangered, including the Georgia spiny mussel (*Elliptio spinosa*), Dwarf wedge mussel (*Alasmidonta heterodon*); 8 species are Vulnerable.

ORDER HETERODONTA

Cockles (family Cardiidae); giant clams (family Tridacnidae), including *Tridacna gigas, T. crocea*; pea shells (family Sphaeriidae), *Pisidium* species; Fingernail clam (family Corbiculidae), *Corbicula manilensis*; Adantic hardshell clam (family Arctidae),

Monoplacophorans

CLASS MONOPLACOPHORA

First of the seven classes in the phylum, the Monoplacophora is a small group of primitive mollusks that were originally thought to have gone extinct about 400 m.y.a. The flattish caplike shell of monoplacophorans resembles that of limpets, and the groups used to be classified with the gastropods.

In 1952 living monoplacophorans were collected 3,750m (11,700ft) down in a Pacific Ocean deepsea trench off South America, and a new species of monoplacophoran, *Neopilina galathea*, was described. The shell is pale, fairly thin, caplike in shape and about 2.5cm (1in) long. On its inner surface, instead of the single horseshoe-shaped muscle scar of limpets, there are several pairs of muscle scars in a row on either side.

The particularly interesting feature of *Neopilina galathea* is the repetition of pairs of body organs: there are eight pairs of retractor muscles attaching the animal to the shell, 5–6 pairs of gills, 6–7 pairs of excretory organs, a primitive ladderlike pedal-nervous system with 10 connectives across, and two pairs of gonads. Although there is a parallel in chitons (see below), in monoplacophorans this repetition is taken much further. In consequence, it has been suggested that mollusks evolved from an annelid/arthropod ancestor, rather than from an unsegmented flatworm, and that the original segmentation of the body was lost during early molluskan evolution. Some other researchers disagree, considering the repetition of body organs to be a more recent, secondary character, rather than a primitive one.

In *Neopilina galathea* there is a molluskan radula and posterior mantle cavity and anus, showing that torsion (the twisting of body organs found in gastropods) did not occur in the monoplacophorans. Since the original discovery, further living species of monoplacophorans have been found in deepwater trenches in other parts of the world such as Aden, Yemen, and now five living species are described.

Solenogasters and Chaetoderms

CLASS APLACOPHORA

The shell-less aplacophorans are curious wormlike creatures found in the mud of marine deposits, usually offshore. This small and little-understood group was once classified with the chitons, but is now placed in a group of its own. Indeed, recent research suggests that the class Aplacophora should be divided into two classes, the solenogasters (class Solenogastres) and the chaetoderms (class Caudofoveata).

Aplacophorans do not have an external shell, although there may be tiny, pointed calcareous spicules in the skin, sometimes of a silvery, "furlike" appearance. In common with other mollusks, most possess a radula, a mantle, mantle cavity, a foot, and a molluskan-type pelagic larva. There are dorsoventral muscles crossing the body, reminiscent of similar structures in flatworms, flukes and tapeworms.

Most species are small, but the solenogaster *Epimenia verrucosa* can reach 30cm (12in) in length. Solenogasters are fairly mobile and can twist their bodies around other objects; the foot is reduced to a ventral groove. Chaetoderms (named for their spiny skin), live in mud, moving like earthworms but spending much of their time in a burrow. The radula is often reduced in this group.

Above *Hatching eggs of the Garden snail* (Helix aspersa). *Newly hatched snails have a tiny, fragile shell, and take about two years to reach maturity.*

Left *Most chitons are herbivorous, but this species,* Craspedochiton laqueatus, *is a carnivore that feeds primarily on small crustaceans.*

Chitons or Coat-of-mail Shells

CLASS POLYPLACOPHORA

Chitons have a dinstinctive oval shell consisting of eight plates bounded by a girdle. They are exclusively marine and, with the exception of a few deepwater species, mostly limited to shores and continental shelves. Beneath the shell with its low profile and stable shape, the animal attaches to the rock by a suckerlike foot. The plates of the shell are well articulated – chitons can roll up into a ball when disturbed. The articulations are also an advantage when moving over the uneven surface of rocks.

Although there are no obvious eyes, chitons are sensitive to light through receptors in the shell. They are found mostly on rocky shores. When a boulder is turned over, chitons on the underside quickly move down again out of the light.

Chitons have remained substantially unchanged since the Cambrian period 543–490 m.y.a. The different species are identified by the relative width of the girdle protecting the mantle, by the sculpturing of the shell valves and the bristles they bear, and also the teeth and the surfaces of the joins between the valves. Most chitons are 1–3cm (0.4–1.2in) long, but some, like the Giant Pacific chiton can reach 20–30cm (8–12in). The larger and more spectacular species are found on the Pacific coast of the USA and off Australia.

Chitons are browsers, rasping algae and other encrusting organisms off the rock with the hard teeth of the radula. One family, the Mopaliidae, is carnivorous, feeding on crustaceans and worms.

The anatomy of the chiton is closer to that of the primitive ancestor than the more highly evolved gastropods. The mantle cavity and anus are situated toward the rear. The mantle extends forward and houses several pairs of gills, rather more than in most other classes of mollusks. Chitons resemble monoplacophorans and the more primitive groups of prosobranchs, such as the ormers and the top shells, in the ladderlike nervous system with paired ventral nerves and cross-connections. Sexes are separate in the chitons and the eggs are fertilized externally.

Slugs, Snails and Whelks (Gastropods)
CLASS GASTROPODA

This largest class of mollusks contains three-quarters of the living species and shows the greatest variation in body and shell form, function, and way of life. Unlike the other classes, which are all aquatic, gastropods have also adapted very successfully to life on land and they have achieved greater diversity in freshwater than the bivalves. Gastropods occur in all climatic zones of the world, colonizing the sea, brackish and freshwater habitats, and land. They are among the earliest molluskan fossils.

In the more primitive prosobranchs, gastropods with a caplike shell, such as slit shells and ormers, which have a trochophore larva with only a short pelagic phase, torsion occurs after the larva has settled. In the more advanced prosobranchs, such as winkles and whelks, the newly hatched veliger larva already has the mantle cavity to the front. Sea slugs and bubble shells do not retain torsion in adult life; loss of shell was influential in the development of this trend. Land and pond snails and slugs have retained torsion, but their nervous system is not twisted.

For the larva, torsion may provide a space into which the animal can quickly contract, enabling it to sink out of danger, or to reach the bottom for settling when it metamorphoses. Advantages of torsion for the adult may include the use of mantle cavity sensors for testing the water ahead or possibly the intake of cleaner water not stirred up by the foot, and providing a space into which the head can be withdrawn. Besides the looping of the

⮣ **Below** *Body plan of a lung-breathing freshwater snail. Characteristic of gastropods are the flat, creeping foot sole, the distinct head with tentacles, mantle, and coiled shell made of one piece (univalve). In most gastropods, rotation (torsion) of the body in the developing embryo (**1–3**) has brought the opening of the mouth cavity, anus, and other organs to the front, and the nervous system is twisted. Sea slugs and Bubble shells lose torsion in adult life, and the nervous system of land gastropods is not twisted.*

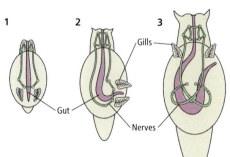

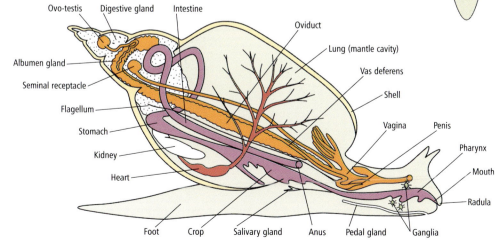

alimentary canal and reorientation of the reproductive organs, torsion causes the twisting of the prosobranch nervous system (streptoneury).

The spiral coiling of the gastropod shell is a separate phenomenon from torsion. Coiling occurs also in some of the cephalopods (e.g. nautiluses), which do not exhibit torsion, and is a way of making a shell compact. If the primitive caplike shell had become tall it would have been unstable as the animal moved along. Spiral coiling is brought about by different rates of growth on the two sides of the body. During their evolutionary history, various spirally coiled mollusks in the gastropods, extinct ammonites and nautiloids have uncoiled, producing loosely coiled shells, tubular forms or, in for example limpets, a return to the caplike shape.

Prosobranchs
SUBCLASS PROSOBRANCHIA

The prosobranchs include most of the gastropod seashells – limpets, top shells, winkles, cowries, cones and whelks – as well as a number of land and freshwater species. The prosobranchs, or operculates, have separate sexes, unlike the two other subclasses of gastropod which are hermaphrodite, and the mouth of the shell is usually, except in limpet forms, protected by a lid or operculum (see below). Aquatic prosobranchs have a gill in the mantle cavity, together sometimes, especially in the carnivorous groups, with a chemical sense organ (osphradium) and slime-secreting hypobranchial gland. The mantle and associated structures exhibit torsion and as a result of this the principal nerves are twisted into a figure-8 in the more highly evolved orders (Mesogastropoda and Neogastropoda).

In marine species there is usually a planktonic trochophore or veliger larval stage which helps to distribute the species.

Prosobranchs live in sea, brackish and fresh water and on land and have an ancient fossil history going back to the Cambrian. Terrestrial prosobranchs are more abundant and varied in the tropical regions than in temperate zones. Shells vary in shape from the typical coiled snail shell to the caplike shells of limpets and the tubular form of the warm-water vermetids (family Vermetidae) that look from the shell more like marine worm-tubes than mollusks. This diverse group exploits most opportunities in feeding from a diet of algal slime, seaweed, detritus, suspended matter and plankton (ciliary feeders), to terrestrial plants, dead animal matter and other living animals.

The lid or operculum is secreted by glands on the upperside of the back of the foot. It is the last part of the animal to be withdrawn and therefore acts as a protective trapdoor. It keeps out predators and also prevents water loss in land prosobranchs and intertidal species. The operculum is present in the veliger larvae, even in limpets and slipper limpets which later lose the operculum.

⬤ **Above** The Warted egg cowry (Calpurnus verrucosus) lives only on Leather coral; the spots on its mantle blend perfectly with the coral for camouflage.

◗ **Right** An interesting defensive strategy is adopted by the Rough keyhole limpet (Diodora aspera). When threatened by a starfish, it raises itself and extends its mantle over its foot and the edge of its shell. This makes it hard for the starfish to gain any purchase.

The opercula of most prosobranchs are horny, but hard calcareous ones are found in some of the turban and pheasant shells. The thick operculum of the Tapestry turban shell is green and may be up to 2.5cm (1in) across: this is the "cat's eye" used for jewelry. The much smaller pheasant shell *Tricolia pullus* from northern Europe and the Australian pheasant shell and others have conspicuous white calcareous opercula.

The different shapes of opercula usually fit the form of the mouth of the shell. Shells with a narrow aperture like cones, for example, have a tall narrow operculum. In some species, such as the whelk *Bullia tahitensis*, there are teeth on the operculum. In the Pink conch shell these teeth are thought to be defenses against attack by predators that include tulip shells. In some species, particularly the land prosobranchs, the operculum may indeed be small, enabling the animal to retreat further inside its shell.

Sea slugs and Bubble shells (Opisthobranchs)
SUBCLASS OPISTHOBRANCHIA

Sea slugs and bubble shells are hermaphrodite – both male and female reproductive systems function in the same individual – and usually have a reduced shell, or none at all. Bubble shells do

CONES – THE VENOMOUS SNAILS

The 400–500 species of cone shells are found mostly in tropical and subtropical waters. These great favorites among collectors are unusual exceptions among mollusks, in that they are directly harmful to humans.

Cones are carnivores, taking a range of prey, from marine worms to sizable fish, and those feeding on fish are most dangerous. In common with other carnivorous gastropods, such as whelks, cones have a proboscis. This muscular retractable extension of the gut carries the mouth, radula and salivary gland forward to reach food in confined spaces or for other reasons at a point distinct from the animal. When the probing, extended proboscis of a cone touches a fish, it embeds one of the harpoonlike teeth on the tip of the radula into the prey, accompanied by a nerve poison which paralyzes the fish: the cone swallows the fish whole.

The Geographer cone, Textile cone (RIGHT), and Tulip cone have been known to kill humans, while others like the Courtly cone, Marble cone, and *Conus striatus* can cause an unpleasant, although not fatal, sting.   JEC

have a normal external shell, which in the Acteon shell looks very like that of a prosobranch, as it is fairly solid with a distinct spire. Most of the bubble shells, such as *Hydatina*, *Bullaria* and canoe shell species, have an inflated shell which consists mostly of body whorl with little spire, is rather brittle and houses a large animal. Other opisthobranchs have a reduced shell that is internal, for example the thin bubble shells of *Philine* and *Retusa* species. The sea hares have a simple internal shell plate in the mantle that is largely horny. A few species have a bivalve shell (see below). The rest of the sea slugs have lost their shell altogether. They include *Hedylopsis* species with hard spicules in the skin, *Hermaea* species and other sacoglossans such as *Limapontia*, and the large group of the nudibranchs (meaning "exposed-gills") or sea slugs, including the sea lemons, the family Aeolidiidae and Dendronotidae, and many others.

The bodies of opisthobranchs, particularly nudibranchs, can be very colorful. Although they may function as warning coloration or camouflage, little is known of the function of such bright colors, which are less vivid at depth under water. Some sea lemons emit acid from glands in the mantle as a defense against predators.

Opisthobranchs reproduce by laying eggs, often in conspicuous egg masses. The eggs hatch to veliger larvae.

Some species of bubble shells, such as *Retusa* and Acteon shells, have a blunt foot which they use to plow through surface layers of mud or sand. The round shell-less sea lemons creep slowly on the bottom with the flat foot, but many of the sea slugs are agile and beautiful swimmers, capable of speed. Sea butterflies or pteropods swim in surface waters of the oceans.

In 1959 a malacological surprise came to light – an animal with a typical bivalve shell but a gastropod body, complete with flat creeping sole and tentacles. This was *Berthelinia limax*, which was found living on the seaweed *Caulerpa* in Japan. Other bivalve gastropods have since been discovered, also on seaweed, in the Indo-Pacific and Caribbean as well as Japanese waters. They are classed with the sea slugs of the order Ascoglossa.

Bivalve gastropods have a single-coiled shell in the veliger larva. In mature shells this is sometimes retained at the prominent point (umbone) of the lefthand valve. This development of a bivalve shell in gastropods is an example of convergent evolution rather than evidence of an ancestor shared with the class Bivalvia.

Lungbreathers or Pulmonates
SUBCLASS PULMONATA

In pond snails, land snails and slugs the mantle wall is well supplied with blood vessels and acts as a lung. In parallel with this specialization, the lungbreathing snails have specialized in colonizing land and freshwater, although a few continue to live in marine habitats. Like the sea slugs and bubble shells, pulmonates are hermaphrodite, with a complex reproductive system: the free-swimming larval stage is lost in land and freshwater species and, except in the marine genus *Salinator*, there is no operculum.

The shell is usually coiled, although the varied shapes include the limpet form and in several unrelated families the shell is reduced or lost altogether, leading to the highly successful design of slugs. The thin shell of land snails still offers some protection against drying out, but is more portable and requires less calcium than do the shells of marine gastropods. Both snails and slugs further conserve body water by being active chiefly at night and by their tendency to seek out crevices. The shell-less slugs are freed from restriction to calcareous soils and can also retreat into deeper crevices.

The body is differentiated into a head with tentacles (one or two pairs), foot and visceral mass. The mantle and mantle cavity are at the front (still showing signs of torsion) but the entrance is sealed off except at the breathing pore (pneumostome), which can open and close. The mouthparts and their muscles (buccal mass) may incorporate both a radula and a jaw. Pulmonates are predominantly plant feeders although there are a few carnivores.

The subclass may be divided into three superorders. In the mostly tropical Systellommatophora the mantle envelops the body. The pond snails (superorder Basommatophora) have eyes at the

○ **Right** *The Blue dragon sea slug (Pteraeolina ianthina) is common in Southeast Asian and Australian waters. If disturbed, it sheds several of its cerata in the defensive strategy known as autotomy.*

base of their two tentacles, while the land snails and slugs have two pairs of tentacles and eyes at the tips of the hind pair.

Pulmonates succeed in less stable environments than the sea by their opportunistic behavior and the fact that they can enter a dormant state during adverse periods of cold (hibernation) or drought (estivation). A solidified plug of hardened mucus (epiphragm) can seal off the mouth of the shell and in some species, such as the Roman snail becomes hardened. Unlike the operculum of a prosobranch, the epiphragm is neither permanent nor attached by muscle tissue to the animal.

▌Tusk shells or Tooth shells
▌CLASS SCAPHOPODA

The tusk shells are a small group of around 900 species which are entirely marine and live buried in sand or mud of fairly deep waters. Only their empty shells are to be found on the beach. Tusk shells or scaphopods occur in temperate as well as tropical waters: the large Elephant tusk shell can be up to 10–13cm (4–5in) long. There are two families, the Dentaliidae, which include the large examples more commonly found, and the Siphon-odentaliidae (e.g. *Cadulus* species), which are shorter, smaller and less tubular in shape. The oldest fossil tusk shells known from the Ordovician period 490–443 m.y.a. Like the chitons, they have changed little and show very little diversity of body form and way of life.

The shell is tubular, tapering, curved and open at either end. Scaphopods position themselves in the sand with the narrow end protruding above the surface, and through this pass the inhalant

and exhalant currents of seawater, usually in bursts rather than as a continuous flow. The broader end of the shell is buried in the sand. From it the head and foot emerge: the foot creates a space in front into which the animal extends the tentacles of the head that pick up detritus, foraminiferans and

other microorganisms from the sand. The tentacles are sensory as well as collecting food and conveying it to the mouth. Food can be broken up by the radula, and the shells of forminiferans are further crushed by plates in the gizzard.

The anatomy of scaphopods is rather simple. The tube is lined by the mantle. There are no gills, oxygen being taken up by the mantle itself, which may have a few ridges with cells bearing tiny hair-like cilia that help to create a current. Oxygen may also be taken in through the skin of other parts of the body. There are separate sexes, fertilization takes place externally in the sea, and the egg hatches into a pelagic trochophore larva.

▌Clams, Mussels, Scallops (Bivalves)
▌CLASS BIVALVIA (OR PELECYPODA)

Members of this, the second largest class of mollusks with around 20,000 living species, are recognized by their shell of two valves which articulate through a hinge plate of teeth and a horny ligament which may be inside or outside the shell.

The bivalve shell can vary considerably in shape, from circular, as in dog cockles, to elongate, as in razor shells. It can be swollen (e.g.

BIVALVE BORERS

An important number of bivalves, from seven different superfamilies, have adapted from burrowing into soft sand and mud to boring into hard surfaces like mudstone, limestone, sandstone and wood, the woodboring habit being the most recent to evolve.

Boring developed from bivalves settling in crevices which they subsequently enlarged – one of the giant clams, *Tridacna crocea*, does this. Rock borers of the genus *Hiatella*, while able to use crevices, also erode tunnels of circular section. They push the shell hard against the wall of the burrow by pressure of water in the mantle cavity. At low tide, the red siphons can be seen protruding from holes in the rock low on the shore – they are sometimes known as red noses.

Most rock borers make their tunnels mechanically by rotation of the shell, often aided by spikes on the shell surface, which erodes the rock. The foot may attach the animal to the end of the burrow, as in piddocks. Closure of the siphons helps keep up fluid pressure. Rock raspings are passed out from the mantle as pseudofeces. While some borers form a tunnel of even width, flask shells (*Gastrochaena* spp.) are surrounded by a jacket of cemented shell fragments and live in a rock tunnel that is narrower at the entrance. The contracted siphons dilate outside the shell to form an anchorage during boring.

The date mussels of warm seas and other bivalves have an elongated smooth shell. They make round burrows in limestone by an acid secretion from mantle tissue which is applied to the end of the burrow. The thick, shiny brown periostracum protects the shell from the mollusk's own acid.

Among rock borers, *Botula*, *Platyodon* (gapers) and false piddocks drill in clays and mudstone, *Fungiacava* species in coral, and rock borers, flask shells, piddocks and oval piddocks, in rock. The piddocks are recognized by a projecting tooth (apophysis) inside, to which the foot muscles are attached.

Wood piddocks and shipworms burrow into wood. Wood in seawater is only a transitory habitat, and boring bivalves have thus adapted in many ways to make the most of what may be a short stay – high population densities, early maturation, prolific breeding and dispersal by pelagic veliger larvae.

Wood piddocks use the wood only for protection, feeding on plankton by normal filtration of seawater, while shipworms exploit the wood further by ingesting the shavings, from which with the aid of cellulase enzymes, they obtain sugar. Shipworms also feed by filtration, but in some species where most food comes from the wood gills are reduced in size. **JEC**

▶ **Right** *Body plan of a bivalve. The bivalve body consists of the mantle, often extended into one or two siphons, the visceral mass and relatively small foot. It lacks a developed head. Usually the siphons and foot can be seen protruding from the shell, but in mussels (*Mytilus, illustrated here*), they remain largely inside.*

◑ **Left** *Donax gouldii* bean clams mass on a Californian beach. Their super-abundance varies – in some years, there are thousands, in others hardly any.

◑ **Above** *Jet swimming by a scallop,* Pecten maximus, *to escape from a star-fish. It flaps its two shell valves, expelling jets of water from its mantle cavity.*

cockles) or flat (e.g. tellins) and can have radial or concentric shell sculpture (ridges, knobs and spines), bright colors and patterns.

The shell is closed by adductor muscles passing from one valve to the other. Where these attach to the shell, distinctive muscle scars are formed on the inside of the shell. The muscle scars are very important in the identifying and classifying of bivalves. In fossils they can provide clues to the way of life of long extinct species (fossil bivalves are known from the late Cambrian period). Some bivalves, such as oysters and scallops, have a single centrally placed muscle scar (monomyarian), but most have two adductor scars, one at each end of the valves, which may be of similar size, as in cockles, or of different sizes, as in mussels. Also on the inner surface of the shell the pallial

line, the scar of attachment of the lobes of mantle lining the shell, runs from one adductor muscle scar to the other. In those bivalves with small projecting mantle tubes (siphons), living on the surface or in shallow burrows, the pallial line is unbroken and parallel to the ventral margin of the shell, opposite the hinge. In the shells of burrowers (for example, venus shells and tellins) which have a long siphon, the pallial line is indented to provide an extra area for attachment of the muscles involved in contracting the siphon when the animal withdraws.

In most bivalves the pair of gills is large and fills the mantle cavity, performing a dual role of respiration and feeding. The primitive nut shells, however, have small gills which are respiratory only nut shells shovel detritus into the mouth with a

pair of labial palps. The carnivorous and more highly evolved dipper clams (septibranchs, e.g. *Cuspidaria* species) have replaced gills with a wall which controls water flow into the mantle cavity. They feed on very small crustaceans and worms drawn in with water.

The bivalve reproductive system is very simple. The sexes are usually separate, although some, like oysters, do alter sex during their lives. The eggs are fertilized externally, in the sea or in the mantle cavity, by sperm taken in with surrounding water. There is a pelagic bivalve veliger larva in most species.

Most species live in the sea, but some have colonized brackish and freshwater. The adults lead a relatively inactive life buried in the substrate, or firmly attached to rock by cement or byssus threads, or boring into stone and wood. A few, like scallops and file shells, flap the valves and swim by jet propulsion.

Octopuses, Squids, Cuttlefishes, and Nautiluses

CLASS CEPHALOPODA

Cephalopods are quite different from the rest of the mollusks in their appearance and their specializations for life as active carnivores. The estimated 900 living species are all marine and include pelagic forms, swimmers of the open sea, and bottom-dwelling octopuses and cuttlefish. While octopuses can be found in rock crevices on the lower shore, most cephalopods usually occur further out and some penetrate deep abyssal waters,

Heart
Kidney
Digestive gland
Ganglion
Stomach
Muscle
Mouth
Exhalent (dorsal) siphon
Muscle
Inhalent (ventral) siphon
Palps
Gills
Shell
Mantle
Foot
Ganglia
Intestine
Gonad

like *Vampyroteuthis infernalis*, which lives 0.5–5km (0.3–3 miles) below the surface.

The cephalopods that flourished in the seas of the Mesozoic period over 65 m.y.a. included nautiloids, ammonites and belemnites. With the exception of nautiluses, these groups, most of which possessed shells, are now extinct.

Most modern cephalopods are descended from the extinct belemnites, which had internal shells.

Cephalopods are typically good swimmers, catching moving fish, and have evolved various buoyancy mechanisms. They are very responsive to stimuli, due to special giant nerve fibers (axons) with few nerve cell junctions (synapses). This enables messages to pass quickly to and from the brain. (Giant axons are also found in annelid worms and some other invertebrate groups.) The well-developed cephelopod eye focuses by moving its position rather than changing the shape of the lens. The high metabolic rate of cephalopods is also aided by a particularly efficient blood system with arteries and veins (other mollusks have arteries only) and extra branchial hearts.

All cephalopods except nautiluses have an ink sac opening off the rectum which contains ink, the original artists' sepia. Discharged as a cloud of dark pigment, this confuses an enemy. The cephalopod can also change color while escaping. Body color and tone are changed by means of pigment cells (chromatophores) in the skin. These are operated under control of the nervous system by muscles radiating from the edge of the chromatophore which can contract it, concentrating the pigment. Stripes and other patterns appear in the skin of cephalopods under certain conditions.

The possibility that these are a means of communication, for example in recognizing sex, is being investigated. In bottom-living species like cuttlefish (*Sepia* species), the chromatophores function as camouflage.

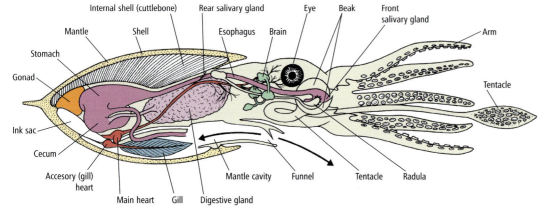

⬦ **Above** California market squid (Loligo opalescens). mating. Grasping the females from below, the males use their third arm (hectocotylus) to insert the spermatophore into the females' mantle cavity.

◁ **Left** Cephalopod body plan. A prominent head region is marked by mouth, eyes, arms, and a cartilage-protected brain.

● **Right** *The Paper nautilus (Argonauta nodosa) is not in fact a nautilus, but an octopus. The 'shell' is a thin egg-case produced by the female.*

● **Below** *With a mantle length of 30cm (12in), the Maori octopus (Octopus maorum) is the largest octopus found in Antipodean waters.*

The sexes are separate and the male fertilizes the female by placing a sperm package (spermatophore) inside her mantle cavity, where the sperm are released. The yolky eggs are large and there is often a pelagic stage like a miniature adult. Cuttlefish come to inshore waters to breed and after egg laying the spent bodies may be washed up on beaches.

Nautiluses have a brown and white coiled shell. When the nautilus is active, some 34 tentacles protrude from the brown and white coiled shell, and to one side of these are the funnel and hood. The hood forms a protective flap when the nautilus retreats into its shell.

Cuttlefishes are flattened and usually have a spongy internal shell. They often rest on the sea bottom but also may come up and swim. They have 10 arms, eight short and two longer ones, as in squids, for catching prey. The internal shell or "bone" is often found washed up on the seashore.

Squids are torpedo-shaped, active, and adapted for fast swimming. Unlike cuttlefishes, which are solitary, squids move around in shoals in pursuit of fish. The suckers on the 10 arms may be accompanied by hooks. The internal shell or pen is reduced to a thin membranous structure. Oceanic or flying squids can propel themselves through the surface of the water.

Octopuses have adapted to a more sedentary lifestyle, emerging from rock crevices in pursuit of prey. They can both swim and crawl, using the eight arms. Female octopuses often brood their eggs. The female Paper nautilus is rather unusual in secreting, from two modified arms, a large, thin shell-like eggcase in which she sits protecting the eggs. The male of the species is very small, only one tenth of the size of the female, and does not produce a shell. **JEC/AC**

LEARNING IN THE OCTOPUS

Octopuses have memory and are capable of learning. A food reward, coupled with a punishment of a mild electric shock, has successfully been used to train octopuses to respond to sight and touch. Sight is important to cephalopods in the recognition of prey. The well-developed eye of cephalopods approaches the acuity of the vertebrate eye more closely than that of any other invertebrate. Presented with two distinct shapes, one leading to a food reward and the other to an electric shock, the octopuses in the above test learned the "right" one after 20–30 trials, although they found some shapes easier to recognize than others, and mirror images of the same shape difficult to separate.

Similar experiments using only the tactile stimulus of cylinders with different patterns of grooves, have shown that octopuses distinguish between and respond differently to rough and smooth objects, different degrees of roughness, and objects with differing proportions of rough and smooth surfaces. Touch is perceived by tactile receptors in the octopus's suckers. Octopuses do not distinguish between objects of different weight, but they can recognize sharp edges and distinguish between inanimate objects and food.

Other researches into the brain and nervous systems of octopuses have led to important advances in knowledge of how nervous systems work in general. **JEC**

Sipunculans

SIPUNCULANS OCCUPY A VARIETY OF MARINE *habitats. Many live in temporary burrows in soft sediment, while others can bore into chalky (calcareous) rocks, as in the genera* Phascolosoma *and* Aspidosiphon, *or corals, as in* Cloeosiphon *and* Lithacrosiphon. *Some, such as* Phascolion, *inhabit empty gastropod shells. Most that have been studied so far are found in shallow waters.*

All sipunculans have an extensible introvert up to ten times the length of the trunk, with the mouth at its tip, which can be withdrawn completely into the trunk. It allows feeding at the substrate surface while the body remains protected, and can be readily regenerated if lost. The introvert is extended by fluid pressure brought about by contraction of the musculature of the trunk wall. In some cases, for example *Sipunculus* species, the circular and longitudinal muscle layers may be arranged in separate bundles. Up to four special muscles retract the introvert. The majority of sipunculans consume sediment, although some are thought to filter material from the water using cilia on their tentacles.

Excretion occurs through the one or two nephridia, which connect the large fluid-filled coelomic space to the exterior, opening on the front of the trunk. They also serve as storage organs for gametes immediately before spawning. Sipunculans have no blood vascular system; rather, the coelomic fluid performs the circulatory function.

Externally, sipunculans may have hooks or spines on the introvert and small protrusions (papillae) and glandular openings on the introvert and trunk. In many boring forms a horny or calcareous shield is present at the front end of the trunk, protecting the animal as it lies retracted in its burrow.

Asexual reproduction is known in only two species, sexual reproduction with separate sexes being the rule. Some populations of *Golfingia minuta* are hermaphrodite. In all sipunculans studied, much of the germ cell development occurs free in the coelomic fluid. At spawning, eggs and sperm are released via the nephridia, and fertilization occurs in the sea. The mode of larval development, however, varies between species and may include a free-swimming trochophore-

⬤ *Above* Phascolosoma annulatum, *with its introvert extended. This proboscis-like structure enables sipunculans to feed while keeping their bodies buried.*

⬤ *Below* Phascolion strombi, *a sipunculan that lines empty shells (e.g. that of* Turitella) *with mud and forms a burrow inside.*

type larva, or may be direct, with juvenile worms emerging from egg masses. In several species, the floating stage occupies a period of months, and long distance transportation of such larvae across the Atlantic has been suggested.

The genus *Golfingia* received its remarkable name from two famous 19th-century zoologists, Ray Lankester and W. C. McIntosh, who discovered a specimen of an animal new to science while playing golf on the Old Course at St Andrews, Scotland. This sipunculan was about the size of a human finger. PRG/AC

FACTFILE

SIPUNCULANS

Phylum: Sipuncula

About 250 species in 17 genera.

Distribution Worldwide. exclusively marine; intertidal down to 6,500m (21,000ft).

Size Trunk 1–50cm (0.4–20in); introvert half to 10 times as long as trunk.

Features Unsegmented worms with coelom; body divided into introvert and trunk; mouth at tip of retractable introvert; gut U-shaped with anus usually at front of trunk; possess 1–2 excretory nephridia; ventral nerve cord unsegmented; trunk wall of outer circular and inner longitudinal muscles; asexual reproduction rare; usually unisexual; larvae free-swimming. Families: Sipunculidae, including genus *Sipunculus*; Golfingiidae, including genera *Golfingia, Phascolion, Themiste*; Phascolosomatidae, genera *Phascolosoma, Fisherana*; Aspidosiphonidae, including genus *Aspinosiphon*.

Echiurans

IN COMMON WITH THE SIPUNCULANS AND *priapulans, echiurans are only really known to scientists – hence the lack of common names for these animals! They are wormlike, but their bodies are not segmented as in annelid worms. The small hooks at their posterior end gives the phylum its scientific name, which literally means 'spine-tails'.*

▶ **Right** Thalassema neptuni, *with its body buried in the substrate.*

▶ **Below** Metabonellia haswelli *extends its forked proboscis and generates mucus. In some species, the proboscis may measure as much as 1.5m (almost 5ft).*

Although they are mainly found in marine environments, a few echiuran species penetrate into brackish waters, and many members of the family Bonelliidae are found at very great depth.

Echiurans are delicate, soft-bodied animals that live either in soft sediments or under stones in semipermanent tubes, or inhabit crevices in rock or coral. Food, usually in the form of surface detritus, is caught up in mucus and transported by cilia down the muscular proboscis to the mouth. In *Urechis* species, a net of mucus is used to filter bacteria out of water pumped through the burrow, and the net is then consumed along with the food.

In *Urechis* the rear end of the gut is modified for respiration, rhythmic contractions of the hind gut

drawing in and expelling water. This may be linked to the absence of a blood circulatory system in this genus, the coelomic fluid containing blood cells having taken over this function. In all other echiurans the blood circulatory system is separate from the coelom.

FACTFILE

ECHIURANS OR SPOON WORMS

Phylum: Echiura

About 140 species in 34 genera.

Distribution Worldwide, largely marine but with a few brackish water species; intertidal down to 10,000m (33,000ft).

Size Length usually between 3 and 40cm (1.2–16in; trunk length excluding proboscis), occasionally up to 75cm (30in).

Features Unsegmented worms with coelom; trunk with muscular proboscis at front; mouth at base of proboscis; gut coiled; anus terminal; blood vascular system usually present; unsegmented ventral nerve cord; usually a pair of bristles (setae) just behind mouth; one to several excretory nephridia and a pair of anal excretory organs; sexes separate with extreme sexual dimorphism in some; produce free-swimming trochophore larva in some others. Families: Bonellidae, including genus *Bonellia;* Echiuridae, including genus *Echiurus, Thalessema;* Ikedaidae, including genus *Ikeda;* Urechidae, including genus *Urechis.*

The musculature of the trunk wall includes an outer circular layer and an inner longitudinal layer. An additional oblique layer may be present, its position being a key feature in defining families.

Reproduction in echiurans is always sexual, the sexes being separate. Mature gametes are collected into the excretory nephridia just prior to spawning, in certain cases by complex coiled collecting organs. Where fertilization occurs in the water (families Echiuridae, Urechidae), a free-swimming trochophore larva results, gradually changing to the adult morphology. In the Bonelliidae, where the male lives in or on the female, fertilization is presumed to be internal and larval development takes place essentially on the sea floor. In *Bonellia*, if the larva comes into contact with an adult female, it tends to become male, and if not, female.   PRG/AC

Segmented Worms

WORMS THAT CAN SUCK BLOOD; WORMS *that can be 3m (10ft) long and worms that are vaguely reminiscent of a strip of rag – leeches, earthworms and ragworms. These are representatives of the three groups of worms known collectively as annelids. Annelids are characterized by a long, soft body and cylindrical or somewhat flattened cross-section.*

An annelid worm is basically a fluid-filled cylinder, with the body wall comprising two sets of muscles, one circular, the other longitudinal. The fluid-filled cavity (the coelom) is effectively a hydrostatic skeleton (fluid cannot be compressed) upon which the muscles work antagonistically to produce changes in width and length of the animal.

Annelids are divided into a number of segments which in some forms give rise to a ringed appearance of the body, hence the name "ringed worms" sometimes applied to this group. Although some annelids can be broken up into individual segments and each of these can regenerate from the front or back into a completely new worm, the segments of which the normal adult is composed are not really independent. The gut, vascular system and nervous system run from one end of the segmental chain to the other and coordinate the whole body. The series of segments is bounded by a nonsegmental structure at each end: the prostomium and a pygidium. The mouth opens into the gut immediately behind the prostomium, while the gut terminates at the anus on the pygidium. The prostomium and the pygidium are variously adapted: the prostomium, lying at the front, naturally develops organs of special sense such as the eyes and tentacles and hence contains a ganglion or "primitive brain," which connects with the nerve cord that runs from one end of the body to the other. The segments too, although primitively similar, are variously adapted, and the annelids demonstrate the variety of changes that can be rung on this apparently simple and monotonous body plan.

Earthworms
CLASS CLITELLATA

Earthworms and other oligochaete worms have a worldwide distribution. Earthworms may be found in almost any soil, often in very large numbers, and sometimes reaching a great size (*Megascolecides* of Australia, reaches 3m (10ft) or more in length). The commonest European earthworms are *Lumbricus* and *Allolobophora* species. The aquatic oligochaetes, sometimes known as blood-

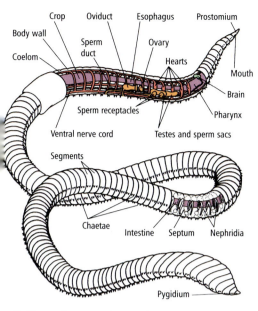

Crop, Oviduct, Esophagus, Prostomium, Body wall, Sperm duct, Ovary, Coelom, Hearts, Mouth, Sperm receptacles, Brain, Pharynx, Ventral nerve cord, Testes and sperm sacs, Segments, Chaetae, Intestine, Septum, Nephridia, Pygidium

○ **Above** *Structure of an earthworm, cut away to show the internal structure, in particular the digestive system, reproductive organs, and the nerve and circulatory systems.*

○ **Left** *An earthworm pulling a leaf down into its burrow. Leaves are used to block the burrow entrance, and also as food.*

FACTFILE

SEGMENTED WORMS

Phylum: Annelida

Classes: Clitellata, Polychaeta, Clitella

About 16,500 species in 3 classes (some authorities put earthworms and leeches in one class).

Distribution Worldwide in land, water and moist habitats.

Fossil record Polychaete tubes (burrows) known from Precambrian (over 600m years ago).

Size Length 1mm–3m (0.04in–10ft).

Features Body typically elongate, divided into segments and bilaterally symmetrical; body cavity (coelom) present; gut runs full length of body from mouth to anus; nerve cord present in lower part of body cavity; excretion via paired nephridia; appendages, when present, never jointed.

EARTHWORMS Class Clitellata; order Oligochaeta
About 6,000 species in 284 genera. **Distribution:** worldwide in terrestrial, freshwater, estuarine and marine habitats. **Size:** 1mm–3m (0.04in–10ft) long. **Features:** no head appendages; few bristlelike chaetae usually in 4 bundles per segment; coelom spacious and compartmented; has blood vascular system, well developed body-wall musculature and ventral nerve cord with giant fibers in some; hermaphrodite with reproductive organs confined to a few segments; glandular saddle (clitellum) present which secretes cocoon in which eggs develop; no larval stage.

RAGWORMS, LUGWORMS AND BEARD WORMS
Class Polychaeta
About 10,000 species in c. 80 families. **Distribution:** worldwide, essentially marine. **Size:** 1mm–2m (0.04–6.6ft) long. **Features:** morphology very variable; various feeding and sensory structures may be present at front end; body segments with lateral appendages (parapodia) bearing bristle-like chaetae; coelom spacious; has blood vascular system, nephridia and ventral nerve cord with giant nerve fibers in some; usually sexual reproduction, with or without free-swimming larval phase.

Includes the specialized family of beard worms (Pogonophoridae). 150 species in all oceans, usually at considerable depths. **Size:** length 5cm to 1.5m (2in–5ft), usually 8–15cm (3.2–6in); diameter up to 3mm (0.1in). **Features:** bilaterally symmetrical, solitary, tube-dwelling worms; body divided into 3 zones – head (cephalic) lobe bearing tentacles, trunk, and posterior opisthosoma; gill slits, digestive tract and anus all lacking; protostome development.

LEECHES Class Clitella; order Hirudinea
About 500 species in 140 genera. **Distribution:** worldwide, mainly freshwater, some terrestrial or marine. **Size:** 5mm–12cm (0.2–4.7in) long. **Features:** 33 segments; suckers at front and rear; coelom much reduced; blood vascular system often restricted to remaining coelomic spaces (sinuses); hermaphrodite with one of mating pair transferring sperm; glandular saddle (clitellum) produces cocoon; no larval stage.

See The 3 Classes of Segmented Worms ▷

DARWIN AND EARTHWORMS

In 1881 Charles Darwin published *The Formation of Vegetable Mould through the Action of Worms*, summarizing 40 years of observation and experiment. After discussing the senses, habits, diet, and digestion of earthworms, he concluded that they live in burrow systems, and feed on decaying animal and plant material, as well as quantities of soil. They produce casts, forming a layer of vegetable mold, thereby enriching the surface soil.

He noted that earthworms often plug their burrow entrances with small stones or leaves, the latter also serving as a food source. Darwin saw signs of intelligence in the way in which leaves are grasped. When the leaf tip is more acutely pointed than the base, most are dragged by the tip, but where the reverse is true, the base is more likely to be grasped. Pine needles are almost invariably pulled by the base, where the two elements join.

The habit of producing casts at the burrow entrance results in the gradual accumulation of surface mold, and Darwin estimated that annually some 20–45 tonnes of soil per hectare (8–18 tonnes per acre) may be brought to the surface in pasture. This soon buries objects left on the soil surface, and may aid the preservation of archeological sites, but under certain conditions cast formation may also hasten soil erosion. Burrowing affects the aeration and drainage of the soil, which is beneficial to crop production.

Darwin failed to distinguish between earthworm species (only relatively few British earthworms make permanent burrows or produce surface casts), but he was one of the first to recognize their important ecological role. He firmly established their beneficial effects on soil, which have subsequently been largely confirmed. **PRG**

worms because of their deep red color, are smaller than earthworms and generally simpler in structure. Some are found in the intertidal zone, under stones, or among seaweeds. But many of the aquatic genera are found in freshwater habitats, living, for example, in mud at the bottom of lakes (*Tubifex*). Such worms commonly have both anatomical and physiological adaptations that equip them to withstand the relatively deoxygenated conditions commonly found in polluted habitats.

Oligochaetes are remarkably uniform. They entirely lack appendages, except for gills in a few species. Some families are restricted to one type of environment, for example where there are fungi and bacteria associated with the breakdown of organic material; some may eat just microflora.

Oligochaetes are exclusively hermaphrodite, with reproductive organs limited to a few front segments. Male and female segments are separate, with segments containing testes always in front of those with ovaries (the reverse is true in leeches). The clitellum, a glandular region of the epidermis (outer skin), is always present in mature animals. It secretes mucus to bind together copulating earthworms, and produces both the egg cocoon and the nutritive fluid it contains. The exact position of the clitellum and the details of the reproductive organs and their exterior openings is of

○ **Right** *An earthworm pair (Lumbricus terrestris) mating. Earthworms are hermaphrodite and during mating mutually exchange sperm.*

fundamental importance in the classification and identification of oligochaetes.

During copulation two earthworms come together, head to tail, and each exchanges sperm with the other. The sperm are stored by each recipient in pouches called spermathecae until after the worms separate. A slimy tube formed by the clitellum later slips off each worm, collecting eggs and the deposited sperm as it goes, and is left in the soil as a sealed cocoon. The eggs are well supplied with yolk, and are also sustained by the albumenous fluid surrounding them. In earthworms there is a tendency for the eggs to be provided with less yolk and rely more on the albumen. Development of the earthworms is direct (unlike most polychaetes), that is, there are no larval stages.

Parthenogenesis (development of unfertilized eggs) and self-fertilization are known in some species, and the aquatic members of the Aeolosomatidae and Naididae almost exclusively reproduce asexually.

Some earthworms are potentially longlived, but the majority of oligochaetes probably have one- to

two-year lifecycles. Cocoon production occupies much of the year, interrupted by unfavorable environmental conditions, such as dryness, or by a seemingly fixed dormancy in some earthworms, that is apparently unrelated to outside conditions.

An earthworm moves by waves of muscular contraction and relaxation which pass along the length of the body, so that a particular region is alternately thin and extended or shortened and thickened. A good grip on the walls of the burrow is aided by the spiny outgrowths of the body wall called chaetae which project from the body wall. Chaetae are found in both polychaetes and oligochaetes; but, as their names imply, polychaetes have many chaetae in each segment, whereas oligochaetes have relatively few. Furthermore, the number of chaetae in each segment of an oligochaete is not only small but constant. The earthworm *Lumbricus*, for example, has eight chaetae in each segment. In the aquatic oligochaetes the chaetae may be longer and more slender than those of an earthworm.

The earthworm feeds either on leaves pulled into the burrow with the aid of its suctorial pharynx, or by digesting the organic matter present among the particles of soil it swallows when burrowing in earth otherwise too firm to penetrate. A muscular gizzard near the front end of the gut serves to break up compacted soil particles into smaller ones, with the result that digestion and absorption of the organic material within the intestine is more efficient. Undigested matter is extruded from the anus on to the surface of the soil as the familiar worm casts. These casts give some indication of the valuable effects earthworms have upon the soil (see Darwin and Earthworms).

Ragworms and Lugworms
CLASS POLYCHAETA

In contrast to the other annelids, polychaetes, such as ragworms, have extremely diverse forms and biology, although a common pattern is usually recognizable for each family. Polychaetes are almost all marine and they are often a dominant group, from the intertidal zone to the depths of the oceans. Planktonic, commensal and parasitic forms are also found.

Basically a polychaete is composed of a series of body segments, each separated from its neighbor by partitions (septa). Externally, each segment bears a pair of bibbed muscular extensions of the body wall known as parapodia containing internal supports (acicula), two bundles of chaetae, and a pair of sensory tentacles (cirri). The parapodia are most highly developed in active crawling forms, for example, ragworms.

Many polychaete families have an eversible pharynx which is most conspicuous in those species that are carnivorous, feed on large pieces of plant material or suck body fluids of other organisms. The pharynx in such families may be armed with jaws. Families with feeding tentacles or crowns use cilia to collect food from the sediment surface or water column and convey it to the

❍ *Left Representative species of polychaete worms, a major element in the benthic fauna of the world's oceans:* **1** *Eulalia viridis, North Atlantic (15cm/6in);* **2** *Marphysa sanguinea, North Atlantic (60cm/24in);* **3** *Spirorbis borealis, a fanworm, North Atlantic (3.5mm/0.1in);* **4** *Pomatoceros triqueter, a fanworm, North Atlantic (2.5cm/1in);* **5** *Harmothoë inibricata, a scaleworm, North Atlantic (5cm/2in);* **6** *Hermodice carunculata, Mediterranean (30cm/12in);* **7** *Perineritis nuntia, a ragworm, Indo-Pacific (2.5cm/1in);* **8** *Tentacles of Reteterebella queenslandica, Indo-Pacific (3.5cm/1.4in);* **9** *Sabellastarte intica, Indo-Pacific (2.5cm/1in);* **10** *Spirobranchus gigantens, Indo-Pacific (1.5cm/0.6in).*

mouth. Many other forms ingest sediment, selecting food particles to a greater or lesser degree.

Small polychaetes respire through the body surface, but larger forms often have gills, which tend to be concentrated near the front in tube-dwelling forms; feeding appendages may also serve a respiratory function. In many tube and burrow dwellers, water is drawn through the tube past the gills by special respiratory movements. Gills are usually associated with the parapodia, and may be simple or threadlike or branched in structure.

The blood system consists of dorsal and ventral longitudinal vessels, connected by segmental vessels and capillaries, or blood sinuses around the gut. It is reduced or absent in many of the smaller forms, and even in some large ones, for example members of the Glyceridae, its function being taken over by the coelomic fluid. Loss of the blood system is often associated with reduction or loss of walls (septa), allowing free passage of coelomic fluid. A variety of blood pigments may be present in polychaetes, either in cells or free in the blood.

Active crawling forms often show a reduction in the circular muscle layer of the body wall with corresponding development of the parapodia and

their musculature and reduction or loss of the septa. This is correlated with a switch from peristaltic locomotion (as in earthworms) to the use of parapodia as the main propulsive organs.

Connecting the coelomic fluid to the exterior are a pair of excretory nephridia and a pair of genital ducts, the coelomoducts, in each segment. The nephridia pass through a septum, the external pore occurring in the segment behind that in which the nephridium originates. In most polychaetes the coelomoducts and nephridia are fused in fertile segments to produce urinogenital ducts, although often only at sexual maturity. Fertilization is generally external, and may lead to a free-swimming larva which may or may not feed, or development may be entirely on the sea floor (benthic). Adults protect the brood in a number of species, and this is not restricted to those with benthic development. Polychaetes may be hermaphrodite, eggs may develop into larva within the body (viviparous) or internal fertilization may take place. Asexual reproduction, by fragmentation or fission followed by regeneration, occurs in some 30 species.

Ragworms are familiar through their use by sea anglers. Some species are carnivorous, feeding on

dead or dying animals; some are omnivorous; others feed only on weed. Polychaete worms predominate among bait species. In Europe ragworm and lugworm are most commonly used for bait, and the catworms occasionally collected. In North America the sandworm and the bloodworm are widely used, as are the long beachworms (species of the family Onuphidae) in Australia. All these species live in intertidal soft sediment, although ragworms are often found in muddy gravel.

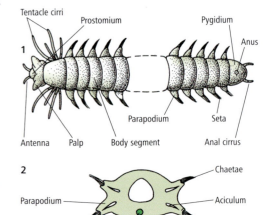

◁ **Left** *Commonly known as the Social feather duster or Cluster duster, the polychaete tubeworm* Bispira brunnea *(family Sabellidae) is found in abundance in the Caribbean and the Gulf of Mexico..*

▷ **Right** *The Bearded fireworm* Hermodice caruncu-lata *is a voracious predator that attacks living soft corals, engulfing their tips with its eversible pharynx. It is seen here on a Purple sea fan* (Gorgonia ventalina).

They live for protection in the mud or muddy sand from which they emerge or partially emerge to feed on the plant and animal debris on the surface. The burrows may be located by the holes on the surface of the mud. The burrows themselves are U-shaped or at least have two openings, for the worms must irrigate them in order to respire. They do this by undulating their bodies, and this serves not only to renew the water within the burrow, but enables them to detect in the incoming water signs of food in the vicinity. Vast populations may occur in suitable habitats. Some species can tolerate the stringent conditions in estuaries and some are found in very low salinities.

Scaleworms also occur on the seashore and below the low-water mark. Their backs are covered or partly covered by a series of more or less disk-shaped scales. The scales are usually dark in color and overlap slightly. They are protective not only in providing concealment but also in their ability to luminesce. The luminescent organs are under nervous control, so that the animal can "flash" if alarmed. Not all scaleworms do this, however.

Another polychaete worm is the sea mouse which is found below low tide level on sandy bottoms. It is often brought up by fishermen in the dredge. The body is covered with a fine "felt" of silky chaetae, and it is to this apparently furry appearance that its common name is due.

Sea mice live for the most part just beneath the surface of the sand or mud. They are rather lethargic although they can scuttle quite rapidly for a short distance when disturbed. If the matted "felt" over the back is removed a series of large disk-shaped scales will be seen overlapping the back: the sea mouse is nothing more than a large scaleworm in which the characteristic scales are concealed by the hairlike chaetae.

Fanworms are the most elegant of all the marine polychaete worms. Pinnate or branched

◁ **Left** *Diagram of a polychaete worm, showing:* **1** *the whole body and* **2** *a cross-section. The basic structure is a series of body segments, each separated from its neighbor by the septa.*

▷ **Right** *Heads of polychaete worms:* **1** Nothria ele-gans, *in which the prostomium is well developed and bears a small number of sensory antennae;* **2** *member of the family Terebellidae, with feeding appendages in the form of extensible tentacles;* **3** *member of the family Sabellidae, with a stiff crown;* **4** *member of the family Sabellariidae, in which specialized chaetae form part of a lid-like opercular structure.*

filaments radiate from the head to form an almost complete crown of orange, purple, green or a combination of these colors. The crown is developed from the prostomium. It forms a feeding organ and, incidentally, a gill. The remainder of the body is more or less cylindrical.

All fanworms secrete close-fitting tubes which provide protection. Although their often gaily-colored crowns must tempt predatory fish, they can all contract with startling rapidity. These startle responses are made possible by relatively enormous giant nerve fibers which run from one end of the body to the other within the main nerve cord. In *Myxicola* this giant fiber occupies almost the whole of the nerve cord. Almost 1mm across, it is one of the largest nerve fibers known. Giant nerve fibers are associated with particularly well developed longitudinal muscles which enable the worm to retract promptly when danger threatens. Other movements are relatively slow.

▌ Beard Worms

CLASS POLYCHAETA; FAMILY POGONOPHORIDAE

The evolutionary position of the beard worms has been extensively researched. Most biologists now concur that the beard worms' possession of a coelom and the segmentation of the opisthosoma makes them close relatives of the annelid worms. Consequently, they are placed in the specialized family Pogonophoridae, in the class Polychaeta.

Beard worms are the most unlikely of animals. They are a zoological curiosity of comparatively recent discovery. Their anatomy was not fully known until 1963, when the first whole specimens were obtained. The name Pogonophoridae comes from the Greek *Pogon* ('beard') – an allusion to the shaggy tentacles carried on the front of the body.

These long, thin animals – often 500 times as long as broad – live in tubes that are generally completely buried in the mud or ooze of the ocean floor. There are two exceptions to this:

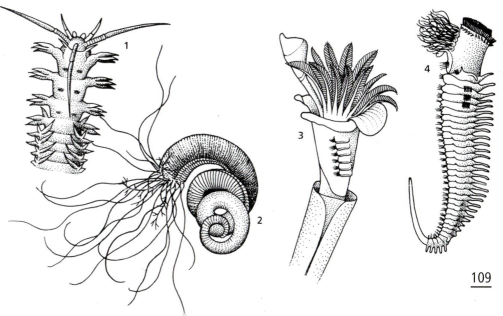

The 3 Classes of Segmented Worms

Earthworms
Class: Clitellata; order Oligochaeta

About 6,000 species in 284 genera. Families: Aeolosomatidae, 4 genera; Alluroididae, 4 genera; Dorydrilidae, 1 genus; Enchytraeidae, 23 genera, including *Enchytraeus, Marionina, Achaetus*; Eudrilidae, 40 genera; Glossoscolecidae, 34 genera; Haplotaxidae, 1 genus; Lumbricidae, 10 genera, including earthworms (*Lumbricus, Allolobophora, Eisenia*); Lumbriculidae, 12 genera; Megascolecidae, 101 genera, including *Megascolex, Pheretima, Dichogaster*; Moniligastridae, 5 genera; Naididae, 20 genera, including *Chaetogaster, Dero, Nais*; Opistocystidae, 1 genus; Phreodrilidae, 1 genus; Tubificidae, 27 genera, including some bloodworms (*Tubifex* species), *Peloscolex*. 6 species are threatened: *Phallodrilus mac-masterae* (family Tubificidae) is Critically Endangered; 4 species are classed as Vulnerable, including the Washington giant earthworm (*Driloleirus americanus*; family Megascolecidae) and the Giant Gippsland earthworm (*Megascolides australis*; family Megascolecidae); and *Lutodrilus multivesiculatus* (family Lutodrilidae) is Lower Risk Near Threatened.

Ragworms, Lugworms and Beard Worms
Class: Polychaeta (includes aberrant groups myzostomes and beard worms)

In the region of 10,000 species in around or so 80 families. Families include: sea mice (Aphroditidae); Arenicolidae, including lugworm (*Arenicola marina*); Cirratulidae; Eunicidae; Glyceridae, including some bloodworms (*Glygcera* species); Nephthyidae, including catworms (*Nephthys* species); Nereididae, including ragworm or sandworm (*Nereis virens*); beachworms (Onuphidae); Opheliidae; beard worms (Pogonophoridae), including *Lamellibrachia, Lamellisabella, Sclerolinum, Spirobrachia*; Sabellariidae; scaleworms (Polynoidae); fanworms (Sabellidae); Serpulidae; Spionidae; Syllidae; Terebellidae (including some bloodworms). *Mesonerilla prospera* (family Nerillidae) is Critically Endangered.

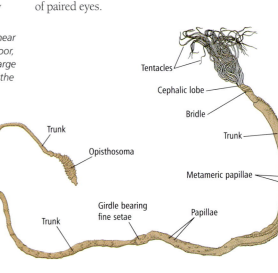

△ **Above** Leech suckers attach alternately to the substrate, are lifted and move forward. This removes the need for chaetae and a fluid-filled coelom, features of other annelid worms.

Leeches
Class: Clitella, order Hirudinea

About 500 species in 140 genera. Families: Acanthobdellidae, genus *Acanthobdeila*; Americobdellidae, genus *Americobdella*; Erpobdellidae, including *Erpobdeila*; Glossiphoniidae, including *Glossiphonia, Theroemozon, Placobdeila*; Haemadipsidae, including *Haemadipsa*; Hirudidae, including Medicinal leech (*Hirudo medicinalis*), *Haemopis*; Piscioli-dae, including *Pisciola, Brancheilion, Ozobranchus*; Semiscolecidae, including *Semiscolex*; Trematobdellidae, including *Trematobdella*; Xerobdellidae, including *Xerobdella*. The Medicinal leech is classed as Lower Risk Near Threatened.

Scierolinum brattstromi lives inside rotten organic matter like paper, wood, and leather in Norwegian fjords; and *Lamellibrachia barhami* builds tubes that project from the sediment.

Beard worms have a front head (cephalic) lobe bearing between one and 100 or more tentacles. Immediately behind the head is the forepart, or bridle, which appears to be important in tube building. Behind this lies the trunk, which comprises the main part of the body. It is covered with minute tentacles (papillae) which toward the front are arranged in quite regular pairs. They become more irregular further back along the trunk and some may be enlarged. These papillae are thought to enable the worm to move inside its tube, and they are associated with plaques, hardened plates that probably assist in this respect. Further along the trunk there is a girdle where the skin is ridged and rows of bristles, similar to those of annelid worms, occur on the ridges. These probably help the worm maintain its position inside the tube.

The distinct rear region of the body, the opisthosoma, is easily broken from the rest of the body, and because of this its presence was not appreciated for many years. It comprises between five and 23 segments, each of which carries bristles larger than the ones on the girdle. The opisthosoma probably protrudes from the bottom of the tube in life and acts as a burrowing organ.

The tube is made from chitin; depending on the species, lengths range from several centimeters to about 1.5m (5ft). Beard worm tubes are very narrow, never exceeding 3mm (0.1in) in diameter.

One of the most peculiar features of the beard worms is the lack of a gut within the body. It is probable that nutrients are absorbed directly from the environment as organic molecules.

The sexes are separate and the sperms are released in packets (spermatophores) which are trapped by the tentacles of the females. The packets gradually disintegrate, and the freed sperms fertilize the eggs, which develop into larvae while still inside the female tube. When large enough they move out and settle nearby.

Leeches
CLASS CLITELLA

Leeches are easily recognized. Their soft bodies are ringed, usually without external projections and with a prominent often circular sucker at the rear. At the front there is another sucker around the mouth, and although this may be quite prominent, as in fish leeches, it often is not. The skin is covered with a thin cuticle onto which mucus is liberally secreted. In front there is usually a series of paired eyes.

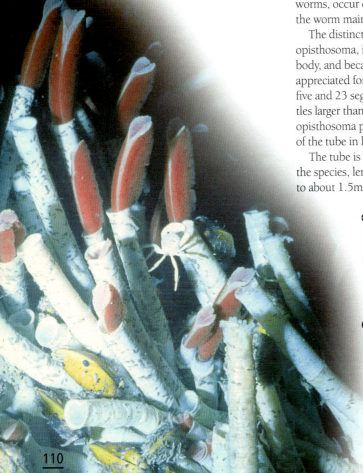

◁ **Left** Large beard worms thrive near hydrothermal vents on the ocean floor, in temperatures up to 40°C. Their large surface-area-to-volume ratio favors the uptake of nutrients, which they obtain from commensal bacteria around the vent.

▷ **Right** Beard worm body plan. A typical pogonophoran, showing the whole worm, most of which is normally buried in its narrow tube in the sea bed.

Tentacles

Cephalic lobe

Bridle

Trunk

Trunk

Trunk

Opisthosoma

Metameric papillae

Girdle bearing fine setae

Papillae

Leeches lack chaetae (except in the Acanhobdellidae) and have a fixed number (33) of segments. Like oligochaetes, they possess a clitellum, involved in egg cocoon production.

Leeches are divisible into two types: those that have an eversible proboscis (Glossiphoniidae and Fisciolidae) and those that have a muscular sucking pharynx, which may be unarmed (Erpobdellidae, Trematobdellidae, Americobdellidae, Xerobdellidae) or armed with jaws (Hirudidae, Haemadipsidae).

Not all species feed in the same way as the Medicinal leech (see Bloodsucker – The Medicinal Leech). Some species feed on other invertebrates, either sucking their body fluids (e.g. Glossiphoniidae) or swallowing them whole (e.g. Erpobdellidae). The Hirudidae, including the Medicinal leech, and the terrestrial Haemadipsidae feed on vertebrate blood. The Pisciolidae are mostly marine, living on fishes' body fluids.

As well as circular and longitudinal muscles in the body wall, diagonal muscle bundles form two systems spiralling in opposite directions between these layers and opposing both. Muscles running from top to underside are well developed and are used to flatten the body, especially during swimming and movements associated with respiration.

The coelomic space is largely invaded by tissue, leaving only a system of smaller spaces (sinuses). The internal funnels of the excretory nephridia open into this system and may be closely associated with the blood system, playing a part in blood fluid production. The blood vascular system is intimately connected with the coelomic sinuses, and may be completely replaced by them.

At copulation, one animal normally acts as sperm donor, and in the jawed leeches, a muscular pouch (atrium) opening to the outside acts as a penis for sperm transfer to the female gonadal pore. In other leeches, sperm packets formed in the atrium attach to the body wall of the recipient, and the spermatozoa make their way through the body tissues by a poorly understood mechanism. Fertilization is internal or occurs as gametes are released into the cocoon, which is secreted by the clitellum and slipped over the leech's head. A small number of zygotes are put in each cocoon, which is full of nutrient fluid secreted by the clitellum. In the Glossiphoniidae, cocoons are protected by the parent, and the juveniles may spend some time attached to the parent. Most leeches only go through one or two breeding periods, with one- to two-year lifecycles.

Leeches are generally accepted as having been derived from oligochaetes, specializing as predators or external parasites. The fish parasite *Acanthobdella* shows many features intermediate between the two groups. PRG/AC

BLOODSUCKER – THE MEDICINAL LEECH

The most familiar leech is the Medicinal leech, native to Europe and parts of Asia. Its use in blood letting in the 18th and 19th centuries led to its introduction to North America. However, it is now thought to be extinct there, as well as in Ireland. The practice of using leeches for "blood letting" to cure almost all conceivable ills ("vapors and humors") has long been discredited, but leeches' ability to drain blood makes them highly valuable allies in plastic surgery, helping restore circulation to grafted tissues.

The Medicinal leech eats blood, usually mammalian but also that of amphibians and even fishes. Once attached to a potential blood source by means of its suckers, its three jaws come into contact with the skin. Each is shaped like a semicircular saw, with numerous small teeth. Sawing action of the teeth results in a Y-shaped incision through which blood is drawn by the sucking action of the muscular pharynx. Glandular secretions are released through each tooth which dilate the host's blood vessels, prevent coagulation of the blood, and act as an anesthetic.

A feeding Medicinal leech may take up to five times its body weight in blood, which passes into its spacious crop. Water and inorganic substances are rapidly extracted and excreted through the excretory cells (nephridia), but digestion of the organic portion may take 30 weeks. It was once thought that the Medicinal leech entirely lacked digestive enzymes, relying on bacteria in its own gut for digestion. However, although the involvement of bacteria is still recognized the leech does produce its own enzymes. The time taken to digest this highly nutritious food means that leeches need to feed only infrequently – not much more than one full meal per year may be sufficient to permit growth.

Although little is known of its life history, the Medicinal leech is thought to take at least three years to mature. Cocoons, containing 5–15 eggs, are laid in damp places 1–9 months after copulation: they hatch 4–10 weeks later. PRG

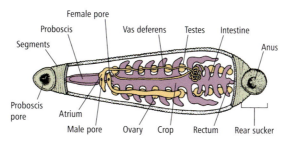

Female pore
Proboscis
Segments
Proboscis pore
Atrium
Male pore
Vas deferens
Testes
Intestine
Anus
Ovary
Crop
Rectum
Rear sucker

❶ **Left** Structure of a leech. Leeches are protandrous hermaphrodites, with one pair of ovaries and 4–10 pairs of testes, each gonad lying in a sac in the body cavity (coelom).

❷ **Below** A swimming Horse leech (Haemopis sanguisuga). This species does not suck blood, but feeds on smaller worms such as earthworms.

Rotifers or Wheel Animalcules

bORNE ON A RETRACTABLE DISK THE CROWN *of cilia known as the corona is the rotifers' most conspicuous structure. When the cilia beat they resemble a wheel spinning in opposite directions when viewed under the microscope. Thus the early microscopists termed rotifers "wheel animalcules."*

Rotifers constitute quite a large phylum with many species living in fresh water and soils all over the world. They inhabit lakes, ponds, rivers and ditches as well as gutters, puddles, the leaf axils of mosses and higher plants and damp soil. Most are freeliving but a few form colonies and some live as parasites. A smaller number of species are marine.

A Hidden Life
BIOLOGY
Rotifer bodies are generally divided into a head, a long middle section or trunk housing most of the viscera, and a tailpiece or foot ending in a gripping toe. The head is not well developed in comparison with those of the higher animals but it does bear an eye spot sometimes colored red. The beating cilia on the corona draws in a stream of water to the head bringing in other microorganisms as food which are then passed into the muscular esophagus. The chewing structure is technically termed the mastax and the teeth and jaws are made of strong cuticle for chewing

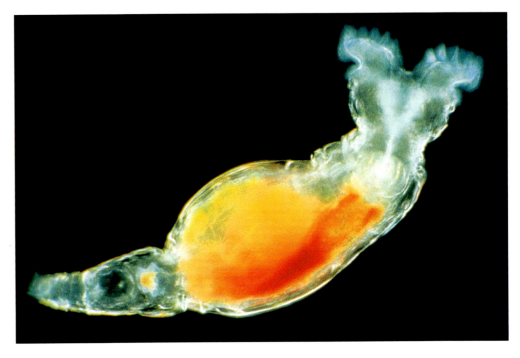

and grinding the food. In some predatory species long teeth may protrude out of the mouth and help seize protozoans and other species of rotifer.

The trunk houses the internal organs including the mastax. Its contents appear complex: they include elements of the gut, excretory system and reproductive system as well as the musculature for

🔺 *Above Little animals of great endurance, Antarctic rotifers (Philodina gregaria) have survived being frozen for over a hundred years. They can withstand immersion in liquid nitrogen.*

🔻 *Below Body structure of the most common rotifer genus Brachionus. It has a distinct cuticle and bilateral symmetry. Its two toes can clearly be seen on the foot.*

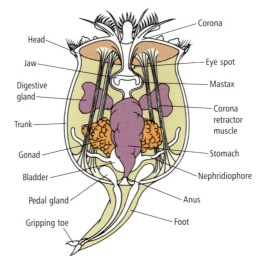

Head —
Jaw —
Digestive gland —
Trunk —
Gonad —
Bladder —
Pedal gland —
Gripping toe —
— Corona
— Eye spot
— Mastax
— Corona retractor muscle
— Stomach
— Nephridiophore
— Anus
— Foot

retracting the corona. The tailpiece is important for posture and stance – many rotifers use it to cling to fronds of aquatic plants or other substrates while they feed or rest. The tail may also serve as a sort of rudder.

The breeding strategies of rotifers typically include a phase of reproduction where females lay unfertilized eggs which develop and grow into other females (parthenogenetic). When the sexual season dictates or when adverse environmental conditions prevail some of the females lay eggs which need to be fertilized by a male. At the same time others lay smaller eggs which develop into males for this purpose. The males then fertilize the new females by injecting them with sperm through the body wall. The resulting fertilized eggs are tolerant of harsh conditions and can withstand drought, an important attribute for species dwelling in temporary pools of water. They can also serve as a dispersal phase when blown about by the wind. Once hatched only females develop from the eggs. Survival over difficult times is also helped by the ability of many rotifers to tolerate water loss and to shrivel up into small balls and remain in a state of suspended animation referred to as cryptobiosis or "hidden life."

Despite their obscurity rotifers are of ecological and direct economic importance. Millions of them may exist in a small body of water and their populations may rise and fall rapidly. They are crucial members of numerous aquatic food webs. Soil-dwelling rotifers aid soil breakdown. **AC**

FACTFILE

ROTIFERS OR WHEEL ANIMALCULES

Phylum: Rotifera

Classes: Monogononta, Digononta, Bdelloidea

About 1,800 species in 100 genera and 3 classes.

Distribution Worldwide, mainly freshwater, some marine, and damp soils.

Fossil record None.

Size Microscopic, 0.04–2mm (0.002–0.08in).

Features Solitary or colonial; body cavity a pseudocoel (now described as blastocoelomate); head bears a crown of cilia; trunk houses internal jaws (mastax); tailpiece in some forms bears gripping toes; excretion by means of flame cell protonephridia; body sometimes encased in a lorica, males often reduced or absent, females sometimes capable of reproduction by themselves.

CLASS MONOGONONTA
Genera include: *Keratella, Hexarthra, Collotheca*

CLASS DIGONONTA (OR SEISONIDA)
Genus: *Seison*

CLASS BDELLOIDEA
Genera include: *Philodina, Rotaria*

Spiny-headed Worms

WORMS IN THE ACANTHOCEPHALA ARE ALL *parasites living in the intestines of various groups of vertebrates. Spiny-headed worms are particularly successful at parasitizing the bony fish and the birds but they have completely failed to conquer the cartilaginous fishes (skates and rays).*

Unlike the parasitic flatworms (flukes and tapeworms) and the parasitic roundworms (nematodes), spiny-headed worms are of little medical or economic significance. However, they are known to cause ill-health to domestic livestock. Acanthocephalans' relative insignificance is probably because the insects and crustaceans that serve as secondary hosts to the juveniles are not eaten by man. In a few species another vertebrate may serve as a secondary host.

Two-host Parasites
BIOLOGY

Spiny-headed worms are elongate, dorsoventrally flattened forms which are typically dull in color. They completely lack a gut. Food digested by the host's gastric system is absorbed across the body wall and nourishes them. The body wall is composed of a fibrous epidermis which contains channels, sometimes referred to as lacunae, which are not connected to the interior or the exterior of the animal. They probably

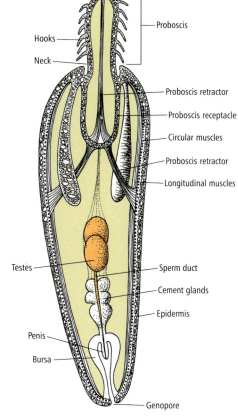

◑ **Above** *Body structure of a spiny-headed worm showing the eversible pharynx. Note the numerous hooks on the proboscis which are used to help the worm embed itself deeply in its host's tissues.*

Labels: Proboscis, Hooks, Neck, Proboscis retractor, Proboscis receptacle, Circular muscles, Proboscis retractor, Longitudinal muscles, Testes, Sperm duct, Cement glands, Epidermis, Penis, Bursa, Genopore

function to circulate absorbed food materials. The front is equipped with a strange reversible proboscis clad with hooks. The proboscis is extended to attach the worm to the lining of the host's gut. It is retracted by muscles into a special proboscis sac and everted by fluid pressure by a reduction in the proboscis sac volume. Beside the sac are two bodies called lemnisci, filled with small spaces and thought to be food storage areas. There are excretory nephridia in some spiny-headed worms. The nervous system is simple; there is a ventral mass of nerve cells at the front of the body from which arise longitudinal nerve cords.

Spiny-headed worms need two parasites where one is used as an intermediate invertebrate host for their larval stages. The sexes are separate and males are often larger than females. Internal fertilization takes place with the male using a penis to transfer sperm to the female. The fertilized eggs develop within the female pseudocoel until they reach a larval stage encased in a shell. These larvae are liberated and pass out with the feces of the host. If eaten by the appropriate secondary host, they emerge from the egg cases, penetrate the secondary host's gut wall and come to lie in its blood space where they remain until the secondary host is eaten by the primary host in a prey-predator relationship or by casual accident, as when water containing a small infected crustacean is drunk. At this point the primary host is reinfected.   AC

SPINY-HEADED WORMS

Phylum : Acanthocephala

Classes: Arahiacanthocephala, Palaeacanthocephala, Eoacanthocephala

About 1,100 species in 3 classes.

Distribution Widespread as gut parasites of terrestrial, freshwater and marine vertebrates; arthropods are intermediate hosts.

Fossil record Only 1 species from Cambrian (600–500 million years ago).

Size About 1mm–1m (0.04in–3.3ft) but mainly under 20mm (0.8in).

Features Worms lacking a mouth, gut and anus; cavity a pseudocoel; peculiar protrusible proboscis ("spiny head") armed with curved hooks; sexes separate.

CLASS ARAHIACANTHOCEPHALA
2 orders; genera include: *Gigantorhynchus*.

CLASS PALAEACANTHOCEPHALA
2 orders; genera include: *Polymorphus*.

CLASS EOACANTHOCEPHALA
2 orders; genera include: *Pallisentis*.

ZOOLOGICAL HIGHLIGHT OF THE 1990S

In 1995 a new species, *Symbion pandora* was discovered living symbiotically on the mouthparts of Norway Lobsters (*Nephrops norvegicus*) in northern Europe. The organism caused excitement as it was so unusual that it could not be classified into any of the existing metazoan phyla. A new phylum was suggested and named Cycliophora, a Greek derivative referring to the circular mouth ring. Although originally believed to be affiliated with the Ectoprocta and Endoprocta, a recent DNA review of the phylum has revealed that its closest relatives may well be members of the phyla Rotifera and Acanthocepha.

S. pandora is marine, inhabiting waters in northwest Europe and the coastal areas of Norway, Sweden and Denmark. Females grow to 0.35mm (0.14in) long while the dwarf males only reach 0.0085mm (0.0003in) in length.

Adults are attached to their hosts setae (bristles) by an adhesive pad, body acoelomate and divided into an anterior, ciliated, moveable, buccal funnel, an oval trunk and a posterior adhesive disc. The trunk and disk are covered by cuticle. They suspension feed by generating currents in the buccal funnel using the cilia carried there. The gut is U-shaped and is ciliated along its whole length. There is a distinct stomach. The regions between the gut, other organs and the body wall are filled with packing tissue. The dwarf males live attached to the female and lack a gut; presumably they derive sustenance from the female. Diffusion is probably responsible for the exchange of respiratory gasses and the circulation of dissolved food substances around the body. There is a nervous system in the females.

The lifecycle is little understood and may involve alternation between sexual and asexual phases. The females produce a Pandora larva, possibly by asexual means, which leave the mother's body and then eventually settles on the same individual host and subsequently develops into a new female. Sexual reproduction appears complex and synchronized with the molting cycle of the crustacean host. A crucial aim for the species is to infect the same or new hosts after they have molted and cleared their previous cycliphoran symbionts, which remain attached to the old exoskeletons. Scientists still have a lot to learn about *S. pandora*.   AC

Endoprocts

e NDOPROCTS WERE ONCE CLASSIFIED WITH *the ectoprocts (moss animals) in one phylum, the Polyzoa. Yet several significant differences (for instance, in the type of body cavity, lophophore structure, and reproductive stages) have persuaded most authorities to regard them as separate phyla.*

However, above all it is the excretory system that forms the single most significant contrasting character; in the ectoprocts (phylum Bryozoa) the anus opens outside the ring of tentacles, not within the calyx, while in the endoprocts the anus (proctodeum in anatomical terms) lies within the ring of tentacles. This explains the meaning of the two names: Endoprocta – anus inside; Ectoprocta – anus outside.

Tentacular Feeders
FORM AND FUNCTION

Endoprocts are small inconspicuous animals that are usually less than 1mm (0.04in) in length. Most inhabit the sea but one genus lives in fresh water. They are sedentary and live attached to hard surfaces or other organisms by a stalk. In the latter case they live as commensals neither receiving benefit from nor giving benefit to the host. Some of the commensal species, such as *Loxosomella phascolosomata*, are catholic and dwell on various marine invertebrates such as the sipunculids *Golfingia* and *Phascolion* as well as on some bivalve shells. Others, like *Loxomespilon perenzi*, are host-specific living on

the polychaete worm *Sthenelais*. Some are even specific to certain parts of the host like the exhalent pores or oscula of sponges or the segmental appendages or parapodia of polychaete worms. Preferences for these specific habitats among endoprocts may reduce competition for survival between endoproct species and place individuals where they can most benefit from water currents.

Individual endoprocts are called zooids and live, according to species, either as solitary animals or in a colony where many zooids are linked together by creeping rootlike stolons. The zooids have a fairly simple structure, each one consisting of a cuplike body called the calyx supported on a stalklike peduncle. The calyx and peduncle are comprised of body wall tissue, which is soft and flexible, cloaked with a thin protective layer of cuticle under which lies a thin layer of epidermis and a thin layer of muscle. The muscle brings about the nodding movements of the calyx on the peduncle. Towards its top the calyx is slightly constricted by a rim above which radiate about 40 hollow tentacles. These can be folded over the top of the calyx and partially retracted so that the muscular web of tissue which connects their bases affords them some protection in unfavorable circumstances. The tentacles are covered with cilia, minute beating threads projecting from the skin.

On top, inside the circlet of tentacles, the calyx is penetrated by the mouth and anus, between which runs a U-shaped gut. The space inside the

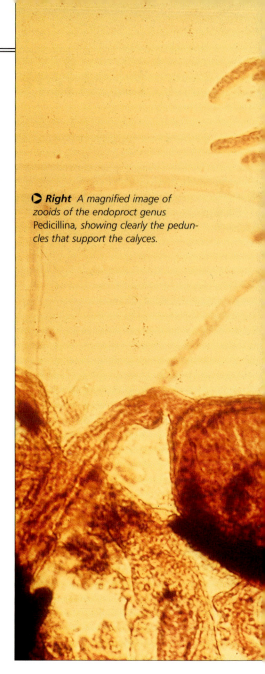

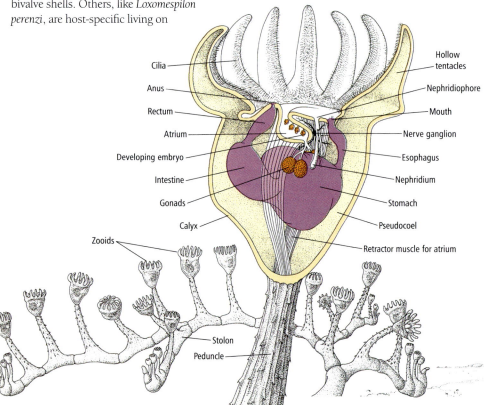

Cilia
Anus
Rectum
Atrium
Developing embryo
Intestine
Gonads
Calyx
Zooids

Hollow tentacles
Nephridiophore
Mouth
Nerve ganglion
Esophagus
Nephridium
Stomach
Pseudocoel
Retractor muscle for atrium

Stolon
Peduncle

calyx is filled with cells so the animals are functionally acoelomate although this space may originally have been formed from the blastocoel in development (a pseudocoel). The reproductive organs lie close to the gut and their short ducts discharge into a fold, the atrium, in the top of the calyx; embryos may be brooded in the atrium. Endoprocts lack an internal circulatory system and have no special respiratory structures; oxygen dissolved in the surrounding water simply diffuses into the zooid. A pair of nephridia are responsible for excretion of nitrogenous waste and these discharge through a single nephridiophore on the top of the calyx just behind the mouth.

Endoprocts are suspension feeders utilizing small organic particles and micro-organisms borne in the water currents to supply them with food. The cilia on the tentacles drive water in

◖ **Left** *A section showing the internal structure of a zooid (genus* Pedicillina). *In the background is part of a colony of the same organism, showing each zooid linked by a creeping stolon.*

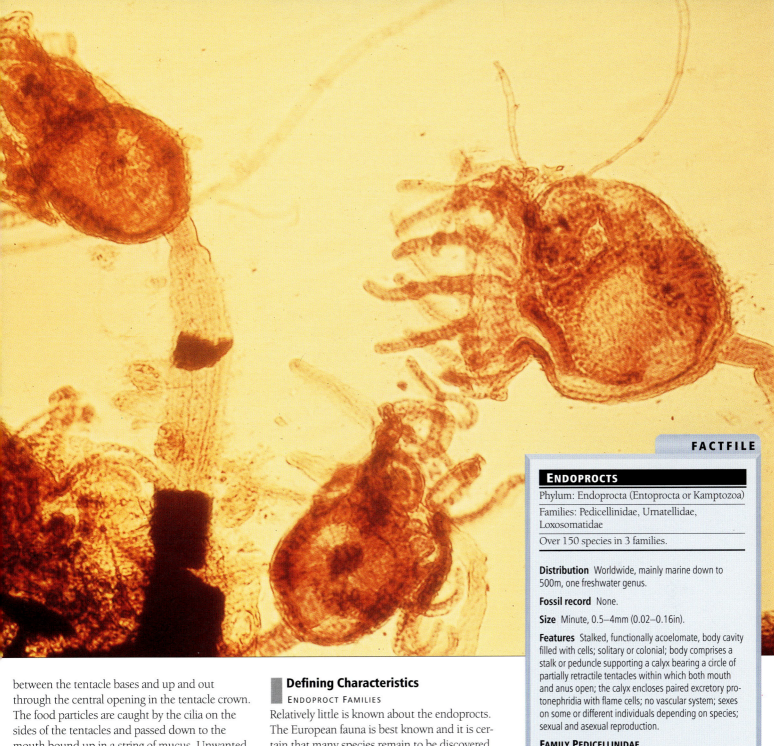

ENDOPROCTS

Phylum: Endoprocta (Entoprocta or Kamptozoa)

Families: Pedicellinidae, Urnatellidae, Loxosomatidae

Over 150 species in 3 families.

Distribution Worldwide, mainly marine down to 500m, one freshwater genus.

Fossil record None.

Size Minute, 0.5–4mm (0.02–0.16in).

Features Stalked, functionally acoelomate, body cavity filled with cells; solitary or colonial; body comprises a stalk or peduncle supporting a calyx bearing a circle of partially retractile tentacles within which both mouth and anus open; the calyx encloses paired excretory protonephridia with flame cells; no vascular system; sexes on same or different individuals depending on species; sexual and asexual reproduction.

FAMILY PEDICELLINIDAE
Includes: *Pedicellina*, *Myosoma*, *Barentsia*, and 3 other genera.

FAMILY URNATELLIDAE
Sole genus *Urnatella*.

FAMILY LOXOSOMATIDAE
Includes: *Loxosoma*, *Loxocalyx*, *Loxosomella*, *Loxomespilon*, *Loxostemma*.

between the tentacle bases and up and out through the central opening in the tentacle crown. The food particles are caught by the cilia on the sides of the tentacles and passed down to the mouth bound up in a string of mucus. Unwanted particles are flicked into the water current leaving the tentacle crown.

Many species undergo asexual reproduction by budding. The style of budding, for example directly from the calyx or from the peduncle (as well as the pattern of growth form in colonial types), is characteristic of particular genera. Budding from the calyx is customary in solitary forms like *Loxosomella*. When the buds reach an advanced stage they drop off to occupy a new site and live independently.

Some endoproct species are hermaphrodite, while others have separate sexes. Fertilization is believed to be within each zooid. The resulting embryos are then brooded in the atrium until they are released as free-swimming larvae. Following the planktonic phase the larvae settle and grow into new zooids.

Defining Characteristics

ENDOPROCT FAMILIES

Relatively little is known about the endoprocts. The European fauna is best known and it is certain that many species remain to be discovered, particularly in the tropics.

The three families of endoproct can be distinguished by the form of the zooids and the growth habit. In the Pedicellinidae there are no solitary species. Here the calyx is separated from the peduncle by a diaphragm so that when conditions are unfavorable or when damaged by predators, such as small grazing arthropods, the calyx can be shed. It can be regrown: examples of this family are frequently seen showing a range of regenerating calyces.

The Urtanellidae contains only one genus, *Urtanella*, which is the only freshwater one. Here the stolon is small and disklike and the calyces may be shed and show regeneration frequently. One species occurs in both western Europe and the eastern USA; a second is known from India.

The Loxosomatidae, which are the most abundant endoproct species, are all solitary, usually with a short peduncle attached by a broad base with a cement gland or a muscular attachment disk. The former type cannot move, being cemented down, but the latter can detach and reattach themselves as conditions require. The peduncle and calyx are continuous and there is no diaphragm. The calyx cannot be shed in the Loxosomatidae.   AC

Horseshoe Worms

UNLIKE THE MOSS ANIMALS, TO WHICH THEY *are probably related, the horseshoe worms form a small and relatively insignificant phylum. These worms are the least diverse and least familiar of the larger-bodied marine phyla. Only some 11 species are known as adults and they are not of any ecological or commercial importance.*

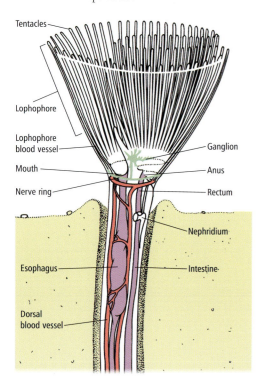

Tentacles

Lophophore

Lophophore blood vessel

Mouth

Nerve ring

Ganglion

Anus

Rectum

Nephridium

Esophagus

Intestine

Dorsal blood vessel

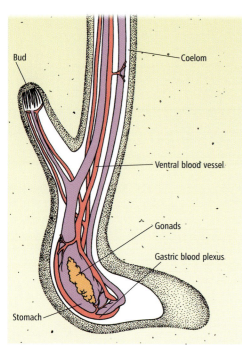

Bud

Coelom

Ventral blood vessel

Gonads

Gastric blood plexus

Stomach

Horseshoe worms live attached to the substrate, in secreted tubes of chitinlike substance which quickly become decorated with fragments of shells and grains of sand. These animals are small and obscure and are normally discovered only by accident when for example items of substrate are being carefully examined. They live in shallow temperate and tropical habitats. None dwell in fresh water. Their known distribution in America, Australia, Europe and Japan is more likely a reflection of where marine biologists are active in discovering them rather than an accurate delineation of where they actually dwell. A number of larvae, technically known as actinotrochs, have been collected, the adults of which are unknown. It is certain that the development of marine biology will see an increase in the number of known species.

Life in the Tube

FORM AND FUNCTION

The horseshoe worm body is essentially wormlike. At the front is a well developed horseshoe-shaped lophophore which in plan resembles two crescents, a smaller one set inside a larger one with their ends touching. The mouth lies between the two crescents. From these crescentlike foundations a number of ciliated tentacles arise to form the lophophore crown, and in some species the crescent tips may be rolled up as spirals thus increasing the extent of the lophophore. The beating of the cilia drives currents of water down the tentacles and out between their bases. Any small food particles are rolled up with secreted mucus and passed to the mouth.

The gut itself is U-shaped, a long esophagus leads back from the mouth to the stomach which is situated near the rear of the animal. From this the intestine leads back to the front and the rectum opens by the anus which is situated on a small protrusion (papilla) just outside the lophophore. The body cavity, a true coelom, houses paired excretory nephridia whose openings lie near the anus, and the gonads. Most species are hermaphrodites, and the sex cells are liberated into the coelom and find their way to the exterior via the excretory ducts.

The body wall consists of an outer tissue (epithelium) covering a thin sheath of circular muscles, which when they contract make the animal long and thin. Inside the circular muscles is a thick layer of longitudinal muscle which is responsible for contracting and shortening the body. The muscles enable the animal to move inside the tube and they are controlled by a simple nervous system. There is a nerve ring at the front set in the epidermis at the base of the lophophore. From this nerves arise and innervate the lophophore tentacles and the muscles of the body wall.

One interesting feature of the horseshoe worms is their clearly defined blood system with red pigment (hemoglobin) borne in corpuscles in the otherwise colorless blood. Blood is carried forward by a dorsal vessel which lies between the limbs of the gut and back to the posterior by a ventral vessel. Small branches penetrate each tentacle of the lophophore. The blood is moved around the system by contractions that sweep along the dorsal and ventral vessels.

One species, *Phoronis ovalis*, is known to reproduce asexually and to establish large aggregations by budding. In sexual reproduction the eggs are generally fertilized in the sea. Typically an actinotroch larva develops which lives in the plankton for several weeks before undergoing rapid change to settle on the sea bed, form a tube and take up the adult mode of life.

◖ **Left** *Internal structure of a Phoronis species. As tube-dwellers horseshoe worms have a U-shaped gut and there is a tiny gap betweeen the mouth and anus.*

◗ **Right** *A colony of horseshoe worms feeding. Hemoglobin is visible in the blood vessels of some of the individuals.*

Oligomerous Worms
EVOLUTION AND TAXONOMY

One aspect of interest which zoologists attach to the horseshoe worms is their evolutionary position in general and their relationship in particular with the phyla of moss animals and lampshells. In the course of development embryos of species in all these phyla show a form of development where the body becomes divided into three sections, each with its own region of body cavity (coelom). As the animals develop the front section becomes progressively reduced and all but disappears. The middle region with its own coelom forms the lophophore and the rear section forms the bulk of the body of the adult. Zoologists have described these animals as oligomerous, that is they have few sections or segments. They are thus quite different from groups like the annelid worms and the arthropod phyla where there are many segments to the body (metamerous). The general pattern of development in these groups is inclined toward that of the protostome groups, for example the annelid worms, but occasional features, such as the way in which the coelom is formed, are inconsistent with this suggesting that in evolutionary terms they may occupy a position among the coelomate groups intermediate between the annelids and the arthropod phyla on the one hand, and the echinoderms on the other.   AC

⬤ **Above** *Actinotroch larvae like this* Phoronis *species swim with their hood upright and ciliated tentacles spread. The ciliary band at the rear acts as a propeller.*

Moss Animals

t HE MOSS ANIMALS ARE AN IMPORTANT GROUP *of sedentary aquatic invertebrates. They live attached to the substrate, either on rocks or empty shells, or on tree roots, weeds or other animals where they can find a hold. They are of interest because of their number and diversity. Some types, for example Flustra, may dominate conspicuous regions of the sea bed and have particular groups of organisms living alongside them. Others, such as Zoobotryon, are important because they can foul structures such as piers, pilings, buoys, and ships' hulls.*

Most moss animals are marine, inhabiting all depths of the sea from the shore downward, in all parts of the world. A smaller group inhabit fresh water, where they are relatively inconspicuous. Moss animals are colonial. This means that many individuals termed zooids live together in a common mass. In a colony the first individual (formed from the larva, itself the result of sexual reproduction) is the founder. From the founder, all other individuals are produced by asexual reproduction and thus share a common genetic constitution.

Colonial Cooperation
FORM AND FUNCTION

In many colonies of moss animals, the individuals are all similar and all participate in feeding and sexual reproduction. Each individual is housed in a protective cup known as a zoecium, whose walls

○ **Below** *An encrusting colony of bryozoans (genus Electra). Such colonies depend on currents flowing close to the rocks to bring them their food.*

are reinforced with gelatinous horny or chalky secretions. The particular nature of these individual cup walls is conferred on the texture of the colony as a whole, so that some, such as *Alcyonidium*, may feel soft and pliant while others (e.g. *Pentapora*) feel hard, sharp, and stiff. Equally, the form of the colonies varies. Some genera, such as *Electra*, adopt a flat encrusting habit, while others like *Myriapora* grow up from the substrate in order to exploit stronger water currents flowing above the substrate.

Each feeding individual in a colony is constructed on a similar plan. There is no head as such. A crown of hollow tentacles, filled by the coelom, forms a food-collecting and respiratory surface. (This parallels the tentacles of lampshells and horseshoe worms.) This crown is termed the lophophore. At the center of the lophophore, the mouth opens and leads in to a simple U-shaped gut with esophagus and stomach. The anus lies close to, but outside the lophophore – the ectoproct condition (compare the Endoprocts, where the anus too lies inside the ring of tentacles).

The lophophore can be withdrawn for protection by a set of muscles and it can be extended by other muscles which deform one wall of the cup. This is often the upper or frontal wall, which includes a flexible, frontal membrane. When special muscles pull the frontal membrane in, fluid pressure in the coelom increases and the lophophore is protracted. Many interesting evolutionary developments have been explored by moss animals to ensure that a flexible frontal membrane to the cup, or some other means of adjusting the cup volume, is retained while making sure that

FACTFILE

MOSS ANIMALS OR SEA MATS

Phylum: Bryozoa (or Ectoprocta)

Classes: Gymnolaemata, Phylactolaemata, Stenolaemata

About 4,000 species in about 1,200 genera and 3 classes.

Distribution Worldwide, some freshwater but mainly marine; sedentary bottom-dwelling animals found in all oceans and seas at all depths but mainly between 50–200m (165–655ft).

Fossil record From Ordovician period (500–440 m.y.a.) to recent times; about 15,000 species.

Size Individuals 0.25–1.5mm (0.01–0.06in), colonies 0.5–20cm (0.2–8in) wide.

Features Microscopic colonial animals attached to substrate, living within a secreted tube or case (zoecium); body cavity a coelom; mouth encircled by hairy (ciliated) tentacle crown (lophophore); gut U-shaped; anus outside lophophore; no nephridia or circulatory system.

CLASS GYMNOLAEMATA
2 orders – Ctenostomata and Cheilostomata. Marine. Genera include: *Alcyonidium*, *Memranipora*.

CLASS PHYLACTOLAEMATA
1 order Plumatellida. Fresh water. Genera include: *Cristatella*, *Plumatella*.

CLASS STENOLAEMATA
4 living orders – Trepostomata, Cryptostomata, Fenestrata, Cyclostomata – 3 extinct. Marine. Genera include: *Crisia*.

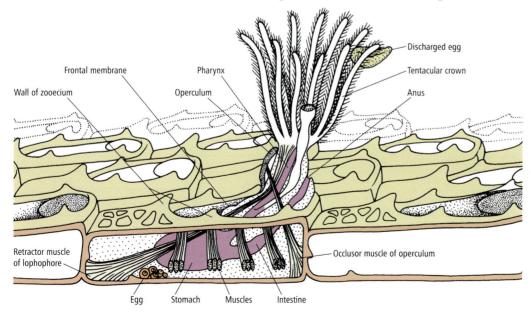

Frontal membrane — Pharynx — Discharged egg

Wall of zooecium — Operculum — Tentacular crown

Anus

Retractor muscle of lophophore — Occlusor muscle of operculum

Egg — Stomach — Muscles — Intestine

⬣ **Above** *Close-up of the individual zooids of* Bugula flabellata. *This erect, foliose bryozoan is a highly evolved moss animal, equipped with aviculariae.*

◖ **Left** *Colonies of* Canda folifera *species of bryozoans off the island of Bali, Indonesia. The bodies of moss animals contain no circulatory or excretory mechanisms; since they are of such small volume, these roles are performed by diffusion.*

◗ **Below** *The forms of some genera of colonial moss animals:* **1** *Flustrellidra;* **2** *and* **3** *Bugula;* **4** *Alcyonidium;* **5** *Pentapora;* **6** *Cellaria;* **7** *Flustra;* **8** *Myriapora;* **9** *Sertella;* **10** *Cupuladria.*

predators are deterred from gaining entry through what is potentially a weak spot. Clearly the requirements of rigid protection and flexibility are not easily reconciled. It is the epidermis of the animal that secretes the horny or gelatinous cuticle and in the chalky ectoprocts this, in turn, is reinforced with calcium salts.

The lophophore tentacles are covered with beating cilia to make efficient filter-feeding organs. When the lophophore is withdrawn the hole it goes in by may be covered over with a flaplike operculum or lid, which is present in some groups but not in others.

Specialized Zooids
BREEDING AND FEEDING

Most animals are hermaphrodite, with male and female organs developing from special regions of the body cavity's inner lining. Ripe sperm and eggs are liberated into the coelom and find their way out of the body by separate pores. In many species the fertilized egg is brooded in a large chamber or ovicell, but in some a free-swimming larva (often called a cyphanautes) spends a period in the plankton feeding on minute algae before settling, metamorphosing, and founding a new colony.

In some more highly evolved moss animals

(class Gymnolaemata, order Cheilstomata) colonies contain several forms. Here, some zooids have given up feeding and are supplied with food by others. Rather, their role is to defend the colony against predators like amphipod crustacea and against clogging by silt. There are two such forms: aviculariae and vibraculae. The first are named for their resemblance to tiny birds' heads with snapping beaks. Modified into tiny jaws with delicate sense organs, the cup and the operculum can seize small animals. The others have a large, elongated, bristle-like operculum that generates a current, vibrating to and fro to sweep away silt. AC

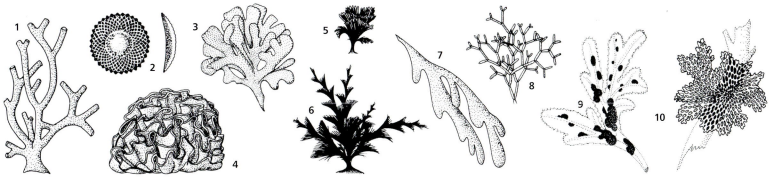

Lampshells

t HE COMMON NAME "LAMPSHELL" EXPRESSES the superficial resemblance of the shells of some of these animals to Roman oil lamps. Lampshells are really animals of the past, for although they are present in modest numbers in various marine habitats the world over, nowhere today do they dominate the seas of the world as they did in the late Paleozoic. Over 30,000 fossil species of lampshells have been identified between the Cambrian and recent times.

Shelf Dwellers
DISTRIBUTION

Lampshells resemble bivalve mollusks, and indeed were classified with them until the middle of the 19th century. Their bodies are ensheathed in a mantle and enclosed by two hinged valves (shells) which protect the soft animal within. The two lobes of the mantle secrete the shells and also enclose and protect the crown (lophophore). However, there are some startling differences between lampshells and mollusks which begin with the issues of symmetry and orientation.

Today lampshells are found living mainly on the continental shelves either attached to rocks or other shells (for example *Crania*) or some (for example *Lingula*) living in burrows in mud. Attachment may be direct or by a cordlike stalk. Some occur in very shallow water, even on shores. Few prosper at any depth. The distribution of these animals is sporadic but where they do occur they may exist in great numbers.

Complex Creatures
FORM AND FUNCTION

The anatomy of lampshells is variable and quite complex. A salient feature is that the upper (dorsal) valve is smaller than the lower (ventral) one.

In most forms the shells are both convex, and the apex of the lower one may be extended to give the effect of the spout of the Roman lamp that the common name alludes to. In some of the burrowing forms the shells are more flattened. The shells themselves may be variously decorated with spines, concentric growth lines fluted or ridged, and their colors range from orange and red to yellow or gray.

The two valves are hinged along the rear line and the manner of their contact forms the basis for a division of the phylum into two classes: Inarticulata and Articulata. In the inarticulate lampshells the valves are linked together by muscles in such a way that they can open widely, but in the articulate lampshells they carry interlocking processes and these limit the extent of the gape. In inarticulate lampshells as many as five pairs of muscles control the movements of the valves while in articulates two or three sets of muscles are involved.

There are other differences between the two classes. In inarticulates the shells are formed from calcium phosphate and the gut terminates in a blind pouch, there being no anus. In articulates the shell is made of calcium carbonate and the gut is a "through" system with an anus. The stalk or pedicle by which most species are attached to the substrate is itself attached to the lower valve. The animals often position themselves so that the lower valve is uppermost, thus adding confusion to the ideas of orientation and symmetry. In a few species the pedicle has been completely lost and here the animals are directly attached to the substrate by the lower valve with the upper valve uppermost.

The body of the animal lies within the valves sheathed in mantle tissue, which are extensions of

FACTFILE

LAMPSHELLS

Phylum: Brachiopoda

Classes: Articulata, Inarticulata

About 335 species in 69 genera and 2 classes.

Distribution Worldwide, marine.

Fossil record Very extensive, early Cambrian (about 600 million years ago) to recent, with greatest profusion in the late Paleozoic (up to 225 m.y.a.).

Size Shell length usually from less than 1mm to 4cm (0.3–1.5in) plus stalk, 9 cm in some extreme cases. Some extinct species reached 30cm (12in).

Features Stalked animals with bilaterally symmetrical shells in two halves (bivalve), comprising dorsal and central valves; body cavity a coelom; circulatory system open with contractile dorsal vessel; excretion via one or two pairs of nephridia, which also serve to release the reproductive cells; conspicuous loop-shaped ciliated respiratory and filter-feeding tentacle crown (lophophore).

CLASS ARTICULATA
3 living orders, 4 extinct. Valves locked at rear by a tooth and socket; lophophore has internal support; anus absent. Genera include: *Terebratella*.

CLASS INARTICULATA
2 living orders, 3 extinct. Valves held together by muscles only; lophophore lacks an external skeleton; anus present. Genera include: *Lingula*.

◐ **Right** *A lampshell (Terebratulina retusa). Inside the shells, it is possible to make out the lophophore, with its numerous fine tentacles. This species occurs at depths ranging from 15m to 1500m, and particularly favors habitats that are sheltered from wave action and strong currents.*

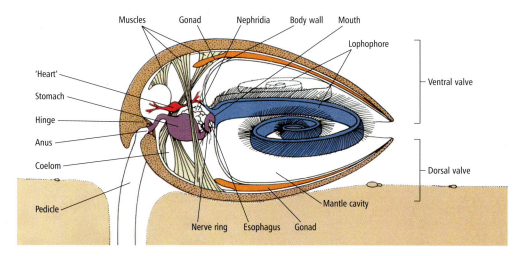

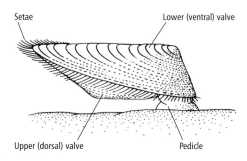

◐ **Left and above** *Body plan of a lampshell, showing the internal organs. The external view shows its attachment to the substrate via the pedicle.*

the body wall. A true body cavity (coelom) lies between the body wall and the gut. The epidermis of the exposed inner mantle surface is hairy (ciliated). The lophophore is suspended in the mantle cavity and consists of a folded crown of hollow tentacles surrounding the mouth. It is supported by the upper valve of the shell and in some species there is actually a special skeletal structure to carry it. For feeding, the valves gape to the front allowing water to flow over the lophophore. The individual tentacles, which are hollow and ciliated on the outside, can reach to the front margin of the valves. They tend to be held close to the upper valve. Suspended food material is trapped in mucus and swept to the mouth via a special groove. Special currents carry away rejected particles. The mouth leads to an esophagus, which in turn gives on to the stomach.

There is an open circulatory system with a primitive pumping heart sited above the stomach. Blood channels supply the digestive tract, tentacles of the lophophore, the gonads and the nephridia. There is no pigment and few blood cells. Circulation of absorbed food is thought to be the main function of the blood system, while oxygen transport would appear to be undertaken by the coelomic fluid.

For excretion, lampshells have one or two pairs of nephridia, which discharge through pores situated near the mouth. The nervous system is rather simple, with a nerve ring around the esophagus and a smaller dorsal and larger ventral ganglion. From these ganglia nerves supply the lophophore, mantle lobes, and the various muscles that control the valves.

There are very few hermaphrodite lampshells. There are generally up to four gonads per individual and the ripe gametes are discharged into the coelom and leave the body via the nephridiopores. The eggs are generally fertilized in the sea. In most cases the embryo develops into a free-swimming larva, but in a few species it may be brooded. The larval development and planktonic period vary considerably between species.   AC

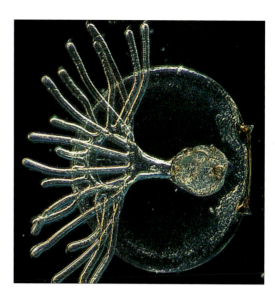

◐ **Above** Larva of the genus Lingula. The large, disklike structure marks the development of the mantle and shells, while the developing lophophore crown shows as the group of tentacles.

Spiny-skinned Invertebrates

FACTFILE

LTERNATIVELY KNOWN AS ECHINODERMS, *spiny-skinned invertebrates are distinct from all other animal types and easily recognizable. The name echinoderm actually means "spiny-skinned," as most members of the group have defensive spines on the outside of their bodies.*

Echinoderms are found only in the sea, never having evolved to cope with the problem of salt balance that life in freshwater would impose on them. As adults they virtually all dwell on the seabed, either, like sea lilies, being attached to it, or, like the starfishes, brittle stars, sea urchins and sea cucumbers, creeping slowly over it. These five groups or classes represent the types of echinoderms found living in the seas and oceans today.

Crystalline Skeletons
FORM AND FUNCTION

For animals relatively high on the evolutionary scale, it is remarkable that a head has never been developed. Echinoderms show a peculiar body symmetry known as pentamerism. This is effectively a form of radial symmetry with the body arranged around the axis of the mouth. Superim-

---

SPINY-SKINNED INVERTEBRATES

Phylum: Echinodermata

About 6,000 species in 3 subphyla and 5 classes (at least 17 in total when including the 12 extinct classes). There is also a fourth subphylum – Homalozoa – but this is extinct.

Distribution Worldwide, exclusively marine.

Fossil record Some 13,000 species known, extensively from pre-Cambrian to recent times.

Size 5mm–1m (0.2in–3.3ft).

Features Adults coelomate (body originally made up of 3 layers of cells), mostly radially symmetrical and 5-sided; no head, body star-shaped or more or less globular, or cucumber-shaped; calcareous endoskeleton gives flexible or rigid support, often extends into spines externally; tentacled tube feet, associated with water vascular system unique to phylum, used in respiration, food-gathering and usually locomotion (not crinoids or ophiuroids); no complex sense organs; nervous tissue dispersed through body; no nephridia; nearly all species sedentary bottom-dwellers; generally separate

sexes, fertilization external; fertilized eggs and larvae generally planktonic; larval stages bilaterally symmetrical.

SEA LILIES AND FEATHER STARS
Subphylum Crinozoa
About 650 species; one living class among the 6 classes and most species known from fossils. Sedentary, mostly stalked, at least in young even if adults freeliving; branching main nervous system; anal opening on same surface as mouth.

STARFISHES, BRITTLE STARS, AND BASKET STARS
Subphylum Asterozoa
About 4,000 species (including the sea daisies) in 2 classes. Stemless, mobile, freeliving; mouth surface faces down, nervous system on mouth surface; usually have arms (rays).

SEA URCHINS AND SEA CUCUMBERS
Subphylum Echinozoa
About 1,250 species in 2 living classes (making up the 6 fossil classes). Stemless, mobile, freeliving; mouth surface downward or to front; main nervous system on oral surface; without arms or rays, external madreporite away from under surface.

See The 3 Subphyla and 5 Classes of Living Echinoderms ▷

○ **Below** *The Western spiny brittle star* (Ophiothrix spiculata) *is found in large groups on the Pacific coast of N and S America. Anchoring itself with one or more arms, it extends the others for filter feeding.*

◐ **Right** Oxycomanthus bennetti, *a species of feather star or crinoid, traps food in its sticky, brittle, fernlike arms. Crinoids are the only surviving echinoderm group that is primarily sessile.*

---

posed on this radial pattern is a five-sided arrangement of the body – epitomized by the starfish. The result is that the echinoderm body usually has five points of symmetry arranged around the axis of the mouth. These points are very often associated with the locomotory organs or tube feet.

While five-pointed symmetry or pentamerism is largely displayed by most present-day adult echinoderms, it is interesting to note that their larvae are bilaterally symmetrical (symmetrical on either side of a line along the length of the animal), and that their primitive ancestors, which appeared in the preCambrian seas, were also bilaterally symmetrical. The causes of pentamerism are unclear, but some authorities have suggested that it leads to a stronger skeletal framework.

The body of echinoderms shows a deuterostome coelomate level of organization. This means that they are relatively highly evolved invertebrates with a body constructed originally from three layers of cells.

The echinoderm skeleton is made of many crystals of calcite (calcium carbonate). It is unusual because these crystals are perforated by many spaces in life (reticulate) so that the tissue which forms the crystals actually invades them. Such a reticulate arrangement leads to a lightening of the

crystal structure and hence a reduction in weight of the animal without any loss of strength. One side effect of this crystal structure is that it is easily invaded by mineral after the death of the animal and thus it fossilizes beautifully.

The skeleton supports the body wall or test. This reinforced structure may be soft (as in sea cucumbers) or hard (sea urchins) but it should never be thought of as a shell because it is covered by living tissue.

The exterior of each class of echinoderm appears different, and so too is the way in which the skeleton has been deployed. In the sea cucumbers the calcite crystals are embedded in the body wall and linked by flexible connective tissue in a way that does not occur in the other classes. In the starfish there is sometimes a flexible body wall, but more often the crystals are grouped close together, sometimes being "stitched" together by fibers of connective tissue running through the crystal perforations. Individual crystals may be extensively developed to form spines or marginal plates. The sea urchins have carried the skeletal process further, for in almost all the skeleton is rigid, being composed of many interlocking crystals. At the same time there is a reduction in the soft tissue of the body wall. The sea urchins have some of the most complex arrangements of muscle and skeleton in the phylum, for example the chewing teeth or "lantern teeth," as Aristotle called them, and the pedicellariae.

In the sea lilies and feather stars, and the brittle stars, the skeleton is massive and arranged as a series of plates, ossicles and spines with a mini-mum of soft tissue. In both these classes the major internal organs or viscera are contained in a reduced area, the cuplike body (theca) of the crinoids and the disklike central body of the brittle stars. Here the skeleton reinforces the body wall, which remains flexible; but in the arms the ossicles become massive, operating with muscles and connective tissue in a way rather reminiscent of the vertebrae of the human backbone. In the arms of both types there is relatively little soft tissue. In the sea lilies the arms branch near their bases into two or more main axes, each bearing lateral branches called pinnacles. The arms of brittle stars branch only in the basket stars.

The drifting echinoderm larvae also have a skeleton, which serves to support their delicate swimming processes.

Sophisticated Hydraulics
WATER VASCULAR SYSTEM AND TUBE FEET

Another unique feature of echinoderms is their water vascular system. This probably arose in the primitive echinoderms as a respiratory system pointing away from the substratum which could be withdrawn inside the heavily armored test. As the echinoderms became more advanced it was arranged around the mouth, but still held away from the substratum. Branching processes developed, forming a system of tentacles that became useful for suspension-feeding as well as respiration. It is in this state that the water vascular system is seen in present-day sea lilies and feather stars. Their branched tentacles, also called tube feet (although in the crinoids they have no locomotory role), are arranged in a double row along the upper side of each arm, bounding a food groove, and along the branches of the arms (pinnules). The tube feet can be extended by hydraulic pressure from within the animal, and much of the water vascular system is internal. They are supplied with fluid from a radial water canal which runs down the center of each arm, just below the food groove, and which sends a branch into each pinnule. The radial water canal of each arm connects with that of its fellows via a circular canal running around the gullet of the animal. Pressure is generated inside the system by the contraction of some of the tube feet, and also by special muscles in the canal itself which generate local pressure increases to distend the neighboring tube feet. The water vascular system in crinoids is associated with several other tubular networks, notably the hemal and perihemal systems (whose role is less easy to define) and the radial water canal also runs close to the radial nerve cord which controls the tube feet.

The activities of the tube feet relate to gas exchange (respiration) and food gathering. The tube feet are equipped with mucous glands in crinoids and when a small fragment of drifting food collides with one, the fragment sticks to the tube feet, is bound in mucus and flicked into the food groove by which it passes down to the central mouth. The tube feet are arranged in double rows alternating with small nondistendable lappets. This arrangement assures their efficient use in feeding.

Crinoids exploit currents of water in the sea. They do not pump water to get their food, but gather it passively. They "fish" for food particles using the tube feet and select mainly those in the 0.3–0.5mm (0.01–0.02in) size range.

In all the remaining groups of echinoderms, the orientation of the body is reversed with respect to the substrate. The tube feet actually make contact with the ground over which the animals are moving and thus take up an additional role in locomotion. This happens in the starfishes, sea urchins, and sea cucumbers but not in the basket and brittle stars, where movement is

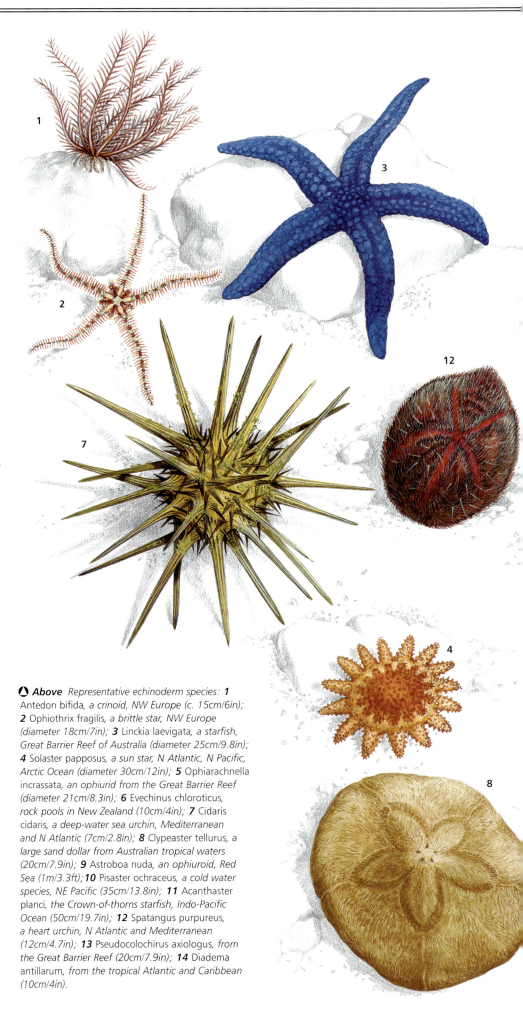

⚫ **Above** Representative echinoderm species: **1** Antedon bifida, *a crinoid, NW Europe (c. 15cm/6in);* **2** Ophiothrix fragilis, *a brittle star, NW Europe (diameter 18cm/7in);* **3** Linckia laevigata, *a starfish, Great Barrier Reef of Australia (diameter 25cm/9.8in);* **4** Solaster papposus, *a sun star, N Atlantic, N Pacific, Arctic Ocean (diameter 30cm/12in);* **5** Ophiarachnella incrassata, *an ophiurid from the Great Barrier Reef (diameter 21cm/8.3in);* **6** Evechinus chloroticus, *rock pools in New Zealand (10cm/4in);* **7** Cidaris cidaris, *a deep-water sea urchin, Mediterranean and N Atlantic (7cm/2.8in);* **8** Clypeaster tellurus, *a large sand dollar from Australian tropical waters (20cm/7.9in);* **9** Astroboa nuda, *an ophiuroid, Red Sea (1m/3.3ft);* **10** Pisaster ochraceus, *a cold water species, NE Pacific (35cm/13.8in);* **11** Acanthaster planci, *the Crown-of-thorns starfish, Indo-Pacific Ocean (50cm/19.7in);* **12** Spatangus purpureus, *a heart urchin, N Atlantic and Mediterranean (12cm/4.7in);* **13** Pseudocolochirus axiologus, *from the Great Barrier Reef (20cm/7.9in);* **14** Diadema antillarum, *from the tropical Atlantic and Caribbean (10cm/4in).*

achieved by bending the arms, while the tube feet are still important in respiration and food gathering. In the basket stars they are well developed for suspension feeding in a way which has interesting parallels with the crinoids. The basket stars, too, exploit currents of water, and arrange their complex branching arms with tube feet as a parabolic net sieving the water currents for particles in the $10–30\mu m$ size range. Thus they do not exactly compete with the crinoids in the same habitat. They are able to withstand stronger currents than the crinoids. In the remaining types of brittle stars there is a range of feeding habits. Some, like *Ophiothrix fragilis*, are suspension feeders, often living in huge beds. Others are detritus or carrion feeders. In many species the tube feet, which are suckerless, are very important in transferring food to the mouth and have a sticky mucous coating which helps this. Water pressure for their extension is derived partly from the head bulbs associated with each tube foot and partly from the effects of other tube feet retracting.

In the starfishes, sea urchins, and sea cucumbers each tube foot is associated with its own reservoir or ampulla. The ampulla is thought to play a role in filling the tube foot with water vascular fluid. It has its own muscle system and connects to the foot by valves to control the flow. However it seems certain that fluid pressure within the water vascular system is also important. The shafts of the tube feet are equipped with muscles for retraction and for stepping movements.

Suckered tube feet occur in all sea urchins and many sea cucumbers. Some asteroids, for example *Luidia* and *Astropecten* species, lack suckers on the tube feet, and most of these burrow in sand. Other starfishes, inhabiting hard substrates, have suckered tube feet and use them for locomotion

Below An eleven-armed seastar (Coscinasterias muricata) *regenerating from a severed arm; starfish can regrow a whole new body if part of the animal's central disk is attached to the dismembered arm.*

Below *Sperm is released from a spawning male Velvet seastar (Petricia vernicina). Seastars can reproduce either asexually (through regeneration) or sexually, with females producing 10-25 million eggs a year.*

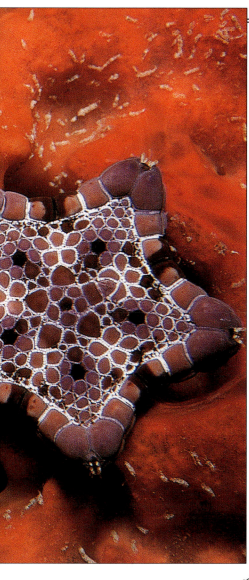

○ **Left** *The aptly named Biscuit seastar (Tosia australis) varies widely in color – ranging from orange and purple to a vivid yellow – and in pattern.*

and for seizing prey. In the burrowing sea urchins, such as *Echinocardium* species, some of the tube feet are highly specialized for tunnel-building and for ventilating the burrow. In the sea cucumbers the ambulacral tube feet may be used for locomotion and respiration, while those surrounding the mouth have become well developed for suspension or deposit feeding and form the characteristic oral tentacles. There are many closely related sea cucumbers which feed in slightly different ways, each having slightly modified oral tentacles so they can exploit food deposits of detritus particles of different sizes.

The fluid within the water vascular system is essentially seawater with added cellular and organic material. Water vascular fluid is responsible for other tasks apart from driving the tube feet. It transports food and waste material and conveys oxygen and carbon dioxide to and from the tissues of the body. It contains many cells. These are mainly amoeboid coelomocytes which have a role to play in excretion, wound healing, repair and regeneration. No excretory organs have been identified in the echinoderms.

The water vascular system of starfishes, basket and brittle stars, and sea urchins appears to communicate to the exterior of the animal via a special

sievelike plate, the madreporite. In sea cucumbers the madreporite is internal, while in the crinoids it is lacking altogether. It used to be thought that seawater entered and left the water vascular system via the madreporite, but more recent research in sea urchins shows that in fact very little water actually moves across this special structure. In starfish and sea urchins the madreporite may be associated with orientation during locomotion (see below).

Sensitive and Self-righting

NERVOUS SYSTEM

The nervous system of echinoderms is peculiar to the group. Because of the absence of a head, there is no brain and no aggregation of nerve organs in one part of the body. In fact, with the exception of the rudimentary eyes (optic cushions) of starfishes, the balance organs (statocysts) of some sea cucumbers, and the chemosensory receptors of pedicellariae of sea urchins (see Grooming Tools of Echinoderms), there are no complex sense organs in echinoderms. Instead, there are simple receptor cells responding to touch and chemicals in solution. These appear to be widely spread over the surface of the animals. Some authorities suggest that all the external epithelial cells of starfish and sea urchins may have a sensory function.

In all living echinoderms the main part of the nervous system comprises the nerve cords which run along the axis of each arm close to the radial

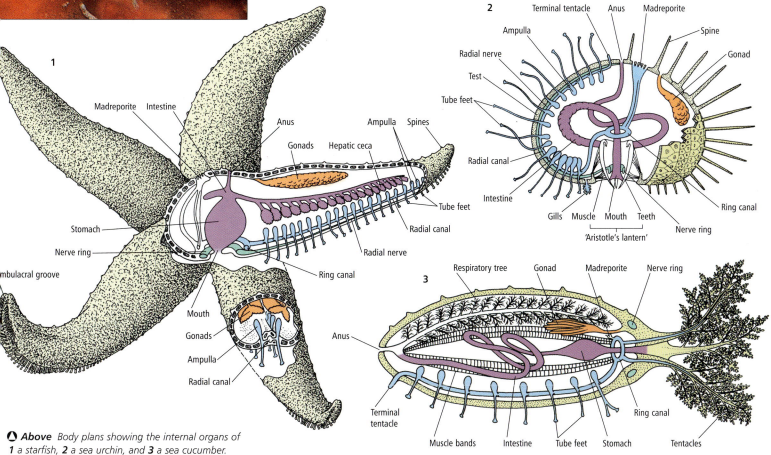

○ **Above** *Body plans showing the internal organs of 1 a starfish, 2 a sea urchin, and 3 a sea cucumber.*

◖ **Left** *A starfish moves in for the kill on a Queen scallop* (Aequipecten opercularis). *Starfishes use their tube feet to pry open the shells of bivalves.*

◖ **Below left** *The arms of brittle stars are made up of many ossicles that fit together rather like the vertebrae of the chordate spine. Here, a snake star* (Ophiothrix *sp.*) *is wrapped around a gorgonian sea fan.*

◖ **Below** *A Southern basket star* (Conocladus australis). *Unlike their relatives in the class Ophiuroidea, the carnivorous brittle stars, basket stars are highly specialized echinoderms that are adapted for suspension feeding on plankton.*

water canal. These radial nerve cords are linked together around the esophagus by a circumesophageal nerve cord so that the activities of one arm or ray may be integrated with the activities of the others.

The control of the tube feet and body-wall muscles is under the command of each radial nerve cord. The responsibilities for coordinated locomotion and direction of movement lie here too. In directional terms echinoderms may move with one arm or ray taking the lead, or even with the space between two acting as a leading edge. Where there is a need to back away, the animal may either go into reverse or actually turn around. In the starfish and sea urchins there is some evidence to suggest that the space between two rays containing the madreporite may often act as the leading edge, possibly because the madreporite has some, as yet unknown sensory function.

Echinoderms are all extremely sensitive to gravity and generally show a well-defined righting response if they are turned upside down. It has been suggested that in the sea urchins, small club-like organs known as sphaeridia act as organs of balance. All other echinoderms, apart from a few sea cucumbers, lack the balance organs (statocysts) that are frequently encountered in mollusks and in crustaceans.

In starfishes and sea urchins the outer surface of the body is covered by a well-developed epithelium at the base of which lies a network of nerves. This nerve plexus controls the external appendages of these two groups which are richly developed in many species. The appendages include various effector organs, movable spines, pedicellariae (minute tonglike grasping organs), sphaeridia in sea urchins and paxillae and papulae in starfishes. These organs are concerned with defending the animal against intruders and keeping the delicate skin of the test clean from deposits of silt and detritus.

The basi-epithelial nerve plexus connects with the radial nerve cords of each arm or ray, thereby forming a system of fine nerves that link the receptor site of the epithelium with the various effector organs.

Efficient Predators

FEEDING AND BEHAVIOR

The various groups of existing echinoderms show characteristic patterns of behavior. All echinoderms are sensitive to touch, and to waterborne chemicals which signal the presence of desirable prey or of potential predators which must be avoided. Most starfish species are efficient predators, feeding on other invertebrates, such as worms, mollusks, and other echinoderms. Recent research has shown that not only are starfish and sea urchins able to "smell" the presence of suitable food in the water and move efficiently towards it,

but they can discriminate between the scent of undamaged members of their own species and ones which have been injured, and thus escape the attacks of other predators upon them.

For the common European starfish, mussels and oysters are significant prey items. The sun stars *Solaster endeca* and *Crossaster papposus* also feed on bivalves, but may attack *Asterias* too. In tropical waters starfishes exhibit a variety of tastes, but the Crown-of-thorns (*Acanthaster planci*) is well known for its selection of certain species of reef-building coral as prey. All these echinoderm predators will move efficiently toward the source

of chemical scent in the water. When they have arrived at it they will commence attack. Some excitement attended the discovery of a new group of echinoderms in the early 1980s. These deep sea forms, the sea daisies (genus *Xyloplax*) were initially grouped in a new class of their own but are now thought to be aberrant starfish belonging to the order Spinulosida.

Some of the burrowing starfish (e.g. *Astropecten* species) will ingest their prey of gastropods whole. *Crossaster* species may attack *Asterias* by hanging on to one ray with the mouth and eating it while the prey drags the predator about. *Acanthaster*

△ *Above* *Purple sea urchins* (Stronglyocentrotus pupuratus) *are a key element in the ecosystem of the North American west coast; they keep kelp forests in check, but themselves are preyed upon by sea otters.*

▷ *Right* *The Fire urchin* (Asthenosoma varium) *is well equipped to defend itself against even large predators such as starfishes. Each of its spines is tipped with a white venom sac.*

feeds on objects too large to be ingested whole, so it everts the stomach membranes through its mouth and smothers the prey with these, digesting the victim outside its body. When the process of digestion is complete, the stomach membranes are withdrawn.

Members of the genus *Asterias*, like other starfishes which prey on bivalves, are able to use their tube feet with their suckers to prize open the valves of a mussel or oyster.

They do this by climbing on to the prey and attaching some tube feet to each valve. The two valves are then pulled apart by the persistent actions of the tube feet. The muscles which keep the shells closed eventually tire, so that they gape ever so slightly. A gap of one or two millimetres is all that is needed for the starfish to insert some of its stomach folds passed out through its mouth. Once this has been done, digestion of the victim will begin and in the end only the cleaned empty shell will remain.

It is interesting to note that in both tropical starfish (for example *Acanthaster* species) and temperate species (for example *Asterias*), solitary individuals display a different type of feeding behavior from that of individuals feeding together in groups. In these starfishes, regular feeding tends to be solitary and at night, the individuals being well spaced one from the next. In some populations, individuals will gather periodically in large numbers at a superabundant food source and feed by day as well as by night; as a result of such social feeding, the growth rate of individuals considerably surpasses the norm. To what extent these differences are acquired or inherited is not yet clear.

In the sea urchins there is a range of feeding behavior. Many of the round (or regular) echinoids (e.g. the genera *Strongylocentrotus*, *Arbacia* and *Echinus*) are omnivores. They browse on algae and encrusting animals such as hydrozoans and barnacles, using their Aristotle's lantern teeth. In many places echinoids are important at limiting the growth of marine plants and compete very successfully with other types of algal grazers, including gastropod mollusks and fish, as recent research in the Caribbean has shown.

The irregular sea urchins, including the sand

dollars and heart urchins, are more specialized feeders. The sand dollars live partly buried in the sand and use their modified spines and tube feet to collect particles of detritus for food. These are then passed to the mouth along ciliated tracts. The heart urchins burrow quite deeply in sand and gravels and ingest the substrate entire. They have lost the Aristotle's lantern. As the substrate

◑ Above *The Pencil sea urchin* (Goniocidaris tubaria) *is a generalist feeder. While algae and seabed detritus make up most of its diet, it will also take carrion. These two urchins are devouring a dead seahorse.*

◐ Overleaf *Close-up of the respiratory gills and tube feet of a Green sea urchin* (Psammechinus miliaris). *This regular echinoid species typically grazes on beds of brown kelp* (Laminaria saccharina).

GROOMING TOOLS OF ECHINODERMS

Between their spines, most starfishes and all sea urchins carry unique small grooming organs like microscopic tongs or forceps. These intriguing organs were once thought to be parasites on the tests of the animals that bear them, but are in actual fact an integral part of the animal. Each consists of two or more jaws supported by skeletal ossicles called valves. Some starfish types are directly attached to the test. Others, like those of sea urchins, are carried on stalks, so that the jaws are able to reach down to the surface of the test.

The jaws are caused to open or close by muscles attached to nerves from both the base of the epithelium of the test and from special receptors responsive to touch and certain chemicals. Most of these receptors are situated on the inside of the jaw blades, but some lie on the outside.

In an undisturbed animal, the epithelial nerves may close down most of the pedicellariae (except some on the sea urchins; see below), so that they are inactive with the jaws closed. If an intruding organism strays onto the test, such as a small crustacean or a barnacle larva seeking a place to settle, the resultant tactile stimuli cause the pedicellariae to gape open and thus expose the special touch receptors. If these are stimulated, the jaws rapidly snap shut, trapping the intruder. The pedicellariae of starfish (skeletal parts only) **1** and the tridentate (three-jawed) **2** and

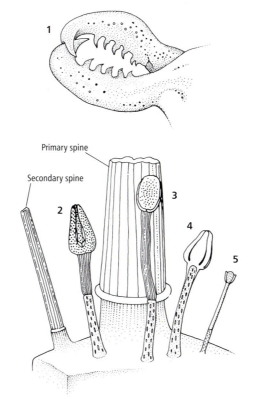

Primary spine

Secondary spine

ophiocephalous (snakehead) **3** ones of sea urchins are all specialized for such activities and often have fearsome teeth to grip their victims.

In the globiferous (roundheaded) pedicellariae **4** of the sea urchin class Echinoidea, there are venom sacs. Here the jaws close only on objects which carry certain chemicals. The venom is injected into the victim via a hollow tooth in many echinoids and in species such as *Toxopneustes pileosus* it has a powerful effect. Globiferous pedicellariae detach after the venom is injected and remain embedded in the tissue of the intruder. They seem to be mainly deployed by the sea urchins as defenses against larger predators such as starfish.

In the sea urchins, sand dollars and heart urchins the smallest class of pedicellariae are known as trifoliate (three-leaved) **5**. They differ from all the others in having spontaneous jaw movements, "mouthing" over the surface of the test in grooming and cleaning activities. This persists even when these pedicellariae are removed from the test.

Far from being the parasites they were once believed to be, pedicellariae therefore perform a highly beneficial function, by keeping the surface of the echinoderm free from other animal, or plant, organisms. Their complex structure is a good example of the intricacies of echinoderm biology, but their various roles are not yet all understood. AC

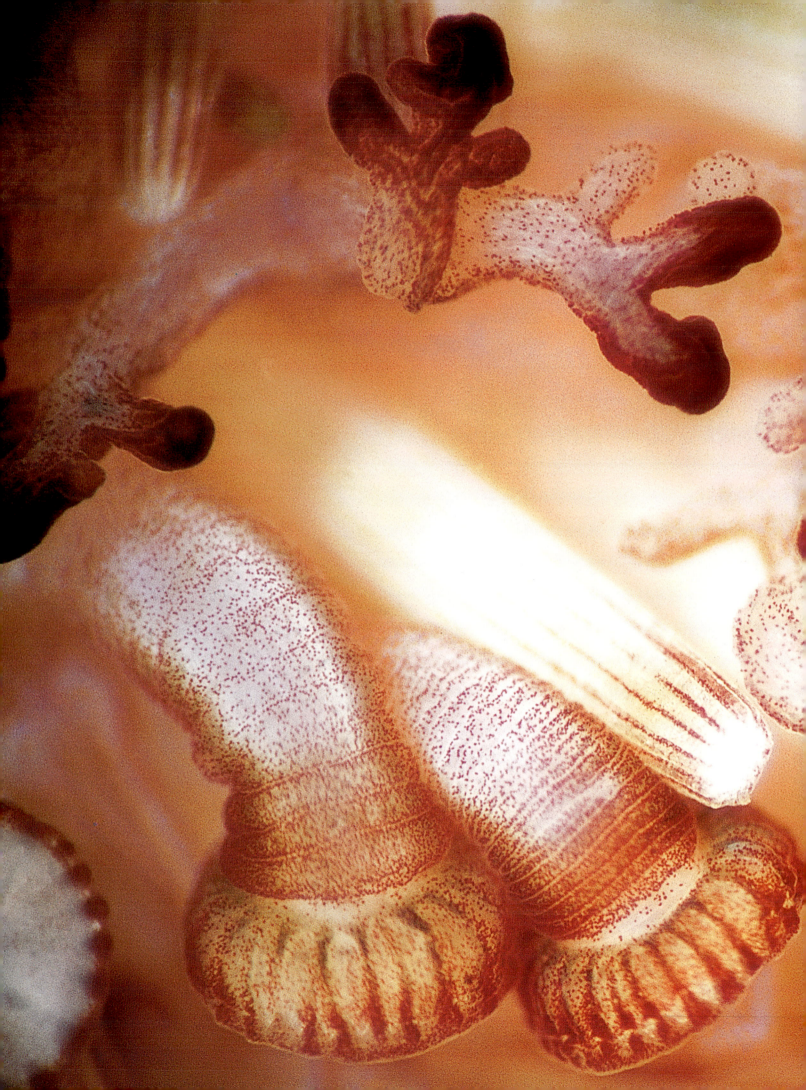

particles pass along their guts any organic material is digested and "clean" substrate is passed out from the anus.

The sea cucumbers have diversified to exploit a number of food sources. In virtually every case the form of their oral tentacles, the specialized tube feet arranged round the mouth, is adapted to gathering food.

Some groups sweep the surface of sand and mud for particles of detritus and thus live as deposit feeders. Others are suspension feeders relying on currents of seawater to sweep suspended particles of food into their oral tentacles. In both cases the size of the sweeping or filtering fronds and the gap between will dictate the sizes of the particles collected.

Synchronized Spawning
BREEDING

The majority of echinoderm species are dioecious – the sexes are separate. A few are hermaphrodite, passing through a male phase before becoming functional females. In one genus, *Archaster* from the western Pacific, pseudocopulatory activity occurs, with the one partner climbing on top of the other, but even here fertilization is external. Sperm and eggs are released into the seawater via short gonoducts. In many species, this is almost a casual affair, and the partners do not come close together. However, synchrony of spawning is essential and this is usually governed by water temperature, and chemical stimuli operating between participants.

Antarctic and abyssal echinoderms often brood their eggs, and a direct development of juveniles occurs in brood pouches or between spines. In the remaining species – the vast majority – the fertilized eggs drift in the oceanic plankton and develop through characteristic larval stages, usually feeding on minute planktonic plants such as diatoms and dinoflagellates. After a period of larval life that may range from a few days to several weeks, depending on different species, metamorphosis occurs, and the juvenile echinoderms settle on the sea bed.

◁ Left *Sea potatoes (Echinocardium spp.) are a form of heart urchin. Mass mortality of this species sometimes occurs, either through storms disturbing the seabed or decaying plankton robbing the water of oxygen.*

Unusual Delicacies
CONSERVATION AND ENVIRONMENT

The fascinating and often beautiful echinoderms inhabit all the world's seas, from the intertidal zone down to the ocean abyss. They are also present in all latitudes from the tropics to the poles. In temperate intertidal zones such as the North Atlantic and North Pacific starfishes and sea urchins are familiar organisms. In some places, sea urchins may be harvested for use as food, for example *Paracentrotus lividus* in Ireland and the Mediterranean and *Tripneustes gratilla* in Mauritius. Brittle stars and sea cucumbers, though present, are less conspicuous intertidally. The shallow seas overlying the continental shelves are particularly good habitats for echinoderms where coastal currents, rich in nutrients, sweep detritus and plankton for suspension feeders such as the crinoids and sea cucumbers and nourish prey suitable for starfishes. In tropical areas the development of reefs allows a great diversity of echinoderm species to develop because of the variety of niches. Certain tropical species of sea cucumber are fished commercially and sold to far eastern markets as *Trepang* or *Beche-de-mer*. Although all groups of echinoderms inhabit the ocean abyss, it is here that the sea cucumbers flourish, often in great densities, moving over the benthic ooze in search of detrital food. Here, too, some highly unusual epibenthic sea cucumbers have taken to a swimming life, moving along in deep currents and collecting food as they go. AC

◁ Above and below *Sea cucumbers play a vital role in the ecology of the seabed. Their feeding churns up sediments, so oxygenating the water, and also recycles nutrients. Above, the colorful* Bohadschia graeffei *and below, a* Stichopus *sp. holothurian.*

The 3 Subphyla and 5 Living Classes of Echinoderms

SUBPHYLUM CRINOZOA

Crinoids
Class Crinoidea

650 species. Comprises the order Articulata, lacking madreporite, spines and pedicellariae appendages. Genera include: Sea lily (*Metacrinus*), feather star (*Antedon*).

SUBPHYLUM ASTEROZOA

Starfishes
Class Asteroidea

About 2,000 species in 2 subclasses; flattened, star-shaped with 5 unbranched arms which blend into the central body (a few with more); endoskeleton flexible; arms contain digestive ceca; branching madreporite.

SUBCLASS SOMASTEROIDEA
Almost exclusively fossil but including one living genus *Platasterias*.

SUBCLASS EUASTEROIDEA
5 orders include: Platyasterida, including genus *Luidia;* Spinulosida, including the Crown-of-thorns (*Acanthaster planci*) and sea daisies (genus *Xyloplax*); Forcipulatida, including the European starfish (*Asterias rubens*).

Brittle stars, Basket stars
Class Ophiuroidea

About 2,000 species in 3 orders; flattened, 5 sided with long flexible arms rarely branched, clearly demarked from central "control" disk; madrepore on underside; no anus or intestine; tube feet lack suckers.

Order Oegophiurida
Includes the genus *Ophiocanops*.

Basket stars
Order Phrynophiurida
Includes the genus *Gorgonocephalus*.

Brittle stars Order Ophiurida
Includes the genus *Ophiura*.

SUBPHYLUM ECHINOZOA

Sea urchins, Sand dollars, Heart urchins
Class Echinoidea

About 750 species in 2 subclasses; mainly globular or disk-shaped, without arms; covered with numerous spines and pedicecellariae; tube feet usually ending in suckers; endoskeleton comprises close-fitting plates.

SUBCLASS PERISCHOECHINOIDEA
1 living order Cidaroida, including the genus *Cidaris*.

Subphylum Crinozoa
Sea lilies, feather stars

Subphylum Asterozoa
Class Asterozoa
Starfishes

Class Ophiuroidea
Brittle stars, basket stars

SUBCLASS EUECHINOIDA

Superorder Diadematacea
Includes genera *Asthenosoma*, *Diadema*.

Superorder Echinacea
Includes genera *Echinus*, *Psammechinus*, *Paracentrotus*, *Toxopneustes*. *Echinus esculentus* is the sole endangered echinoderm species (Lower Risk/Near Threatened).

Upperorder Gnathostomata
Orders: Holectypoida, including *Echinoneus*, *Micropetalon* and Clypeasteroida, including *Rotula*, *Clypeaster*, *Echinocyamus*; Atelostomata with suborders Holasteroidea, including *Pourtalesia*, *Echinosigria*, and Spatangoida, including *Spatangus*, *Echinocardium*, *Brissopis*.

Sea cucumbers
Class Holothuroidea

About 500 species in 3 subclasses; long, saclike, without arms; bilaterally symmetrical; mouth surrounded by tentacles; no

Subphylum Echinozoa

Class Echinoidea
Sea urchins, sand dollars and heart urchins

Class Holothuroidea
Sea cucumbers

spines or pedicellariae; endoskeleton reduced to microscopic spicules or plates, or absent, internal madreporite.

SUBCLASS DENDROCHIROTACEA

Order Dendrochirotida
Genera include: *Cucumaria*, *Thyone*, *Psolus*

Order Dactylochirotida
Genera include: *Rhopalodina*.

SUBCLASS ASPIDOCHIROTACEA

Order Aspidochirotida
Genera include: *Holothuria*.

Order Elasipodia
Genera include: *Pelagothuria*, *Psychropotes*.

SUBCLASS APODACEA

Order Molpadiida
Genera include: *Moipadia*, *Caudina*.

Order Apodida
Genera include: *Synapta*, *Leptosynapta*.

Acorn Worms and Allies

HEMICHORDATES ARE A MINOR PHYLUM OF *marine invertebrates; they are not abundant and relatively few species are known. Yet they fascinate zoologists, displaying as they do several characters that indicate similarities to the chordates (lancelets, fish, mammals, etc.), a group with which they were once classified. These characters include gill slits and a nerve cord on the upper (dorsal) side of the body. In some species the nerve cord is hollow and like those of vertebrates. At no stage of their development, however, does a rudimentary backbone (notochord) appear, which excludes them from the phylum Chordata.*

Hemichordates are divided into three classes: Enteropneusta (acorn worms); Pterobranchia; and Planctosphaeroida , which have no common names. The pterobranchs are regarded as being more primitive than the acorn worms and some of these lack gill slits and have solid nerve cords. Hemichordates also show similarities to echinoderms; the larva is a tornaria, which has features in common with some echinoderm larvae, for example the asteroid bipinnaria. Intriguingly, the pterobranchs, with their appendages clothed with tentacles, display similarities to the sea mats, horseshoe worms, and lampshells.

Acorn Worms
CLASS ENTEROPNEUSTA

The wormlike acorn worms are the only hemichordates likely to be encountered other than by a scientist, and then only rarely. They grow to 2.5m (5.2ft) in length but are often smaller. Their bodies are made up of three sections, the proboscis at the front, the collar, and the trunk at the rear (which

forms the bulk of the body). The group's common name derives from the way in which the proboscis joins the collar, resembling an acorn sitting in its cup. The proboscis is a small conical structure connected to the collar by a short stalk. The collar itself is cylindrical and runs forward to ensheath the proboscis stalk. The collar bears the mouth on its underside. The trunk makes up most of the body length and at the front end this contains a

⏵ **Right** *The front region of the acorn worm* Balanoglossus australiensis, *a species found in waters around Australia, living in sand under stones.*

⏷ **Below** *Body plans of hemichordates.* **1** *A colony of individuals of the pterobranch genus* Rhabdopleura, *showing individuals within tubes that are connected by a stolon;* **2** *Close-up of the head of* Rhabdopleura *protruding from its tube;* **3** *General body plan of the acorn worm* Saccoglossus; **4** *Front end of the acorn worm* Protoglossus, *showing water currents (as arrows) carrying food particles;* **5** *Burrow system of the acorn worm* Balanoglossus.

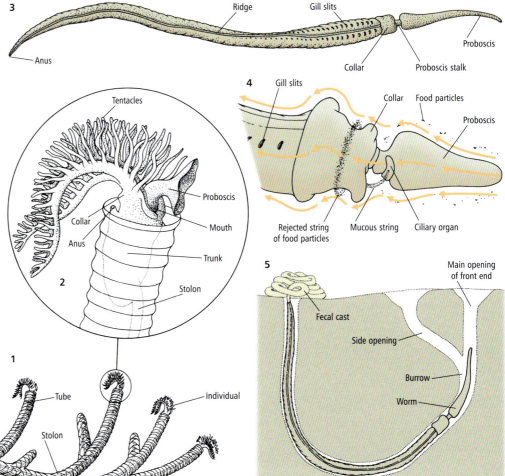

3 Ridge Gill slits Proboscis Anus Collar Proboscis stalk

2 Tentacles Proboscis Collar Mouth Anus Trunk Stolon

4 Gill slits Collar Food particles Proboscis Rejected string of food particles Mucous string Ciliary organ

1 Tube Individual Stolon

5 Fecal cast Main opening of front end Side opening Burrow Worm

The acorn worms' nervous system is primitive in comparison to the chordates, and the animals are not highly active. The sexes are separate and the eggs are fertilized in the sea. Early development is like that of the echinoderms. In some species, it proceeds to a tornaria larva, which lives in the plankton before it metamorphoses. Other types develop directly, with a juvenile worm appearing.

Pterobranchs and Planctosphaeroids
CLASSES PTEROBRANCHA AND PLANCTOSPHAEROIDA

The pterobranchs are very different, although their bodies still show the three zones. The proboscis is smaller and shield- or platelike, while the collar has well-developed outgrowths of tentacles. According to the group, there may be two backward-curving arms bearing tentacles (e.g. *Rhabdopleura*) or between five and nine (*Cephalodiscus*). The tentacles may play a food-gathering role.

The gill slits are few and inconspicuous and none is present in *Rhabdopleura*. In this group the gut is U-shaped with an anus opening on the top side of the collar. Again the sexes are separate and many individuals may live grouped together.

The solitary species *Planctosphaera pelagica* of the Planctosphaeroida drift in the plankton of the Atlantic and Pacific oceans. Their body form is quite unlike any other hemichordate; this organism might well be the larva of an as yet unknown adult hemichordate living on the ocean floor.   AC

THE ENIGMATIC XENOTURBELLA

The primitive marine worm *Xenoturbella*, which DNA sequencing has shown to be related to the hemichordates, may be a common ancestor to all bilaterally symmetrical animals. First described in 1949, *Xenoturbella bocki* was found in marine muds off the Swedish coast. The external surface of the animal is covered with cilia and it is small enough to be confused with some large ciliate protozoans. The taxonomic affinities of *Xenoturbella* were long disputed – it was speculated that it was a flatworm, a cnidarian, or a mollusk.

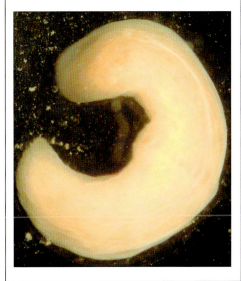

row of gill slits on each side. A ridge runs down the middle of the back of the trunk. The reproductive organs are borne outside the gill slits; in some forms the trunk is extended as winglike genital flaps to contain them. The body cavity (coelom) is present in all three parts of the body. There is a single cavity in the proboscis, a pair of cavities in the collar and a pair in the trunk.

Acorn worms live in shallow water and some species may be found burrowing in sandy and muddy shores, identifiable by their characteristic coiled fecal casts. The burrows may be more or less permanent. Other species can live under stones and pebbles. Most burrowing acorn worms feed on the organic material in the sand or mud in which they live, simply by ingesting the sediment

as an earthworm ingests soil. Some feed by trapping suspended plankton and particles of detritus in the mucus covering on the proboscis. Cilia then pass these particles back to the mouth and the collar plays a role in rejecting unsuitable particles.

The gut runs from the mouth on the collar, via the pharynx of gill slits in the front trunk, to the rear of the trunk where the anus is situated. There is a long, thin blind-ended branch (diverticulum) running from the gut near the mouth into the proboscis, which once was mistaken for a notochord. The gill slits were originally probably feeding mechanisms, which have since become involved in gas exchange. The cilia they bear pump in water through the mouth and out through the gills.

Sea Squirts and Lancelets

VERTEBRATES, FISHES, AMPHIBIA, REPTILES, *and mammals (subphylum Craniata or Vertebrata) are the most familiar members of the phylum Chordata. These animals possess a definite backbone and bony braincase. Yet there are a number of lowly chordates that display the phylum's characteristics at a simple level. All aquatic, they are included in the two other subphyla of the chordates, the Urochordata and Cephalochordata.*

Chordates are "higher animals" possessing a single, hollow, dorsal nerve cord and a body cavity that is a true coelom. However, in the Urochordata and Cephalochordata the dorsal nerve cord is only present during the embryonic development of the animal.

Sea squirts and Allies

SUBPHYLUM UROCHORDATA

The adult sea squirts look nothing like vertebrates. They are bottom-dwellers growing attached to rocks or other organisms. Their bodies are encased in a thick tunic made of material which resembles cellulose, the main constituent of plant cell walls. At the top of the body lies the inhalant siphon, and on the side is the exhalant siphon. There is no head. Water is pumped in via the inhalant siphon and passes through the pharynx and out between the gills into the sleevelike atrium. From the atrium it is discharged via the exhalant siphon. The gills serve as a respiratory surface and also act as a filter, extracting suspended particles of food. They are ciliated, the microscopic cilia providing the pumping force to maintain the respiratory and filter current. Acceptable food particles are collected in sticky mucus secreted by the endostyle, a sort of glandular gutter running down one side of the pharynx, and they are then passed into the gut for digestion. Waste products are liberated from the anus which opens inside the atrium near the exhalant siphon.

Sea squirts may be solitary or colonial. In a colony the exhalant siphons of individuals open into a common cloaca, and each individual retains its own inhalant siphon. Colonial squirts may be arranged in masses, as in *Aplidium* species, where the individuals are hard to recognize, or in encrusting platelike growth, for example *Botryllus* species, where the individuals can easily be made out.

◗ **Right** *Sea squirt species of different genera (*Polycarpa, *the large central organism,* Didemnum, *and the solitary, translucent-blue* Rhopalaea) *on a reef. Some colonial tunicates can be highly invasive.*

SEA SQUIRTS AND LANCELETS

Phylum: Chordata

Around 3,020 species in 2 subphyla.

SEA SQUIRTS AND ALLIES

Subphylum Urochordata (or Tunicata)

About 3,000 species in 4 classes. **Distribution:** worldwide; bottom-dwelling and pelagic at all depths and in all oceans. **Fossil record:** very few, from the Cambrian to the Quaternary (600–500 million years ago to recent). **Size:** individuals from less than 1cm (0.4in) to about 20cm (8in) long. **Features:** chordate characteristics – hollow, dorsal nerve cord, enterocoelic body cavity, gill slits, tail behind anus, and notocord – are all present in the larvae; adults show no segmentation, lack hollow dorsal nerve cord and notochord, and most have the gills surrounded by a large cavity (atrium) and are ensheathed in a test or tunic of tunicin, a substance related to cellulose; hermaphrodite; reproduction often involves budding and an asexual phase; lifecycles complex in Thaliacea and Larvacea.

SEA SQUIRTS Class Ascidiacea

Genera include: *Aplidium*, *Botryllus*, *Ciona*, *Clavelina*.

SALPS OR PELAGIC TUNICATES Class Thaliacea

Genera include: *Pyrosoma*, *Salpa*.

CLASS APPENDICULARIA (= LARVACEA)

Sexually mature adults resemble larvae. Genera include: *Fritillaria*, *Oikopleura*, *Stegasoma*.

SORBERACEANS Class Sorberacea

Genera include: *Octanemus*.

LANCELETS Subphylum Cephalochordata (or Acrania)

Fewer than 20 species in 2 families. **Distribution:** temperate to tropical shallow seas , adults bottom-dwellers, burrowing in sand and fine gravels. **Fossil record:** none. **Size:** up to 5cm (2in) long. **Features:** simple fishlike chordates lacking a recognizable head, with hollow dorsal nerve cord similar to vertebrates, but no vertebrae, instead a notochord, muscle blocks segmented; enterocoelic coelom and well-developed gills; can swim; sexes separate; planktonic tornaria larva produced.

FAMILY BRANCHIOSTOMIDAE

Contains one genus, *Branchiostoma* (or *Amphioxus*).

FAMILY ASYMMETRONIDAE

Contains one genus, *Asymmetron*.

The heart is situated in a loop of the gut and services the very simple blood system. Sea squirts are hermaphrodite, each having male and female organs. In some species the eggs are retained within the atrium, where the sex ducts open, and where they are fertilized by sperm drawn in with the feeding and respiratory currents. The embryos are able to develop here in a protected environment. In other species the eggs and sperm are both liberated into the sea where fertilization occurs. The embryo quickly develops into a tadpole-like larva. This process may take from a few hours to a few days, a timescale that makes these animals ideal specimens for observation and experimental embryology.

The "tadpoles" of sea squirts are small, independent animals like miniature frog's tadpoles. They are sensitive to light and gravity, enabling the animal to select an appropriate substrate for settlement, attachment and metamorphosis. These tadpoles obviously serve to distribute the species too. It is the ascidian tadpole with its chordate characters of dorsal hollow nerve cord, stiffening notochord supporting the muscular tail, and features of the head which tells us much more of the likely evolutionary position of the sea squirts than does the adult.

Some sea squirts are of economic importance because they act as fouling organisms encrusting the hulls of ships and other marine structures. They are also of considerable evolutionary and zoological interest.

The other urochordates, thaliaceans (salps and others), and the larvalike appendicularians, have characters fundamental to the group but have evolved along pelagic and not bottom-dwelling lines. Members of one thaliacean order, the Pyrosomidae, are commonly found in warmer waters and emit phosphorescent light in response to tactile stimulation. These pelagic animals (for example *Pyrosoma* species) live in colonies, but some other types exist as solitary individuals. They have complex life histories. *Oikopleura* is an appendicularian genus of small animals like the tadpoles of sea squirts. Rhythmic movements of the tail draw water through the openings of the gelatinous "house" in which they live and which is secreted by the body. Members of the class Sorberacea resemble the sea squirts, but they are predators living in the deep ocean and they possess dorsal nerve cords as adults.

Lancelets

SUBPHYLUM CEPHALOCHORDATA

The lancelets (named for their elongate, bladelike form) are a minor group of chordates with only two genera and under 20 species. These small, apparently fishlike animals show primitive chordate conditions. The notochord, which in sea squirt larvae merely supports the tail, extends into the head (hence the term cephalochordata). There is

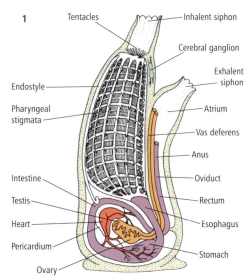

1

Tentacles — Inhalent siphon — Cerebral ganglion — Exhalent siphon — Endostyle — Pharyngeal stigmata — Atrium — Vas deferens — Anus — Intestine — Oviduct — Testis — Rectum — Heart — Esophagus — Pericardium — Stomach — Ovary

no cranium as in the craniates or vertebrates, and the front end, although quite distinct, lacks the well-developed brain, eyes and other sense organs as well as the jaws associated with vertebrates.

In species of *Branchiostoma*, a hood extends over the mouth equipped with slender, tentacle-like cirri instead of jaws. These form a sieve that assists in rejecting particles of food too large for the lancelet's suspension-feeding habit. The oral hood leads to the extensive pharynx via a thin flap of tissue, the velum. The pharyngeal wall is composed of many gill bars and it is the action of the cilia situated on those bars that draws the water and suspended food particles into the body by way of the oral hood. The gill bars act as a filter for food as well as providing a surface for the absorption of oxygen. When water passes through the gill bars, food particles are trapped and passed down to the floor of the pharynx, where they are swept into the endostyle. In this ciliated gutter trapped food is collected up, bound into mucus strands, and passed into the midgut. The filtered water passes out into the atrium and leaves the body via the atrial pore. The midgut has a blind diverticulum leading forward. Backward the midgut leads to the intestine and eventually to the anus.

The anatomy of these coelomates is complex compared to most invertebrates, and has some unusual features. The excretory system consists of saclike nephridia lying above the gill bars. Each lancelet nephridium has a number of flame cells reminiscent of those seen in the flatworms, annelids, and mollusks. In evolutionary terms the nephridia (which do not occur in other primitive chordates) are a far cry from the vertebrate kidneys, which must have evolved via a different route.

The muscle blocks are arranged in segments (myotomes) along either side of the body. A hollow dorsal nerve cord runs the length of the animal and shows very little anterior specialization or brain. As it passes back along the body it branches to supply muscles and other organs.

There is a simple circulatory system with blood vessels passing through the gills to collect oxygen and distribute it to the body. The sexes are separate. In *Branchiostoma* the gonads are arranged on both sides of the body at the bases of the muscle blocks, but in *Asymmetron* they lie only on the right side. Sperms and eggs are released into the atrium by rupture of the gonad wall. They pass out to the sea through the atriopore. Fertilization occurs in the open water and a swimming larva or tornaria type develops. This lives a dual life for several months as it feeds and matures. In the daytime it lies on the seabed but when darkness comes it swims and joins the plankton. When it has attained a length of about 5mm (0.2in) it metamorphoses and becomes bottom-dwelling and more sedentary. The tornaria is the chief distributive phase.

The characters of *Branchiostoma* have helped further our understanding of vertebrate organization, and its simple structure makes it quite easy to identify the basic chordate features, many of which are seen in humans themselves.   AC

2

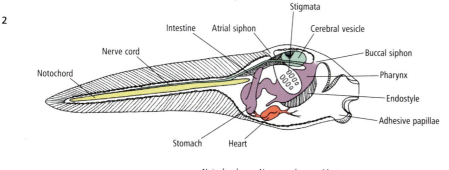

Nerve cord · Notochord · Intestine · Atrial siphon · Stigmata · Cerebral vesicle · Buccal siphon · Pharynx · Endostyle · Adhesive papillae · Stomach · Heart

3

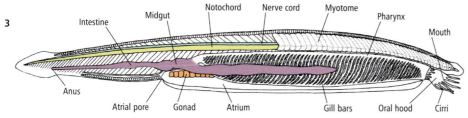

Intestine · Midgut · Notochord · Nerve cord · Myotome · Pharynx · Mouth · Anus · Atrial pore · Gonad · Atrium · Gill bars · Oral hood · Cirri

What is a Fish?

IN ALL PROBABILITY LIFE STARTED IN OUR *planet's waters around 3,000 million years ago. For a very long time not much seems to have happened. The first known multicellular, or many-celled, invertebrates (animals without backbones) evolved about 600 million years ago. After a much shorter interval (in geological terms), about 120 million years, the first aquatic vertebrates (back-boned animals) – the fishes – appeared. From these early fish groups arose the animals most familiar to us today: birds, reptiles, and mammals.*

Over half of the vertebrates alive today are fishes. They do just about everything that the other vertebrates do and also have many unique attributes. Only fishes, for example, make their own light (bioluminescence), produce electricity, and have complete parasitism, as well as having the largest increase in volume from hatching to adulthood.

Different people have different impressions of fishes. To some, the image of the perfect fish is the sharp-toothed shark, elegantly and effortlessly hunting its prey in the sea. To others, fishes are small, entrancing animals kept in home aquaria. For anglers, fish are a cunning quarry to be outwitted and caught. For commercial fishermen, fishes are a mass of writhing bodies being hauled on board the fishing vessel. Biologists regard fishes as representing a mass of challenges concerning evolution, behavior, and form, the study of which results in more questions than answers.

It is the very diversity of fishes, the large number of species and the huge numbers of individuals of some species that make them so interesting, instructive, and useful to us. It is easy to see that the huge shoals of many species (provided they are maintained by careful management) form a valuable food resource for us and other animals, but it is not so generally realized that fishes are also valuable research animals that may help us solve many complex surgical and medical problems. For example, in making transplants of hearts and lungs in humans, there are problems of tissue rejection. How much might we learn from the fusion of the male angler fish onto the female's body, seemingly without any rejection problems? Studies on a few small closely related fishes that exist as eyed coloured surface forms and eyeless

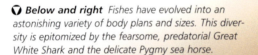 **Below and right** *Fishes have evolved into an astonishing variety of body plans and sizes. This diversity is epitomized by the fearsome, predatorial Great White Shark and the delicate Pygmy sea horse.*

SUPERCLASSES:
AGNATHA AND GNATHOSTOMATA
5 classes; 58 orders; c.469 families

SUPERCLASS AGNATHA (Jawless fishes)
2 families, 12 genera, C.90 species

CLASS CEPHALASPIDOMORPHI

LAMPREYS Order Petromyzontiformes   p156
c.40 species in 6 genera and 1 family

CLASS MYXINI

HAGFISHES Order Myxiniformes   p160
c.43–50 species in 6 genera and 1 family

SUPERCLASS GNATHOSTOMATA (Jawed fishes)
c.467 families, c 4,180 genera, c. 24,510 species

CLASS CHONDRICHTHYES (Cartilaginous fishes)
34 families, 138 genera, c. 915 species in 14 orders

FRILLED SHARK Order Chlamydoselachiformes p276
1 species *Chlamydoselachus anguil*

SIX- AND SEVEN-GILLED SHARKS
Order Hexanchiformes   p276
5 species in 3 genera and 1 family

CATSHARKS Order Scyliorhyniformes   p276
87 species in c.15 genera and 3 families

SMOOTH DOGFISH SHARKS Order Triakiformes p276
30 species in 5 genera and 1 family

PORT JACKSON SHARKS
Order Heterodontiformes   p278
8 species in 1 genus and 1 family

ORECTOLOBOIDS Order Orectolobiformes p278
31 species in 13 genera and 7 families

REQUIEM SHARKS Order Carcharhiniformes p279
c.100 species in 10 genera and 1 family

GOBLIN SHARKS & ALLIES
Order Odontaspidiformes   p279
7 species in 4 genera and 3 families

THRESHER SHARKS & ALLIES Order Isuriformes p281
10 species in 6 genera and 3 families

SPINY DOGFISH & ALLIES Order Squaliformes p281
c.70 species in c.12 genera and 1 family

ANGEL SHARKS Order Squatiniformes   p283
10 species in 1 genus and 1 family

SAWSHARKS Order Pristiophoriformes   p283
5 species in 2 genera and 1 family

SKATES, RAYS & SAWFISHES Order Batiformes p284
c.465 species in c.62 genera and 12 families

CHIMAERAS Order Chimaeriformes   p289
31 species in 6 genera and 3 families

CLASS ACTINOPTERYGII (Ray-finned fishes)
c.428 families, c.4,037 genera, c.23,600 species in 39 orders

BICHIRS Order Polypteriformes   p268
10 species in 2 genera and 1 family

CLASS SARCOPTERYGII (Lobe-finned fishes)
5 families, 5 genera, 8 species, and 3 orders

COELACANTHS Order Coelacanthiformes p269
2 species in 1 genus and 1 family

AUSTRALIAN LUNGFISHES
Order Ceratodontiformes   p270
1 species *Neoceratodus forsteri*

SOUTH AMERICAN AND AFRICAN LUNGFISHES
Order Lepidosirenifomes   p270
5 species in 3 genera and 3 families

STURGEONS AND PADDLEFISHES
Order Acipenseriformes   p162
27 species in 6 genera and 2 families

BOWFIN Order Amiiformes   p165
1 species *Amia calva*

GARFISHES Order Semionotiformes   p164
7 species in 2 genera and 1 family

TARPONS & ALLIES Order Elopiformes p166
8 species in 2 genera and 2 families

BONEFISHES, SPINY EELS, & ALLIES
Order Albuliformes   p167
29 species in 8 genera and 3 families

EELS Order Anguilliformes   p168
738 species in 141 genera and 15 families

GULPER EELS & ALLIES
Order Saccopharyngiformes   p178
c.26 species in 5 genera and 4 families

HERRINGS AND ANCHOVIES
Order Clupeiformes   p182
c357 species in 83 genera and 4 families

BONYTONGUES & ALLIES
Order Osteoglossiformes   p184
c.217 species in 29 genera and 6 families

PIKES AND MUDMINNOWS Order Esociformes p186
10 species in 4 genera and 2 families

SMELTS & ALLIES Order Osmeriformes   p191
c.241 species in 74 genera and 13 families

SALMON, TROUT, & ALLIES
Order Salmoniformes   p196
66 species in 11 genera and 1 family

BRISTLEMOUTHS & ALLIES Order Stomiiformes p204
c.320 species in 50 genera and 4 families

LIZARDFISHES Order Aulopiformes   p210
c.225 species in c.40 genera and 15 families

LANTERNFISHES Order Myctophiformes   p213
c.25 species in c.35 genera and 2 families

CHARACINS & ALLIES Order Characiformes p215
c.1,340 species in c.250 genera and c.15 families

CATFISHES Order Siluriformes   p218
c.2,400 species in c.410 genera and 34 families

CARPS & ALLIES Order Cypriniformes   p222
c.2,660 species in c.279 genera and 5 families

NEW WORLD KNIFEFISHES
Order Gymnotiformes   p225
c.62 species in 23 genera and 6 families

MILKFISHES & ALLIES
Order Gonorhynchiformes   p225
c.35 species in 7 genera and 4 families

TROUT-PERCHES & ALLIES
Order Percopsiformes   p229
9 species in 6 genera and 3 families

CUSKEELS & ALLIES Order Ophidiiformes p230
c.355 species in 92 genera and 5 families

CODFISHES & ALLIES Order Gadiformes p231
c.482 species in 85 genera and 12 families

TOADFISHES Order Batrachoidiformes p234
69 species in 19 genera and 1 family

ANGLERFISHES Order Lophiiformes p234
c.310 species in 65 genera and 18 families

SILVERSIDES Order Atheriniformes   p240
290 species in 49 genera and 6 families

KILLIFISHES Order Cyprinodontiformes p240
800 species in 84 genera and 9 families

RICEFISHES & ALLIES Order Beloniformes p243
200 species in 37 genera and 5 families

PERCHLIKE FISHES Order Perciformes p244
c.9,300 species in c.1,500 genera and c.150 families

FLATFISHES Order Pleuronectiformes p256
c.570 species in c.123 genera and 11 families

TRIGGERFISHES & ALLIES
Order Tetraodontiformes   p258
c.340 species in c.100 genera and 9 families

SEAHORSES & ALLIES Order Syngnathiformes p260
c.241 species in 60 genera and 6 families

SQUIRRELFISHES & ALLIES Order Beryciformes p262
c.130 species in 18 genera and 5 families

DORIES & ALLIES Order Zeiformes   p263
c.39 species in c.20 genera and 6 families

PRICKLEFISHES & ALLIES
Order Stephanoberyciformes   p264
c.86 species in 28 genera and 9 families

SWAMP EELS & ALLIES
Order Synbranchiformes   p264
c.87 species in 12 genera and 3 families

STICKLEBACKS Order Gasterosteiformes p265
c.216 species in 11 genera and 5 families

MAILCHEEKED FISHES Order Scorpaeniformes p266
c.1,300 species in c.266 genera and 25 families

OARFISHES & ALLIES
Order Lampriformes   p267
c.19 species in 12 genera and 7 families

pink-bodied cave types may help us understand the relationship between the genetic code and the environment. There are many similar examples.

Fishes, then, are many things to many people and for millennia they have fascinated humanity in many ways, not least because they have conquered an environment that is alien to us. Yet all these associations between humans and fishes beg the most vital question of all: What is a Fish?

What is a Fish?

BASIC PARAMETERS

Incredible as it may sound, there is actually no such thing as a "fish." The concept is merely a convenient umbrella term to describe an aquatic vertebrate that is not a mammal, a turtle, or anything else. There are five quite separate groups (classes) of fish alive today – plus three extinct ones – not at all closely related to one another. Lumping these together under the umbrella term "fishes" is like lumping all flying vertebrates – namely, bats (mammals), birds, and even the flying lizard – under the single heading "birds," just because they all fly. The relationship between a lamprey and a shark is no closer than that between a salamander and a camel!

However, the fact that "fish" has become hallowed by usage over the centuries as a descriptive term dictates that, for convenience's sake, it will be used here. It is worth remembering, however, that employing this term to describe the five different living groups is equivalent to referring to all other vertebrates as tetrapods (four-legged animals), even if some have subsequently lost or modified their legs.

The five living groups consist of two groups of jawless fishes, the hagfishes and the lampreys, and three groups with jaws, the cartilaginous fishes (sharks and rays), the lobe-finned fishes (the coelacanths and lungfishes) and the bony fishes (all the rest). The last two of these possess bony, rather than cartilaginous, skeletons.

The five living groups differ widely in their numbers of species. There are about 43 species of hagfish and about 40 of lamprey. Today the jawed fishes predominate: the sharks, rays, and chimaeras comprise about 700 species, whereas the greatest flowering is in the bony fishes, with over 26,000 species.

A Brief History of the Major Groups

EVOLUTION

The first identifiable remains of fishes are small, broken and crushed plates in rocks of the middle Ordovician era 490–443 million years ago. (Possible traces from the upper Cambrian era, more than 500 m.y.a., have not been confirmed as belonging to fishes). These plates represent parts of the bony external armor of jawless fishes. Although none of the living jawless fishes has any external protection, large defensive head-shields were not uncommon in the early forms. However, it is not known what the overall body shape of the first known fishes was like.

About 150 million years after they first appeared, the jawless fishes radiated into many widely varying forms, quite unlike the eel-like forms alive today. In some species of the Devonian era (417–354 million years ago) the armor was reduced to a series of thin rods allowing greater flexibility of the body and, in one poorly known group, represented now by mere shadowy outlines on rocks, the armor consisted solely of tiny isolated tubercles (nodules).

Although most of these Devonian jawless fishes were small, the pteraspids, fishes with the front half of the body covered with a massive plate, often with a backward pointing spine, were exceptional and could reach 1.5m (5ft) in length. The cephalaspids, with their shield-shaped head plates, are the best-known fossil jawless fishes (agnathans), a group well known from fossils in the Old Red Sandstone formations of the Devonian. A fortunate discovery of some well-preserved

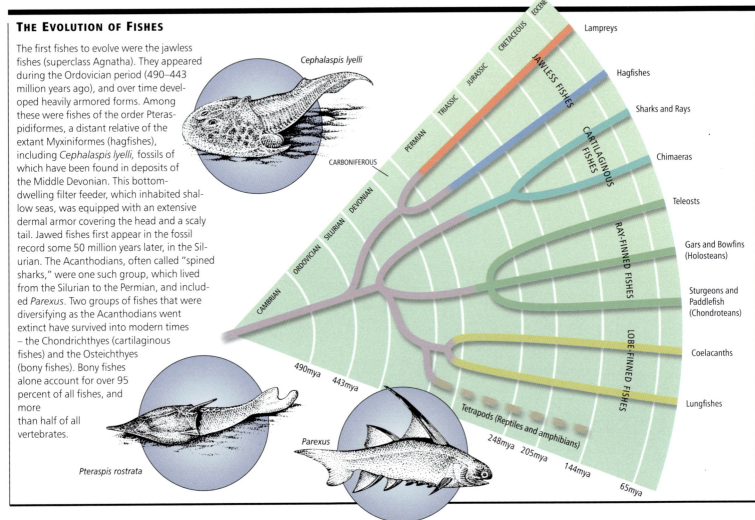

THE EVOLUTION OF FISHES

The first fishes to evolve were the jawless fishes (superclass Agnatha). They appeared during the Ordovician period (490–443 million years ago), and over time developed heavily armored forms. Among these were fishes of the order Pteraspidiformes, a distant relative of the extant Myxiniformes (hagfishes), including *Cephalaspis lyelli,* fossils of which have been found in deposits of the Middle Devonian. This bottom-dwelling filter feeder, which inhabited shallow seas, was equipped with an extensive dermal armor covering the head and a scaly tail. Jawed fishes first appear in the fossil record some 50 million years later, in the Silurian. The Acanthodians, often called "spined sharks," were one such group, which lived from the Silurian to the Permian, and included *Parexus*. Two groups of fishes that were diversifying as the Acanthodians went extinct have survived into modern times – the Chondrichthyes (cartilaginous fishes) and the Osteichthyes (bony fishes). Bony fishes alone account for over 95 percent of all fishes, and more than half of all vertebrates.

Cephalaspis lyelli

CARBONIFEROUS

PERMIAN

DEVONIAN

SILURIAN

ORDOVICIAN

CAMBRIAN

EOCENE

CRETACEOUS

JURASSIC

TRIASSIC

490mya

443mya

248mya

205mya

144mya

65mya

JAWLESS FISHES

CARTILAGINOUS FISHES

RAY-FINNED FISHES

LOBE-FINNED FISHES

Lampreys

Hagfishes

Sharks and Rays

Chimaeras

Teleosts

Gars and Bowfins (Holosteans)

Sturgeons and Paddlefish (Chondroteans)

Coelacanths

Lungfishes

Tetrapods (Reptiles and amphibians)

Pteraspis rostrata

Parexus

Above *The limestone quarries at Solnhofen, in Bavaria, Germany have yielded a huge variety of fossils. Among them is this Jurassic fish, Gyrodas circularis, which strongly resembles the body shape of modern bony fishes.*

cephalaspids buried in fine mud enabled, with careful preparation, the course of their nerves and blood vessels to be discovered.

The first recognizable fossil lampreys have been found in Carboniferous (Pennsylvanian) rocks of Illinois, USA (dating from 325–290 m.y.a.). To date, however. no indisputable fossil hagfishes have been found.

The earliest of the true jawed fishes were the acanthodians. Spines belonging to this group of large-eyed, scaled fishes have been reported from rocks 440 million years old, from the Silurian period. They are thought to have hunted by sight in the upper layers of the water. Some of the largest species, which grew to over 2m (6.5ft) long, have jaws which suggest that they were active predators, much like sharks today. The majority of the acanthodians, though, were small fishes. The earliest acanthodians were marine; the later species lived in freshwater.

Acanthodians had bony skeletons, ganoid scales (typical of primitve fishes and containing several top layers of enamel, followed by dentine – a hard elastic substance also known as ivory –

and, finally, by one or more layers of bone) and a stout spine in front of each fin except the caudal. Most species had a row of spines between the pectoral and pelvic fins. The tail was shark-like (heterocercal), that is, the upper lobe was longer than the lower. The tail shape and the presence of spines have led to them being called "spiny sharks," despite the presence of bone and scales. Recent research has suggested that they may, however, be more closely related to the bony fishes. Acanthodians never evolved flattened or bottom-living forms. One hundred and fifty million years after they appeared, they became extinct.

The other group of extinct fishes is the placoderms, a bizarre class that may be related to sharks, or to bony fishes, or to both, or to all other jawed fishes; no one knows for certain. The front half of their body was enclosed in bony plates, formed into a head shield that articulated (formed a joint) with the trunk shield. Most had depressed bodies (i.e. flattened) and lived on the bottom. One order, however, the arthrodires, were probably fast-swimming active predators growing to 6m

(20ft) long. They probably paralleled the living sharks in the same way that the very depressed rhenanids paralleled rays and skates. Another group of placoderms, the antiarchs, are among the strangest fishes ever to have evolved. About 30cm (1ft) long, they had an armor-plated trunk that was triangular in cross section. The eyes were very small and placed close together on the top of the head. The "pectoral fins" are most extraordinary and unique among vertebrates. Whereas all other vertebrates had developed an internal skeleton, the "pectoral fin" of these antiarchs had changed to a crustacean-like condition, resembling the legs of a lobster – a tube of jointed bony plates worked internally by muscles. The function of these appendages is unknown, but they may have been used to drag the fish slowly over mud or rocks. The antiarchs also had a pair of internal sacs, which have been interpreted as lungs. In another

FISH BODY PLAN

The oldest vertebrates on Earth, fishes display a number of intriguing physiological adaptations to life in water. The fins give fishes control over their movement by directing forward thrust and providing lift. The swimbladder provides buoyancy. The complex respiratory system – the gills and gill arches – enables fishes to absorb and concentrate the scant oxygen available in the water, while the ultra-sensitive lateral line allows them to detect predators or prey items.

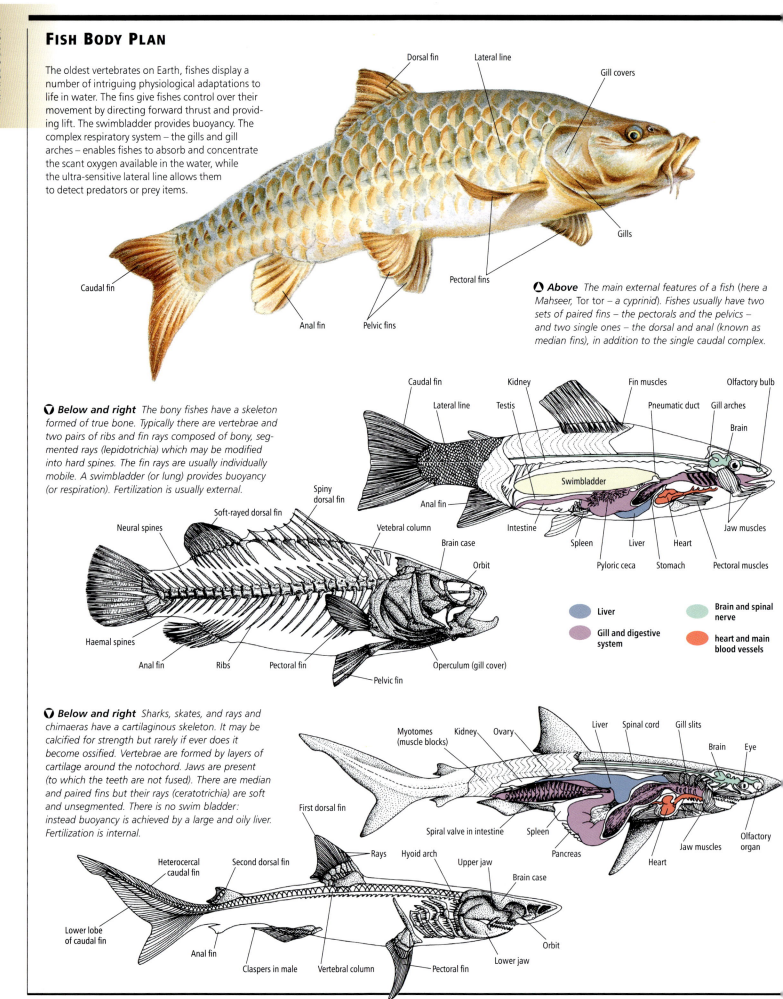

Dorsal fin
Lateral line
Gill covers
Gills
Pectoral fins
Anal fin
Pelvic fins
Caudal fin

◐ *Above* *The main external features of a fish (here a Mahseer, Tor tor – a cyprinid). Fishes usually have two sets of paired fins – the pectorals and the pelvics – and two single ones – the dorsal and anal (known as median fins), in addition to the single caudal complex.*

◑ *Below and right* *The bony fishes have a skeleton formed of true bone. Typically there are vertebrae and two pairs of ribs and fin rays composed of bony, segmented rays (lepidotrichia) which may be modified into hard spines. The fin rays are usually individually mobile. A swimbladder (or lung) provides buoyancy (or respiration). Fertilization is usually external.*

Caudal fin
Lateral line
Kidney
Testis
Fin muscles
Pneumatic duct
Olfactory bulb
Gill arches
Brain
Swimbladder
Anal fin
Intestine
Spleen
Liver
Heart
Jaw muscles
Pyloric ceca
Stomach
Pectoral muscles

Soft-rayed dorsal fin
Neural spines
Spiny dorsal fin
Vetebral column
Brain case
Orbit
Haemal spines
Anal fin
Ribs
Pectoral fin
Operculum (gill cover)
Pelvic fin

Liver
Brain and spinal nerve
Gill and digestive system
heart and main blood vessels

◑ *Below and right* *Sharks, skates, and rays and chimaeras have a cartilaginous skeleton. It may be calcified for strength but rarely if ever does it become ossified. Vertebrae are formed by layers of cartilage around the notochord. Jaws are present (to which the teeth are not fused). There are median and paired fins but their rays (ceratotrichia) are soft and unsegmented. There is no swim bladder: instead buoyancy is achieved by a large and oily liver. Fertilization is internal.*

Myotomes (muscle blocks)
Kidney
Ovary
Liver
Spinal cord
Gill slits
Brain
Eye
Spiral valve in intestine
Spleen
Pancreas
Jaw muscles
Heart
Olfactory organ
First dorsal fin

Heterocercal caudal fin
Second dorsal fin
Rays
Hyoid arch
Upper jaw
Brain case
Lower lobe of caudal fin
Anal fin
Claspers in male
Vertebral column
Pectoral fin
Lower jaw
Orbit

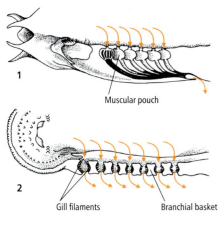

1 — Muscular pouch

2 — Gill filaments, Branchial basket

3 — Gill filaments, Gill slits

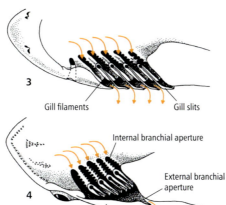

4 — Internal branchial aperture, External branchial aperture, Operculum

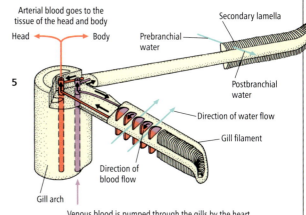

Arterial blood goes to the tissue of the head and body
Head ← → Body
Prebranchial water
Secondary lamella
Postbranchial water
Direction of water flow
Gill filament
Direction of blood flow
Gill arch
5
Venous blood is pumped through the gills by the heart, to which these vessels are directly connected

◑ **Right** *The four basic types of fish scales:* **1** *Ctenoid scales, found in most modern bony fishes, overlap one another in the manner of roof tiles, and have a comb-like posterior margin;* **2** *Cycloid scales – found, for example in salmon – have a rounded appearance and a smooth posterior margin ;* **3** *Rhomboid-shaped ganoid scales are found in certain "primitive" modern fishes, such as bichirs, gars, and bowfins;* **4** *Placoid scales, or 'dermal denticles,' found in sharks, rays and other cartilaginous fishes.*

1
2
3
4

◐ **Above** *Gill structures in fishes:* **1** *In the hagfishes water passes through a series of muscular pouches before it leaves through a single common opening;* **2** *In the lampreys each gill has a separate opening to the outside and the gills are supported by an elaborate cartilaginous structure called the branchial basket;* **3** *In the living Chondrichthyes (namely, the sharks, skates, and chimaeras), the gills (except in the chimaeras) primitively open directly to the outside via five slits. (In the chimaeras an operculum or cover is developed);* **4** *In bony fishes the gills are protected externally by a bony operculum (cover);* **5** *Detailed diagram of blood flow through the filaments and the lamellae of fishes' gills. Note that the blood flows through the lamellae in the direction opposite to that of the water flowing over it to maximize the efficiency of exchange – the so-called "countercurrent system."*

EXTREME FISH FACTS

- **Smallest** The Dwarf pygmy goby (*Pandaka pygmaea*), length (mature male) 9mm (0.4in).
- **Largest** The Whale shark (*Rhincodon typus*), a cartilaginous fish, length 12.5m (41ft).
- **Fastest** A Sailfish (*Istiophorus platypterus*) swimming near the Florida coast was timed at 110km/h (68mph).
- **Fastest reflexes** It takes toadfishes only 6 milliseconds to swallow a passing fish – so fast that other fishes in the shoal will not even have noticed.
- **Commonest** Deep-sea bristlemouths (*Cyclothone* spp.) are found in great abundance throughout the world's oceans, at depths of over 300m.
- **Largest number of eggs** The Oceanic sunfish (*Mola mola*) lays some 250 million eggs in a single spawning.
- **Lowest reproduction rate** The Sand tiger shark (*Carcharias taurus*) gives birth to only one or two large young every two years.
- **Shortest lifespan** The Turquoise killlifish (*Nothobranchius furzeri*), which lives in seasonal pools, has a 12-week lifespan, the shortest of any vertebrate.
- **Longest lifespan** The Lake sturgeon (*Acipenser fulvescens*) can reach 80 years of age.
- **Most venomous** The Estuarine stonefish (*Synanceia horrida*) delivers venom that can kill a person.

◑ **Right** *The lateral line organ of fishes comprises a series of fluid-filled ducts just beneath the scales. The receptors are highly sensitive, and detect the slightest vibrations.* **1** *a longitudinal section through the lateral line shows the connections of the canal to the outside and the position of the receptors;* **2** *detail of a single pressure receptor.*

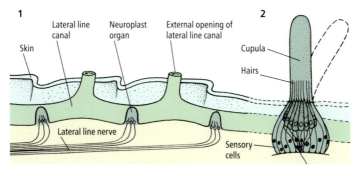

1
Lateral line canal
Neuroplast organ
External opening of lateral line canal
Skin
Lateral line nerve

2
Cupula
Hairs
Sensory cells

◑ **Right** *The mouths of fishes display an enormous variety of forms, adapted to the ecology and feeding strategy of individual species:* **1** *The air-breathing Siamese fighting fish (Betta splendens) has an upturned mouth ideal for catching the larvae of mosquitoes and other insects;* **2** *The Angel squeaker (Synodontis angelicus), a catfish, displays the long mouth barbels characteristic of this group. The fleshy protuberances help these suctorial bottom-feeders locate food;* **3** *The Moorish idol (Zanclus cornutus) has a small, protruding mouth equipped with many elongate, bristle-like teeth, with which it scrapes encrusting animals off rocks;* **4** *The Gulper eel (Eurypharynx pelecanoides), which feeds on crustaceans, has a huge backward extension of the jaws.*

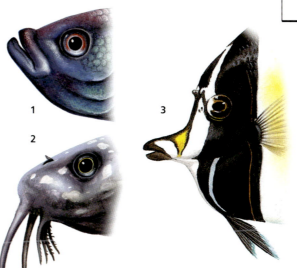

1
2
3
4

THE FASCINATION OF FISHES

Four thousand years of myth and mystery

HUMANS HAVE AN ENIGMATIC RELATIONSHIP with fishes. To start with, fishes live in a medium that we cannot enter without relying on technology that allows us to take some of our medium (air) with us. Yet many people's awareness of fishes extends only as far as their use as food items, or as decorative aquarium or pond inhabitants.

It was not always so. Fishes were sacred to the ancient Egyptians – one form of the major deity Isis has a fish head. Moreover, a giant native fish, the Nile perch, was deified and the town of Esueh renamed Latopolis, from the Greek word for a fish, after several thousand of them were found embalmed there during the Hellenic period.

In Ancient and Medieval times, fishes were often associated with miraculous occurrences. A legend common to several cultures tells how a ring, accidentally dropped or deliberately thrown into a body of water, later returns to its rightful owner in the belly of a fish served up for dinner. This story recurs in such diverse sources as the Greek myth of the tyrant Polycrates of Samos, *The Arabian Nights,* and the Life of St Kentigern.

The sheer size of certain fishes has always held a special fascination – as witness the perennial angler's tale of "the one that got away." In 1558, the Swiss naturalist Conrad Gesner recounted how a man took his mule to a lake to drink, whereupon a pike bit the mule's lips and clung on. It was supposedly only after a fierce struggle that the mule prevailed and pulled the pike from the water. Somewhat better attested is the same author's account of the so-called "Emperor's pike," of which several paintings exist. Apparently, in 1497 in Germany, a pike was caught, around the "neck" of which was a copper ring bearing the inscription that it had been put there by Frederick II in 1230.

This huge fish was 5.8m (19ft) long and weighed about a quarter of a tonne. To verify the catch and preserve it for posterity, the pike's skeleton was kept for centuries in Mannheim cathedral. Yet when it was examined by scientists in the 19th century, it was found to be a hoax – the skull came from one pike, but the body was made up of several pike bodies joined together!

Later fish forgeries were even more imaginative, feeding the popular superstition of grotesque hybrid creatures under the sea. From the 16th to the 19th century, a trade arose in "Jenny Hanivers," diabolical-looking sea monsters with humanoid heads. They were made either by stitching together fish and monkey carcasses to resemble a mermaid, or manipulating a ray or guitar fish to create a winged "sea devil". Mummified by drying in the sun, these morbid curios were brought back from their travels by European and American sailors and voyagers and exhibited in circuses or sideshows.

Other extraordinary aquatic phenomena have their basis in fact rather than fraud. Showers of fishes have been witnessed many times in the last thousand years, causing great alarm and consternation. Yet we now know that they are the result of freak weather conditions. A tornado passing over the sea and turning into a waterspout has the ability to suck up fishes along with the water so that, when the wind drops, the fishes fall from the sky. Most fishes that are caught up in waterspouts are small, but in India, a rain of fishes is reported to have contained individual specimens weighing up to 3kg (6.6lb)! Occasionally, small fishes may be carried up to the height at which hail forms, and so come down embedded in ice.

Mariners' tales once abounded of monsters of the deep and sea serpents. Fanciful artists' impressions of these terrifying beasts appear on countless Medieval maps and nautical charts. Such creatures are thought to have had their origins in misinterpretations of rarely-seen fishes such as the Oar fish (*Regalecus glesne*). sunfishes (*Mola* spp.), the Whale shark (*Rhincodon typus*) and the Megamouth shark (*Megachasma pelagios*). Likewise, a school of dolphins or porpoises swimming in line and surfacing periodically to breathe might well resemble a sea serpent, if seen in poor conditions or from afar. Even so, stories of sea serpents persisted into modern times. In 1892, Dr A.C. Oudemans, Director of the Zoological Gardens in The Hague, recorded over 160 cases of what he considered

Above This 2nd-century BC mosaic from the House of the Faun in Pompeii, gives evidence of the keen appreciation (and observation) of fishes by the Ancient Romans. Red and gray mullets, electric rays, dogfishes, and wrasses are all accurately depicted, as is a Moray eel, much prized by the Roman aristocracy.

Left Conrad Gesner's Historia Animalium, published in 1551–58, contained many accurate engravings of real animals alongside completely fanciful illustrations, such as this unidentified aquatic vertebrate.

History of Fishes in Captivity
FOOD AND AQUARIA

Some 70 percent of the earth's surface is covered with water, which, unlike the land, offers a three-dimensional living space, very little of which is devoid of fish life. The overall contribution that fish make to the total vertebrate biomass is therefore considerable. Yet, because they are not as obvious a part of the environment as birds and mammals, fish have not been as generally appreciated as they deserve, though people have been interested in them for at least 4,000 years.

It is not known when fishes were first kept in captivity; nor is the reason for doing this known, although it seems likely that it was to provide an ready source of fresh food, rather than for esthetic purposes. Around 4,000 years ago, the Middle East in general, and the fertile crescent of the rivers Tigris and Euphrates in particular, were far wetter and more fertile than in modern times. It was in this period that the first identifiable fish ponds were built by the Sumerians in their temples. The Assyrians and others followed later. It is conceivable that the idea of fish ponds came from the sight of fishes that had been left behind after a flood and survived for some time in natural, water-filled depressions. It is not, however, known which types of fishes were kept in these ponds. The Assyrians depicted fishes on their coins, but not accurately enough for them to be identified.

The story of fishes kept by the Egyptians is quite different. Their high standard of representational art has enabled the fishes in their ponds to be identified. Even more conveniently, they mummified some of their important species, allowing the accuracy of the drawings to be checked. Various species of *Tilapia* (still a highly valued food fish in the region), Nile perch and *Mormyrus* (Elephant nose) are among those depicted. The Egyptians added a new dimension to the functional aspect of fish ponds, that of recreation. Murals depict fishing with a rod and line, which must have been for fun, because it is not as efficient as netting for catching fish in commercial quantities. The Egyptians also worshiped their fish.

The Roman Marcus Terentius Varro (116–27 BC) wrote in his book *De Re Rustica* of two kinds of fish ponds: freshwater ponds (*dulces*) kept by the peasantry for food and profit, and saltwater ponds (*maritimae* or *sales*) which were only owned by wealthy aristocrats who used them for entertainment. Red mullet were especially favored because the dramatic color changes of the dying fish were admired by guests before the fish was cooked and eaten. Large moray eels were also kept and, in the most extreme examples, were decorated with jewelry and fed on unwanted or errant slaves (See Tarpons, Bonefishes, and Eels).

Although the Romans possessed glass technology, there is no record of any form of aquarium having been constructed. The Romans' involvement with fish was not totally for show, though.

genuine recent sightings in his book *The Great Sea-Serpent*. Some of the reports came from the captains of Royal Navy vessels, who could be relied upon for their sobriety and, moreover, were equipped with telescopes

Shark attacks, however infrequent, generate powerful myths. In a celebrated Internet hoax of 2001, a manipulated photo showed a hapless diver, suspended on a ladder beneath a helicopter, about to be eaten by a huge Great White shark leaping from the water!   KEB/JD

group of placoderms, the ptyctodontids, the pelvic fins show sexual dimorphism – that is, they are different in males and females, those of the males being enlarged into shark-like claspers. From this it is assumed that fertilization of eggs was internal.

Most of the early, and a few of the later, placoderms lived in freshwater; the rest, including the fascinating antiarchs, were marine. This enigmatic group appeared about 400 million years ago and became extinct some 70 million years later.

They explored fish culture methods and were known to have transported fertilized fish eggs, which they may well have fertilized externally by stripping male and female fish.

Records of fishes are few in the western world after the fall of the Roman Empire, and with the onset of the Dark Ages. The historian Cassiodorus (c.AD490–c.AD585) notes that live carp were taken from the Danube to the Goth king Theodoric at Ravenna in Italy, while Charlemagne marketed the live fishes he kept in ponds.

The tradition had doubtless been kept alive, however, by clergy and nobles. It is, for example, stated in the Domesday Book (1086) that the Abbot of St Edmund's had fish ponds providing fresh food for the monastery table and that Robert Malet of Yorkshire had 20 ponds taxed to the value of 20 eels. Stewponds were common in monasteries during the Middle Ages, and indeed were regarded as essential, since the church forbade the eating of meat on Fridays. The word "stew" in this context comes from the Old French

estui, meaning "to confine," and is not connected – as is widely believed – with the means of preparation of the fish for consumption.

Modern-style aquaria were developed in the first half of the 19th century. At a meeting of the British Association for the Advancement of Science in 1833, it was shown that aquatic plants absorbed carbon dioxide and emitted oxygen, thereby benefiting fishes. The first attempt at keeping marine fish alive and the water healthy by using plants was, however, made by Mrs Thynne in 1846. Only six years later came the first sizeable public aquarium, built in the Zoological Gardens in London. In late Victorian times, as now, many homes had aquaria and the invention of the heater and thermostat later allowed more exotic fishes to be kept.

The best known of all aquarium fishes is the Goldfish. This species is native to China and has been bred for its beauty for over 4,500 years. In 475BC Fan Lai wrote that carp culture had been associated with silkworm culture (silkworms are the caterpillars of the Silk Moth - *Bombyx mori*) –

the fish feeding on the feces produced by the caterpillars – since 2,689BC. About 2,000BC, the Chinese were, according to fishery experts, artificially hatching fish eggs. Red Goldfish were noted in AD350 and during the T'ang dynasty (about AD650) gold-colored fish-shaped badges were a symbol of high office. By the 10th century, basic medicines for fishes, such as poplar bark for removing fish lice from Goldfish, were available.

In the wild state, goldfish are coppery brown, but when first imported into Britain (probably in 1691) gold, red, white and mottled varieties were already available. By 1728, trade in the goldfish had grown considerably, with the merchant and economist, Sir Matthew Dekker, importing the fishes in large numbers and distributing them to many country houses. Goldfishes reached America in the 18th century and shortly thereafter became one of the most familiar fishes. Today, the Goldfish is believed to be not only the most popular fish kept in aquaria, but also the most popular of all pet animals.

○ **Above left** *Kaiyukan Aquarium in Osaka, Japan, has the world's largest indoor tank, some 30ft (9m) deep. It contains fauna of the Pacific Ocean, including two huge Whale sharks.*

○ **Above right** *Some varieties of the universally popular Goldfish, created by selective breeding: 1 Bristol shubunkin; 2 Common goldfish; 3 Ranchu; 4 Veiltail; 5 Bubble-eye; 6 "Pom-pom".*

Endangered Fishes

ENVIRONMENT AND CONSERVATION

In 1982, the Fish and Wildlife Service of the USA proposed removing the Blue pike (*Stizostedion vitreum glaucum*) and the Longjaw cisco (*Coregonus alpenae*) from the American 'List of Endangered and Threatened Wildlife' – not, however, because numbers of both species had recovered to their former abundance, but ,on the contrary, because the two species were deemed extinct. The Blue pike, which formerly lived in the Niagara River and Lakes Erie and Ontario, had not been seen since the early 1960s. The Longjaw cisco, from Lakes Michigan, Huron and Erie, was last reported in 1967. What caused their terminal disappearance after thousands of years of successful survival? Both species, directly and via their food chain, were severely depleted by pollution; in addition, the Longjaw cisco, in particular, suffered from predation by parasitic Sea lampreys that gained increasing access to its habitat after the Welland Canal was built, linking Lake Ontario with Lake Erie.

In South Africa a small minnow, called *Oreodaimon quathlambae*, was described in 1938. A few years later, it was extinct in its original locality in Natal. No canals had been dug, pollution was minimal, but an exotic species, the Brown trout (*Salmo trutta*), had been introduced to provide familiar sport for British expatriates. Small trout ate the same food as *Oreodaimon* while large trout ate the *Oreodaimon* themselves. Fortunately, in the late 1970s, a small relict population was discovered living above a waterfall on the Tsoelikana River in the Drakensberg mountains, Lesotho. The fall had prevented the spread of trout, but they had recently been transplanted above the falls. Although this population is protected as far as possible from predation, a more serious threat to its survival is the overgrazing of the land adjoining the river, causing the silting up of the river and changes in the river's flow.

In parts of Malaysia, Sri Lanka, and in Lake Malawi some of the more brightly colored freshwater fishes are becoming ever harder to find. In the past, on top of any other pressures that may have existed, numbers were thought to have fallen because of collecting for the aquarium trade and concomitant environmental damage. Today, large-scale commercial breeding programs meet most of the global demand for these fishes. However, while captive breeding may relieve some of the pressure on wild stocks, others – for example direct and indirect damage to natural habitats – remain as serious threats.

Formerly, large parts of the US southwest were covered with extensive lakes. With post-Pleistocene

STEALTH FISHES
Underwater camouflage strategies

FISHES HAVE A REMARKABLE RANGE OF methods for concealing themselves from predators or prey – or for mimicking the food items of other species, the better to hunt them.

Perhaps the simplest form of camouflage is countershading, as exhibited by sharks. A dark upper surface and a light underside enable them to approach prey unseen, since the light tone, when seen from below, blends in with the sky.

The ability to merge with the background, or cryptic coloration, is common to several species. Active cryptic coloration is used by flatfishes like the Turbot or the Peacock flounder, as they lie in wait on the seabed for their prey. Chromatophores (skin cells that can alter their pigmentation) enable these voracious hunters to change color rapidly to blend in with their surroundings.

The Leafy seadragon uses passive cryptic body shape and coloration, its fragmented outline disguising it perfectly in its weedy habitat. So successful is this strategy that neither predators nor prey recognize the seadragon as a fish. Less spectacular, though just as effective, are those species that burrow into the substrate, showing only their well-camouflaged faces, or that tone in almost imperceptibly with rocks. In the latter

Above Hidden in the gravel of the sea floor, an Atlantic stargazer (Uranoscopus scaber) *is barely visible. This species has venomous dorsal spines.*

Below The Peacock flounder (Bothus lunatus) *is a predatorial fish that can change its coloration to match the substrate, so concealing itself from its prey. In experiments, this remarkable mimic has even replicated the pattern of a checkerboard.*

category is the Stonefish (*Synanceia verrucosa*), whose body may even, like the surrounding rocks, be mottled with algae. As divers can attest, it is all too easy to step inadvertently on a Stonefish and be injected with its fearsomely powerful venom.

Certain fishes have taken mimicry to a high level of sophistication. Angler fishes (*Antennarius* spp.) are so called for their habit of fishing with a "rod and line" – a stalk and a lure resembling a favored prey item (e.g. a worm) of their target species. This amazing mechanism, which folds away when not in use, is a development of the spine of the first dorsal fin.

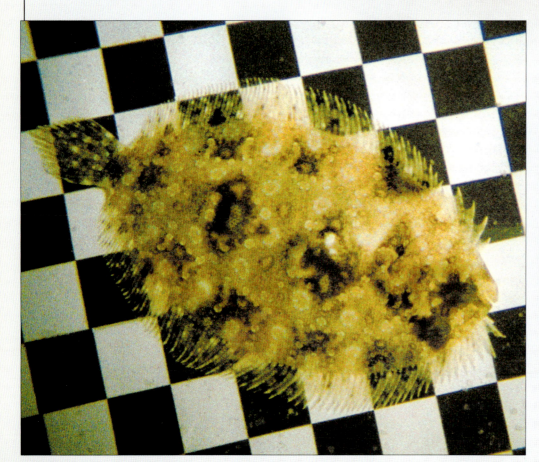

Above The kelp-like body shape of the Leafy seadragon (Phycodurus eques) *camouflages it effectively in the reef environment that is its habitat.*

◗ **Right** A sturgeon catch on the Volga River, Russia, in the 1990s. The construction of dams, together with a growth of illegal fishing for these fishes' valuable caviar, has seen sturgeon stocks plummet.

desiccation (i.e. about 100,000 years ago) the lakes, with their associated fishes, dwindled, and now some pupfish and related species only survive in minute environments. For example, the Devil's Hole pupfish (*Cyprinodon diabolis*) lives only in a pool 3 x 17m (10 x 55ft) located 18m (60ft) below the desert floor in southern Nevada; it is believed to be the vertebrate with the smallest natural distribution in the world. The species depends for its food on the invertebrates living in the algae on a rock shelf 3 x 5.5m (10 x 18ft) wide, close to the surface of the water. Although this habitat is situated in a protected area in the Death Valley National Monument, distant pumping of subterranean water lowered the water table, threatening to expose the shelf and deprive the fish of its only source of food. Attempts to transplant some of the fish to other localities failed. Hastily, a lower, artificial shelf was installed. Three specially-built ponds were also stocked with some pupfishes and the case was brought up before the US Supreme Court. The court ruled that the pumping should cease, whereupon the water level stabilized and the Devil's Hole pupfish was saved.

The examples given above illustrate what is happening and what can be done. All the fishes mentioned live in freshwaters, where the area occupied is small enough for low-level population changes to be monitored. The same detailed knowledge about marine fishes is lacking because they can occupy much greater territories, making the collection of such information very difficult.

For various reasons, then, a disproportionate number of species of fish are in danger of extinction. Several measures have been put in place to attempt to secure their future. Many countries are signatories to CITES (Convention on International Trade in Endangered Species of Wild Fauna and Flora). Member countries produce lists of their threatened animals and plants and all agree that there shall be no unlicensed trade in certain of the species. While mammals and birds occupy the great majority of the pages in the latest editions of the IUCN (World Conservation Union) Red List, some 750 species of fish are also included in the three highest categories of threat: Vulnerable, Endangered, and Critically Endangered. However, enforcing the regulations is a no easy matter, particularly for Customs officers who are largely responsible for the implementation of the rules by ascertaining that the species in a particular shipment are what they purport to be. They are ill-equipped to identify accurately the 5,000 species they might be confronted with – something that even many professional fish specialists find difficult, since the diagnostic characters may be internal. Moreover, if fish are found to be illegal and are

impounded by Customs, there remains the question of what to do with them. Even if it were possible to ship them back to their native land before they died, there is no guarantee they would be released into their original habitat. Public aquaria and zoological institutions are only able to accept a small proportion of illegal imports. As for the rest, the authorities are confronted with the harsh option of destroying the fish, or the expensive alternative of allowing illegal shipments into the

country, but placing a sale embargo on them until the correct documentation is presented.

Some countries follow the spirit of the laws of conservation better than others. For example, in the United States, dam construction on the Colorado River prevented many of the endemic species from breeding and many species quickly became very rare and were in danger of extinction. After prompting from scientists, the Dexter National Fish Hatchery was constructed in New

Mexico and the endangered species were taken there and allowed to breed. The breeding program proved successful and many young were returned to suitable sites each year. But such ventures can only provide partial answers; the Amistad gambusia (*Gambusia amistadensis*), for example, lived and bred in a reed-fringed pool at Dexter but still went extinct in 1996. It could not be reintroduced in the wild because the Goodenough Spring, in which it lived, was lost forever at the bottom of a reservoir! Other species, such as the Gold sawfin goodeid (*Skiffia francesae*) now only survive in captivity, and cannot be reintroduced because their home waters may now be populated by introduced species, or may be highly polluted.

A cynic might question the point of trying to save small fishes from extinction. Altruistically, the response would be that they have as much right to life we have; more selfishly, it could be argued that they might ultimately be of use to us. Living in a cave in Oman, for example, is a small, eyeless fish (*Garra* sp.) whose total population is probably 1,000. It is quite a remarkable fish because it can regrow about one-third of its brain (the optic lobes) – the only vertebrate known to do so. Such a discovery is potentially of great significance in human neurosurgery. Luckily, this fish was discovered. Yet how many more useful attributes were there in fishes that have died out?

The status of some species is more critical than others, but the fate of them all is in our hands. If endangered species are to survive, the right decisions must be taken – and the sooner, the better.

The Future of Fishes
ECOLOGY

For a few years prior to 1882 there was an extensive fishery for a tile fish (*Lopholatilus chamaeleonticeps*) off the eastern seaboard of the USA, particularly from Nantucket to Delaware Bay. This nutritious, tasty species reached about 90cm (3ft) in length and 18kg (40lb) in weight. Tile fishes lived in warm water near the edge of the continental shelf from 90 to 275m (300–900ft) down. During March and April 1882, many millions were found floating, dead, on the surface. One ship reported that it steamed for two whole days through tile fish corpses. For over 20 years no

more were caught, but by 1915 the numbers had recovered enough to sustain a small fishery.

Despite the long gap in records, enough individuals must have survived to be able to rebuild the population, albeit to a lower level. The cause of this carnage is uncertain, but it is believed that ocean currents changed and the warm water in which the tile fish lived was rapidly replaced by an upwelling of deep, cold water in which they died. Although many fish species undergo natural variations in abundance, for no matter what reason, a major natural disaster can affect them all. Should the population be at a low level at such a time, the chance of extinction, and the loss of a resource,

---

HERRINGS AND HISTORY

The humble herring, for long a staple food fish in many counties in northern Europe, has played a major role in the history of the region. The Hanseatic cities on the southern coast of the Baltic prospered greatly during the Middle Ages not only because of the rich supply of herring on their doorsteps, but also because of their commercial expertise in preserving them and exporting them throughout Europe.

Then the herring suddenly quit the Baltic for the North Sea. The Hanseatic states collapsed economically and politically and the Netherlands now had access to the herring. The efficient Dutch fleet proceeded to catch large quantities of herring, often in British waters. Charles I of England realized that a good way of boosting his exchequer would be to tax the Dutch for this privilege. To enforce payment of this unpopular tax and to keep British herring for the

British, Charles had to build up the declining Royal Navy. The Dutch resolved to protect their fleet, and before long the two countries were at war.

An earlier "battle of herrings" occurred in 1429, when Sir John Fastolf routed the French, who tried to prevent him taking herrings to the Duke of Suffolk, who was besieging the city of Orléans.

Although these series of skirmishes were finally resolved, the dispute over the ownership of a "moveable" resource as represented by many fish species, continues. For instance, there is still no international agreement on the exploitation of deep-sea fishes in the North Atlantic. The fierce 1980s wrangles over herring quotas between member states of the European Union were merely modern, politely political equivalents of firing cannon balls at one another. KEB/JD

could occur. Fortunately, the tile fish population was high when the currents changed.

It is largely a self-evident truth that where industries are few, rivers are clean. This is certainly true of parts of Scotland, at least, where communities depend for financial viability on the spawning runs of the Atlantic salmon. For over a century the mainstay of the tourist and hotel business has been the anglers who stay in the hope of hooking a salmon. Nearer the coast are the netsmen, who catch salmon as they begin their upstream migration and sell their luxury food in the markets further south. These communities remained stable and thrived, until an accidental observation was made in the late 1950s.

Before that time, nobody knew where the salmon passed their growing period in the sea, but a US nuclear submarine spotted vast shoals of salmon under the ice in the Davis Strait (between Greenland and Baffin Island). When this information became generally available, commercial fishing boats went after this valuable catch. The stocks were rapidly decimated, leaving progressively fewer fish to return to their home rivers to spawn. There were fewer fish for the netsmen to catch and their livelihood suffered; there were fewer still for the angler to catch and even fewer to spawn and replenish the stocks.

On two famous pools on the River Tay, anglers normally landed about 500 fish before the end of May. In 1983, only 36 were caught. Anglers deserted the area, and hotels that used to open shortly after the New Year did not bother to open until Easter. This resulted in fewer jobs and faster economic decline in an already hard-pressed area that had few other employment opportunities.

Two further factors emphasize the ridiculous artificiality of the situation regarding salmon. First, there is a slow climatic change that tends to reduce the number of fishes involved in the spring spawning runs upriver. Second, salmon farming has reached the point where it can now provide such a large proportion of the market's demands that there is little necessity to continue cropping wild stocks at sea. Biologically, of course, it is also better to conserve vigorous and healthy wild populations as a genetic reserve, in case inbreeding in farmed fish weakens their genetic makeup. This is not such a hypothetical argument as it might at first appear; for example, the number of young farm-bred salmon that are born with foreshortened jaws and, hence, have difficulty in feeding and therefore a slow growth rate, is higher (at least, in some stocks) than in the wild.

The examples given above show how valuable fish stocks are. Fish should not be just a short-term source of profit for a few, but a continuing self-renewing resource; and they would be if used properly. When herring were caught by drift nets, before the Second World War, there were over 1,600km (1,000 miles) of net out in the North Sea each night. Yet, because the shoals moved up

and down in the water, and the nets only occupied the top 6m (20ft), enough herring escaped to spawn and so maintain the stocks. Changing fishing techniques, using echo sounders and adjusting the depth of the net, resulted in a much better yield-to-effort ratio, but also brought a rapid destruction of the stocks. It was only in the early 1980s that drastic measures were taken (such as a fishing ban) to conserve stocks. Stringent, though not total, fishing restrictions are now being implemented to protect the dwindling stocks of another species, the Atlantic cod, in European waters. The lessons learned during the herring crisis may have prompted earlier action and stocks may consequently recover more quickly in this case.

It is not only prime food fish that are under threat. Species living in deeper waters, such as rat-tails and argentines, are now caught; their flesh is shredded, breaded, molded and served as "fish

◁ **Left** A Swordfish (Xiphias gladius) *caught in a net off Sardinia, Italy. This species, much sought after for its firm flesh, is also sometimes taken as bycatch in other fisheries, and some populations are threatened.*

◑ **Below** *Off Gloucester, Massachusetts, a fisherman empties cod from a dragnet. In some parts of the world, overfishing has depleted numbers of this once abundant food fish to below sustainable levels.*

fingers." When it becomes uneconomical to catch these species, what happens? To all these pressures must be added unnatural, that is, human-induced, catastrophes like the dumping of industrial waste, or oil spills. These poison fish locally, but, more importantly, the toxic substances become concentrated up the food chain and can reach harmful levels in the fish that we eat from the top of the chain. Oil spillages also have other less obvious effects like preventing eggs near the surface from hatching. However, for the comfort of our way of life we want waste disposed of and oil transported. Then there are the nets used to catch fish for fertilizer, which have a small mesh, so they also catch the young of larger species before they can spawn. Trawls can also destroy spawning grounds.

Are all these factors, of which many people are unaware, necessarily a recipe for disaster? The answer is not cut-and-dried, but is probably "yes," unless the international compromises that are regularly discussed can be agreed and adhered to. The seas can provide a sustainable crop if treated with care and thoughtfulness. The future of fishes is our responsibility and is intimately linked with the quality of human life. It is up to us to realize this and act accordingly to ensure that the worst scenario never materializes. KEB/JD

Lampreys and Hagfishes

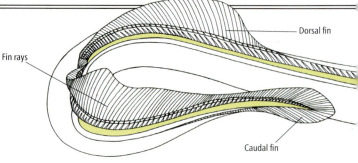

Fin rays

Dorsal fin

Caudal fin

dURING THE DEVONIAN ERA (410–354 million years ago) the world's rivers and seas were occupied by heavily armored jawless vertebrates. Today, their bony plates and head shields are common as fossils, testifying to the success of their radiation. But with the arrival of the jawed fishes, these jawless forms became less common and are now represented by just two groups, lampreys (class Cephalaspidomorphi) and hagfishes (class Myxini).

Neither group bears much resemblance to the Devonian forms; the living forms are eel-like and lack bony plates in the skin. Both are at a similar basal level of organization – at a pre-jaw stage – but both have had long, separate histories and there are many important internal differences. The relationship of the two living groups to each other and to the fossil forms was the subject of much controversy until the discovery of the first hagfish fossil in 1991 signaled that no close relationship exists between the two groups. The association of the two groups here is purely one of convenience.

Lampreys

FAMILY PETROMYZONTIDAE (PETROMYZONIDAE)

Lampreys are found in the cooler waters of both hemispheres. All have a distinct larval stage (ammocoete), during which they hardly resemble the adults in structure or lifestyle. The adult is eel-like, with one or two dorsal fins, a simple caudal fin and no paired fins. The mouth is a disk adapted for sucking, bearing a complex arrangement of horny rasping teeth, the exact arrangement of which is peculiar to each particular species and heavily relied upon in classification. There are seven gills, each of which has a separate opening.

Water enters each side through an opening near the mouth and then flows into any of seven ducts, each of which leads to one of seven external gill openings. Each duct has a muscular pouch which encourages water flow. Between the eyes, on the top of the head and just behind the single median (centrally located) nostril, is a small patch of translucent skin covering the pineal organ. In lampreys this organ is light-sensitive and the light levels it receives control hormone levels. (In higher vertebrates this sensitivity to light is lost, but hormonal control is still exercised by the remaining part of the organ.) The lamprey's skin has glands that secrete a mucus with toxic properties that are thought to discourage larger fish from eating the lamprey. (The mucus should be removed before using lampreys for human consumption, as it can cause severe stomach upsets.)

The inner ear of bony fish and the higher vertebrates consists of three semicircular canals at right angles to each other; these maintain balance as well as being involved in the hearing process. In lampreys only the two vertical canals are present; the horizontal canal is absent.

From a biological point of view there are two interconnected groups of lampreys: those that spend most of their adult life at sea and enter freshwater to breed (compared with those that spend their entire life in freshwater), and those that feed parasitically on fish as adults (compared

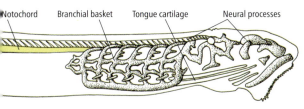

Notochord   Branchial basket   Tongue cartilage   Neural processes

◐ ◑ *Left and below* Lamprey anatomy. In lampreys the notochord does not have developed centra (i.e. the main part of vertebrae) but there is a series of paired arch cartilages. Dorsal and caudal fins are present. Formerly there was bone, but this is lost in the living forms.

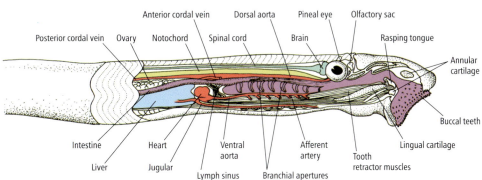

Anterior cordal vein   Dorsal aorta   Pineal eye   Olfactory sac

Posterior cordal vein   Ovary   Notochord   Spinal cord   Brain   Rasping tongue

Annular cartilage

Buccal teeth

Intestine   Heart   Ventral aorta   Afferent artery   Lingual cartilage

Liver   Jugular   Tooth retractor muscles

Lymph sinus   Branchial apertures

with those that feed on small invertebrates).

To some extent, all lampreys move upstream to spawn. The marine species, which are larger than their freshwater relatives, are anadromous – that is, they leave the sea to migrate up rivers. A problem immediately encountered by these species is the need to adjust the concentration of salts in their blood and body fluids as they move from saltwater to freshwater.

The timing of the spawning run varies with species and locality. In northwest Europe, for example, the Brook lamprey commences its run in September or October, but, in the Adriatic region, the peak comes in February and March, while in northwest Russia there are spring and fall runs. Lampreys in the southern hemisphere spend much longer on the spawning run and may not spawn until a year or more after they enter freshwater. The spawning grounds may be several hundred kilometers from the estuary through which

FACTFILE

LAMPREYS AND HAGFISHES

Superclass: Agnatha

Classes: Cephalaspidomorphi, Myxini

About 90 species in 13 genera and 2 families.

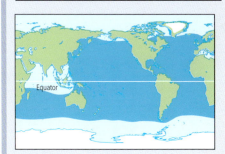

Equator

Distribution Worldwide in cool marine and freshwaters.
Size Length 20–90cm (8–35in).

ORDER PETROMYZONTIFORMES

LAMPREYS
Family Petromyzontidae or Petromyzonidae
About 40 species in 6 genera and 3 subfamilies.

Subfamily Petromyzontinae
About 36 species in 4 genera. Northern hemisphere. Species include: **Brook lamprey** (*Lampetra planeri*), **European river lamprey** (*L. fluviatilis*), **Northern brook lamprey** (*Ichthyomyzon fossor*), **Sea lamprey** (*Petromyzon marinus*). **Conservation status**: The Lombardy brook lamprey (*Lampetra [Lenthenteron] zanandreai*) is classed as Endangered and the Greek brook lamprey (*Lampetra [Eudontomyzon] hellenicus*) is Vulnerable.

Subfamily Geotriinae
Sole member of subfamily **Pouched lamprey** (*Geotria australis*). Southern Australia, Tasmania, New Zealand, Chile, Argentina, Falkland Islands and South Georgia, possibly Uruguay and southern Brazil.

Subfamily Mordacinae
3 species of the genus *Mordacia*, including **Short-headed lamprey** (*M. mordax*). Chile, SE Australia, Tasmania. **Conservation status**: The Non-parasitic lamprey (*M. praecox*) is Vulnerable.

ORDER MYXINIFORMES

HAGFISHES
Family Myxinidae
43–50 species in 6 genera and 2 subfamilies.

Subfamily Myxininae
15–20 species in 4 genera. Atlantic, Pacific, including coasts of Argentina and New Zealand. Genera and species include: **North Atlantic hagfish** (*Myxine glutinosa*), *Notomyxine*, *Neomyxine*, and *Nemamyxine*.

Subfamily: Eptatretinae
28–30 species in 2 genera. Atlantic, Indian and Pacific oceans. Genera: *Eptatretus*, including **Pacific hagfish** (*E. stouti*) and *Paramyxine*.

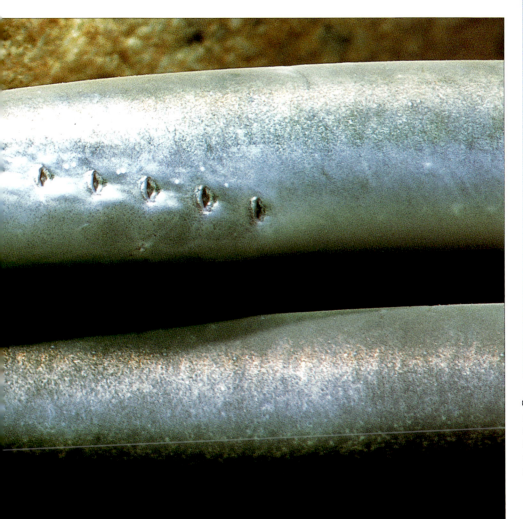

◐ *Left* Clearly displayed on these sea lampreys are not only the tooth-studded sucking mouthparts, but also the seven separate gill openings. When a lamprey latches onto a fish to feed, it is still able to pass water over its gills by drawing it in through the spiracle (the first gill opening).

157

they enter the rivers from the sea. In slow-flowing stretches lampreys may be able to travel at 3km (about 2 miles) each day, overcoming weirs and rapids on the way. When exhausted by these efforts (during which they do not feed) lampreys cope with weariness by temporarily holding on to rocks with their suckers.

During the upstream migration and the subsequent spawning, some changes in body shape occur. These may be as minor as the changes in the relative positions of the two dorsal fins and the anal fin, or as substantial as the enlargement of the disk (sucker) in males of the southern species and genera, such as the Pouched lamprey and the two Australian *Mordacia* species. The males of the Pouched lamprey and the South American species *Mordacia lapicida* (but not of other species of the genus *Mordacia*), also develop a large, spectacular, saclike extension of the throat, whose function is, at the moment, unknown.

The spawning grounds, often used year after year, are chosen for particular characteristics, the most important of which appears to be gravel of the right size for the larvae to live in. Other features are less vital, although water about 1m (3ft) deep and of moderate current is favored. The males of the Sea lamprey arrive first and start building a nest by moving stones around to make an oval, shallow depression with a gravelly bottom. Large stones are removed and the rest graded, with the biggest being placed on the upstream part of the nest. All species of lamprey build similar nests, but in different species, the sex of the nest-builder differs and may not be consistent.

Spawning is usually a group activity, involving 10–30 individuals in the Brook lamprey, and smaller numbers in the Sea lamprey, often a pair to a nest. In the European river lamprey there is courtship: while the male is building the nest, the female swims overhead and passes the posterior part of her body close to the male's head. It is suggested that stimulation by smell may be involved in this behavior. Fertilization occurs externally, the male and female entwining themselves and shedding sperm and eggs, respectively, into the water. Using her sucker, the female attaches herself to a stone and the male then sucks onto her to remain in position during spawning. In the Brook lamprey two or three males may attach to the same female. Only a few eggs are extruded at a time, so mating takes place at frequent intervals over several days. The eggs are sticky and adhere to the sand grains, and the continued spawning activity of the adults covers the eggs with more sand. After spawning, the adults die.

The eggs hatch into burrowing larvae (called ammocoetes) which are structurally unlike the adults. Their eyes are small and hidden beneath the skin, and light is detected by a photosensitive region near the tail. The sucking mouth with its horny teeth is not yet developed. Instead, there is an oral hood, rather like a cowl or a greatly expanded upper lip, at the base of which is the mouth surrounded by a ring of filaments (cirri) which act as strainers. Water is drawn through the oral hood by the action of the gill pouches and of a valvelike structure behind the mouth called the velum. On the inner surface of the hood, there are rows of minute hairs (cilia) and large quantities of sticky mucus. Particles in the water are caught on this mucus and the action of the cilia channels the food-rich mixture through the mouth into a complex glandular duct (the endostyle) at the base of the pharynx. The ability of the ammocoetes to secrete mucus is important, for it enables them, not just to feed, but also to cement the walls of their burrows and stop them from collapsing.

Ammocoetes rarely leave their burrows, and then only at night, but they often change position. They lie partially on their backs inside their burrows, tail down, with the oral hood facing into the current. In this position the importance of the photosensitive tail region can now be appreciated: it helps the ammocoete to orient itself correctly. The longest phase in the life history of lampreys is spent as ammocoete larvae (often called "prides"). The Sea lamprey, for example, can spend seven years of its life in this stage, the Northern brook lamprey six, the Brook lamprey three to six years, and the Short-headed lamprey three years.

Although lampreys live successfully as ammocoetes and as adults, the change from one state to the other is a dangerous one, resulting in high mortality. The changes involved are profound, since the entire mouth and the feeding and digestive systems have to be restructured, eyes have to be developed and the burrowing habit abandoned for a free-swimming one. During this time, which may last for eight months, lampreys do not, and cannot, feed. It was discovered in Russia, for example, that large numbers of metamorphosing lampreys found dead during early spring had been effectively suffocated by the breakdown of the velum, after the skin of the gills and the mouth had become blocked by mucus.

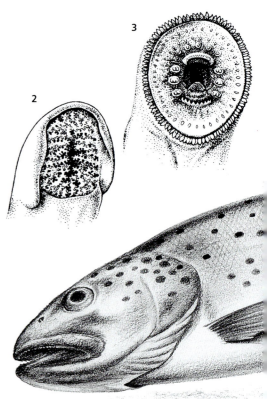

● **Below** *Representative species of lampreys and hagfishes:* **1** *Juvenile – ammocoete larvae – European river lampreys (Lampetra fluviatilis) on the bottom, filtering detritus from water (8–10cm/ 3–4in);* **2** *Head of a juvenile European river lamprey showing the oral hood;* **3** *Mouth of an adult European river lamprey showing horny teeth. During the parasitic phase the many teeth on the rim of the oral disk provide much needed traction to help latch onto the side of the fish host. Once attached, lampreys use the teeth on the tongue in the center of the disk to penetrate the host;* **4** *Brook lampreys (Lampetra planeri) feeding on a sea trout (50–60cm/20–24in);* **5** *A Sea lamprey (Petromyzon marinus) building a nest (1m/3.3ft);* **6** *Head of a hagfish (a species of the genus Myxine) showing the mouth and nostril surrounded by tentacles;* **7** *A hagfish of the genus Myxine, showing its eel-like form (60cm/24in);* **8** *A hagfish (genus Myxine) about to enter the body of its prey. By twisting into a knot it can gain extra leverage for thrusting itself into the fish.*

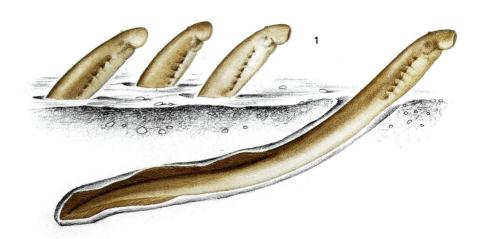

Metamorphosis in northern-hemisphere lampreys usually starts in late summer. In any given area, the ammocoetes start their transformation almost simultaneously, mostly within a couple of weeks. Environmental conditions appear to be the trigger for this; it has been noted, for example, that metamorphosis starts earlier in colder waters. Initially, the newly-eyed adults are inactive, but then a downstream migration begins and it is now that the difference between the parasitic and nonparasitic lampreys becomes important. After metamorphosis, nonparasitic lampreys do not feed; they breed and die. Therefore, all their growth is spent as a larva. Parasitic lampreys, on the other hand, feed on the blood and fluids of fishes for up to two years, sometimes with spectacular effect.

During the parasitic phase, lampreys travel widely. Species that go to sea have been caught many kilometers off the coast and at depths as great as 1,000m (about 3,300ft). Lampreys detect their prey by sight and usually attach to the lower side surface in the central third of the body. They move in with the sucker closed, so reducing water resistance, but open it just before attack. After attachment, they may move to a more favorable position. In Sea lampreys continuous blood flow is ensured by an anticoagulant in their saliva.

◑ **Above** *Anchored against the flow, a European river lamprey uses its sucker to hold itself fast to a rock. The lamprey mouth is efficient and effective; as well as being used for feeding it is also used in carrying stones for the nest and in mating.*

◑ **Right** *The Pacific hagfish is normally sedentary, living in burrows in mud and eating rarely; it has a low metabolic rate and stores a lot of fat. When it is hungry its sedentary habits cease and it swims around tasting odors by lifting its head and spreading its barbels.*

The opening of the disk, which is essential for attachment, brings the teeth into play. The attachment is so strong that only rarely do fish manage to free themselves of lampreys, doing so by coming to the surface and turning over so that the lamprey's head is in the air. During the course of the parasitic phase, it has been calculated that 1.4kg (3lb) of fish blood will suffice to feed the lamprey from metamorphosis to spawning. Scarcely any fish is immune from attack, not even garfishes (family Lepisosteidae), which are covered with tough, diamond-shaped scutes (plates). Several lampreys may attack the same fish and newly metamorphosed individuals are the most voracious.

Lampreys are extremely adaptable and any change in the environment may have unforeseen consequences for other species. For instance, there used to be an extensive and profitable fishery for trout in the Great Lakes of North America in the early 19th century. When the Welland Canal was built to bypass Niagara Falls and thus allow ships to sail from Lake Ontario into Lake Erie (completed in 1829), it gave Sea lampreys access to the Lakes. Even so, they were not noted in Lake Erie for almost a century (1921), but thereafter spread rapidly from Lake Erie into Lakes Huron, Michigan, and Superior. By the mid-1950s, Sea lampreys were well established and had taken a terrible toll on the trout. Considerable efforts were made to control the lampreys and restock the trout, but these attempts were expensive and ultimately futile. The only real hope now is that a biological balance will be achieved before pollution wipes out all the fish life in the Lakes.

Hagfishes
FAMILY MYXINIDAE

Hagfishes are superficially undistinguished and unprepossessing animals. They are eel-like, white to pale brown, with a fleshy median fin on the flattened caudal (tail) region and four or six tentacles around the mouth. However, their apparent simplicity conceals a number of extraordinary, even unique, features. Hagfishes have neither jaws nor stomach, yet they are parasites of larger fishes. They have few predators but defend themselves by exuding large amounts of slime, and when their nostrils clog up with this slime they "sneeze." They can even tie their bodies into knots and also have several hearts.

There are about 50 species, some of which can grow to 90cm (35in) or more in length and live in cold oceanic waters at depths from 20–300m (65–1,000ft) where the sediment is soft. The exact number of species is not known for certain because of the lack of agreed, tangible characters and the unknown degree of individual variability among the species. (The two best-known genera are *Eptatretus* and *Myxine*.) The relationship of the hagfishes to the other extant (living) jawless fishes, the lampreys, is uncertain and the subject of much debate. An important (and so far unique) discovery of a fossil hagfish took place in north-eastern Illinois in 1991. Dating to the Late Carboniferous (Pennsylvanian) period, 300 million years ago, *Myxinikela siroka* shows remarkable similarities to extant forms, indicating that little evolutionary change has occurred in this group.

The mouth is surrounded by four or six tentacles according to species. There are no eyes; instead, there are two pigmented depressions on the head and other unpigmented regions on the head and around the cloaca (genital and anal chamber) that can detect the presence of light. The senses of touch and smell are well developed. There is a single median nostril above the mouth which leads into the pharynx; a blind olfactory sac, which detects odors, is also present.

During breathing, water enters the nostril, from where it is pumped by the velum to the 14 or so pairs of gill pouches leading from the pharynx to

◑ **Right** *Hagfishes have changed little in over 330 million years of evolution and although they have a partial skull, they have no backbone, only an undifferentiated, pliable notochord. What skeleton hagfishes do have is made of cartilage.*

uses. It can, for instance, be used to evade capture, especially when this strategy is combined with slime secretion. Knotting is also used to clear a hagfish of secreted slime that might otherwise clog gill openings and cause suffocation. In this case, it simply wipes itself free of slime by sliding through the knot. The nostril cannot be cleared in this maneuver, however, so a hagfish also has the ability to produce a powerful "sneeze" in order to clear its nose.

Slime is secreted into water as cottonlike cells which, on contact with seawater, rapidly expand, coagulate and form a tenacious mucous covering. A single North Atlantic hagfish measuring 45cm (18in) in length can, when placed in a bucket of seawater, turn the entire contents of the bucket into slime in a few minutes.

Like most fish, hagfishes have a heart to pump the blood through the fine vessels of the gills. However, they also have a pair of hearts to speed the blood after it has passed through the gills, while yet another heart pumps the blood into the liver; there is also a pair of small hearts, like reciprocating pumps, near the tail. These accessory hearts are necessary because, in hagfishes, the blood is not always contained in restraining blood vessels. Instead, there is a series of open spaces or "blood-lakes," called sinuses, in which there is a great drop in blood pressure. The accessory heart that is found after each of these sinuses increases the pressure and pushes the blood on to the next part of the circulatory system. The tail hearts, though, are something of a mystery. They are minute, so they cannot pump much blood, and can be stopped by stimulating the skin. (They are worked by a plungerlike rod of cartilage activated from outside the heart by the movement of the body.) Furthermore, hagfishes are not greatly inconvenienced by their removal. It has also been found that at least some of the hearts double up as endocrine organs (ductless glands) that secrete hormones.

Little is known about the reproduction of hagfishes. Only a few (probably fewer than 30) eggs are laid, which measure some 2.5cm (1in) long, and are oval in shape, with adherent tufts at each end that attach the eggs to each other and to the sea bed. A zone of weakness near the end splits when a young hagfish is ready to hatch about two months later. Hagfish lack copulatory (mating) organs, so it is assumed that the eggs are fertilized externally, but how this is achieved remains a mystery. An adult hagfish has only one gonad (sexual organ), which develops into either an ovary or a testis as the fish matures. Despite few eggs being laid, hagfishes are abundant in some areas; local populations of up to 15,000 have been recorded. They have no larval stage (in marked contrast to lampreys) and their lifespan is unknown, but it may be long, thanks to their amazing resistance to infection of wounds, thought to be engendered by the slime.   KEB/JD

the outside. In the gill pouches, oxygen is taken from the water by the blood which simultaneously releases its carbon dioxide. It is thought that the skin also absorbs oxygen and excretes waste carbon dioxide. Externally, the gill pouches are visible as a series of small pores, increasing in size towards the rear. This row is continued by small openings of the slime glands. The only teeth of the hagfish are on the tongue.

The main prey of hagfishes are dying or dead fish, although they can also be predatory, actively hunting for worms and other invertebrates. When they detect a victim, hagfishes swim rapidly

upcurrent to reach it. Now the tongue and flexible body come into play, with the toothed tongue quickly rasping a hole in the side of the fish. In the case of a large fish, extra leverage is needed, so hagfishes loop their bodies into a half-hitch knot and use the fore part of this loop as a fulcrum to help thrust their head into the body of the fish. Hagfishes feed quickly and may soon be completely inside their victim, voraciously eating the flesh. It is, in fact, quite common for a trawler to catch the grisly and almost-hollow remains of a fish with a sated hagfish inside it.

The hagfish's ability to knot the body has other

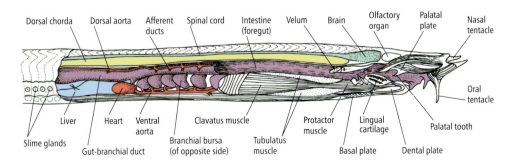

Dorsal chorda — Dorsal aorta — Afferent ducts — Spinal cord — Intestine (foregut) — Velum — Brain — Olfactory organ — Palatal plate — Nasal tentacle — Oral tentacle — Palatal tooth — Dental plate — Basal plate — Lingual cartilage — Protactor muscle — Tubulatus muscle — Clavatus muscle — Branchial bursa (of opposite side) — Gut-branchial duct — Ventral aorta — Heart — Liver — Slime glands

Sturgeons and Paddlefishes

t *HE ONLY SURVIVORS OF AN ANCIENT GROUP of fishes known from the Upper Cretaceous period (95–65 million years ago), sturgeons and paddlefishes form the subclass Chondrostei (together with five extinct orders). Today, they are confined to the northern hemisphere, within which there are two distributions, one centered on the Pacific Ocean, the other on the Atlantic. Sturgeons are the largest of all freshwater fishes, the longest-lived, and produce a roe – caviar – that is beloved of the world's gastronomes.*

The sturgeons and paddlefishes are under a greater degree of threat than any other group of fishes. Overfishing and human despoliation of habitat have brought about a serious decline in many populations, with the result that 23 of the 25 species are classed by the IUCN as Vulnerable, Endangered, or Critically Endangered. Overfishing is especially problematic due to these fishes' late sexual maturity. It is estimated that the number of sturgeon in the world's major river basins has fallen by some 70 percent since 1900. There is particular concern over the plight of sturgeon stocks in the Caspian Sea, victims both of pollution and of poaching for the highly lucrative illegal trade in roe.

Sturgeons

FAMILY ACIPENSERIDAE

Sturgeons have heavy, almost cylindrical, bodies which bear rows of large ivory-like nodules in the skin (scutes or bucklers), a ventral mouth surrounded by barbels (whiskers), a heterocercal tail (where the upper lobe is longer than the lower one) and a cartilaginous skeleton.

Some sturgeons live in the sea but breed in freshwater; others live entirely in freshwater. Little is known of the life at sea of anadromous sturgeons (those fish that migrate from the sea into rivers). They appear to take a wide variety of food including mollusks, polychaete (bristle) worms, shrimps and fishes. Adults have few enemies, though they are known to be attacked and even killed by the Sea lamprey (*Petromyzon marinus*).

The Baltic or Atlantic sturgeon has been found at depths of over 100m (330ft) in submarine canyons off the continental shelf. Although it was known that the Kaluga sturgeon inhabited fishing grounds off Sakhalin Island in the Russian Far East, it was not until 1975 that the first specimens were caught in the well-fished grounds off Hokkaido, northern Japan. The White sturgeon is known to travel over 1,000km (625 miles) during its time at sea. Freshwater sturgeons usually remain in shoal areas of large lakes and rivers feeding on crayfish, mollusks, insect larvae, and various other invertebrates, but rarely on fishes. Seasonal movements are from shallow to deeper waters in the summer and a return to the shallows in winter. In the River Volga, sturgeons overwinter along a 430-km (270-mile) stretch, aggregating in bottom depressions.

Anadromous sturgeons spawn during spring and summer months, though in some species there are "spring" and "winter" forms which ascend the rivers in their respective seasons. The spring form spawns soon after going up the river, whereas the winter form spawns the following spring. Additionally, some adults spawn every year, while others do so intermittently. Freshwater sturgeons make their way from their home streams and lakes into the upper or middle reaches of large rivers for spawning. The North American Lake sturgeon will spawn over rocks in wave conditions when more suitable quiet areas are unavailable. Courtship in this species involves the fish leaping and rolling near the bottom.

Both anadromous and freshwater species cease feeding during the spawning period. Eggs (caviar) are produced in millions – over 3 million in a large female Baltic sturgeon 2.65m (8.7ft) long. The eggs are adhesive, attaching to vegetation and stones. Hatching takes about a week. Few data are available on the development of the young, but growth is generally rapid in the first five years: approximately 50cm (20in).

The size and age of sturgeons are impressive. The White sturgeon of North America and the Russian Beluga are the world's largest freshwater fishes. An 800kg (1,800lb) White sturgeon caught in Oregon in 1892 was exhibited at the Chicago World Fair, but the only great White sturgeon that has actually been weighed and measured came from the Columbia River (Canada and USA). Caught in 1912, it was 3.8m (12.5ft) long and weighed 580kg (1,285lb). When 1.8m (6ft) long, the White sturgeon is between 15 and 20 years old. The largest Lake sturgeon, caught in 1922, weighed in at 140kg (310lb), and the greatest recorded age was 154 years for a specimen caught in 1953. A Beluga caught in 1926 weighed over 1,000kg (2,200lb) and yielded 180kg (396lb) of caviar and 688kg (1,500lb) of flesh; it was at least 75 years old.

STURGEONS AND MAN

In Longfellow's epic poem *Hiawatha* (1855) the Lake Sturgeon was called "Mishe-Nahma, King of Fishes." This mighty fish also made an impression on the early explorers of North America, as shown by the proliferation of place-names such as "Sturgeon river." In ancient America and Russia, sturgeons were a valuable resource. Scutes (the bony plates on the body) were used as scrapers, oils as medicine, flesh as food, and eggs as caviar.

Horrendously, steamboats in North America could trawl large numbers of sturgeons and used their oil as fuel. Thousands more were butchered by 1885, when over 2 million kg (5 million lb) of smoked sturgeon were sold at Sandusky, Ohio.

The eggs or roe provide the sturgeon's most prized product: the expensive delicacy caviar. The center of the caviar trade is the Russian Caspian Sea basin. Here, sturgeons were fished intensively for 200 years, and even by 1900 stocks had declined dramatically. The First World War and internal strife allowed some recovery of stock, but by 1930 feeding grounds were intensively overfished and dam construction further depleted the fishery by precluding breeding migrations. Another product that has contributed to the reduction in sturgeon stocks is isinglass. Derived from the sturgeon's swimbladder and vertebrae, it was used as a clarifier of wines and as a setting agent for jams and jellies. In 1885 about 1,350kg (3,000lb) of isinglass were exported (procured from around 30,000 sturgeons).

The development of sturgeon hatcheries in the 1950s conserved and increased populations; these hatcheries released millions of young (45 million in 1965) into the rivers. Sturgeon fishing is subject to strict quotas, although illegal harvesting has grown apace since the breakup of the Soviet Union. Today in both Russia and the USA the sturgeon's plight is serious: the Aral Sea populations of the Ship and Syr-Darya shovelnose sturgeons are near extinction.

⬤ *Below* *It took five fishmongers from London, UK, to hold up this Beluga, which was caught in the English Channel in 1947 and weighed 181kg (400lb). Belugas produce the best known caviar.*

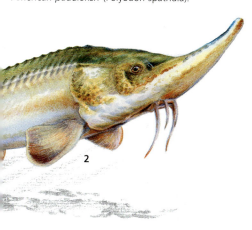

⬤ *Left* *Representative species of sturgeons and paddlefishes: **1** The Critically Endangered Common or Baltic sturgeon (Acipenser sturio) reaches sexual maturity at 7–9 years old; **2** The Pallid shovelnose (Scaphirhynchus albus) is cited on the IUCN Red List as Endangered; **3** Pollution, dams, and intensive fishing have contributed to the Vulnerable status of the American paddlefish (Polyodon spathula).*

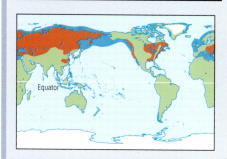
Paddlefishes

FAMILY POLYODONTIDAE

There are two paddlefish species: the American paddlefish of the Mississippi and the Chinese Paddlefish of the Yangtze, but fossils are known from North America from the Cretaceous and Eocene periods (135–38 million years ago).

Paddlefishes are identified by their extended upper jaw, which forms a long, flat, broad snout. The huge mouth is sacklike and opens as the fish swims, scooping up crustaceans and other plankton. The American paddlefish occurs in silty reservoirs and rivers; it exceeds 1.5m (5ft) in length, weighs up to 80kg (175lb) and yields its own type of caviar. This species is largely nocturnal, resting at the bottom of deep pools during the day.

Spawning was first observed in the American paddlefish only in 1961. When water temperature reaches 10°C (50°F) adults are stimulated to move upstream to shallows, where spawning occurs in April and May in temperatures of around 13°C (55°F). About 7,500 eggs are produced per kilo of body weight by females and they take about one week to hatch.

The function of the paddlelike upper jaw is uncertain. It has been suggested that it is an electrical sensory device for detecting plankton swarms; a stabilizer to balance the head against the downward pressure that is created in the huge mouth; a scoop; a mud-digger (though this is no longer believed to be the case); or even a beater to release small organisms from aquatic plants (though individuals that have lost their paddles in accidents are known to feed perfectly, from the evidence of their full stomachs).

The biology of the Chinese paddlefish is poorly known. It has, however, been established that – in contrast to its American plankton-eating relative – this species feeds predominantly on fish. It therefore possesses far fewer gill rakers – the "sieving" structures that filter out suspended food particles from the water. It is also reputed to grow to 7m (23ft); the largest recorded specimen, however, measured 3m (around 9.8ft).   GJH/JD

Garfishes and Bowfin

1

tHE GARFISHES AND BOWFIN ARE LIVING *relics of several widely distributed groups of extinct fishes. For example, garfishes of the extinct genus* Obaichthys *inhabited South America during the Cretaceous period (142–65 million years ago), while fossils of the two living garfish genera have been found in the Cretaceous and Tertiary deposits of Europe, India, and North America. The ancestral group of the bowfin (the Halecomorphi) once contained 50 genera, with a lineage stretching back to the Jurassic (206–142 m.y.a.). During the Tertiary (65–1.8 m.y.a.) bowfins were widespread in Eurasia and North America.*

Nowadays, distribution of the two families is far more limited. Only one species of bowfin survives, in central and eastern North America. *Lepisosteus* gars exist only in North America and Mexico; members of the genus *Atractosteus*, however, are more southern in their distribution, extending from the southern USA into Central America (Costa Rica and Cuba).

Garfishes
FAMILY LEPISOSTEIDAE

Garfishes are long-bodied predators with the habit of lurking in wait for prey alongside submerged branches. They are characterized by their long jaws with numerous pointed teeth and by their heavy, diamond-shaped, armor-like scales. Their swimbladder is connected to the esophagus or gullet, namely the tube that runs from the back of the mouth to the stomach. This arrangement performs like a lung, enabling garfishes to breathe atmospheric air.

The Alligator gar (*Atractostes spatula*) is one of the largest North American freshwater fishes. One specimen weighing over 135kg (300lb) and 3m (10ft) long was caught in Louisiana. This species is, however, now scarce throughout its range (an arc along the Gulf coast plain from Veracruz to the Ohio and Missouri rivers).

Sport fishermen widely hold the Alligator gar responsible for eating game fishes and waterfowl and, thus, for depleting angling stocks and other forms of wildlife. However, careful studies have shown that this species rarely feeds on these animals and preys mostly on forage fishes and crabs, although it will also take some game fishes and waterfowl. It has even been reported as eating other gars and – according to one account – of

◐ *Below The characteristic habitat of the Longnose gar is slow-flowing streams, backwaters, and lakes with plenty of underwater vegetation. Small fishes and crustaceans are its habitual prey. The Longnose gar is rarely caught for eating, and its roe is poisonous.*

FACTFILE

GARFISHES AND BOWFIN

Orders: Semionotiformes, Amiiformes

Families: Lepisosteidae, Amiidae

8 species in 3 genera.

Tropic of Cancer

GARFISHES
Family Lepisosteidae
7 species in 2 genera. C America, Cuba, N America as far N as the Great Lakes. **Length:** 75cm–3m (2.5–10ft), **weight:** 7–135kg (15–300lb). Species: **Alligator gar** (*Atractosteus spatula*), **Cuban gar** (*A. tristoechus*), **Tropical gar** (*A. tropicus*), **Florida Spotted gar** (*Lepisosteus oculatus*), **Longnose gar** (*L. osseus*), **Shortnose gar** (*L. platostomus*), **Spotted gar** (*L. platyrhincus*).

BOWFIN *Amia calva*
Family Amiidae
Sole member of family.
N America from the Great Lakes S to Florida and the Mississippi Valley. **Length:** 45–100cm (18–39in), **weight:** maximum 4kg (9lb).

○ **Left** *Garfish and bowfin species:* **1** *Alligator gar (Atractosteus spatula) – this species can grow extremely large, and there are unconfirmed reports of it attacking humans;* **2** *Longnose gar (Lepisosteus osseus), with Least killifish prey (Heterandria formosa);* **3** *Bowfin (Amia calva).*

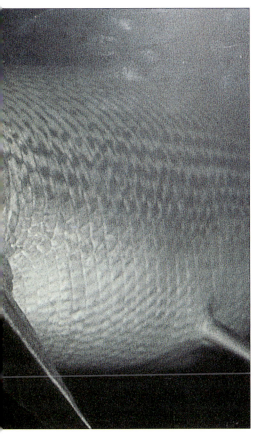

being capable of cutting a small alligator in half! The other two *Atractosteus* species are the Tropical gar (*A. tropicus*) of Nicaragua and the Cuban gar (*A. tristoechus*). Little is known of their biology; the Tropical gar inhabits the shallow, protected areas of Lake Nicaragua, where specimens can grow to over 1.1m (3.6ft) and weigh over 9kg (20lb); the Cuban gar can grow to around 2m (c.6.6ft).

The genus *Lepisosteus* has a wider distribution, from the northern Great Lakes to Florida and the Mississippi basin. The Spotted gar (*L. oculatus*) occurs throughout the Mississippi drainage and grows to over 1.1m (3.6ft) and a weight of 3kg (6.6lb). The distribution of the Longnose gar (*L. osseus*) is wider than that of the Spotted gar and it, too, inhabits brackish water in its coastal range.

The Shortnose gar (*L. platostomus*) covers an area encompassing northeastern Texas, Montana, southern Ohio and the Mississippi, while the Florida Spotted gar (*L. platyrhincus*) occurs there and in the lowlands of Georgia.

The Longnose gar can grow to over 1.8m (5.9ft) and weigh 30kg (66lb). The females are longer than the males, the difference being as much as 18cm (7in) in their tenth or eleventh year. Males rarely survive beyond this period, but females may live for up to 22 years. Group spawning, in which a single female may breed with several males, occurs from March to August, according to locality, in shallow warm water over vegetation or in a female-excavated depression. The adhesive eggs, usually about 27,000 – but as many as 77,000 – per female, are deposited and hatch within 6–9 days. As in the bowfin, the young cling to vegetation by means of an adhesive pad on their snout. Growth is rapid, at 2.5–3.9mm (0.1–0.15in) per day

Bowfin

FAMILY AMIIDAE

The bowfin's position within the historical classification of fishes has been hotly debated for many years, and among bony fishes its anatomy is probably the most thoroughly described. The structure of the skull alone forms the subject of a 300-page monograph (by Edward Allis) published in 1897. Current scientific opinion is that the bowfin is most closely related to the Teleostei, the so-called "perfectly-boned" fishes.

The common name "bowfin" alludes to the species' long, undulating dorsal fin. In the Great Lakes it is known as the dogfish, and in the southern states of the USA as the grindle, while, elsewhere, it is variously referred to as the mudfish, choupique, cottonfish, or – intriguingly – the lawyer! Other distinctive features of the bowfin include its massive blunt head and cylindrical body. At the upper base of the tail is a dark spot, edged in orange or yellow in males (probably a sign for recognition). Females lack the edging and sometimes even the spot itself. Most bowfins grow

to 45–60cm long (18–24in) but a few will reach 110cm (43in) and weigh 4kg (9lb).

Bowfins can use their air bladder as a "lung" and can survive for up to a day out of water, as long as the body is kept moist. This enables them to live in swampy, stagnant, oxygen-poor waters that are unsuitable for other predatory fish. There is also evidence that, during periods of drought, individuals may bury themselves in the bottom mud and enter a state of torpor or dormancy known as estivation.

Bowfins spawn in spring. Males move to shallow water and each prepares a saucer-shaped nest, 30–60cm (12–24in) across, by biting away plants growing in the bed of the river or lake. The males vigorously defend their nesting sites against other males and often spawn with several females. Females lay about 30,000 adhesive eggs, which the male guards and fans. In 8–10 days the eggs hatch and the young fish cling to vegetation by an adhesive snout pad. The male continues to guard the brood until the young are about 10cm (4in) long. Growth of these young is relatively slow; it takes them some 3–5 years to reach maturity.

Bowfins are predators that feed mostly on other fish (sunfish, bass, perch, pike, catfish, and minnows), frogs, crayfish, shrimps, various water insects, turtles, snakes – even leeches and rodents. Bowfin flesh itself is unsavory, and its plundering of sport fishes and comparative abundance do not endear it to anglers and conservationists. Some people, however, argue that, without the presence of bowfins, many stretches of angling water would become overcrowded, thus stunting the growth of the game fish, which – in turn – would make them far less attractive quarry for anglers. GJH/JD

Tarpons, Bonefishes, and Eels

eELS HAVE LONG BEEN PRIZED AND IN THE *Middle Ages were a staple food. From the earliest days, eels were believed to be different, since, unlike other freshwater fish, they did not produce eggs and sperm at the start of the breeding season. This apparent enigma gave rise to some ingenious explanations – all of them fanciful – until the mystery was solved at the end of the 19th century. Today, even though we know a great deal about the biology of eels, their behavior still holds many secrets.*

The subdivision of tarpons, bonefishes, eels, and notacanths comprises four orders, the members of each of which seem to be unlike the others, apart from certain anatomical similarities. They are united in having a larva that is quite unlike the adult: it is transparent, the shape of a willow leaf or ribbon, and is graced with the name of "leptocephalus." The four orders are the Elopiformes, containing the tarpons and tenpounders or ladyfishes; the Albuliformes, containing the bonefishes, halosaurs and spiny eels; the Anguilliformes with about 15 families of eels; and the Saccopharyngiformes, containing the gulpers, swallowers and their allies.

Tarpons and Allies
ORDER ELOPIFORMES

The un-eel-like tarpons and allies (Elopiformes) represent an ancient lineage. Fossils belonging to this group occur in the Upper Cretaceous deposits of Europe, Asia, and Africa (96–65 million years ago). In addition to developing from a leptocephalus larva, they all have gular plates – a pair of superficial bones in the skin of the throat – between each side of the lower jaw. Gular plates were far more common in ancient fishes than they are in living fishes. All members of this order are mainly marine fish, although they are also known to enter brackish water, and even freshwater.

The Tarpon (*Megalops atlanticus*) is the largest fish in the group, weighing up to 160kg (350lb). It is a popular game fish because it gives the angler a fight, leaping into the air, twisting and turning to dislodge the hook. This species lives in tropical and subtropical waters on both sides of the Atlantic. The adults breed at sea and the larvae make

⊙ **Below** *A young European eel (Anguilla anguilla) in freshwater; eels will spend between 6 and 12 years (males) or 9 and 20 years (females) in such habitats before migrating to the sea to spawn.*

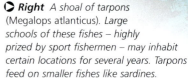

◐ **Right** *A shoal of tarpons (Megalops atlanticus). Large schools of these fishes – highly prized by sport fishermen – may inhabit certain locations for several years. Tarpons feed on smaller fishes like sardines.*

their way inshore where they metamorphose. The young live and grow in lagoons and mangrove swamps. These swampy regions can often be low in oxygen, but the tarpon can breathe atmospheric oxygen and does so at such times.

The Indo-Pacific tarpon (*M. cyprinoides*) is similar in appearance to its Atlantic relative and even has the last ray of the dorsal fin similarly prolonged. Its life cycle is also like that of the Tarpon. Apart from some minor anatomical differences, for example, in the way that processes from the swimbladder lie closely against the region of the inner ear in the skull, or in numbers of fin rays and vertebrae, the most obvious difference is that the

Indo-Pacific tarpon is smaller, rarely reaching 50kg (110lb).

The tenpounders (*Elops* spp.) are also warm-water species, and occur in the tropical and sub-tropical Atlantic. Despite their common name, they can grow up to 6.8kg (15lb) in weight.

Bonefishes, Spiny Eels, and Allies

ORDER ALBULIFORMES

The bonefishes are widespread in shallow tropical marine waters. They are shoaling fishes and feed on bottom-living invertebrates, often in water so shallow that the dorsal fin and upper lobe of the caudal fin stick out of the water. Bonefishes rarely exceed 9kg (20lb) in weight and 1.1m (3.5ft) in length. Despite their poor flavor, they are much sought after angling fish because of their fighting qualities.

The halosaurs (Halosauridae) and the spiny eels or notacanths (Notacanthidae) are scaled, deep-sea fishes rarely exceeding 2m (6.5ft) in length. They have a snout that extends in front of the mouth and which may be sharply pointed. The head is usually the deepest part of the body; the latter is partially eel-like and tapers away to a rat tail. In some species, a minute caudal fin is present, while in others, the anal and caudal fins are confluent., i.e. joined up. The dorsal fin, if present, is short and placed well forward. The nota-canths have a series of isolated spines on the back and in front of the anal fin, hence their other common name of spiny eels; they are also stockier. Notacanths are distributed worldwide and feed on echinoderms (see urchins and starfishes), sponges and sea anemones from the sea floor.

The halosaurs also live worldwide, mostly

FACTFILE

TARPONS, BONEFISHES, AND EELS

Subdivision: Elopomorpha

Orders: Elopiformes, Albuliformes, Anguilli-formes, Saccopharyngiformes

About 800 species in about 156 genera, about 24 families, and 4 orders

Distribution Worldwide in all oceans; tropical and temperate waters.

Equator

See Tarpon, Bonefish, and Eel Orders ▷

at depths down to 1,800m (5,900ft), but one species, *Aldrovandia rostrata*, was caught in 5,200m (17,000ft) of water in the North Atlantic. They feed on invertebrates, mostly deep-dwelling forms, which at least some species are thought to dislodge from the sea floor with their snouts. Other species prey on small squid and one species, the Abyssal halosaur (*Halosauropsis macrochir*) from the Atlantic, has a row of what are thought to be taste buds across the top of its head. Halosaurs are mostly dark-hued fishes, but *Halosaurus ovenii* is pinkish with silvery sheens. This species is also one of several in which the roof of the mouth has alternate light and dark stripes.

The Suckermouth spiny eel (*Lipogenys gillii*) from the western North Atlantic, has a toothless mouth that functions like a vacuum cleaner and sucks up vast quantities of ooze. The amount of organic material in ooze is probably small, but as this species has a long intestine, permitting maximum absorption of nutrients, it apparently survives on such an unpromising diet.

During a research voyage of 1928–30 , the research vessel *Dana* caught a leptocephalus larva 1.84m (6ft) long, off South Africa. Much speculation appeared in the popular and pseudoscientific press along the following lines: "if a 10cm (4in) Conger eel leptocephalus produces an adult 2m (6.5ft) long, then this larva will produce an adult over 30m (100ft) long; hence it is a baby sea serpent and the sea serpent is an eel." Other giant leptocephali were caught and named *Leptocephalus giganteus*. In the mid-1960s, luck came to the aid of science, however, when another giant leptocephalus was caught. This time, however, it was in mid-metamorphosis and it could be established that the adult form was a notacanth. Reexamination of the other giant larvae showed they, too, could be referred to notacanths, thereby establishing the relationships of the notacanths with the eels and dispelling one set of rumours about sea serpents. Unlike other eels, though, notacanths hardly grow after metamorphosis and the 30m (100ft) adult – the sea serpent – is merely a product of imaginative extrapolation.

Eels

ORDER ANGUILLIFORMES

The exact number of families of eels is uncertain. Differences of opinion arise because some groups are poorly known – sometimes on the basis of just one or a few specimens. In addition, there is the problem of matching up the known leptocephali with the known adults.

The larvae of European eels (*Anguilla anguilla*) hatch in the Sargasso Sea and then drift back in the Gulf Stream and take about three years to reach the colder, shallower and fresher European coastal waters. Here they shrink slightly, metamorphose into elvers and move upstream, where they grow and feed until, some years later, the urge to

migrate comes upon them. The American eel (*A. rostrata*) breeds in the western part of the Sargasso and its leptocephali take only one or two years to reach freshwaters.

The breeding grounds have not been found for all anguillid eels, though. The commercially significant Japanese eel (*Anguilla japonica*), for example, has an unknown spawning ground. Eels from the eastern part of southern Africa, for example the Mottled eel (*A. nebulosa*), the Northern eel (*A. bicolor bicolor*) and the East African or Longfin freshwater eel (*A. mossambica*) all breed at depth to the east of Madagascar.

As adults, the European, American, and Japanese eels are widespread. A fourth species of eel in eastern Africa, the Madagascar mottled eel (*A. marmorata*) also occurs on many Pacific islands and as far east and north as Hong Kong and southern Japan. In complete contrast, *Anguilla malgumora* lives in the river Bo in Borneo, *A. anterioris* in mountain streams in New Guinea, and the Celebes longfin eel (*A. celebensis*) only in the northeast of Celebes. Other species have intermediate ranges and all have to find their way to their breeding grounds. How, and why? We do not know the answers, but a few interesting possibilities can be suggested.

◁ **Left** *Representative species of eels and notacanths:* **1** *A bobtail snipe eel* (Cyema atrum), *one of the two species of the family Cyematidae;* **2** *A snipe eel* (genus Nemichthys), *family Nemichthyidae;* **3** *Sea-grass eel* (Chilorhinus suensonii), *of the false moray family* (Chlopsidae); **4** *Undulated moray eel* (Gymnothorax undulatus), *family Muraenidae;* **5** *Northern cutthroat or Kaup's arrowtooth eel* (Synaphobranchus kaupii), *family Synaphobranchidae;* **6** *Spaghetti eel* (Moringua edwardsi), *family Moringuidae;* **7** *A halosaur* (genus Halosaurus, *family Halosauridae, of the order Albuliformes*); **8** *Cape conger eel* (Conger wilsoni), *family Congridae;* **9** *A Gulper or Pelican eel* (Eurypharynx pelecanoides), *sole species of the family Eurypharyngidae.*

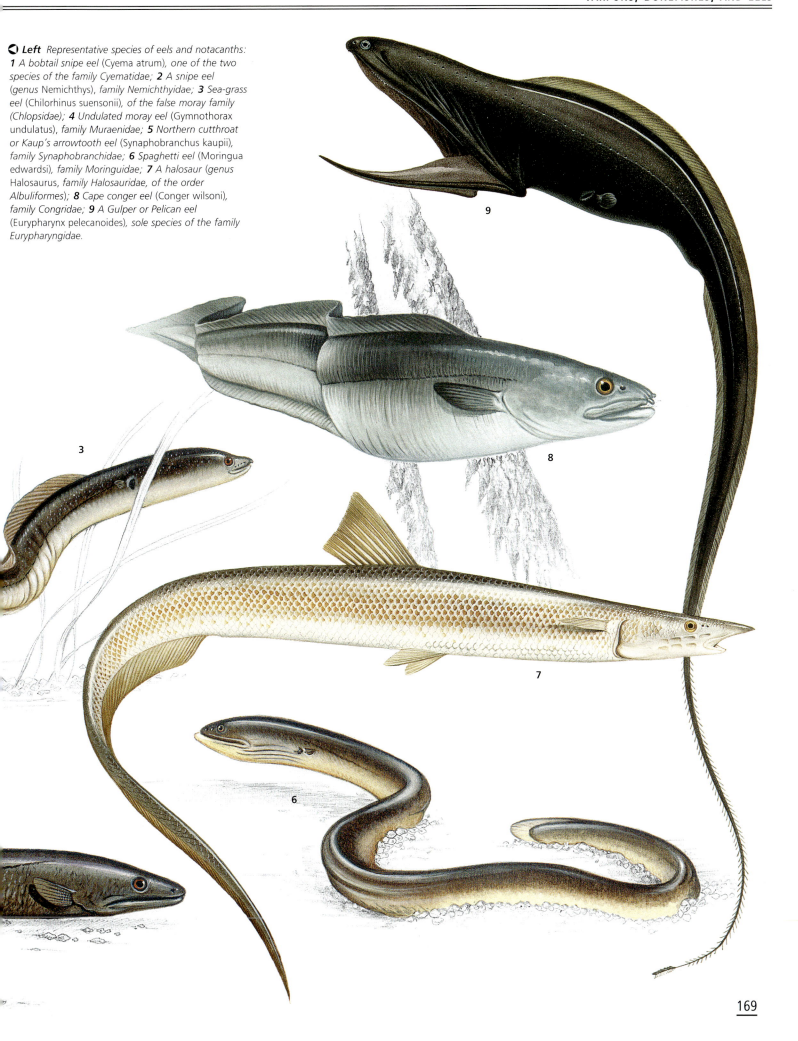

THE SARGASSO SEA MYSTERY

Solving the puzzle of where eels come from

THE BEST-KNOWN EEL IS THE EUROPEAN EEL (family Anguillidae). Although anguillid eels are the only family that spend most of their life in freshwater, the European eel's life history will serve as an illustration for all the other families, not least because the eel's familiarity has, over the centuries, occasioned so much curiosity about eel reproduction.

From before the days of the Greeks and Romans, this eel has been an important source of food. Aristotle and Pliny wrote about large eels going down to the sea and small eels coming back from the sea. Other freshwater fish had been noticed to have eggs and sperm at the start of the breeding season, but not the eel; it was therefore concluded that the eel was "different" and two millennia of speculation were born. Aristotle was certain that baby eels sprang out from "the entrails of the earth," while Pliny, on the other hand, concluded that young eels grew from pieces of the adult's skin scraped off on rocks. Subsequent suggestions continued to be as unrealistic. In the 18th century, for example, the notion of the hairs from horses' tails giving rise to eels was in vogue and, in the 19th, a small beetle was advocated as the natural mother of eels. The truth, when finally resolved, like the denouement of a detective story, was hardly more credible.

Countless millions of eels had been caught and gutted for eating over the centuries, but not until 1777, were developing ovaries identified by Professor Mondini of Bologna. In 1788, his finding was challenged by Spallanzani who pointed out that none of the 152 million eels from Lake Commachio ever showed such structures. Nonetheless, Spallanzani was struck with the determination of the eel to reach the sea, even traveling overland on damp nights. In 1874, indisputable testes were found in an eel in Poland, but it was not until 1897 that an indisputably sexually mature female was caught in the Straits of Messina. The beetle myth was laid to rest; eels must lay eggs in the sea – but where? When the eels reappear on the coasts they are about 15cm (6in) long. Why were smaller specimens never caught?

The answer had been available, but unrealized, since 1763. In that year, the zoologist Theodore Gronovius illustrated and described a transparent fish like a willow leaf, which he called leptocephalus. One hundred and thirty-three years later (1896) Grassi and Calandruccio (the two biologists who found the sexually

| Year 1 | Year 2 | Year 3 | Year 4 |

Above Swimming leptocephali of the common eel. Adult eels of various species arrive in the Sargasso Sea from Europe and North America, sometimes travelling from thousands of miles away, to mate and spawn (only with others from their own native region, it has been found). The larvae then embark on a long journey back to where their parents came from; the map charts the odyssey of the European eel on the Gulf Stream.

Below The transparent leptocephalus larva of an eel, which is shaped like a willow leaf, shrinks before metamorphosing into its adult form.

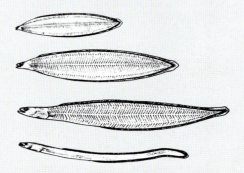

mature female eel) caught two leptocephali and kept them alive in aquaria. The leptocephali, being caught near the coast, were on the point of metamorphosing; their transformation in the aquaria, therefore, tied up, at least, a part of the story.

The hunt was now on for leptocephali and the eel breeding grounds. Johannes Schmidt took leptocephali samples and followed their decreasing size. Finally, he found the smallest of all, 1cm (0.4in) long, in an area of the west Atlantic between 20 and 30° N, 48 and 65° W: the Sargasso Sea.

On the basis of much subsequent research, we now know that the European Eel probably breeds from late February, probably to May or June, at moderate depths of around 180m (600ft) – the eyes of the adults enlarge on their 4,000 mile journey – and at a temperature of about 20°C (68°F). The Sargasso Sea is one of the few areas where such a high temperature extends to such a depth. There are, throughout the world, 16 species of the genus Anguilla and all are thought to breed in deep warm waters, although only two, the European and the American eel (Anguilla anguilla and A. rostrata) in the Sargasso Sea. No adult eels, however, have been captured in the Sargasso...and no eggs have ever been collected in the area.

In the European eel, as the larvae are carried by the Gulf Stream, might not the adults also follow it back to the breeding grounds? However, if the breeding grounds are characterised by three parameters – temperature, salinity and pressure – could these be guides? But these latter possibilities present difficulties. For example, an adult eel leaving northern Europe could follow a temperature gradient and reach the Sargasso, but an eel leaving Italy would not (the Mediterranean is warmer than the adjacent parts of the Atlantic). The appropriate pressure (as a measure of depth) could be reached very much closer to European shores than the other side of the Atlantic. Also, it should not surprise anyone that adult eels are not particularly sensitive to salinity changes, as they have already had to cope in their earlier migration with change from freshwater to saltwater.

Our ignorance is considerable, but we cannot leave the problems without some potentially exciting speculations. The first is that many animals are known to be able to navigate using the earth's magnetic field and although no magnetic-field detectors have yet been found in the eel, the possibility remains. A second possibility involves the movements of continents – Continental Drift.

Most of Europe and North America were once joined together as one continent, as were Africa and South America. At one stage in the shaping of the present continents, there was a narrow sea between the two. Is it possible that when eels first appeared, they bred in this sea and still need its physical conditions to ensure successful reproduction, even though it entails a journey of thousands of kilometers by an inefficient swimmer?

From tagged migrating eels it has been extrapolated that they take 4–7 months to make the journey and, during that time, they do not eat. Further enigmas occur with the allegedly passive journey of the leptocephali in the water currents that bring them back to the feeding grounds. It appears that they do not eat; yet, it takes them two to three years to migrate across the ocean. No food has been found in the guts and they develop peculiar forward-pointing teeth, mostly on the outside of their jaws, which are ill-adapted to catching food. However, they grow as they migrate, until, at

⬤ **Below** *Between leptocephalus and adulthood, eels pass initially through a phase where the body form is developed but still transparent. These "glass eels" and the next phase, the elver, are culinary delicacies.*

metamorphosis, they shrink and lose their teeth.

A few clues are available that hint at partial solutions to these conundra. A Conger eel (*Conger conger*) larva that was studied was shown to be able to absorb nutrients and vital minerals from the seawater. The mouth of this species is lined with minute projections (villi) which are thought to absorb the nutrients. However, this has not yet been shown to be the case in anguillid eels. The metamorphosis is rapid, and a lot of calcium must be made available very quickly to mineralize the bones and convert them from the juvenile to the adult state. The forward-pointing teeth of the leptocephalus, which disappear at metamorphosis, contain a great deal of calcium, and so it is possible that these may act as the necessary calcium reservoirs.

As the leptocephalus metamorphoses, it modifies its compressed body into the adult's shape and develops pigment, pectoral fins and scales. Before pigmentation develops, the young fish is called a glass eel and latterly an elver. Depending upon local conditions, it is either the glass eels or the elvers that ascend the rivers in vast numbers. In the 19th century, before estuarine pollution had its effect, millions of elvers were caught and

eel fairs were held. Elvers caught on the River Severn in England were particularly famous. There, elvers were used principally for food, but in Europe, they were also used to make preservatives and glue. Elvers are still caught today but their fate is to be taken to eel farms and grown to maturity in less time than it would take in the wild. Adult eels are very nutritious and are popular in many parts of the world, smoked or stewed; jellied eels were once widely eaten in the poor East End of London.

The popularity of eels remains high, even though their blood contains an ichthyotoxin (fish toxin) which can be dangerous. It is particularly important not to let eel blood come into contact with the eyes or any other mucous membrane. However, the poison is quickly destroyed by cooking, so most eel eaters remain blissfully unaware of their toxicity.

Moray eels were favorite pets of the ruling class in Ancient Rome. The scientific name of the Mediterranean moray (*Muraena helena*) commemorates a rich and powerful Roman citizen, Licinius Muraena, who lived toward the end of the 2nd century BC. According to the writer Pliny the Elder, Licinius kept moray eels in captivity as an ostentatious public display of his wealth. Later, in the time of Julius Caesar, one Gaius Herrius is said to have constructed a special pond for his morays, which so impressed the emperor that he offered to buy the eels. Gaius refused but, presumably to retain favor with Caesar, did lend him 6,000 morays to display at a banquet. Other stories recount how wealthy owners bedecked their pet eels with jewelry.

Perhaps the most notorious account of eels in the decadent society of Imperial Rome concerns a certain Vedius Pollo, who would entertain his dinner guests by feeding recalcitrant or superfluous slaves to his morays. This and similar stories about the voracity of these eels may be the source of some pervasive myths, principally that morays find skin divers irresistible. Tales abound of moray eels attacking divers, delivering a poisonous bite and refusing to loosen their grip once they have clamped their teeth onto their victims. Little credence can be given to such rumors. First, a moray's bite is not poisonous, and any infection of the wound is secondary. Second, Moray eels' teeth are adapted for holding small prey – they are long and thin and the larger teeth are hinged to permit the smooth passage of prey into the stomach. This does not, however, mean that they will not release after biting, especially if the quarry is too large to swallow.

Most morays have teeth like those of the Mediterranean moray , but species of the tropical

● **Right** Nestling amid Tubastraea *sun corals, two Spotted moray eels* (Gymnothorax moringa) *strike a characteristic pose, with their heads just protruding from their lair. This species is common around reefs.*

genus *Echidna* have blunt, rounded teeth adapted for crushing crabs which are their major food item. The ribbon morays (genus *Rhinomuraena*) are characterized by having the anterior nostrils expanded into tall, leaf-like structures. The Blue ribbon eel (*Rhinomuraena quaesita*) is brilliantly colored and much prized by aquarists. In males, the body is turquoise-blue, the dorsal fin bright yellow with a white margin, the front and underside of the head yellow and the rest blue; females are yellow with a black anal fin.

Moray eels are found in all tropical seas, usually in shallow waters. They will also occasionally enter freshwater.

The false morays (Chlopsidae - also sometimes referred to as Xenocongridae) are probably close relatives of the morays. Like them, they lack scales and have thick skin covering the continuous median (central) fin. The pectoral fins are reduced or, in at least one case, lost. The coloration is mottled like that of many morays. The pores on the

head are much smaller than in morays and the body is much thinner, this combination being deemed sufficient justification to consider them a separate family. Representatives are found worldwide, but little is known of them because they are secretive fishes.

The leptocephalus of the Bi-colored false moray (*Chlopsis bicolor*) is extremely common in the Mediterranean, but until recently, the adults were poorly known. This species was described over a hundred years ago, but only a very few specimens were in museum collections until divers began using underwater narcotics to drug fish and succeeded in catching large numbers. This species, which also lives off Florida, is a small fish (shorter than 25cm, 10in) that lacks pectoral fins and is dark brown above and paler below.

Chlopsis olokun was known from just a single specimen captured by the research vessel *Pillsbury* off the estuary of the St. Andrews River, Ivory Coast, at a depth of 50m (165ft). (The specific name is derived from Olokun, a sea deity in the Yoruba religion of the region). Fryer's false moray (*Xenoconger fryeri*) is widespread in the Pacific, but *C. olokun* was the first member of this genus to be found in the Atlantic.

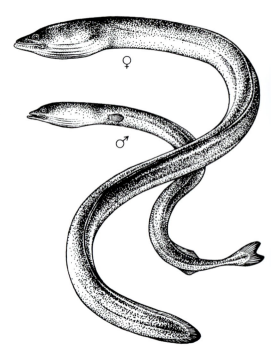

● **Above** *Some eel species, such as the Spaghetti eel (Moringua edwardsi) exhibit pronounced sexual dimorphism; here the size and the configuration of the fins are very different.*

● **Below** *The Blue ribbon moray (Rhinomuraena quaesita; here a male, as indicated by the yellow dorsal fin) is the only moray species that can undergo abrupt changes in sex and coloration.*

COLONIES OF GARDEN EELS

There are about 25 species of garden eels grouped into two genera (*Gorgasia* and *Heteroconger*), and it seems that the daily cycle and life histories of all are very similar. Colonies usually live in shallow water where there is a reasonable current and enough light for the eels to see their food. There, the eels give a passable imitation of prehensile walking sticks facing into the current. The densest colonies are deepest, with perhaps one eel every 50cm (20in). The distance between individuals depends upon the length of the eel, with each fish occupying a hemisphere of water with a radius similar to the eel's body length, so that it is just separated from its neighbor.

A colony of *Gorgasia sillneri* in the Red Sea has been studied intensively and has produced some interesting information. The eels' burrows themselves are twisted and lined with mucus secreted by the skin (during the period of study, no eel ever left its burrow). The day starts about half an hour before sunrise when the eels emerge and, by sunrise, all are out eating. Any disturbance causes the whole colony to disappear. For a period either side of noon, the eels rest in their burrows, but from mid afternoon to sunset, they are out feeding again. An interesting phenomenon is that while the eels are fully retracted in their burrows, their feeding space is taken over by another, totally unrelated fish – a species of sand diver (*Trichonotus nikii*) from the family Trichonotidae, which feeds at the level of where the eels' heads would be. When the eels are out feeding, the sand diver, as its name suggests, hides in the sand.

Even mating is conducted from the security of the burrow with a male stretching out and rippling his iridescent fins at an adjacent female. If she is receptive, she stretches out of her burrow and they intertwine. A few eggs are shed and fertilized at a time and a couple may mate 20 times a day. Detailed study of a plot within a colony showed that females never moved their burrows but some males did, to

be near females. However, as this movement was never observed, it was presumed to take place at night. The males also moved away from the females after breeding.

After going through a leptacephalus stage, small eels settle down together until they are about 25cm (10in) long, when the colony breaks up and individual eels try to find a place in an adult colony. The

adults resent this intrusion and, unless the juvenile can stand up to aggression, it has to move away to a new area or the fringes of the established colony.

A major predator of garden eels is the ray, whose effect as it swims over a colony has been likened to a mower cutting grass. Whether the eels retreat in time or are caught, has not, however, been satisfactorily ascertained.

The common name "spaghetti eels" appositely describes the six or so members of the family Moringuidae. These are long, thin, and scaleless fishes, usually with poorly developed dorsal and anal fins; they are also sometimes referred to as "worm eels," although this common name is probably best reserved for the members of the family Ophichthidae, otherwise also known as the snake eels. They are commonest in the Indo-Pacific, but a few species are found in the Atlantic, mostly in the west. Most unusually for eels, they have a distinct caudal fin which can vary from having distinct forks (with two lobes) to being trilobed.

In some species of spaghetti eels, there are marked differences between the sexes. In the West Indian worm eel (*Moringua edwardsi*), for example, the females are nearly twice as long as the males, have more vertebrae and the heart lies much further back in the body. These differences engendered several misidentifications in the past.

Spaghetti eels are burrowing fishes but, unlike most others, they burrow head-first, preferring a bed of sand or fine gravel. Their life history is

exemplified by the Pacific species *Moringua macrochir*. As the wormlike leptocephalus with its minute eyes and reduced fins metamorphoses, it starts burrowing. It subsequently rarely leaves the burrow and then only at night, until the onset of sexual maturity. At that point, the eyes and fins enlarge and the metamorphosing forms swim around at night to find a mate.

Garden eels (family Congridae, subfamily Heterocongrinae) have acquired their common name because they live in underwater colonies (gardens), rooted in the sea bottom where they wave around like plants. They are closely related to conger eels and are characterized by having a long thin body, small gill openings and a hard fleshy point at the rear of the body with the caudal fin hidden below the skin. They burrow tail-first, their modified tail regions being used to penetrate the sand. Their distribution is similar to that of the spaghetti eels.

The cutthroat eel famiy (Synaphobranchidae) is subdivided into three groups: the arrowtooth or mustard eels (subfamily Ilyophinae or Dysommatinae) – with about 16 species, the cutthroat

eels proper (subfammily Synaphobranchinae) – with around 9 species and the monotypic Simenchelyinae, containing the Snubnose parasitic eel (*Simenchelys parasitica*). All have leptocephali with an unusual characteristic: telescopic eyes, indicating a very close relationship.

Dysomma species are characterized by enlarged teeth in the roof of the mouth (vomerine teeth). There is also a tendency towards the loss of the pectoral fin. These species tend to be laterally compressed and to taper evenly towards the tail. The swimbladder is very long and the nostrils are tubular. The main reason for including this otherwise unremarkable Indo-Pacific subfamily (Ilyophinae or Dysommatinae) is because the following history of the genus *Meadia* sums up some of the problems faced by ichthyologists.

A fish was bought in a fish market near Kochi in Japan. No one knew what it was and it became the type, that is, the specimen on which the scientific description was based, of the new species and genus – the Abyssal cutthroat eel (*Meadia abyssalis*). During the Second World War, this specimen was destroyed and no further specimens were caught until 1950, off Japan and Hawaii. Although the search for this brownish, scaleless eel was not especially assiduous, it does show how fate can so easily eradicate the only representatives available to the scientific world of a species that is probably common in its own particular habitat.

The cutthroat or synaphobranchid eels are characterized by their gill slits being almost joined up ventrally, a feature that gives them their common name. Rare in collections, 12 specimens were caught in the course of one expedition by the deep-sea research vessel, *Galathea*. These were sent, in three separate parcels for safety, to a researcher in New Zealand. Unfortunately, the second parcel, containing five specimens, was destroyed by fire in a mail-storage warehouse in Wellington in July 1961.

Cutthroat eels live in cold, deep waters, where temperatures average 5°C (41°F), and where they feed on crustaceans and fishes. (One specimen of *Synaphobranchus kaupii*, trawled at a depth of 1,000m (3,300ft), had eaten octopus eggs). They are thick-set, scaled eels with large jaws and small teeth. The scale pattern is like that of the Snubnosed parasitic eel and several species have a characteristic nick in the ventral outline of the body just below the pectoral fin. The genus *Haptenchelys* is the odd one out in this subfamily because it lacks scales. The distribution of these eels is worldwide and all come from waters that are 400m to 2,000m deep (1,300–6,600ft). The adults are bottom dwellers and the larvae have telescopic eyes, but beyond that, little is known about their life history.

The third species in this assemblage (the Snubnose parasitic eel) is believed to be the only member of its subfamly. However, as is often the case, there is no universal agreement on this matter. This deep-sea eel, which grows to around 60cm (24in), has been caught off the eastern coast of Canada, in the western and northern Pacific, off South Africa and off New Zealand. Whether these discrete collecting localities reflect different local species, or just the collecting effort, is impossible to say. It seems to be plentiful because it is caught in large numbers, which could mean that it is a gregarious species, or that it may need a particular habitat. It has a blunt head with a small transverse mouth. Jaws and jaw muscles are strong. The gill slits are short and lie horizontally below the pectoral fins. The dorsal fin starts well in advance of the anal fin. The body is cylindrical until the anus and compressed thereafter. The small scales are grouped and angled acutely to the lateral line.

The young eat small crustaceans, but the adult is probably at least partly parasitic, or a scavenger. The stomachs of the first specimens found were full of fish flesh, as are those of most of the subsequent specimens. Evidence from the North Atlantic suggests that these eels feed on the flesh of halibut and other large fish, but probably only injured or moribund specimens.

The remaining families in the order Anguilli-

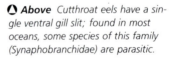

◑ Above *Cutthroat eels have a single ventral gill slit; found in most oceans, some species of this family (Synaphobranchidae) are parasitic.*

◑ Above right *The Stargazer snake eel (Brachysomophis cirrocheilos) can grow up to 1.2m (4ft) and is equipped with extremely strong jaws. This indivdual is devouring a Peacock flounder.*

◑ Far right *A Gold-spotted snake eel (Myrichthys ocellatus). Members of this family (Ophichthidae), which have stiffened tails that allow them to burrow into sand, lie partially buried waiting to attack small fish and crustaceans.*

◑ Left *The large-eye conger eel (Ariosoma marginatum) is a Pacific species. It hunts at night, with its head protruding obliquely from the substrate.*

formes are all deep-sea eels and are modified for their environment in spectacular, if different, ways.

Members of the family of snipe eels (Nemichthyidae) are large-eyed, extremely elongated animals. The rear of the body is little more than a skin-covered continuation of the spine. Here, the vertebrae are weak and poorly ossified, i.e. contain small quantities of bone matter; hence, few complete specimens are known. Undamaged specimens can have over 750 vertebrae, the highest number known. This family's common name alludes to its long and widely flaring jaws, fancifully believed to resemble the bill of the snipe. It had been thought that there were two groups of snipe eels, those with extremely long divergent jaws and those with short divergent jaws. However, enough specimens have been caught by now to show that mature males are short-jawed and mature females and juveniles of both sexes are long-jawed. Before maturity, both the inside and outside of snipe eels' jaws are cov-

ered with small, backward-pointing teeth presenting a passable imitation of sandpaper. It seems likely that because adults have lost many teeth, they eat little; it is also possible that they may die after they have reproduced.

We are still not sure how snipe eels feed, since their jaws can only close posteriorly, i.e. the two tips of the snout cannot be brought together. A few observations of living eels from deep-sea research submarine vessels have shown that they spend their time hanging vertically, mouth down, in the water, either still or with bodies gently undulating. A few specimens caught with food still in their stomachs revealed that the major food source is deep-sea shrimps. Typical of these creatures are very long antennae and legs. It is therefore suggested that snipe eels feed by entanglement, ie that once the long antennae or legs of the crustacean become caught up in the teeth inside or outside the jaws, they are followed down to the body which is then consumed.

There are three recognized genera of snipe eels (*Avocettina*, *Nemichthys*, and *Labichthys*). They are widely distributed in warmer parts of the oceans at depths down to 2,000m (6,600ft). Their lepto-cephali are easily identifed by their thinness and the long caudal filament, a precursor of the adult's prolongation of the caudal region. These larvae metamorphose when they are 30cm (12in) long.

Gulper Eels and Allies
ORDER SACCOPHARYNGIFORMES

The remaining four families are all members of the deep-sea gulper or swallower eels. The two mono-typic genera of bobtail snipe eels (Cyematidae) are especially distinctive. These fish look rather like darts, with a long, thin point divided into diverg-ing dorsal and ventral parts. These eels occur in all tropical and subtropical oceans at depths of 500–5,000m (1,600–16,500ft), but rarely to the great-est depth. They are laterally compressed, small fish that grow up to 15cm (6in) long. *Cyema* has a dark velvety skin and minute, but functional, eyes; *Neocyema* is bright red. Their biology is poor-ly known, though what is known of their breeding has some interesting aspects. Many eels breed in clearly circumscribed areas, where the physical conditions meet the stringent requirements of their physiology. By contrast, in the Atlantic, the bobtail snipe eels spawn over large stretches of the warmer parts of the north section of this ocean.

The leptocephalus is quite different to that of other eels. Whereas the typical leptocephalus is a willow-leaf shape (save for minor variations), the leptocephalus of the curtailed snipe eels can be nearly as deep as long. The little evidence available suggests that these species spend at least two years in the larval phase.

On account of their mouths, three families of deep-sea eels: the single-jawed eels (Monognathi-dae), the swallowers (Saccopharyngidae), and the Gulper or Pelican eel (Eurypharyngidae) are some-times grouped under the name "gulper eels."

Monognathids are known from about 14 species found in the Atlantic and Pacific oceans. Their scientific name, which means "one jawed," alludes to the fact that they lack upper jaw bones and have a conspicuous lower jaw that can be longer than the head. All known specimens are small, the largest individual being just 16cm (6.3in) long. Only one species, *Monognathus isaacsi*, has developed any pigment. It has been suggested that single-jawed eels are in fact juvenile swallow-ers (saccopharyngids), but adult saccopharyngids have many more vertebrae than the monog-nathids. However, the largest monognathids have the most vertebrae, so perhaps vertebral formation continues as the fish grows. This puzzle will only be solved when either a sexually mature monog-nathid is found, or when a clear monognathid–saccopharyngid series of stages can be built up, in other words, specimens showing a spectrum of changes from one type of eel to the other.

◁ **Left** *The elongated jaws of a snipe eel (*Nemichthys *sp). They bear file-like teeth that entangle with the long legs and antennae of deep-sea crustaceans.*

The swallowers are archetypal deep-sea fishes. They have huge mouths, elastic stomachs, toothed jaws, and a luminous organ on the tail. One major enigma is that only nine species are generally recognized (based on fewer than 100 specimens), whereas about 14 species of single-jawed eels are usually admitted. Thus, if single-jawed eels are juvenile swallowers, then there are at least five more swallowers awaiting discovery, or five single-jawed eel species have been wrongly described.

Only a few specimens have been seen alive. One fortunate catch involved a specimen of *Saccopharynx harrisoni* from the western Atlantic. This fish, although trawled in 1,700m (5,600ft) of water, was not in the net but entangled by its teeth in the mouth of the trawl, and so escaped being crushed by the weight of fish during the haul to the surface. Also, lacking a swimbladder, it did not suffer the fate of many deep-water fishes – the massive expansion of swimbladder gas as the water pressure reduces during the ascent to the surface.

For deep-sea fishes, the swallowers are large, growing to over 2m (6.5ft) long, but most of the body is tail. The huge mouth has, unsurprisingly, necessitated some morphological changes. The gill arches, for example, are a long way behind the skull and are dissociated into two separate lateral halves. The opercular (gill cover) bones are not developed and the gill chambers are incompletely covered by skin. These modifications mean that the respiratory mechanism of these eels is unlike

that of other fishes. Another peculiarity of these fishes, apart from the absence of a pelvic girdle, is that the lateral line organs, instead of lying in a subcutaneous canal, stand out from the body on separate papillae or protuberances. It is surmised that this adaptation makes the fish more sensitive to vibrations in the water and enhances its chance of finding a suitable fish to cram into the distensible stomach. The escape of the prey, once in the mouth, is prevented by two rows of conical and curved teeth on the upper jaw and a single row of alternating large and small teeth on the lower jaw.

At the end of the long, tapering tail of all swallowers there is a complex luminous organ whose function is unknown. Indeed, the whole arrangement of the luminous organs is odd. On top of the head are two grooves that run backward towards the tail. These contain a white, luminous tissue that glows with a pale light. The grooves separate to pass either side of the dorsal fin, each ray of which has two small, angled grooves containing a similar white tissue. The tail organ is confined to about the last 15cm (6in) of the body. Where the body is shallowest, there is a single, pink, club-shaped tentacle on the ventral surface. Further back, where the body is more rounded, there are six dorsal and seven ventral scarlet projections (papillae) on pigmentless mounds. The main part of the organ lies behind these and is a transparent leaf-like structure with an ample supply of blood vessels. Its dorsal and ventral edges are prolonged and scarlet, whereas the organ is pink because of the blood vessels. The main organ is split into two zones by a band of black pigment with red spots. There are further fingerlike papillae even nearer

the end of the body where the tail narrows and the black of the rest of the body is replaced by red and purple pigments. The small papillae produce a steady pink light, while the leaf-like tail organ can produce flashes on top of a constant reddish glow.

The organ may be a lure, but this seems unlikely, since the contortions required to place the organ where it will act as a lure, even for such a long, thin and presumably prehensile fish, would leave the body in a position where it would be unable to surge forward to grasp the prey.

Equally bizarre is the last member of this group of deep-sea eels, the Gulper or Pelican eel (*Eurypharynx pelecanoides*), the only member of its family (Eurypharyngidae). The mouth is bigger than that of the saccopharyngids, and the jaws can be up to 25 percent of the body length. The jaws are joined by a black elastic membrane. The eyes and brain are minute and confined to a very small area above the front of the mouth.

Almost nothing is known of the biology of the Gulper eel. The teeth are tiny, so it probably feeds on minute organisms. A small complex organ is present near the tail, but it is not known if it is luminous. There is no swimbladder, but there is an extensive liquid-filled system of vessels (the lymphatic system) which may aid buoyancy. The lateral line organs are external and show up as two or three papillae emerging from a small bump.

Gulper eel larvae metamorphose when less than 4cm (1.5in), but even at this diminutive size have already developed the huge mouth. Interestingly, the larvae live much nearer the surface of the sea (100–200m; 330–660ft) than the adults, which live at great depths.   KEB/JD

Tarpon, Bonefish, and Eel Orders

Tarpons and Allies
Order Elopiformes

Most tropical seas. Rarely brackish or freshwater. Length maximum about 2m (6.5ft), weight maximum 160kg (350lb). About 8 species in 2 genera and 2 families including: **Indo-Pacific tarpon** (*Megalops cyprinoides*), **Tarpon** (*M. atlanticus*), **Tenpounder** or **Ladyfish** (*Elops saurus*).

Bonefishes, Spiny Eels, and Allies
Order Albuliformes

Most tropical seas (bonefishes) and deep seas worldwide (halosaurs and spiny eels). Length maximum about 2m (6.5ft). About 29 species in 8 genera and 3 families including: **Bonefish** (*Albula vulpes*), **Suckermouth spiny eel** (*Lipogenys gillii*).

Eels
Order Anguilliformes

All oceans, N America, Europe, E Africa, Madagascar, S India, Sri Lanka, SE Asia, Malay Archipelago, N and E Australia,

New Zealand. Length maximum about 3m (10ft). About 738 species in c. 141 genera and c. 15 families including: **anguillid** or **freshwater eels** (family Anguillidae), including **American eel** (*Anguilla rostrata*), **European eel** (*A. anguilla*), **Japanese eel** (*A. japonica*); **snipe eels** (family Nemichthyidae); **conger eels** (family Congridae); **moray eels** (family Muraenidae), including **moray eels** (genus *Muraena*); **cutthroat** or **synaphobranchid eels** (family Synaphobranchidae); **worm** or **spaghetti eels** (family Moringuidae); **false morays** or **xenocongrid eels** (family Chlopsidae); **Snub-nosed parasitic eel** (subfamily Simenchelyinae, sole species *Simenchelys parasitica*).

Gulper Eel & Allies
Order Saccopharyngiformes

Mostly deep waters in tropical and temperate Atlantic, Indian and Pacific oceans. Length maximum c. 2m (6.5ft). 26 species in 5 genera and 4 families including: **Gulper eel** (*Eurypharynx pelecanoides*).

Tarpons and allies

Tarpons
Megalopidae

Tenpounders
Elopidae

Bonefishes, spiny eels and allies

Bonefishes
Albulidae

Halosaurs
Halosauridae

Lipogenyidae

Notacanthids
Notacanthidae

Eels

Anguillid or freshwater eels
Anguillidae

Duckbill eels
Nettastomatidae

Heterenchelyidae

Pike congers
Muraenesocidae

Snipe eels
Nemicthyidae

Worm or spaghetti eels
Moringuidae

False morays or xenocongrid eels
Chlopsidae

Gulper eel and allies

Curtailed or bobtail snipe eels
Cyematidae

Gulper eels
Eurpharyngidae

Saccopharyngids
Saccopharyngidae

FISH OUT OF WATER

How fishes are adapted for life on land

THAT HUMANS EXIST ON EARTH REFLECTS THE fact that, in the Devonian period, more than 350 million years ago, some ancient fishes emerged from the water, adapted progressively to a terrestrial environment, evolved and…one of the results is us. Today, some bony fishes leave the water for various lengths of time, although it is not suggested that the end point of their excursions will necessarily be as dramatic as that of their ancestors!

It should be pointed out that the ability of a fish to breathe air does not equate with its ability to leave water. The spectacular attributes of the lungfishes, among others, are dealt with elsewhere . Here, we are concerned with fishes that actively travel out of water. Naturally, there are degrees of extra-aquatic activity, ranging from small fishes that skitter along the water's surface momentarily to escape predation, to the Pacific moray eel which may spend up to ten minutes out of water, and others that spend far longer on land.

What problems do they face? Several, including (not in order of severity): respiration, temperature control, vision, desiccation and locomotion.

An initial problem facing fishes leaving water is that the surface area of the delicate gill filaments is reduced since they clamp together, as they are no longer kept separate by the buoyancy of water. Drying out of the gills also occurs. Consequently, either other means of respiration have to be present, or ways of protecting the gills must exist. This usually involves the development of a sac into which the air is sucked; such sacs or cavities have a moist lining that is richly endowed with blood vessels (vascularized). As is always the case with fish,

◑ **Above** *On their migration back to the sea, mature European eels* (Anguilla anguilla) *will cross wet ground if necessary.*

◐ **Left** *Mudskippers move by "crutching" – the fish swings its pectoral fins forward while supporting its body weight on the pelvic fins. Then, by pressing downward and backward with the pectorals, the body is both lifted and drawn forward.*

there are, of course, exceptions. The Chilean cling fish (*Sicyaces sanguineus*), for example, which spends a substantial part of its life out of water, has a vascularized layer of skin in front of the sucker formed from its ventral fins. When it needs oxygen, it raises the front of its body off the rocks and exposes this skin patch to the air. More 'orthodox' are the anabantoids or labyrinth fishes of the suborder Anabantoidei, which include the Climbing perch (*Anabas testudineus*), and the totally unrelated Walking catfish (*Clarias batrachus*) of the family Clariidae. Both these types of fish have pouches above the gill chamber, with linings expanded into convoluted shapes that increase the surface area. The Electric eel (*Electrophorus electricus*), which spends only a small part of its life out of water, can use its gills for aerial respiration, while the mudskippers (*Periophthalmus* spp.), which spend a lot of their life out of water, can use their skin.

Fishes on land have a problem in keeping cool, a difficulty that is compounded because most

'semiterrestrial' fish live in tropical areas. Although living in a coolish climate, one technique for keeping cool is displayed, once more, by the Chilean cling fish: it doesn't produce heat by muscular activity. At its best, this species has been described, when out of water, as "inactive and difficult to tell when dead." It also lives in a shore zone where waves will, from time to time, wash over it.

The length of time it can stay on land depends very much on the weather. When cloudy, it can stay out for about two days and lose only 10 percent of its body water, while in captivity, it has been shown that it takes about a 25 percent loss of body water to cause death. Chilean cling fish that die in the wild have lost little water, but the sun has driven their body temperatures up to some 24°C (75°F), which is fatal for the species. Adult Chilean cling fish do not breathe continuously through the vascularized skin in front of the sucker, but alternate this with holding air in the mouth and pharynx and exchanging gases through their moist lining.

When on land, fish have to see and, unless modifications occur, they would all be short-sighted. Two physical responses are possible: the first is to change the shape of the lens,

and/or the second, to keep the lens spherical and change the shape of the cornea. Mudskippers have done both and have such excellent vision that they can catch insects on the wing.

Eyes are delicate and must, obviously, be protected on land. Mudskippers achieve this by means of a thick layer of clear skin that protects the eye against physical damage. To keep their eyes lubricated (since fish lack tear ducts), mudskippers roll them back into the moist sockets. The walking catfishes (*Clarias* spp.), which probably cannot see farther than 2m (6.5ft) on land, protect their eyes by a thick layer of clear skin and by confining them to within the body contour – that is, they do not protrude from the side of the head. Since conditions are brighter on land than in water, to cope with excess light hitting the retina, some fishes – notably those of the blenny genus *Mnierpes* –

have developed a layer of pigment – the fishes' equivalent of sunglasses!

For eels and eel-like fishes, locomotion on land is just like swimming. *Clarias* species, for instance, employ waving or swimming movements of the body, but supplement this with the use of the pectoral fin spines as bracers. An African species, the Sharptooth or North African catfish (*Clarias gariepinus*), burrows in drying pools and comes out at night to feed. Migrations of up to a thousand individuals have been recorded and it is suggested that the barbels (whiskers) are used to keep in touch. The Walking catfish originally from Southeast Asia, was introduced into Florida, where it has flourished and its ambulatory habits have, not surprisingly, caused much disquiet among many residents of that state, who occasionally find them "walking" across roads.   KEB/JD

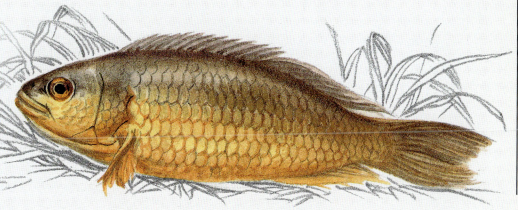

◗ **Right** *The Climbing perch of southern Asia can survive for days or even weeks out of water if its auxiliary breathing mechanism – the "labyrinth organ" – is kept moist.*

Herrings and Anchovies

SOME OF THE MOST FAMILIAR FISH IN THE *world belong to an order comprising just four living families: herrings and anchovies, plus the denticle and wolf herrings. Their influence has been enormous. The economically highly valuable North Atlantic herring has been the subject of wars and its migrations have brought down governments and caused the dissolution of states.*

Herrings and their relatives (Clupeidae) are a cosmopolitan, largely marine group of fishes. Compared with many groups, they are beautifully coherent and easy to diagnose. Freshwater representatives of the herrings and shads occur in the eastern USA, the Amazon basin, West and Central Africa, eastern Australia and occasionally and sporadically elsewhere. The anchovies are coastal forms in all temperate and tropical regions, with freshwater species in the Amazon and Southeast Asia. The wolf herrings are solely marine and the single species in the Denticipitidae lives only in freshwater, occurring in a few rivers in West Africa.

Herrings and Shads
FAMILY CLUPEIDAE

Within this group, the herrings and shads family contains the largest number of species (about 214). They are of great commercial importance. Thanks to their former abundance, highly nutritious flesh and shoaling habits, they became a prime target for fishing fleets. In 1936–37 members of this family made up 37.3 percent by weight of all the fish caught in the world. About half of this weight was from one species, the Pacific Sardine.

In the North Atlantic, the Herring has long been exploited. In 709 AD salted herring were exported from East Anglia in England to the Frisian Islands; the fisheries even appear in Domesday Book (1086). The great advantage of this herring (and others) was that it could be preserved in a variety of ways: pickled in brine, salted, hot and cold smoked (either salted first and split or not, resulting variously in kippers and red herrings). These preservation techniques were devised to keep fish edible before the advent of freezing and canning.

Herrings spawn in shoals in the warmer months, laying a mat of sticky eggs on the sea floor. After hatching, the young become pelagic (free-swimming in the upper and middle layers). Their food, at all stages in their life history, consists of plankton, especially small crustaceans and the larval stages of larger crustaceans. Herrings can swim at a maximum speed of 5.8km/h (3.6mph).

Sprats are small relatives of herrings. The fish often marketed as sardines are the young of the Pilchard, another herring species. Whitebait are the young of both the North Atlantic herring and the Sprat.

Shads (*Alosa* spp.) are larger members of the herring clan. An American Atlantic species (*A. sapidissima*) reaches nearly 80cm (31in) in length. In 1871, they were introduced into rivers draining into the Pacific and are now widespread along the Pacific coast of the USA where they grow to 90cm (35in). In the European North Atlantic there are two species, both now scarce, the Allis shad and the Twaite shad. The latter species has some non-migratory dwarf populations in the Lakes of Killarney (Eire) and some Italian lakes. Freshwater populations of the American alewife are also known.

The external appearance of members of the herring family is very similar. Most are silvery (darker on the back), with no scales on the head. They lack spines in the fins and have scales that are very easily shed (deciduous scales).

Anchovies
FAMILY ENGRAULIDAE

Species in the anchovy family are longer and thinner than many clupeids. They have a large mouth, a pointed, overhanging snout and a round belly without the scute-covered keel that is present in the clupeids.

Engraulis mordax from the eastern Pacific grows to about 18cm (7in). It is in great demand, more as a source of oil and as meal than as a delicacy. Only a very small proportion of the catch is canned or made into paste. It was once far commoner than it is now. There is, for example, a record of a single set of purse-seine nets catching over 200 tonnes in November 1933.

Further south, the Peruvian anchoveta, which is abundant in the food-rich Humboldt Current, is one of the major resources of South American countries on the Pacific seaboard. It is caught in vast shoals off Ecuador, Chile, and especially Peru, but its numbers decline drastically during occurrences of the *El Niño* Southern Oscillation climatic event. The Anchovy is found in the warmer parts of the North Atlantic and the Mediterranean. Before being sold, in whatever form, anchovies are packed into barrels with salt and kept at 30°C (86°F) for three months until the flesh has turned red. Anchovies rarely grow to more than 20cm (8in) long, and may live for seven years, but are usually sexually mature at the end of the first or second year. They are plankton feeders and eat the edible contents of the seawater filtered out by their long, thin gill rakers.

Wolf and Denticle Herrings
FAMILIES CHIROCENTRIDAE, DENTICIPITIDAE

The family Chirocentridae houses only one genus and two species, the wolf herrings. These giants among the herrings grow to over 1m (39in) long and live in the tropical parts of the Indo-Pacific Ocean (west to South Africa and the Red Sea and from Japan to New South Wales). They are elongate fish, strongly compressed and with a sharp belly keel. They have large, fanglike teeth on their jaws and smaller teeth on the tongue and roof of the mouth. Avid hunters, wolf herrings make prodigious leaps. These species are not used for food because they have numerous small intermuscular bones and also, if caught, struggle violently and snap at anything, including fishermen. Within the intestine, these fish have a spiral valve whose function is to increase the absorbtive surface; spiral valves are very rare in bony fishes.

The Denticle herring is the only representative of the Denticipitidae. It measures 8cm (3in) long and is found only in the fastest flowing parts of a few rivers near the Nigerian border with Dahomey. It is silvery with a dark stripe along the side. A seemingly inconspicuous and insignificant fish, it is noteworthy for the presence of a large number of toothlike denticles over the head and front part of the body, hence its common name. Their significance and function are unknown. Fossils, hardly distinguishable from the living species, have been found in former lake deposits in Tanzania – about 20–25 million years old – and named *Palaeodenticeps tanganikae*. The living Denticle herring is believed to be the most primitive member of the clupeomorphs.   KEB/JD

◗ **Right** *Atlantic herrings schooling in a cave in Scotland. Schooling, along with their silvery sides, excellent hearing, and fast escape responses help these fish to fend off predators. Atlantic herrings seek food out by using only their visual sense.*

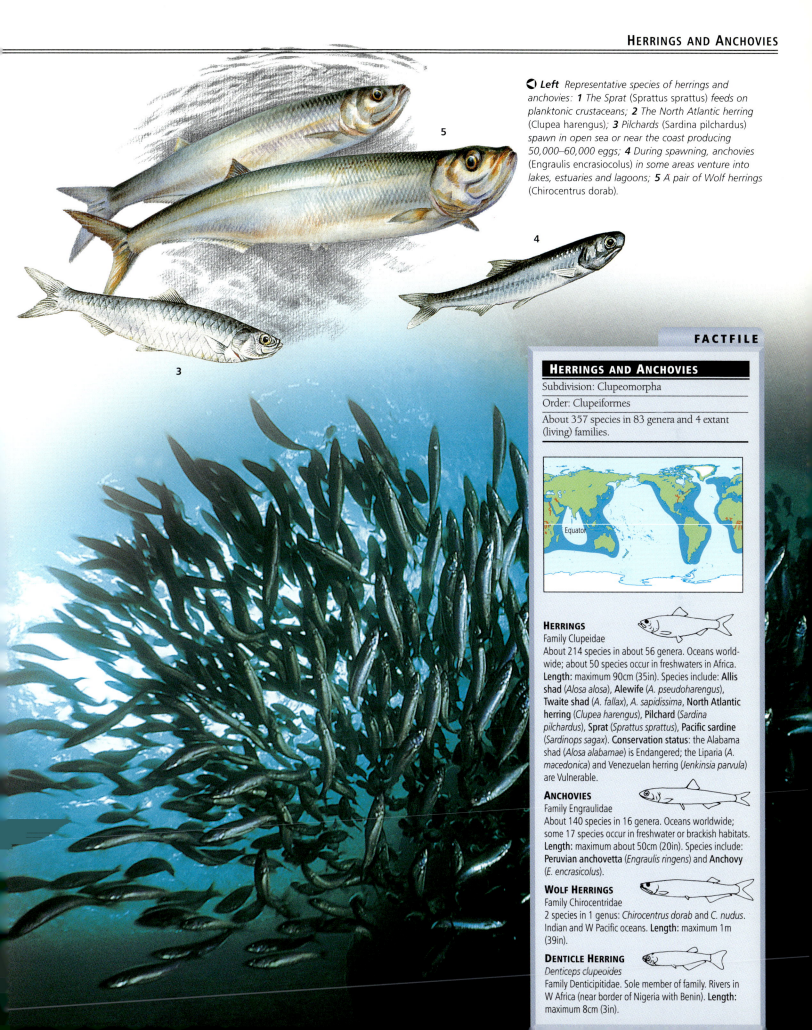

◖ **Left** *Representative species of herrings and anchovies:* **1** *The Sprat* (Sprattus sprattus) *feeds on planktonic crustaceans;* **2** *The North Atlantic herring* (Clupea harengus); **3** *Pilchards* (Sardina pilchardus) *spawn in open sea or near the coast producing 50,000–60,000 eggs;* **4** *During spawning, anchovies* (Engraulis encrasiocolus) *in some areas venture into lakes, estuaries and lagoons;* **5** *A pair of Wolf herrings* (Chirocentrus dorab).

FACTFILE

HERRINGS AND ANCHOVIES

Subdivision: Clupeomorpha

Order: Clupeiformes

About 357 species in 83 genera and 4 extant (living) families.

HERRINGS
Family Clupeidae
About 214 species in about 56 genera. Oceans worldwide; about 50 species occur in freshwaters in Africa. **Length:** maximum 90cm (35in). Species include: **Allis shad** (*Alosa alosa*), **Alewife** (*A. pseudoharengus*), **Twaite shad** (*A. fallax*), *A. sapidissima*, **North Atlantic herring** (*Clupea harengus*), **Pilchard** (*Sardina pilchardus*), **Sprat** (*Sprattus sprattus*), **Pacific sardine** (*Sardinops sagax*). **Conservation status:** the Alabama shad (*Alosa alabamae*) is Endangered; the Liparia (*A. macedonica*) and Venezuelan herring (*Jenkinsia parvula*) are Vulnerable.

ANCHOVIES
Family Engraulidae
About 140 species in 16 genera. Oceans worldwide; some 17 species occur in freshwater or brackish habitats. **Length:** maximum about 50cm (20in). Species include: **Peruvian anchovetta** (*Engraulis ringens*) and **Anchovy** (*E. encrasicolus*).

WOLF HERRINGS
Family Chirocentridae
2 species in 1 genus: *Chirocentrus dorab* and *C. nudus*. Indian and W Pacific oceans. **Length:** maximum 1m (39in).

DENTICLE HERRING
Denticeps clupeoides
Family Denticipitidae. Sole member of family. Rivers in W Africa (near border of Nigeria with Benin). **Length:** maximum 8cm (3in).

Bonytongues and Allies

ESSENTIALLY TROPICAL FRESHWATER FISHES bonytongues, butterflyfish, mooneyes, featherbacks and elephantnoses make up the diverse group known as osteoglossomorphs. Some featherfins, however, may also occur in brackish water. Although they possess toothed jaws, the main bite is exerted by teeth on bones in the tongue pressing against teeth on the roof of the mouth. This feature is responsible for the general name sometimes applied to the whole group – the bonytongues.

Osteoglossomorphs share a number of other structural characteristics, including complex ornamentation or markings of the scales and, unusually, an intestinal arrangement in which part of the gut is arranged on the left side of the gullet and stomach (it passes on the right in most fishes).

A Wide Spectrum

OSTEOGLOSSOMORPH FAMILIES

The **bonytongues** are moderate to very large fishes with prominent eyes and scales and dorsal and anal fins placed well back on their long bodies. The giant Amazonian arapaima is reputed to grow to lengths of 5m (16ft) and weights of 170kg (375lb). These estimates have not been verified, but if they were authenticated, then this species would rank as the giant of freshwater fishes. There is no doubt that it grows to 3m (10ft) and weighs up to 100kg (220lb) in the wild – still a huge size!

In addition to using its gills in the normal way to breathe, the Arapaima is also an air-breather, absorbing oxygen via its swimbladder, a structure that is joined to the throat and has a lunglike lining. A similar bladder condition prevails in the African or Nile arowana (*Heterotis niloticus*), which also has an accessory respiratory organ above the gills. How much these fish use air is uncertain, but both can penetrate inhospitable oxygen-poor swamps for spawning. Both fishes build nests and guard their young. The Nile arowana constructs a walled nest of broken vegetation measuring about 1.2m (4ft) in diameter. By contrast, the two South American arowanas (*Osteoglossum bicirrhosum* and

O. ferreirae), the Asian Dragon fish and the Australian saratogas brood eggs and young in their mouths. In the South American arowanas and Dragon fish, the brooding is carried out by the male. In *S. leichardti*, it is the female that is reported as being the brooder; no details are currently available for *S. jardinii*.

Bonytongues are carnivores that eat insects, other fish, amphibians, rodents and even birds, snakes and bats. *Heterotis*, however, consumes mud, plankton, and plant detritus.

At the other end of the size spectrum of osteoglossomorphs lies the curious West African **Butterflyfish** which is only about 6–10cm (2.4–4in) long. This species, also an air breather, inhabits grassy swamps where it swims close to the surface, trailing below the amazingly long and separated rays of its pelvic fins as it feeds on floating insects and fish. With its ability to leap high out of the water and to skit over the surface, the butterflyfish can also feed on flying insects.

Mooneyes are herringlike fishes of modest size which extend the distribution of osteoglossomorphs into North America. There are only two species in this family: the Mooneye itself and the Goldeye. Both are freshwater species with strongly compressed bodies (that is, flattened from side to side), and silvery scales; they also possess a keel-like belly. Mooneyes are predatory fishes that feed on other fishes and insects. Both are fished commercially, especially the Goldeye.

Featherbacks are laterally compressed fishes that swim by undulating a very long anal fin, extending from the tiny pelvic fins to the tip of the tail. The Clown knifefish, one of two Asian species, can grow to 1m (3.3ft) in length and

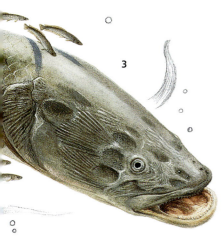

◁ **Left** *Representative species of bonytongues and allies:* **1** *A young specimen of an arowana (genus Osteoglossum) at the water's surface;* **2** *the Butterflyfish (Pantodon buchholzi) was given its name after leaping into a butterfly collector's net;* **3** *the Arapaima (Arapaima gigas) builds a nest about 0.5m (1.6ft) across in the sand for its young;* **4** *Bronze featherback (Notopterus notopterus);* **5** *the Churchill (Petrocephalus catastoma) is a species of snoutless elephantnose and* **6** *Campylomormyrus rhynchophorus is an example of an elephantnose with a long snout.*

3

FACTFILE

BONYTONGUES AND ALLIES

Subdivision: Osteoglossomorpha

Order: Osteoglossiformes

About 217 species in 29 genera and 6 families.

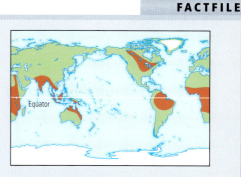

Equator

Distribution N and S America, Africa, SE Asia, Australia in rivers, swamps, lakes.
Size Length 6cm–3m (2.4in–10ft); weight up 100kg (220lb).
Diet Varied, including insects, fish, plankton.

BONYTONGUES
Family Osteoglossidae
7 species in 4 genera. S America, Africa, Malaysia, New Guinea, Australia. Species: **Arapaima** (*Arapaima gigas*), **Nile arowana** (*Heterotis niloticus*), **Dragon fish** (*Scleropages formosus*), **Australian saratogas** (*S. jardinii, S. leichardti*), **South American arowanas** (*Osteoglossum* spp.). **Conservation status:** Dragon fish Endangered.

BUTTERFLYFISH *Pantodon buchholzi*
Sole member of family Pantodontidae. W Africa.

MOONEYES Family Hiodontidae
2 species of the genus *Hiodon* – the Mooneye (*H. tergisus*) and Goldeye (*H. alosoides*). N America.

FEATHERBACKS
Family Notopteridae
8 species in 4 genera.
Africa, SE Asia. Species include: **Bronze featherback** (*Notopterus notopterus*), **African knifefish** (*Xenomystus nigri*).

ELEPHANTNOSES
Family Mormyridae
Nearly 200 species in 18 genera.
Africa. Species include: **Peter's elephantnose** (*Gnathonemus petersii*), **Elephantnose** (*Campylomormyrus tamandua*).

ABA ABA *Gymnarchus niloticus*
Sole member of family Gymnarchidae. Africa.

shows some parental care of spawned eggs. This consists of the male fanning the eggs (which are laid on a sunken branch or other solid surface) and defending them during their 5–6 day development. Other featherbacks are smaller than the Clown knifefish. The African knifefishes, *Papyrocranus* and *Xenomystus*, also have accessory respiratory structures above the gills and can inhabit swampy pools. All of these fishes have large mouths and predatory habits, feeding largely on aquatic invertebrates and other, smaller, fishes.

The **elephantnoses** or mormyrids make significant contributions to the fish stocks of many African lakes, rivers and floodpools. Most are bottom dwellers feeding on worms, insects and mollusks. Some species are long-snouted, but, although there is a tendency in others for a forward and downward prolongation of the snout region, within the family head shapes are highly variable. Some species (many of which are known as "whales") have no snout at all. Small to medium in size, all elephantnoses have small mouths, eyes, gill openings and scales. Dorsal and anal fins are set well back and the deeply forked caudal fin has an exceptionally narrow peduncle. The muscles are modified to form electric organs that emit

a continuous field of weak discharges at varying frequencies around the fish. Moreover, there are electroreception centers in part of the enlarged cerebellum of the brain (giving mormyrids the largest brains to be found among lower vertebrate animals). The cerebellum is so large that it extends over the surface of the forebrain. The electrosensitive system acts as a sort of radar, detecting distortions in the electrical field from objects coming within it. This would seem to be an ideal adaptation for nocturnal activities, including social and breeding interactions, in murky waters.

Much early research into electrogenic activity was conducted on the **Aba Aba**. Recently separated by systematists from the mormyrids and assigned to its own family (Gymnarchidae), it is a large, predatory osteoglossomorph that is reported as growing to 1.6m (65in). The Aba Aba has a remarkable shape in that it lacks anal and caudal fins and moves by undulating a dorsal fin that extends almost the entire length of its eel-like body. The swimbladder serves as a lung and *Gymnarchus* constructs a 1-m (39-in) flask-shaped, often floating, nest of grass which it is reputed to defend with vigor. Around 1,000 eggs are laid and these take about five days to hatch.

Popular but Problematic
CONSERVATION AND ENVIRONMENT

Apart from their scientific interest, humans are involved with osteoglossomorphs at various levels. There are capture fisheries for Arapaima and arowanas in South America, and for the Nile arowana and the Aba Aba, in West Africa and the upper White Nile. Larger mormyrids are more widely fished in Africa, although they are not universally acceptable as food. For example, many women in East Africa avoid eating them due to the superstition that their children might be born with elephantine snouts. Bonytongues, mooneyes, and *Gymnarchus* are all rated as good sport fish by anglers. In pond culture, good growth rates have been achieved, but in the case of the Nile arowana, harvesting may be thwarted by their superb ability to leap the seine net, behavior also exhibited by its South American, Asian, and Australian cousins.

The Butterflyfish, featherbacks and a number of small mormyrids are particularly interesting for aquarists because of their specialized features, but they are not popular, since breeding them in captivity is difficult. Some of the larger species, most notably the Arapaima, are popular in public aquaria. When first introduced into an aquarium, though, large arapaimas can cause problems by trying to swim through the walls of tanks; they too are hard to breed in captivity. However, pond-breeding of several species, including the Arapaima, is now being achieved on a regular basis. In the Far East, the Dragon fish has been bred in captivity for many years and the best, large fish command astounding prices because of the symbolism attached to them.   RGB/JD

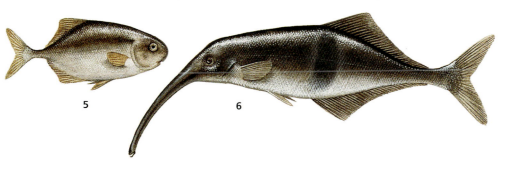

5   6

Index

Initial bold **1** and **2** indicate the volume in which the reference will be found. Page numbers in *italic* type refer to picture captions. Page numbers in **bold** indicate extensive coverage or feature treatment of a subject.

Picture Credits

Prelims Vol 1: OSF: Daniel Cox ii; Prelims Vol 2: Doug Perrine: ii

Ardea: 119, Kurt Amsler 245, Kev Deacon 246-7, Jean-Paul Ferrero 51, JM Labat 253, Ken Lucas 32b, 82, 226-7, P. Morris 160-1, 164-5, Mark Spencer 262, Ron & Valerie Taylor 261b 29, 261b, Ron Taylor 279t; Alissa Arp/ San Francisco State University: 110; Beverly Factor: 21; Biophotos Associates: 115; Bruce Coleman Collection: Franco Banfi 211b, Sven Halling 42, Malcolm Hey 35, 244t, C & S Hood 260, Pacific Stock 4/5, 234-5, Kim Taylor 252c; Coral Reef Research Institute : 38; Corbis: Hal Beral 46, Lester V Bergman 17, Jonathan Blair 145, Brandeon D. Cole 57, Mimmo Jodice 148/9, Jeffrey L. Rotman 155, Stuart Westmorland 78; Corbis Sygma: Thierry Prat 63; Dr G.L. Baron: 71b; Mark Erdmann: 273c; Frank Lane Picture Library: F. Bavendam/Minden Pictures 101, Susan Dewinsky 109, Foto Natura Stock 224-5, W.T. Miller 82 insert, Flip Nicklin/Minden Pictures 47b; Imagequestmarine.com: 142t, Peter Herring 190, 204-5, 208t, 208b, 209t; Natural Visions: Peter David 239, Heather Angel 67; Nature Picture Library: Dan Burton 182-3, Brandon Cole 142b, 152b, Georgette Douwma 32c, 244b, 256-7, 259b, Jeff Foott 241, Jurgen Freund 22, 282t, David Hall 284-5, Alan James 201, Reijo Juurinen 156-7, Avi Klapfer & Jeff Rotamn 254-5, 281, Conrad Maufe 275c, John Downer Productions 152bl, Fabio Liverani 49, 152t, Naturbild 187, Michael Pitts 6b, 141, Jeff Rotman 256, 275b, 278-9, 282b, 283, John Sparks 153, Sinclair Stammers 70; NHPA: A.N.T 195b, ANT Photo Library 266, 289, Pete Atkinson 34, 56b, Anthony Bannister 56t, Bill Coster 64, Daniel Heuclin 263, Image Quest 3D 37b, Scott Johnson 95t, B. Jones & M. Shimlock 32t, 33, 65, 72, 108, 138/9, 140, 211t, Lutra 188-9, 220-1, Trevor McDonald 23t, 58b, 286-7, Ashod Francis Papazian 265, Peter Parks 11, 121t, Tom & Theresa Stack 28t, MI Walker 25, Nobert Wu 28b, 37t, 238, 251, 264-5; Oxford Scientific Films: 3, 4, 10, 12/13, 20, 39, 74-75, 111b, 117t, 132/3, 160, 175, 178, 196t, Doug Allan 230, Kathie Atkinson 52b, 84, 104, 137t, Tobias Bernhard 86/7, 128b, 259b, 274-5, Waina Cheng 8, Paulo De Oliveira 170, 181, 279b, Mark Deeble & Victoria Stone 83b, Dr F. Ehrenstrom & L. Beyer 121b, 220t, 233,

235b, David Fleetham 2, 9, 50b, 52t, 79, 83t, 90/1, 123, 174, 176, 210, 247b, 261t, 278b, Stephen Foote 117b, Jeff Foote/Okapia 202t, 203t, 203b, David Fox 60b, Gary Gaugler 77, Max Gibbs 176/7, Lawrence Gould 177, Karen Gowlett-Holmes 7, 23b, 24, 27, 86t, 92, 94t, 102, 103, 118-9, 126-7, 126b, 126l, 128/9, 134/5, 134b, 258, Green Cape PTY Ltd 50t, Howard Hall 48/9, 167, Mark Hamblin 47t, Richard Hermann 98/9, 100, 122, Frank Huber 202b, Rodger Jackman 128t, 171, Paul Kay 30/1, 130b, Breck P. Kent 186, Richard Kirby 60t, Rudie Kuiter 85, 96/7, 101t, 131, 194, 195t, 213, Zig Leszczynski 180, Alastair MacEwen 18/9, Victoria A. McCornick 198/9, Prof H. Melhhorn/ Okapia 75, Colin Milikins 48, 54/5, 166, Patrick Morris 191, Tammy Peluso 130t, Michael Pitts 172/3, Science Pictures Ltd 196b, Sue Scott 198, 231, Frithjof Skibbe 87, Gerard Soury 85b, 274, 288, Survival Anglia, Harold Taylor 58t, 92/3, Konrad Wothe 6t, Norbert Wu 94/5, 154, 252t; PA Photos: EPA 150; Photomax: Max Gibbs 204, 214, 216/7, 220b, 224, 232, 235t, 240, 241b, 252b, 268; Premaphotos Wildlife: Ken Preston-Mafham 41t, 68, 105, Dr Rod Preston-Mafham 134t; SAIAB: 272c, 272b; Seaphot: John Lythgoe 99; Seapics: Shedd Aquar/Ceisel 209b; Science Photo Library: 273t, Martin Dohrn 111t, Eye of Science 16, 69, Claude Nuridsany & Marie Perennou 271, David Scharf 71t, Andrew Syred 40, John Walsh 112; Still Pictures: Roland Birke 14/15; Welcome Trust Medical Photographic Library : Graham Budd 137b.

Diagrams by: Martin Anderson, Simon Driver

All artwork ©Brown Reference Group plc.

While every effort has been made to trace the copyright holders of illustrations reproduced in this book, the publishers will be pleased to rectify any omissions or inaccuracies.